COUNTDOWN

TO

CRISIS

Also by Kenneth R. Timmerman

The French Betrayal of America

Preachers of Hate: Islam and the War on America

Shakedown: Exposing the Real Jesse Jackson

Selling Out America: The American Spectator *Investigations*

The Death Lobby: How the West Armed Iraq

Weapons of Mass Destruction: The Cases of Iran, Syria, and Libya

Poison Gas Connection: Western Suppliers of Unconventional Weapons and Technologies to Iraq and Libya

COUNTDOWN TO CRISIS

THE COMING NUCLEAR SHOWDOWN WITH IRAN

KENNETH R. TIMMERMAN

CROWN FORUM
NEW YORK

Published in the United States by Crown Forum,
an imprint of the Crown Publishing Group,
a division of Random House, Inc., New York.
www.crownpublishing.com

Crown Forum and the Crown Forum colophon are
trademarks of Random House, Inc.

Library of Congress Cataloging-in-Publication Data
Timmerman, Kenneth R.
Countdown to crisis : the coming nuclear showdown
with Iran / Kenneth R. Timmerman.—1st ed.
p. cm.
Includes bibliographical references and index.
1. Nuclear weapons—Iran. 2. Iran—Military policy.
3. United States—Military policy. 4. World politics—
1995–2005. 5. World politics—21st century. I. Title.
UA853.I7T56 2005
355.02'17'0955—dc22 2005008826

ISBN 1-4000-5368-4

Printed in the United States of America

DESIGN BY BARBARA STURMAN

2 4 6 8 10 9 7 5 3 1

First Edition

TO THE FREEDOM-FIGHTERS
OF TOMORROW

Contents

Prologue

WHAT IF THE AYATOLLAH GOT THE BOMB?

In a cleft between two mountains around 50 kilometers southwest of Natanz, Iran's Revolutionary Guards have constructed a deep underground facility using special tunneling machines imported from Germany.

The blast door giving access to the buried facility measures 18 meters across and nearly 6 meters high. Its surface has been faced with natural rock, making it virtually invisible to outside eyes. It opens onto a well-lit tunnel nearly 60 meters long that leads to an underground traffic circle wide enough for an eighteen-wheel tractor-trailer to turn around without hindrance.

From the circle, six tunnels lead down to separate underground chambers. Two of the hardened storage bunkers house Shahab-3 missiles, each with its own Mercedes-Benz tractor and specially designed launch trailer. The Revolutionary Guards claim that the missiles can be driven outside, fueled, and launched within twenty-five minutes and that they can then scoot underground before any retaliatory strike. In nearly a dozen live tests, they have shown that the missiles can hit targets anywhere in Israel. New versions will soon be capable of hitting America directly.

Two of the storage depots house a secret cascade of uranium-enrichment centrifuges—high-speed spinning machines designed to convert uranium into fuel for nuclear weapons. This is one of several such cascades now operating in Iran.

The other two underground chambers house fifteen nuclear warheads ready to be mated to the missiles.

On March 1, 2005, the deputy director general of the International Atomic Energy Agency, Pierre Goldschmidt, told the IAEA Board of Governors that Iran was continuing to prevent UN inspectors from verifying the activities of key nuclear sites. The suspect sites and capabilities that Iran was protecting coincided precisely with what they needed to build the bomb. They included:

- hardened underground bunkers near Isfahan, where Western intelligence agencies suspected Iran had been secretly producing uranium hexafluoride to be converted into nuclear weapons fuel
- a suspected enrichment plant in the capital of Tehran, which Iran razed in late 2003 to prevent the IAEA from discovering its true purpose
- suspected weaponization labs at Parchin, where Iran's Defense Industries Organization produced HMX, precisely the type of high-powered explosives needed for the non-nuclear "lenses" that trigger a nuclear implosion device

Today, the IAEA is finally pressing Iran's Islamic clerical leaders to account for their nuclear program. But for more than eighteen years, as I document in this book, the UN's nuclear "watchdog" agency and the international bureaucrats who ran it actually *helped* Iran acquire key nuclear technologies, while blocking any effective investigation of Iran's clandestine program.

The IAEA is finally discovering that Iran tapped into a vast network of black-market suppliers affiliated with Pakistani nuclear mastermind Dr. Abdel Qader Khan. But for nearly two decades, the UN agency simply turned a blind eye to his activities. In fact, Dr. Khan made a public visit to Iran in 1986 and signed a nuclear consulting agreement with the regime the following year. Now the IAEA has stumbled upon parts of the contract, including lists of equipment and services being offered by Dr. Khan. As I chronicle in this book, the elusive Pakistani established a veritable Stop & Shop for nuclear wannabes right under the noses of the IAEA and Western intelligence agencies. Today, the shelves are empty and the inventory has been sold.

If the Iranians used the equipment we now know that they purchased from the Khan network over the past eighteen years, today they could have enough fissile material to produce between twenty and twenty-five nuclear weapons, according to publicly available estimates developed by nuclear experts.

What if the Ayatollah got the bomb?

For years, this was a rhetorical question. Today, it is a reality for which Americans must prepare.

But Iran's race for the bomb is just part of the story. This book is about the threat from a regime that has vowed "Death to America" since its foundation and regularly announces it will turn the Persian Gulf into a "sea of blood" and destroy Israel with nuclear missiles. It is a story about capabilities, but also about intentions.

Iran's clerics didn't get out of the terror business when they freed the U.S. hostages in 1981; they merely got better at hiding their traces. Since then, they have launched a series of attacks on America, through proxies and secret intelligence networks. I have drawn on previously classified documents and fresh eyewitness reports to tell the stories of several of these attacks and the Iranian leaders who ordered them. Despite clear intelligence showing Iranian government involvement, the United States has never retaliated. I believe this was a deadly mistake.

Dramatic new evidence—presented here for the first time—suggests that Iran may have been responsible for the destruction of TWA Flight 800 off the coast of Long Island on July 17, 1996. Multiple warnings of impending Iranian terrorist attacks flowed into the U.S. intelligence community beforehand, but they were not considered "actionable" and so were ignored.

Similar intelligence information, revealed here for the first time, shows that top Iranian officials were directly involved in the 9/11 plot, meeting with high-level al-Qaeda operatives and providing them with passports, safe haven, intelligence assistance, secure communications, and training in explosives and airline hijacking.

Many readers will demand to know how the United States missed the collaboration between al-Qaeda and Iran. The short answer is: we didn't. But the conventional wisdom within the intelligence community dictated that Iran's clerics couldn't possibly work together with Osama bin Laden because they came from bitterly opposed sects of Islam. This shortsighted concept had deadly consequences.

Another important thread in this story is the regime's ruthless elimination of its political opponents—those who might challenge the system of *Velayat-e faghih*, absolute clerical rule. But murder is just one tool the ruling clerics use to disrupt the opposition. As I relate in this book, the regime has infiltrated and successfully manipulated virtually every opposition group, both at home and in exile, through "false flag" operations, fake "reform" movements, false promises, and financial inducements. Meanwhile, the United States consistently failed to help the opposition to organize effectively, yet another failure that can be told for the first time.

Iran's ruling clerics realize that their regime is vulnerable, especially from within, where two generations of young people born since the revolution now thirst for Western-style freedoms. The mullahs' greatest fear is that Iran's youth, helped by the United States, will stage a revolt or a referendum to usher in secular government. This is one reason they have acted with such determination to slow the march of freedom in neighboring Iraq, lest it become a pole of attraction and an example to Iran's youth.

And it is why they are desperate to get the bomb, which they view as the ultimate insurance policy against an American or Israeli attack.

A NOTE ON SOURCES

This book relies almost exclusively on sources developed over the past two decades, including present and former U.S. government officials and trusted sources within the intelligence community, who for years have been observing Iran from the far side of the mirror. Some of these sources described classified documents that shed new light on the Iranian regime, and what the United States knew about it.

Wherever possible, I have tried to tell the inside story of the brutality of the clerical regime in Iran and the often inept response from Washington through reconstructed scenes and dialogue. In preparing such passages, I have relied on interviews with direct participants and have paraphrased their accounts. In the rare occasions where that has not been possible, I have used the published writings of participants, public accounts, comments they have made to others, internal documents, and the recollections of friends and colleagues, and so indicate in the text or in the notes.

Defectors from Iran's intelligence services have provided valuable information, including minutes of secret meetings of the Iranian leadership, the location of safe houses, organization charts of various intelligence organs, personal impressions of key figures in this book, and eyewitness accounts of meetings between top al-Qaeda leaders and senior Iranian officials. Thanks to their testimony, readers have a unique opportunity to view the incredible schemes of Iran's clerical leaders from both sides of the mirror.

At times, my relationship to these defectors became a part of the story, as when a leading regime newspaper in Tehran ran a front-page article in

June 2000 naming me as the "head of the CIA's humint [human intelligence] operation" against the regime—a laughable accusation, were the accuser not so prone to murder.

Several times, the CIA tried to steer me away from information these defectors provided. Rather than do me a good turn, the CIA was, I believe, trying to lead me away from their own errors of judgment—errors that I believe cost thousands of American lives. For a case in point, see chapter 1.

A treasure trove of documents that 9/11 Commission staffers discovered by chance just one week before the commission report was scheduled for printing in July 2004 bears out the stories I had been hearing from multiple defectors. The clue to the existence of those documents, produced by the CIA and the National Security Agency, was contained in a single dense report, buried beneath a mountain of highly classified intelligence data, where Agency officials obviously hoped it would never be found. The report summarized what the U.S. intelligence community knew about Iran's pre-9/11 connection to Osama bin Laden and is disclosed for the first time in chapter 24 of this book. Because of the arrogance and willful blindness of our nation's top intelligence officers, America's leaders were misled about the threat from Iran before it was too late.

Groups in the United States supporting a reestablishment of an Iranian monarchy have long believed that I secretly set up a July 1995 meeting between Reza Pahlavi, son of the former shah, and President Clinton. Interested readers will find the truth about that meeting, and how the regime in Tehran felt it could manipulate Pahlavi and neutralize his supporters, in chapter 15.

Iran's clerical leaders have no ambiguity about their intentions. They have no moments of doubt as they lie to the IAEA about their nuclear programs or as they murder their opponents. For more than two decades, they have been playing all the notes on the piano of terror while smiling and pretending they were just playing a waltz.

The Islamic Republic of Iran is not just any other country. It is a regime that thrives in a climate of crisis, that needs war to survive. Seeking to change the behavior of the regime—whether its support for terror, its pursuit of nuclear capabilities, or its abysmal human rights record and suppression of freedom—is tantamount to asking the ruling clerics to willingly abandon power. Nevertheless, many politicians and even governments continue to do so.

Today, Iran's leaders are plotting new attacks on the West with Osama bin Laden, whom they are sheltering inside Iran, and are continuing to finance Abu Musab Zarqawi, the terrorist who became infamous for beheading his victims in Iraq.

After learning of the ruling clerics' direct involvement in the September 11 plot and their continued collaboration with Osama bin Laden today, most Americans will, I believe, demand that our leaders take resolute action in retaliation. Readers will find my prescription for what America can do to counter these grave new threats in the final chapter.

THE DEFECTOR

On July 26, 2001, an Iranian intelligence officer named Hamid Reza Zakeri walked into the U.S. embassy in Baku, Azerbaijan, and asked to speak to the CIA. As a trusted security official, Zakeri had a diplomatic passport with permanent visas, allowing him to leave his country at will. He told the local receptionist that he had important information concerning the security of the United States and wanted to convey it to the station chief in person.

The Azeri shrugged. We have no CIA officers here, he said. But the Marine guard behind him had been trained for this type of occasion and discreetly phoned up to the CIA station. The forty-one-year-old Zakeri was known as a "walk-in" in the intelligence trade. Like an itinerant peddler, he had goods for sale. It was the CIA's job to evaluate those goods.

On the one hand, it was easy to get taken in by the Willy Lomans of the intelligence trade. But on the other, if the peddler's wares were good, it was the station chief's job to pay him a fair price and pass the information on to Langley for further evaluation and exploitation. Walk-ins had provided vital information to Western intelligence agencies during the Cold War, including secrets of Soviet spy rings that specialized in stealing our high-technology secrets. It would be irresponsible to reject a live one without carefully scrutinizing his wares.

Azerbaijan was not exactly what CIA covert operators considered a plum assignment. The tiny station was headed by a junior officer ("Oh, you mean that GS-10 woman they sent out there?" sneered one former clandestine operator I asked about the encounter.) When the station chief finally met Zakeri in an anteroom off the main lobby, she introduced herself as "Joan."

"Joan" may not have been a senior officer, but she was a professional. She listened to his tale, made no promises, and sent a message back to headquarters asking them to dispatch an evaluation team. She didn't have a clue what to make of the claims being advanced by this Iranian of a "huge" impending attack on America, but she figured that at least she should pass it along. There was so much chatter about potential terrorist attacks circulating these days, she felt a bit like the little boy crying wolf.

After several days of debriefings with Joan at a CIA safe house in Baku, the "expert" arrived from Washington to evaluate his intelligence. That meeting did not go well.

The officer introduced himself as "George." He was around forty years old, very tall, and very sure of himself. He had read the five-page letter Zakeri had written in Persian that described what he knew of the impending terrorist attack. He made clear that he thought Zakeri was lying.

You say you work for a "shadow" intelligence organization that operates out of the Supreme Leader's office? he said. That's news to me. A shadow intelligence organization in Iran! How come I don't know about this?

Zakeri drew him an organization chart. Hojjat-ol eslam Ali Akbar Nateq-Nouri, the well-known former Majles speaker,* was the top man in the Leader's office. His official title was "head of inspection." Zakeri's boss, Mustafa Hadadian, reported to him. As head of Section 110, Hadadian ran intelligence operations, including physical security for visiting VIPs, counterintelligence, and planning for overseas terrorist attacks. Each of his twelve deputies was listed by his "real" name and his "work" name and had a unique numeric code, like a telephone extension. Hadadian's code was 2500; his real name was Mustafa Sanaie-pour.

George looked at the chart with Hadadian in the center, his deputies arrayed around him in a circle, and burst out laughing. This is preposterous, he said.

There's going to be a big attack on America on the twentieth of Shahrivar, Zakeri insisted. That's the date my boss told us to be ready. Six people who have been trained as pilots have just left Iran.

George consulted a calendar that gave the corresponding Western dates. So we're talking about September 10, right? I'll mark my date book, he added sarcastically. He paid Zakeri a few hundred dollars for his time and sent him away.

"They were not correct with me," Zakeri complained later, during one of many interviews I conducted with him. "They said unacceptable things. They accused me of lying. They said I was telling them false stories to confuse them."

---

*The Majles-e Shoura-ye Eslami, or Islamic Consultative Assembly, is frequently called Iran's "parliament" in the West, although its powers are far more limited.

On nearly a dozen occasions over a two-year period, including face-to-face debriefings over five days in Paris and a Middle East country I have agreed not to disclose, Zakeri never contradicted the extremely detailed information he had provided to me. He provided documents and photographs to buttress his claims. As I investigated his claims during this time I discovered that other defectors—and intelligence reports that surfaced well after the September 11 attacks—independently corroborated key parts of his story.

But thanks to "CIA George" and his bosses back in Langley, Zakeri's warnings were never taken seriously.

THE TARGET WALL

There's an old saying in the intelligence business as in life: the more things change, the more they stay the same.

For nearly four years after the violent birth of the Islamic Republic of Iran in 1979, the nation's ruling clerics failed to establish a formal ministry of intelligence. It wasn't that Ayatollah Khomeini and his followers refused to engage in skullduggery. Nor did they have any qualms about using extreme violence to seize and maintain their grip on power. In a way, they were victims of their own success.

Before the revolution, Iran's future rulers had complained about the brutality of SAVAK, the National Organization for Intelligence and Security, getting reporters and human rights activists to refer to it universally as the shah's "dreaded" intelligence service. To establish a successor too soon after the revolution would give the lie to the bogus claims they had peddled to sympathetic reporters and foolish Western leaders that their revolution had replaced one of the world's most horrific tyrannies with a new form of democracy.

When they finally announced the creation of the Ministry of Information and Security (MOIS) in 1983, Iran was mired in war on so many fronts that no one cared about the old lies anymore. Nor did anyone seem to notice when the new minister, Hojjat-ol eslam Mohammad "Nick" Reyshahri, a Soviet-trained intelligence professional, drafted entire overseas networks formerly run by SAVAK. He generalized the use of torture, which SAVAK had in fact used quite sparingly, notwithstanding the loud complaints from international human rights organizations.[1] Reyshahri further showed his respect for his predecessors by taking over the former SAVAK headquarters in Sultanatabad, in northern Tehran, whose enormous underground holding pens now resounded with the screams of the damned.

The display area in the entry hall of the *majmoueh etelaat* building in Sultanatabad was well known to Zakeri and his colleagues. It was here that their bosses posted photographs of Iranian dissidents shortly before MOIS or Iranian Revolutionary Guard hit squads assassinated them in Europe. This "target wall," as they called it, was a not-so-subtle way of spreading the word to insiders as to who was going to become the regime's next target—a typically Persian bit of braggadocio. It was one of those things that Western intelligence officers found so difficult to understand about Iran.

Hamid Reza Zakeri didn't share the visceral hatred of all things American that animated many of his colleagues at MOIS. Indeed, a four-year stint in Canada from 1988 to 1992, where he could see firsthand how well his compatriots were doing in exile, had given him a certain respect, even envy, for the United States. So a chill went down his spine that hot afternoon in the early summer of 2001 when he saw the huge display along the target wall. He understood instantly that the planning phase was over.

On the left was a blow-up of the World Trade Center, nearly 5 feet high, mounted on foamboard. Next to it stood a 3-D model of the White House, lit from inside by a red light as if it was running with blood. To the right was a photograph of CIA headquarters; then a huge, 7-foot-high model of the Pentagon, canted upward so he could see into the inner courtyard. The target display was completed by a smaller photograph of three low buildings, which a printed label identified as Camp David.

Suspended from the ceiling, a missile with a black warhead was bearing in on the Pentagon. Nearly 3 meters long, it was hung so that anyone who walked down the hallway would pass directly beneath it. Along the body of the missile a phrase had been written in blood-red ink. It read, "*Al-mohtal America*"—"Death to America"—in Arabic, not Farsi.

As Zakeri looked at the display, he understood that his government was preparing to help the Arabs who had come to Iran seeking assistance earlier that year and that their goal was to murder as many Americans as possible.

THE HAMBURG LINK

Zakeri was a security specialist, not a high-ranking clandestine operator or intelligence planner. He began working immediately after the revolution as a bodyguard, in charge of the close protection detail of the top five leaders of the Islamic Republic.[2] When MOIS was established in 1983 (known to Iranians by its Persian acronym, VEVAK, and later, VAJA), he left the Revolutionary Guards Corps and moved there, eventually getting an overseas posting in 1988.

The CIA tried to recruit him in Ottawa, Canada, in 1992, and when he returned to Iran he told his immediate boss, a family member, the whole story. He also revealed that the CIA had recruited an Iranian named Tavakoli who was working as an MOIS department director. Zakeri's boss, who headed Department 12 at MOIS headquarters, was pleased at this sign of loyalty and promoted him to office director. The CIA never forgot Zakeri's betrayal.

According to a note presented to a federal court in Hamburg, Germany, on January 21, 2004, by the Bundeskrimalamt (BKA)—the German equivalent of the FBI—Department 12 was responsible for "the protection of persons and institutions." It was clear from the dismissive tone of the note that the BKA thought this was too lowly a position for someone claiming knowledge of international terrorist operations, as Zakeri was doing. He was little more than a glorified bodyguard, in the eyes of the BKA.

Two other German intelligence agencies did a similar evaluation of Zakeri's credentials in preparation for his appearance as a government witness in the trial in Hamburg of a thirty-year-old Moroccan named Abdelghani Mzoudi, who was facing 3,066 counts of accessory to murder for having allegedly provided material assistance to 9/11 hijackers Mohammad Atta, Marwan al-Shehhi, and Ziad Jarrah.[3] Both agencies confirmed his employment at MOIS and noted that in 1999, Zakeri said he had been transferred to the newly formed Intelligence Office of the Supreme Leader, the "shadow" intelligence outfit whose existence the CIA found "preposterous."

In his new position, Zakeri once again handled security arrangements for the nation's top leaders and most senior intelligence operators.[4] That was how he got to meet Osama bin Laden's chief deputy, Dr. Ayman al-Zawahri, and bin Laden's eldest son, Saad. "I organized the security for their meetings with my bosses," Zakeri told me.

When I traveled to Karlsruhe, Germany, to talk with German prosecutors about Zakeri, they said he was "unreliable." I was curious whether they meant he was an imposter who had lied about his past employment with Iranian intelligence. No, they said: German intelligence had confirmed his employment record. It was his testimony on Mzoudi that was unreliable, because he claimed Mzoudi was in Iran in 1997 when the Germans had confirmed that he was actually in Germany. I pointed out that in my conversations with Zakeri leading up to the trial, he had never mentioned Mzoudi. That information came from an e-mail Zakeri had received on December 17, 2003, from a source in Iran. (See appendix.) Zakeri casually mentioned Mzoudi's training in Iran at a lunch with a German intelligence officer. Two days later, he listened with astonishment as the Voice of America announced he was a "surprise new witness" in the 9/11 trial in Hamburg. Without him, the Germans didn't have a case.

In fact, once the Germans told him they planned to put him on the stand, Zakeri pleaded with them to give him enough time to get his source out of Iran to provide detailed testimony. They agreed to postpone Zakeri's court appearance by ten days, but no more. It wasn't enough.

A few weeks after the trial, Zakeri did manage to get his source out of Iran and took a videotaped deposition of his testimony at a location I have agreed not to disclose, along with Andreas Schultz, a lawyer for the German victims of the September 11 attacks. Zakeri showed me the 18-minute videotape. His source was part of the Revolutionary Guards security detail that handled foreign terrorists coming to Iran for special training. He picked out Mzoudi from a series of eleven photographs and said he first saw him arriving at Tehran's Mehrabad Airport in early November 1999—two years *after* the date Zakeri had understood from his cryptic e-mail. Mzoudi was coming in from Damascus on an Iran Air flight, along with five other Arab "trainees." Zakeri's source took them to the former U.S. embassy in Tehran, where the IRGC keeps its main computers. "They have a special place there for teaching transmissions and codes," he said. "Number Six [Mzoudi] received that training." He also recognized Mzoudi's codefendant, Moatesseq, among the trainees.

"Zakeri did say something about meetings in Iran before 9/11," the lead prosecutor acknowledged, "but he didn't say if the 9/11 attacks were planned there. And he didn't participate in those meetings directly. He was in charge of security for the people who attended the meetings." I could detect a note of contempt in the prosecutor's voice, although he had just confirmed one of the most astonishing—and previously unknown—details about the planning phase of the 9/11 attacks. The 9/11 hijackers and al-Qaeda planners had been in constant contact with senior Iranian officials and intelligence officers *before* September 11. It was not a casual relationship or a chance encounter here and there, but a steady stream of contacts.

The Germans never asked Zakeri about those meetings during the Mzoudi trial. They didn't care.

PLANNING SESSION

The first of the planning sessions took place in January 2001, when Zawahri arrived in Iran from Afghanistan accompanied by twenty-nine other al-Qaeda leaders. "Zawahri told my boss, Mustafa Hadadian, that they were planning a major operation against the United States and Israel," Zakeri told me.[5] The four-day meeting was held at a luxurious mountain guesthouse near the town of Varamin, just south of Tehran, that was reserved for use by senior regime officials. The three-story villa was built to blend into the mountain if viewed from the air and was protected by a 5- to 10-kilometer exclusion zone. In preparing the site, Zakeri went door to door in the nearby villages, collecting names and phone numbers so he could keep tabs on the local residents. The villa itself could only be reached via a tunnel leading from the cemetery.

Very few people knew about the Varamin guesthouse, according to an old friend who had worked on Iran for various U.S. intelligence agencies for more than thirty years. He considered that Zakeri's intimate knowledge of this safe house argued in favor of his credibility.

"Zawahri and his men were talking about their 'plans for the future,' and said they had the 'same enemy' as the Iranians," Zakeri said. "They said they were trying to build up one movement [of Sunnis and Shias] to cooperate together and were asking Iran for additional operational support."

Bin Laden's top deputy asked the Iranians for special equipment and help in laundering money in Dubai, as well as assistance with travel documents so al-Qaeda operatives could move from Iran to Europe without attracting the attention of customs and immigration. "Ayman al-Zawahri told my boss that al-Qaeda was very soon going to make a major operation against the United States and Israel," Zakeri said.

Nateq-Nouri, the head of the Office of the Supreme Leader, led the Iranian delegation during the initial four-day meeting with Zawahri. Also present was Ali Akbar Parvaresh, a former education minister and top operative in Section 43, the MOIS outfit that handled overseas terrorist operations and that controlled the Varamin safe house. Parvaresh was wanted by the Argentine government for his alleged involvement in the bombing of the Argentine Israeli Mutual Association in Buenos Aires that killed eighty-six people in July 1994.

As a show of respect for Zawahri and al-Qaeda, the Iranians had made available top regime leaders. They had big hopes and big plans.

Arguably the most important member of the Iranian team was not even Iranian, at least by birth. He was a Lebanese named Imad Fayez Mugniyeh, a top operative with the Qods Force, a special branch of the Revolutionary Guards that carried out foreign terrorist operations. He arrived separately at the safe house in a canvas-covered livestock truck. Zakeri had known him for years and they talked frequently. His operational involvement with the 9/11 plot has never been documented before by an eyewitness account.

The four-day meeting went so well that twelve of Zawahri's men stayed on in Iran, setting up an operational headquarters in the city of Karaj. They stayed in a safe house known as "3,000 Mountain"—another obscure place whose existence was known only to a few, my friend at a U.S. intelligence agency said.

Among those who remained in Iran, Zakeri recognized Saif al-Adel, an Egyptian who had worked with Mugniyeh for several years. Still in Iran today, al-Adel assumed control of al-Qaeda's military operations after U.S. air strikes killed his predecessor in Afghanistan in November 2001, the United States believes.

A second, unrelated defector from Iran's Revolutionary Guards Corps, whom I have agreed to identify only as Colonel B, told me independently of Zawahri's meeting with Nateq-Nouri. He learned of the meeting from a relative who was physically present and who hand-carried messages from Zawahri to Supreme Leader Ali Khamenei after September 11. "At the time, I didn't know about al-Qaeda," he told me. "We called them all Taliban." But both he and his source referred to Zawahri by name.

BIN LADEN'S SON

On May 4, 2001—exactly four months and seven days before September 11—another al-Qaeda delegation arrived in Iran from Afghanistan. Zakeri believed they crossed near Tayebad, east of Mashad, a border post frequently used by Iranian intelligence to facilitate al-Qaeda travel. A senior Revolutionary Guards commander flew the al-Qaeda men by helicopter from eastern Iran to a small military airport near Damavand Mountain, south of Tehran. Zakeri met them when they touched down.

Salaam, he said to the tall young Arab who emerged from the helicopter. It was one of the few Arabic words Zakeri knew.

When the young man replied in English, Zakeri made small talk. Is this the first time you come to Iran?

It is, said the young Arab. Zakeri learned later that the young man was Osama bin Laden's eldest son, Saad. Zakeri thought he carried himself like a king. "He was very confident, very much at ease with himself," he recalled. "He was always carrying a Koran, like the Prophet Mohammad." The other Arabs who climbed out of the helicopter were his bodyguards.

Zakeri accompanied Saad bin Laden in an armored Mercedes to the intelligence headquarters in Parchin, just south of Tehran. The bodyguards followed in a separate car. To enhance security, they had closed off the main highway from Damavand to Tehran to all other traffic. They sped along at breakneck speed.

We give you some time to relax, freshen up, Zakeri said, as he showed them to a special suite in the underground complex. "We move again at one-thirty in the morning."

At 2:15 a.m. he drove the younger bin Laden and two bodyguards to Ayatollah Khomeini's former residence in Jamaran, the Tehran suburb in the foothills of the Elburz mountains where top regime officials lived.

During daylight hours, parts of Jamaran are a museum dedicated to Khomeini's memory. At night, access to the area is tightly controlled. Former president Ali Akbar Rafsanjani lives next door and other top clerics live nearby. Just like the underground intelligence headquarters in Parchin, Jamaran was part of a parallel universe, created solely for top officials of the regime. For this meeting, security was even more rigorous than normal.

Zakeri's boss, Hadadian, welcomed the Arab guests at the door, but only Saad bin Laden was shown inside. Zakeri stayed outside with the bodyguards and watched the leaders arrive one by one. "I know who they are because I recognize their cars and know all the bodyguards," he told me. "We talked outside while the meeting is going on."

Inside, the younger bin Laden met for nearly three hours with all five members of the Leadership Council: Supreme Leader Ali Khamenei; Rafsanjani, who now headed the Expediency Council; Mohammad Yazdi, head of the Council of Guardians, which overseas the parliament; Mahmoud Hashemi Shahroudi, the Judiciary chief; and Ayatollah Ali Meshkini, the head of the Assembly of Experts, the group that picks the Supreme Leader.

It was an extraordinary event. These were the unelected men who ruled Iran. They were the ones who decided if dissidents got picked up on the streets or were gunned down in Europe. They had ordered the bombing of the U.S. Air Force barracks in Dhahran. And they were about to give assent and assistance for a far more devastating attack on America.

Zakeri believes it was at this meeting, on May 4, 2001, that Iran's leaders learned the specifics of bin Laden's plans for the September 11 attack and decided to provide operational assistance. "Everything changed after this," he told me.

When the predawn call to prayers sounded from a nearby *muezzin*, the Iranian leaders departed one by one. At around 6 a.m. Zakeri drove Saad bin Laden back to Parchin. For the next three weeks he handled security for the young Saudi as he met with operational leaders from Section 43—the detail men of Iran's foreign terrorist organization.

THE TASKING MEMOS

On May 14, 2001, Nateq-Nouri sent a memorandum to Mustafa Pourghanad, the director of Section 43, laying out the guidelines established by the Supreme Leader for joint operations with al-Qaeda. It was the equivalent of a Presidential Decision Directive in the United States, the top-secret documents that guide policy makers in developing specific operational plans.

Zakeri gave me a copy of this document. Stamped "Top Secret" in red, it bears Nateq-Nouri's personal signature seal in green ink and a rectangular blue stamp showing that it had been filed after a copy had been sent to MOIS Section 43 on the same date. The original, which he also showed me, is on high-rag-content paper with a silvery watermark bearing the seal of the Islamic Republic of Iran at top, and at bottom, the phrase *Sazeman-e etelaat-e Rahbari*—Leader's Intelligence Office. The watermark is of currency quality.

In the memorandum, written in Persian, Nateq-Nouri says that Khamenei personally has seen the latest report "regarding support and help for the future plan" of al-Qaeda. Any attack, Khamenei ordered, must "strike at [America's] economic structure, their reputation . . . and their internal peace and security."

"Our emphasis should be the struggle with the Great Satan and Israel," Khamenei said. "This is our main agenda." Whatever operation Section 43 put together, it was essential that Iran "not leave any evidence behind that can impact negatively on us in the future."

In closing the letter, Nateq-Nouri instructed MOIS to work to "improve our plans, especially in coordination with fighters of al-Qaeda and Hezbollah to find one objective that is beneficial to both sides." Above all, he stressed, "the Leader mentioned that we should limit our relations with al-Qaeda to just two people as before—Imad Mugniyeh and Ayman al-Zawahri—and deal only with them."

Deniability was key to the Iranian plans, as was an intelligence operative who has been on the U.S. Most Wanted List for over twenty years: Lebanese-born Hezbollah terror master Imad Mugniyeh.

Zakeri's boss, Hadadian, sent a follow-on tasking memo to Pourghanad three weeks later as the plans become more precise. In this June 3 memo, which Zakeri also made available, he ordered Pourghanad to mobilize all Section 43 operations cells to prepare for the attack, which was then planned to take place on the tenth of Shahrivar—September 1.

"If there is going to be an attack on the American government," he wrote, "we have to ensure we can defend against U.S. retaliation." By defense, he clearly meant more terrorist attacks against the United States and U.S. interests around the world.

It was around the time this second letter was sent that Zakeri recalls seeing the display on the target wall at MOIS headquarters in Tehran showing a missile aimed at the Pentagon.[6]

In early July, Zakeri's boss asked him if he wanted to go back to the border with Afghanistan with Mugniyeh to pick up the al-Qaeda men. Zawahri was returning to Tehran for a final operational meeting.

Zakeri declined. Zawahri gave him the creeps. "He never smiles. He never moves his lips when he speaks. You could put a hundred pounds of honey on his face and no one would eat him. He doesn't move his hands when he walks."

Zakeri became increasingly nervous. Something big was coming down. He knew he had to get out of Iran.

CIA CYA

I spoke with Zakeri on several occasions after he fled to Europe in May 2002, and walked him through his story repeatedly. No matter whether I began at the beginning or asked him to clarify an obscure detail he had mentioned, his story never varied in the many times he told it. I quizzed him about details of the MOIS headquarters where he saw the model of the 9/11 targets, then asked other former Iranian intelligence officers to describe the building they knew. The descriptions matched. I asked him to describe the safe houses where the January and May 2001 meetings took place, and ran those by friends in the U.S. intelligence community who had been tracking Iran for decades. Again, his story appeared credible under such scrutiny. Similarly, I ran the details of his more discursive account of Iran's foreign terrorist apparatus—names, dates, titles, and attributions; and in every case the information tracked.

In describing another defector who provided extraordinary information on al-Qaeda's future plans in 1996, a former CIA analyst who worked on the staff of the 9/11 Commission told me, "If 25 percent of a defector's information checks out with things you know from other sources, then you had damn well better pay attention to the other 75 percent." Ignoring claims from such a defector, no matter how wild, was contrary to good intelligence practice.

And yet, when I called the CIA for its reaction to the warning Zakeri said he had delivered in Baku in late July 2001, I was greeted with unusual hostility. A female intelligence officer returned my call with a shaking voice. "This man is a serial fabricator," she said, more nervous than indignant. "I have to warn you off of this story."

A few hours later, I received another call, this one from a higher-ranking official. When I asked him to comment on the veracity of Zakeri's warning, he replied angrily, "We have no record that he made any such claim. And he is a fabricator of monumental proportions." But when I asked him whether Zakeri was lying about meeting with U.S. officials in Baku on July 26, 2001, this senior official pointedly refused to answer.[7]

It wasn't as if the Agency hadn't been warned before. The covert war that Iran's leaders were waging against the United States had been raging for well over twenty years.

Increasingly, that war is becoming more open.

2

THE INTERCEPT

Colonel Timothy J. Geraghty woke up well before 5:30 a.m., as was his habit, and went outside to enjoy the early-morning calm. It was Sunday, October 23, 1983. By Beirut standards, the previous six months had been relatively uneventful. Geraghty remembers being asked when he first arrived in Lebanon in May what uniform he would be taking ashore "for the social side" of his duties. As commander of the U.S. contingent of the multinational force then in Beirut, he was expected to attend a wide variety of ambassadorial and diplomatic functions, but he made an early decision "that I wasn't going to take any uniforms that weren't combat gear." It wasn't a premonition of things to come so much as a matter of principle, Geraghty told me. He didn't want to pretend that he was in Beirut as anything other than a marine.

What he couldn't know was that others, too, intended to remind him that he was a combatant.

No one could blame Colonel Geraghty for believing that Beirut—the marines nicknamed it "The Root"—was the mission of mercy the Reagan administration and its partners in France, Britain, and Italy portrayed it as being. The president decided to redeploy the marines to Beirut after the massacre of Palestinian women and children in the Sabra and Shatilla refugee camps in September 1982—a decision, Geraghty told me, Reagan made "with his heart, against hard information from some quarters." It was a humanitarian mission, not dictated by a clear U.S. national security interest.

The marines were concentrated into a large, exposed building with a Hyatt Hotel–style atrium near the Beirut international airport, within easy mortar range of Syrian- and Iranian-backed militia groups in the surrounding hills. Although the U.S. embassy in Beirut had been blown apart by a truck bomb in April that killed sixty-three people, Geraghty and his superiors were not unduly worried, since at that time the embassy bombing appeared to be an isolated event. "Marines were going on liberty. They were going in town to eat. They were—it was just a lot more relaxed environment and they were generally being accepted very much by the people," Geraghty recalls. "When we would go on patrols we were met—the kids were coming out and very friendly. And I have to add, it wasn't just the Americans. Troops from the other members of the multinational peacekeeping force were similarly greeted as protectors."[1]

On August 28, 1983, the Israelis withdrew their troops from the Beirut area, creating a security vacuum and ushering in a period Geraghty later called the "September Wars." Militia groups began shelling the marines randomly almost every day, but the peacekeepers' mission hadn't changed. Every marine under Geraghty's command was handed a small printed card with the rules of engagement: "When on post, mobile or foot patrol, keep loaded magazine in weapon, bolt closed, weapon on safe, no round in chamber."

When Geraghty went out that morning sometime before six o'clock, he was struck by how quiet it was, especially after the almost daily shelling of recent weeks. "There weren't too many things moving. No songbirds or anything else. It had cleared up. It was just very quiet."

Less than a half hour later that quiet was shattered.

Geraghty had gone back up to his office, a short distance away from the marine barracks, known as the BLT1-8 (Eighth Marines Battalion Landing Team), when a tremendous explosion blew out windows and doors and hurled him against the far wall. Geraghty ran downstairs to the command center, but all he could see was a fog of dust and dirt. He felt his way outside, where he heard his logistics officer, Major Melton, call out to him.

"My God, sir, the BLT building is gone."

SITTING DUCKS

Steve Edward Russell, an E-5 sergeant with the Second Marine Division out of Camp Lejeune, North Carolina, was in the sandbag-protected guard post directly in front of the BLT building when he heard a loud snap behind him, by the main gate—"like a two-by-four breaking," he later recalled. At first he thought nothing of it. "I must have said to myself, well, it's Sunday morning, 0630, whatever. You know, there had been construction throughout the week behind us at the airport terminal. You know, trucks came out. A lot of construction noise. So I didn't really think anything of it at first."

But when Russell looked over his shoulder, he law a large Mercedes water truck "coming through an open gate and bouncing." Russell whipped around "and I said out loud to myself, 'Where the f—k did he come from?' "

As he got up from the swivel chair inside the guard post to take a better look, his .45 sidearm caught on the arm of the chair. The gun was not loaded—in keeping with the peacekeeping mission's rules of engagement as they applied to marines inside the compound. By the time Russell got outside with his unloaded weapon, the truck was leaning heavily as it swerved around traffic barriers and began heading straight toward his guard shack and the barracks. As it closed in, Russell got a clear look at the driver's face. "We made eye contact and he had what I call a shitty grin on his face." The driver, who Russell thought was around twenty-five or thirty, was wearing a patterned shirt that could have been camouflage. "He had a grubby—perhaps what I call a scrubby seven-day beard, not full beard but a scrubby seven-day beard. Mustache. Curly black hair."

At that point something snapped inside Russell, "and the only thing on my mind was to warn," he says. He began running, screaming to a marine he encountered to get out of the way, and headed into the lobby to warn those who were sleeping upstairs in rooms ringing the atrium. He got one last look at the driver as the truck followed him into the lobby, just twenty or thirty feet behind him. He had "a smile of success, you might say." Russell made it to the far side of the building when the truck stopped inexplicably in the center of the lobby. The windshield was broken, the driver appeared to reach down, and the next thing Russell saw was "a bright flash, a yellow flame," followed almost instantaneously by "heat and confusion and that was it." When he woke up a few minutes later, Russell was lying on his stomach and all he could see was gray dust. "The very first thing I said to myself is 'That son of a bitch did it. He f—kin' did it.' "

As his senses returned, Russell heard the voice of a black marine screaming for help, but he couldn't move. When he finally managed to roll onto his back, he saw that his left foot was reversed and that his left hand was split in two. He lay there helpless for two or three minutes until the screaming stopped. That's when help finally arrived.

Twenty years later, in March 2003, Russell testified before a Washington, D.C., courtroom packed with family members of his fellow marines. At the end of his testimony, he burst into tears, releasing the burden of guilt he had been carrying for the past two decades for not having been able to stop the truck. "I hope I've done some good today," he said finally, "and if I step down right now and drop dead I'd be happy because I've been a good marine." The entire courtroom erupted into applause.[2]

Russell's sidearm was not loaded because the marines were on a "peacekeeping" mission. Asked by attorney Thomas Fortune Fay what that meant, Russell hesitated. "At the time we really didn't know. To this day I really can't—"

Judge Royce C. Lamberth gently cut him off. "Well, you know today it's to be sitting ducks," he said.

THE UNITED STATES FAILS TO STRIKE BACK

The blast that killed 241 U.S. Marines that morning in Beirut was so powerful that it snapped the reinforced concrete support columns of the building "like rubber bands," according to FBI explosives expert Danny A. Defenbaugh, who was brought in from the United States to examine the evidence after the attack. The terrorists had used government-issue PETN explosive enhanced by butane gas canisters in an effort to generate the massive destructive power of a fuel-air explosive, he said. Fifty-eight French peacekeepers died in a parallel truck-bombing just minutes later, less than two miles away.

If the U.S. Marines had no clear idea what they were doing in Beirut, the Islamic Republic of Iran had no doubt as to its goal, which was to drive the United States out of Lebanon, tail between its legs. The nearly simultaneous, coordinated attacks were the handiwork of Iranian government agents. Their previously unheard-of technique found a distant admirer in Osama bin Laden, who later quizzed his Iranian and Hezbollah contacts to learn its secrets.[3]

It wasn't the Iranian government's first attack on America since the 444-day Tehran hostage crisis. But it was the first time that Iran's involvement was crystal clear to U.S. policy makers. The story of just how much we knew at the time can now be told for the first time, thanks to four men who shared their knowledge with the court and with me for this book: Vice Admiral (ret.) James ("Ace") Lyons, former deputy chief of naval operations; former secretary of the navy John Lehman; former CIA operations officer Robert Baer; and Maryland trial lawyer Thomas Fortune Fay.

On or about September 26, 1983—four weeks *before* the attack—the National Security Agency (NSA) intercepted a message sent from Iranian intelligence headquarters in Tehran to Hojjat-ol eslam Ali Akbar Mohtashemi, the Iranian ambassador in Damascus. The message "directed the Iranian ambassador to contact Hussein Musawi, the leader of the terrorist group Islamic Amal, and to instruct him . . . 'to take a spectacular action against the United States Marines,'" as Judge Lamberth summarized.[4]

The intercept was never delivered to Colonel Geraghty and his men so they could improve base security. "Generally, yes, we knew the problem," he told me. "But we never got a warning mentioning a possible attack on the barracks or mentioning Iran."

Thousands of messages involving threats to U.S. forces in Lebanon were being processed by the NSA and other intelligence agencies. Because this particular intercept "did not mention a specific time or place, it was not considered [by CIA managers] to be actionable," former CIA operations officer Robert Baer told me. As a result, the warning never was sent on to Beirut. It was a fatal oversight—precisely the type of preventable intelligence failure that was highlighted by the 9/11 Commission twenty years later.

Admiral Lyons, then deputy chief of naval operations for plans, policy, and operations, remembers well when he first learned of the NSA intercept. It was exactly two days *after* the attack. "The director of naval intelligence carried the transcript to me in a locked briefcase," he told me. "He gave it to me, to the chief of naval operations, and to the secretary of the navy all in the same day." In a personal tribute to the slain marines and their families, Lyons presented a copy of the highly classified NSA transcript in a sealed envelope to the court. "If ever there was a 24-karat gold document, this was it," Lyons said. "This was not something from the third cousin of the fourth wife of Muhammad the taxicab driver." The message "should have set off all the bells and whistles."

Lyons still cannot understand why it was not sent up the chain of command until after the attack. "I've asked that question a thousand times."

After the bombing, the CIA launched its investigation, and soon managed to identify the Hezbollah operative who built the bomb in the truck. "His name was Ibrahim Safa," says Bob Baer. "He was working with the Pasdaran—the Iranian Revolutionary Guards—out of the southern suburbs of Beirut. In the hierarchy of things, he was just a thug who'd found God. He'd been a bang-bang man in the civil war in the 1970s who knew explosives."

The driver of the truck—the unshaven man with the "shitty" grin—was an Iranian named Walid, also known as Asmail al-Askari ("the Soldier"). Iranian ambassador Mohtashemi didn't fully trust his Lebanese allies to carry out the plot to the very end—their own suicide—and wanted to make sure that one of his own countrymen had final responsibility for piloting the truck on its death run.

After the bombing, President Ronald Reagan privately demanded retaliation, asking the U.S. Navy and the Joint Chiefs of Staff to draw up target lists. According to several participants in these internal and highly classified deliberations, the Syrian government also played a role in the plot, and so several Syrian officers were put on the target list. So were the Syrian defense ministry and the Iranian Revolutionary Guards headquarters in the Sheikh Abdallah barracks in Lebanon's Bekaa Valley.

"It is my recollection that I had been briefed on who had done it and what the evidence was," former navy secretary John Lehman told me. "I was told the actual names of the Syrians and where they were. I was told about the evidence that the Iranian government was directly behind it. I was told that the people who had done it were trained in Baalbek and that many of them were back in Baalbek. I recall very clearly that there was no controversy who did it. I never heard any briefer or person in the corridor who said, 'Oh, maybe we don't know who did it.'"

Within three weeks of the attack, enough intelligence had been gathered to determine exactly where and how to hit back, and the president was briefed on a counterstrike package. Planners say it included eight Tomahawk missiles launched from the battleship *New Jersey* against the Syrian defense ministry and other command targets in Syria. Carrier-based A6-A Intruders were assigned to bomb the Sheikh Abdallah barracks in a joint strike with the French. It also included selected "snatches" of Syrian officers based in Lebanon who had helped carry out the operation.[5]

Coordinates were already being programmed into the Tomahawks, and the A6 pilots and snatch teams were being briefed, intelligence and defense officials involved in the planning told me, when someone pulled the plug. By all accounts, that someone was Defense Secretary Caspar Weinberger.

What prompted Weinberger to blink? When I put that question to him point-blank, twenty years later, Weinberger said that the intelligence on who was behind the attacks was unclear. "We had nothing before the bombing, although I had warned repeatedly that the security situation [in Beirut] was very bad. We were in the middle of the bull's-eye, but we didn't know who was attacking the bull's-eye."

Weinberger insists that he has "never heard of any specific information" about Iranian responsibility for the attack. "If I had known, I wouldn't have hesitated" to approve retaliatory action, he says. "Clearly the attack was planned. But it was hard to locate who had done it out of all the different groups. The president didn't want some kind of carpet bombing that would kill a lot of innocent civilians. There were so many groups, and not all of them were responsible to the government of Iran. All we knew was that they were united in their hatred of America."[6]

Weinberger's account surprised several other participants who had firsthand knowledge of the intelligence information. "Perhaps Weinberger was never given the intercept by his staff," one participant suggested.

At the time, highly classified NSA material such as the Damascus intercept would have been given to the chairman of the Joint Chiefs of Staff, General John Vessey, and to the military aide to the secretary of defense, who would determine whether the secretary would be apprised of the information personally. Weinberger's aide at the time was Major General Colin Powell.

But Vessey told me he had "no recollection" of seeing the intelligence on Iran's involvement in the attack. "It is unbelievable to me that someone didn't bring it through the director of the Defense Intelligence Agency up to me and the secretary of defense," he said. Somewhere along the line, the system broke down. "I just don't know what happened," Vessey said. Powell's chief of staff at the State Department, who spent thirty-one years in the military and was well versed in how this type of highly classified intelligence was processed, suggested that the intercept never made it into the president's daily brief, the all-source intelligence summary, which was shared with the secretary of defense. Powell, Vessey, and Weinberger all agreed that if the intercept had reached them, they would have ordered retaliatory raids without hesitation.

On November 16, 1983, Weinberger received a telephone call from Charles Hernu, the French minister of defense, informing him that French Super-Etendard fighter-bombers were getting ready to attack Iranian Revolutionary Guards positions in Baalbek. In his memoirs, Weinberger states that he "had received no orders or notifications from the president or anyone prior to that phone call from Paris," which he said gave him too short a notice to scramble U.S. jets.[7]

I was covering the fighting between Yasser Arafat and Syrian-backed PLO rebels in Tripoli, Lebanon, at the time, and I vividly recall watching the French warplanes with their clearly recognizable silhouette roar overhead en route to Baalbek. The raid was a total failure, killing a local shepherd but none of the Iranian Revolutionary Guards in the Sheikh Abdallah barracks, who had been evacuated just as I was watching the planes head toward the Bekaa Valley. It was later reported that someone in the French Foreign Ministry had warned the Iranians of the impending raid just minutes before the planes took off.

Whatever the reasons behind America's refusal to join that French retaliatory raid, there can be no doubt that the terrorists and their masters took the U.S. failure to retaliate forcefully as a sign of weakness. Just five months later, the same terrorist who organized the marine barracks bombing took CIA station chief William Buckley hostage and hideously tortured him for more than a year until he died.

Osama bin Laden has referred to the U.S. withdrawal from Beirut as a clear demonstration of "the weakness of the American soldier, who is prepared to fight cold wars and unprepared to fight long wars."[8] Syrian foreign minister Abdel Halim Khaddam drew a similar conclusion during negotiations over the U.S. pullout from Lebanon a few months later. "The United States is short of breath. You can always wait them out."[9]

"The first shots in the war on terror we are in now were fired in Beirut in October 1983," says Colonel Tim Geraghty. "The [Bush] administration is now doing exactly what we need to be doing, attacking the enemies of freedom where they live instead of letting them attack us in our home."

But the failure to strike back against Iran and Syria in 1983 was a dreadful mistake, he says. "This was an act of war. We knew who the players were. And, because we didn't respond, we emboldened these people to increase the violence."

In Arlington National Cemetery, across the Potomac River from Washington, D.C., a small memorial marks the graves of the 241 marines, seventeen U.S. embassy personnel, and a half-dozen U.S. hostages who died in Lebanon in the 1980s. A cedar of Lebanon stands over the site. Every year on October 23, families gather for a memorial service to commemorate the lives of these first American victims of Islamic Iran's vicious, relentless, and unending war on America.

3

THE HIJACKER

Ken Stethem realized that the dead man was his younger brother, Robbie, when he saw the bloodied shirt on the tarmac. It was the same distinctive, checked shirt he had given Robbie just weeks earlier, during his last visit home for a family reunion in Waldorf, Maryland. Now Robbie lay lifeless beneath a TWA jetliner in Beirut, his face bruised and swollen beyond recognition.[1]

Robert Dean Stethem was a twenty-three-year-old U.S. Navy petty officer, trained as a diver and an underwater construction specialist. On the morning of Friday, June 14, 1985, Stethem and six fellow divers assigned to a navy underwater construction team boarded TWA Flight 847 in Athens, Greece, bound for Rome, Italy. After a variety of overseas assignments, they were heading back home to the United States.

Ten minutes into the flight, two hijackers stormed the forward section of the plane and assaulted a flight attendant. Brandishing a pistol and hand grenades, they shouted in English, "Americans, come to die!"[2]

The next twenty hours were a roller-coaster ride of unimaginable torment for Stethem and his navy comrades. The hijackers ordered pilot John Testrake to fly first to Beirut, where they took on fuel and released seventeen women and two children, then to Algiers, where, after a tense five hours of negotiations, they eventually released another twenty passengers. The hijackers herded all the passengers toward the rear of the aircraft and forced them into the "847 position"—head down, with hands locked behind their necks and elbows on their knees—whenever the plane was airborne. The survivors never forgot the stifling heat of the Algerian desert, when the plane sat on the runway without air conditioning, toilets overflowing, the hijackers screaming and threatening to kill them if a fuel truck didn't arrive. During that first stop in Algiers, Stethem and fellow diver Knut Carlson were marched blindfolded, at gunpoint, to the forward cabin, their arms bound behind them. The hijackers beat Stethem brutally about the head, shoulders, back, and arms with a club as they shouted, "One American must die."

After refueling, the hijackers ordered Testrake to fly back to Beirut, where he arrived well after midnight on June 15. Rival Christian and Shiite militiamen battled for control of the runway, and for several hours the Boeing 727 circled overhead, unable to land. Finally, with just six minutes of fuel remaining, Testrake put down and taxied toward waiting reporters and fuel trucks.

Inside the plane, the hijacker the passengers referred to as "Hitler" grabbed Robbie Stethem, who was bleeding profusely, and hauled him toward the passenger door at the front of the aircraft. Once "Hitler"—later identified as Mohammad Ali Hamadeh—was sure the news cameras were running, he kicked open the door and appeared wearing a ski mask and holding a gun against Stethem's head. Other passengers heard the twenty-three-year-old petty officer cry out, "Oh God!" just before Hamadeh pulled the trigger and pushed Stethem out the door. For several hours the navy officer lay at the foot of the stairway, in a pool of his own blood.

The hijackers then demanded that the airport authorities and news media douse all the lights, and under cover of darkness a dozen more militiamen joined the hijackers, including the man who was identified later as their ringleader. Inside the plane, they singled out six passengers with Jewish-sounding names and led them away.

After yet another round-trip flight to Algiers, where the remaining women and older passengers were disembarked, TWA 847 returned to Beirut so the hijackers could disperse the male passengers to hiding places in Beirut's treacherous southern suburbs. Lebanese Shiite leader Nabih Berri was ostensibly in charge of negotiating their release. But as President Reagan's national security adviser, Robert McFarlane, testified in a U.S. court seventeen years later, it wasn't until approval was given by Iranian Majles speaker Ali Akbar Hashemi-Rafsanjani that the hostages were driven to Damascus and turned over to the Syrian government to be released, two weeks after the ordeal had begun.

The hijacking and hostage crisis were yet another attack on America by the Islamic Republic of Iran.

Many Americans still remember the haunting image of Captain Testrake being interviewed on ABC News through the open cockpit window on the ground in Beirut, while a masked hijacker grabbed him and waved a pistol at his head. Once again, America was being held hostage, and the U.S. government appeared powerless to do anything about it.

With the hijacking of TWA Flight 847, Rafsanjani and his fellow mullahs in Tehran were taunting President Reagan. Where were the marines? Iran had chased them from Lebanon. Where was the Delta Force, rumored to be just offshore, waiting to storm the plane? As Ayatollah Khomeini had said during the Tehran hostage crisis, "America can't do a damn thing." An aura of invincibility buoyed the hijackers and their Iranian masters. They were openly defying the greatest power on earth, and America seemed powerless to stop them.

EMERGING OUT OF THE SHADOWS

With the hijacking of TWA 847, the man who had become the Iranian government's top terrorist agent stepped out of the shadows for the first time. TWA 847 was his perverse premiere on the world stage. Until then he had worked behind the scenes, blowing up the U.S. embassy in Beirut on April 18, 1983, and truck-bombing the marine barracks six months later. In 1984 he began kidnapping westerners in Beirut, starting with CNN correspondent Jeremy Levin and, on March 16, CIA station chief William Buckley. Now he wanted all the world to see him. Wearing a thick beard and blue jeans, with cartridge belts slung around his neck, he brandished an assault rifle at the foot of the aircraft like some Islamic Che Guevara.

Although no one yet knew his name or anything about the mysterious group he commanded, the young Lebanese Shiite put a face on Islamic terror that persists to this day.

CIA director William Casey had had a personal interest in discovering his identity ever since Buckley was whacked on the head outside of his apartment building in Beirut and bundled into a car to become a hostage. Casey tasked CIA operatives in the field to report back every sliver of information they could find about Buckley's kidnappers.

One of the first pieces of the puzzle was a set of fingerprints an FBI forensics team found in the rear lavatory of the TWA jetliner in Beirut once the hijacking/hostage crisis was over. The Lebanese authorities identified the prints as belonging to a young Lebanese Shiite named Imad Fayez Mugniyeh and provided a copy of the passport he had been issued on September 7, 1984.

The eldest of four children, Mugniyeh was born in the village of Tir Diba in the mountains above the Lebanese coastal city of Tyre on July 12, 1962. At first glance, he seemed an unlikely candidate to become a star terrorist or an agent of the Islamic Republic of Iran. His father, Sheikh Muhammad Jawad Mugniyeh, was a local cleric who won renown as a writer. In a 1979 book, *Khomeini wa al Dawla al Islamiyya* (*Khomeini and the Islamic State*), Sheikh Jawad condemned the principle of an Islamic state led by a Supreme Guide (*faghih*), arguing that such a leader would be "vulnerable to obliviousness, pride, and vanity." If anything, his writings urged Lebanese Shiites to withhold support from Ayatollah Khomeini and Iran, not become their agents.

But the young Imad rejected his father's caution. As a high school dropout during Lebanon's civil wars, he traveled up to Beirut and joined the elite Force 17, Yasser Arafat's personal security guard. According to former CIA officer Bob Baer, who helped track Mugniyeh while posted to the shattered CIA station in Beirut in 1986, Mugniyeh began his career at the age of fourteen or fifteen as "a low-level bang man, one of dozens who spent their days and nights sniping at Christians across the Green Line."[3]

While living among Shiite refugees in a blighted Beirut suburb known as 'Ayn Al-Dilbah, Mugniyeh became friends with a handsome, half-paralyzed young man his own age, Mustafa Badr-el-Din. To compensate for his handicap (which prevented him from proving himself through street combat), Badr-el-Din learned a trade that made a virtue of a steady hand and a cool head, rather than an itchy finger.

He became a bomb maker.

Mugniyeh would frequently use Badr-el-Din's specialty: truck bombs boosted by bottles of butane gas to enhance their explosive yield. To seal their friendship, Badr-el-Din offered Mugniyeh his sister in marriage, Western intelligence officers I consulted in Europe told me.[4]

When Arafat was forced to leave Beirut after the 1982 war, he handed over Mugniyeh and the network of Force 17 security operatives he worked with to Iranian Revolutionary Guards commander Hossein Mosleh, who was operating out of Baalbek. At that point, Mosleh reported to Iran's ambassador in Damascus, Mohtashemi—the same man who ordered Mugniyeh's truck-bombing of the U.S. Marines in October 1983. Some 1,500 Revolutionary Guards troops of the newly organized "Qods Force" were encamped in the Lebanese army barracks on the outskirts of town.

The Iranian Revolutionary Guards imposed dour new rules on the people of Baalbek, a cosmopolitan town where Christians and Muslims had mingled and done business for centuries. Christian girls were required to wear Muslim-style headscarves at school; singing, dancing, and alcohol were banned; contacts with westerners were discouraged. Just seven years earlier, Baalbek had won international fame for hosting international dance troops and multimedia performances in its spectacular Roman ruins. By the time Mugniyeh began working with the Iranians, the Revolutionary Guards had set up tents and a latrine within the Temple of Jupiter and had hoisted sheets to cover naked statuary in the Temple of Bacchus.

Mugniyeh's crippled brother-in-law was captured and sentenced to death by the Kuwaiti authorities after a botched bombing attempt in Kuwait City in December 1983. (The Iranians were furious at Kuwait for its support of Saddam Hussein and also tried to assassinate the Kuwaiti emir.) One year later, Mugniyeh hijacked a Kuwaiti airliner to Tehran in an effort to win his release. When the Kuwaitis refused to buckle, Mugniyeh tried pressuring the French, hoping they would be able to persuade Kuwait to release his brother-in-law and sixteen other co-conspirators affiliated with the Islamist ad-Dawa party. In March 1985, Mugniyeh took two French diplomats, a researcher, and a journalist hostage in Beirut, and he reiterated his demand that Kuwait release the so-called Dawa 17 during the two-week ordeal of TWA 847.

David Jacobsen was one of a dozen Americans and Frenchmen kidnapped in Beirut in the mid-1980s by Mugniyeh and his pro-Iranian militiamen. At one point he shared a cell with the CIA's William Buckley in the Sheikh Abdallah barracks. "I was chained to the floor; I was blindfolded," Jacobsen recalled. "The person at my feet, I later learned, was [Associated Press bureau chief] Terry Anderson, and the person at the head was Bill Buckley."

Their guards tried to keep them from speaking to one another. "One of the chilling moments for me and for Terry Anderson was to hear Bill Buckley cough," says Jacobsen. "He was very, very sick. He was delirious. I heard him say, 'I don't know what happened to my body; it was so strong thirty days ago.' "

Mugniyeh's younger brother Jihad died in March 1985 when a car bomb intended for Hezbollah leader Sheikh Muhammad Hussein Fadlallah killed seventy-five people outside Fadlallah's home in Beirut. Hezbollah blamed the CIA for the attack. The CIA came to believe that Mugniyeh murdered Buckley some months later as an act of personal revenge, after he and his Iranian masters had extracted whatever secrets they could from the CIA officer during months of vicious torture.*

The United States twice spotted Mugniyeh on international flights

*Buckley was honored by CIA director William H. Webster at a posthumous ceremony at Arlington National Cemetery on May 13, 1988, and a star in his honor was carved into the wall of CIA headquarters—the fifty-first.

and sought to have him arrested. In 1985 he was photographed at Orly airport outside Paris, apparently headed back to Lebanon after several days of secret negotiations with the French government. Although the CIA provided a copy of the passport he was using, the French declined to stop him as happened again a year later at Roissy. French security officers, disgusted by their government's cowardice, gave me copies of those pictures not long afterward, which I published in a confidential newsletter called *Middle East Defense News* (*MEDNEWS*). The same photographs are reproduced in this book's appendix.[5]

Those pictures now appear on television networks, Web sites, and law enforcement most-wanted lists around the world as the only confirmed images of the younger Mugniyeh. "Hajj Imad was always a pretty boy," a former Iranian intelligence operative said. His good looks were almost feminine and made him the butt of jokes.

In 1995 Mugniyeh was on a commercial flight from Khartoum to Beirut after meeting with Osama bin Laden in the Sudan. The United States arranged with the air carrier—French-owned Middle East Airlines—to have the plane make an unscheduled stopover in Jedda, Saudi Arabia, so U.S. agents could arrest Mugniyeh on the basis of a sealed indictment issued against him by the U.S. Justice Department for his involvement in the TWA 847 hijacking and the murder of Robbie Stethem. But the Saudi authorities refused to haul him off the plane, fearing reprisals from bin Laden and their own radical clerics. Neither the French nor the Saudis wanted him on their hands.

In the 1990s Mugniyeh shifted focus from Lebanon to launch a series of dramatic international operations on Iran's behalf. On March 17, 1992, a Hezbollah strike team under his command leveled the Israeli embassy in Buenos Aires, killing twenty-nine people and wounding 242. A follow-on attack against the Argentine Israeli Mutual Association (AMIA) building in Buenos Aires in July 1994 took eighty-six innocent lives. U.S. and Israeli intelligence sources believe Mugniyeh parachuted into Argentina on an Iranian service passport shortly before the AMIA bombing, to activate the sleeper networks who did the dirty work. "There was lots of Iranian diplomatic activity just before the attack which remains unexplained," Argentinean judge Juan José Galeano told me. The Iranian diplomats and undercover operators involved in the attack "all got out before the bomb went off."[6]

In 1996 Mugniyeh wanted to hit another commercial airliner, this time from the Israeli airline El Al. The name on the expertly forged British passport used by Mugniyeh's operative was Andrew Jonathan Neumann.

Israel's much-vaunted security guards failed to notice anything suspicious about him or to detect the kilogram of military-grade RDX explosive he was carrying when he boarded a Swissair flight in Zurich in April 1996, bound for Israel.

Neumann wasn't British. He was a Lebanese Shiite named Hussein Mohammad Mikdad. Luckily for his intended victims, he failed Bomb-Making 101. While assembling the bomb in an East Jerusalem hotel room, Mikdad blew off his lower body. From the hospital bed where the Israelis struggled to keep him alive after the explosion, he affirmed that he had been trained in Iran to become "a heroic human flying bomb," on board an El Al flight departing from Tel Aviv. "The operation was a special gift" to Israel from Imad Mugniyeh, he said.

Before September 11, the Israelis had picked up numerous signs that Mugniyeh was planning new operations against Israel and the United States. A top Israeli military-intelligence official, Major General Amos Malka, went on Israeli television in June 2001 to warn that "bin Laden has tried, will try to reach us and may even reach us here in Israel." He described recent attempts by bin Laden to establish terrorist cells in Gaza and the West Bank, and said bin Laden's group was "planning an attack on U.S. and Israeli interests within the next few weeks." Mugniyeh was believed to be involved in several of these infiltration attempts.

Russian president Vladimir Putin has fingered Mugniyeh and Iran for helping to train Chechen rebels who fight against the Russian government. Speaking in Germany just ten days after the September 11 attacks, Putin said he had given specific information to the United States on Arab fighters in Chechnya whom Mugniyeh had trained. "As a rule, activities of terrorists are very coordinated," he said. "For example, on one Arab mercenary in Chechnya we found instructions for flying a Boeing."

"Bin Laden is a schoolboy in comparison with Mugniyeh," an Israeli intelligence officer told me. "The guy is a genius, someone who refined the art of terrorism to its utmost level. We studied him and reached the conclusion that he is a clinical psychopath motivated by uncontrollable psychological reasons, which we have given up trying to understand. The killing of his two brothers by the Americans only inflamed his strong motivation."*

After the TWA 847 hijacking, Mugniyeh rarely left fingerprints behind him and never again appeared in public.

---

*The second brother, Fuad, died when a car bomb exploded outside his shop in December 1994, across the street from the Beirut mosque where Hezbollah leader Sheikh Fadlallah was preaching his weekly sermon.

He has long since undergone a series of plastic surgery operations in Iran to alter his appearance. "They made him so he looks a bit like Richard Gere, but with a potbelly," a former Iranian colleague said. Today he lives in Qom with his Iranian wife, a cleric's daughter from the Hosseini clan. They have three children.

"Mugniyeh is a killer," the former colleague said. "Even at home he enjoys killing. He personally slaughters the lambs for the Muslim feasts, and takes pleasure in slitting their throats. From morning to night, he is planning to kill."

Such was the man the Iranians had chosen to become their chief operational liaison to Osama bin Laden and al-Qaeda. He was skilled and deadly. Most important of all, he was deniable.

ATOMIC AYATOLLAHS

It is your duty to build the atomic bomb for the Islamic Republican Party. . . . Our civilization is in danger and we have to have it.

—Ayatollah Mohammad Beheshti, speaking to the head of the shah's clandestine nuclear procurement effort, Dr. Fereidoun Fesharaki, in Tehran in May 1979

On November 6, 1985, the foreign edition of Tehran's *Keyhan* newspaper ran an Iranian government advertisement inviting Iranian nuclear scientists who had fled their country after the revolution to return home to attend a nuclear science and technology conference. Not only was the regime promising that their past sins would be forgiven, it even pledged to handle all the scientists' expenses and to make all the necessary travel arrangements.

Coming at a time when many exiles no longer had Iranian passports and were greeted with suspicion—and, frequently, jail—if they dared return home using foreign travel documents, the government offer was unusual. The keynote speaker for the March 14–19, 1986, conference was Hojjat-ol eslam Ali Akbar Hashemi-Rafsanjani, the powerful speaker of the Majles and a top aide to Ayatollah Khomeini.

Before 1979, the Atomic Energy Organization of Iran (AEOI) had more than 4,500 scientists; by 1985, all but an estimated 800 had fled.[1] If Iran wanted to jump-start its nuclear programs, it was absolutely critical to lure the exiles home.

The conference was to be held in the Persian Gulf port of Busheir, not far from the border with Iraq, where Siemens subsidiary Kraftwerkunion (KWU) had contracted with the former shah's government to build twin nuclear power reactors. KWU was ordered out of Iran by Ayatollah Khomeini at the start of the 1979 revolution. Iran didn't need nuclear power or Western weapons and shouldn't waste money buying them, Khomeini argued. Although the Iranian government already had spent 5.8 billion Deutschmarks (well over $3 billion) on the nuclear power station, work ground to a halt and squatters took over the site.

Rafsanjani's patronage of the event and the venue he had chosen sent a powerful message—and not only to the exiles the regime was hoping to lure home. It also set off alarm bells in intelligence agencies around the world. It was the first open statement by a top official in Iran that crystallized what intelligence reporting had been suggesting for a number of years: Iran had a secret program to get the bomb.

THE FIRST SIGNS

Saddam Hussein was worried enough by Iran's nuclear efforts that he ordered Iraqi warplanes to bomb the Busheir plant on March 24, 1984. Iraqi pilots managed to punch a hole in one nearly completed reactor dome, apparently hoping to replicate Israel's crippling June 1981 air strike against the Osirak reactor that set Iraq's program back by several years.

Rafsanjani had won Ayatollah Khomeini's approval to restart the nuclear project, and shortly after the Iraqi raid, he arranged for a team of forty KWU technicians to visit Busheir to assess what it would take to complete at least one of the reactors.

There were other troubling indications of undisclosed nuclear activity in Iran. Just a month after the initial raid on Busheir, Iraqi jets attacked the Amir Kabir Technical College in Tehran, which housed a 5-megawatt nuclear research reactor the United States had built in the 1960s. In contrast to its behavior after the Busheir bombing, the Iranian government failed to submit a damage report to the International Atomic Energy Agency (IAEA) in Vienna even though the reactor was under international safeguards and was regularly visited by IAEA accountants to ensure that none of its weapons-grade uranium fuel was missing.

Also that year, Rafsanjani inaugurated a new nuclear research center associated with the University of Isfahan. Designed initially by the French in the 1970s, the labs were completed in 1984 with help from the People's Republic of China. The Isfahan Nuclear Technology Center had been designed "large with room for expansion" and included "many buildings, some underground," according to contemporary accounts.[2] Some reports claimed that the Iranians were conducting uranium conversion and enrichment experiments, enabling them to master the processes of manufacturing bomb-grade material. But no one knew for sure what was going on in Isfahan since the Iranian government refused to declare the new center to the IAEA, as expected under the Nonproliferation Treaty, which Iran ratified in 1970.

China's nuclear cooperation with Iran so alarmed Senator John Glenn, the architect of key U.S. nonproliferation legislation, that in 1984 he requested a confidential briefing from the State Department's top official in charge of nonproliferation issues and relations with the IAEA, Ambassador Richard Kennedy.

Iran was probing suppliers around the world through a variety of intermediaries to obtain a broad spectrum of nuclear gear, including production equipment to build uranium milling, processing, and conversion plants. It sought high-precision centrifuge manufacturing tools, electromagnetic isotope separation units, and a small training reactor from Communist China. At one point the Iranian government approached a company in Argentina in an attempt to acquire weapons-grade uranium, ostensibly to resupply the 5-megawatt research reactor in Tehran. To prove their innocence, the Iranians pointed out, correctly, that the IAEA had suggested they negotiate a nuclear supply agreement with Argentina, since the United States was refusing to refuel the Tehran reactor.

The United States responded to these reports of clandestine nuclear procurement activities by convening a rare meeting of the Nuclear Suppliers Group in London, but the ad hoc group of the nuclear "haves" refused to end sales of uranium enrichment and reprocessing equipment, because it was inherently "dual-use" (meaning it could be used for energy purposes, not just for weapons). And it was profitable.

In his office in the leafy Munich suburb of Pullach, Eberhard Blum, the head of Germany's Federal Intelligence Service, the Bundesnachrichtendienst (BND), mulled over the file his analysts had pulled together on a nearby German company and its latest contract with Iran. The company and several others like it had sold high-tech gear to Tehran directly and through South Africa, ostensibly for civilian purposes. Although the equipment was not controlled by Germany, making the exports legal, the high-temperature vacuum furnace was exactly the type of specialized equipment Iran needed to build uranium enrichment centrifuges.

Shortly after the initial Iraqi air strike against Busheir, Blum had a deputy make discreet phone calls to a few trusted journalists. Recent intelligence reports suggested that Iran had made dramatic progress in uranium enrichment and could conceivably field a nuclear device within two to three years if nothing was done to stop them. Although that conclusion turned out to be premature, the message was clear, and it was ominous. Germany's foreign intelligence service had concluded that Iran was engaged in a top-secret program to develop nuclear weapons.

1984. The first warning.

THE INIMITABLE DR. KHAN

In February 1986, Pakistan's top nuclear scientist, Dr. Abdul Qadeer Khan, paid a discreet visit to Busheir, just weeks before Rafsanjani's nuclear technology conference was scheduled to take place. The sudden appearance of Dr. A. Q. Khan fueled suspicions of nuclear cooperation between Iran and Pakistan.

There are two routes to the bomb: highly enriched uranium and plutonium. Both paths are difficult and require expensive, sophisticated technologies and industrial-sized facilities.

The world's major nuclear powers pursued them both.* But to most proliferation analysts it was unthinkable that a third-world country lacking a modern technology base could afford the luxury of twin nuclear weapons programs. They changed their tune when Dr. Khan emerged on the scene.

Abdul Qadeer Khan was trained as a metallurgist in Europe and took a Ph.D. at Belgium's Catholic University of Leuven in 1972. For fifteen years he worked in the European nuclear industry, helping to build a uranium centrifuge enrichment plant in the Dutch town of Almelo. It was here, while he worked for a supplier to the Urenco consortium, that Dr. Khan acquired the contacts to build a far-flung network of nuclear suppliers. When Dr. Khan went back to Pakistan in 1976, he knew what to buy and where to get it. Many of the companies that produced parts and supplied equipment to Urenco soon began working for Dr. Khan, delivering the goods that allowed Pakistan to build a top-secret uranium enrichment plant in the mountains at Kahuta, outside the capital, Islamabad. Western suppliers "literally begged us to buy their equipment," Dr. Khan revealed later.[3]

Dr. Khan's identity was first revealed in a BBC television documentary that aired in 1980 called "Project 706—The Islamic Bomb." Project 706 was the code name for the Kahuta plant. BBC correspondent Steve Weissman teamed up with American investigative reporter Herbert Krosney to tell Dr. Khan's extraordinary story in a groundbreaking 1981 book, *The Islamic Bomb*.

The Dutch government prosecuted Dr. Khan in absentia for espionage in 1983, but he won an appeal and the charges were dropped. By the time he traveled to Iran to visit the unfinished Busheir nuclear reactors, Dr. Khan had become a legend throughout the Muslim world.

*The U.S. "Little Boy" weapon dropped on Hiroshima on August 6, 1945, used highly enriched uranium; "Fat Man," dropped on Nagasaki three days later, was a plutonium design.

He was known as the father of the Islamic bomb.

The Iranians didn't seek out Dr. Khan solely for his expertise in uranium enrichment. They also were keen to benefit from his knowledge of how the civilian fuel cycle could be manipulated to produce weapons-grade material. Unlike his mentors in the West, who, in their desire to export nuclear power plants to the developing world, claimed that civilian reactors could not produce nuclear weapons, Dr. Khan revealed the truth in a stunning article that appeared in a Pakistani daily just six months after his first visit to Busheir. "After all, there is only a weak, transparent screen between the two," he wrote. "Once you know how to make reactors, how to produce plutonium and to reprocess it, it becomes a rather easy task to produce nuclear weapons."[4]

A large nuclear power reactor, such as the ones the Iranians wanted to complete at Busheir, was a perfect vehicle for a clandestine nuclear weapons program. Not only did it provide a "legend," or cover story, that allowed Iran to purchase vast quantities of dual-use equipment legally on the international market, but it also gave Iran an excuse to master the nuclear fuel cycle, from the mining, conversion, and enrichment of uranium to the extraction of plutonium from the nuclear waste. This knowledge, and the technology that went with it, ultimately gave Iran the keys to the bomb. From the very beginning, A. Q. Khan was Iran's mentor.

The Iranian regime was so keen on cultivating Dr. Khan that the intelligence ministry dispatched an executive Fokker jet to Islamabad to fetch him in January 1987 and offered him a consulting contract to perform a study on the feasibility of using the Busheir reactors to produce weapons-grade plutonium. Dr. Khan met with top Iranian officials at an intelligence ministry guesthouse in Parchin, just south of Tehran, according to an eyewitness I interviewed recently in Europe.

If Iran wanted to use Busheir to produce plutonium, it needed to find a supplier that would allow the fuel from the reactor to be reprocessed in Iran, Dr. Khan said. But there was always the possibility that the ruse would be uncovered by international inspections, since the power plant was covered by a safeguards agreement with the IAEA, which regularly sent nuclear accountants to count the fuel.

There was a better option, Khan suggested. Why not produce the fuel domestically in Iran, starting with recently discovered supplies of natural uranium that Iran could mine and secretly refine on its own? That would keep the entire nuclear fuel cycle safe from nuclear safeguards. Iran could build small pilot plants to test the process, then mass-produce components for a centrifuge enrichment plant locally, using production plans Dr. Khan's network had acquired from helpful German businessmen. No one would be the wiser, because IAEA accountants would not detect any change in the amount of nuclear materials Iran declared it was holding.

Rafsanjani was following Dr. Khan's talks closely. As soon as the Pakistani had returned home, Rafsanjani convened a top-secret meeting at the Amir Kabir nuclear research center, a guarded compound not far from Tehran University, to discuss the next steps. With him were Revolutionary Guards leader Mohsen Rafiq-Doust, financial adviser Mohsen Nourkhbash, and Reza Amrollahi, a Rafsanjani relative who was catapulted to the head of the AEOI in 1982. Amrollahi brought with him some of the top scientists working on the nuclear program, including a key exile who continued to travel back and forth to Iran.

That meeting marked a turning point in Iran's nuclear future, for it was there that Rafsanjani decided to dramatically increase spending on nuclear projects with the ultimate goal of developing an atomic device.

His first decision was to purchase the production blueprints of the Urenco gas centrifuge (known as the P-1 design) that Dr. Khan was offering. Rafsanjani knew that things were no longer quite as simple as they had been for Dr. Khan. Western governments were becoming more careful in regulating enrichment and reprocessing equipment. Given the problems in procuring off-the-shelf technologies, Rafsanjani gave orders that separate research teams should pursue both the plutonium and the highly enriched uranium tracks to the bomb until it became clear who had the best chance of success. Rafiq-Doust was put in charge of procurement, and a special section of the Revolutionary Guards was created to supervise building, staffing, and protecting all clandestine nuclear facilities. Amrollahi was given control over "declared" nuclear plants, such as the Busheir reactor, and relations with the IAEA. Nourkhbash, who later became finance minister and then governor of the Central Bank, was put in charge of financing the overseas procurement networks through Iranian state-owned banks, cutouts, fake contracts, and front companies.

Rafsanjani himself had overall control. He was the driver behind the revived nuclear effort, the chief backer, and the ultimate end-user. As Majles speaker, he was able to hide the funds needed for nuclear projects in a variety of ways by padding Iran's public budget. Most important, he had Ayatollah Khomeini's ear.[5]

Shortly after this meeting, Dr. Khan, working through intermediaries, submitted a formal offer to supply sample certrifuges, drawings, specifications, and calculations for a "complete plant" to enrich uranium that would contain two thousand centrifuge machines. In addition, Dr. Khan offered to provide "auxiliary vacuum and electric drive equipment" for the enrichment plant as well as "uranium re-conversion and casting capabilities" so Iran could shape bomb cores out of the material it obtained.[6]

It was the complete "paint by numbers" version of the Islamic bomb. And at just a few million dollars, it was a bargain.

The countdown had begun.

THE FOX

After Khomeini, Rafsanjani was the regime official best known in the West. A key architect of Iran-Contra, he was portrayed as a "moderate" in the West. Iranians referred to him as "the Fox," because of his wily political ways, or "the Shark," because of his greed. He had adopted the turban much as scions of prominent families in the Middle Ages in Europe took up the scepter of the Catholic Church. It was his path to power.

When he left his family in the city of Rafsanjan in southeastern Iran at the age of sixteen, his father told relatives that he had gone to Qom not to study theology but to become a shah. Before the revolution, he bought rundown buildings, remodeled them, and flipped them at a profit.

Since coming to power as a top aide to Khomeini in 1979, he had amassed vast personal wealth. In his home province of Kerman he owned large agricultural tracts and dominated the pistachio trade, one of Iran's most lucrative non-oil exports. (As a gesture to Rafsanjani, pistachios were specifically exempted from U.S. sanctions during the last year of the Clinton administration.) He also owned fish canneries, supermarket chains, and a good chunk of the caviar business. Rafsanjani was believed to be the richest man in Iran, and even today he sends his sons to manage real estate investments in Canada and Las Vegas and to stash the family billions in numbered bank accounts in the Cayman Islands.

It always amused Rafsanjani to read Western press accounts of the power struggle between "moderates" and "hard-liners" in Tehran. There was plenty of jockeying for power and influence among rival factions of Iran's Shiite clergy. But Rafsanjani knew he had more in common with his most hated clerical rival than he did with any secular politician.

They could differ at the fringes—on relations with the United States, central planning versus free markets, the need for foreign investment, or sexual segregation in schools and universities—but no member of the ruling elite would ever agree to do away with the founding principle of the Islamic Republic, the infallibility of the Supreme Leader. Known as the *Velayat-e Faghih*, this was the bedrock of the Islamic Republic, the red line they could allow no one to cross. It guaranteed the mullahs' exclusive grip on power against all comers.

Another goal Iran's ruling clerics shared had become Rafsanjani's preoccupation: acquiring nuclear weapons and the means to deliver them throughout the region. They believed nuclear weapons would provide the ultimate guarantee against American and Israeli plots. Without nukes, they were vulnerable. One day the exiles might stop fighting among themselves and win foreign support to overthrow the regime. Or the Israelis might make mischief. Or the Americans might decide to punish them for one too many terrorist attacks. All this was possible if they didn't have a nuclear arsenal. But with it, who would dare to attack? As Khomeini liked to say, "America can't do a damn thing!"

More than anyone else, Rafsanjani saw clearly just how vital this work was to the survival of the regime.

"WE NEED IT NOW"

Shortly after the planning session Rafsanjani held with his nuclear team, President Ali Khamenei (who today is Iran's Supreme Leader) gave a pep talk to officials at AEOI headquarters in Tehran. They were the public face of Iran's nuclear research efforts, the scientists who were sent to conferences around the world to converse with their voluble colleagues in the international scientific community.

"Regarding atomic energy, we need it now," Khamenei said. But what he meant by "energy" had little in common with how the term is used in the West. "Our nation has always been threatened from outside. The least we can do to face this danger is to let our enemies know that we can defend ourselves. Therefore, every step you take here is in defense of your country and your evolution. With this in mind, you should work hard and at great speed."[7]

From the very start, the mullahs were clear about their goals in seeking nuclear technology. There was none of the ambiguity one frequently hears today, no distinction between "civilian" and "military" nuclear technology. They knew, as Dr. Khan had instructed them, that there was virtually no line dividing the two.

Later that year, Iran signed a nuclear cooperation agreement with Pakistan, approved personally by President Zia ul-Haq, that included the training of Iranian technicians in Pakistan. By mid-October 1987, the first thirty-one engineers from the AEOI arrived in Pakistan to work in research labs and institutes controlled by the Pakistani Atomic Energy Organization. Some followed doctoral programs at the Nuclear Studies Institute at Nowlore and at the Institute for Nuclear Sciences and Technology in Islamabad. Others worked directly under Dr. Khan to learn nuclear fuel processing techniques.[8]

President Zia claimed that the cooperation in Iran was limited to civilian nuclear technologies. Dr. Khan had other ideas.

SIREN SONG

Rafsanjani's ads in London newspapers calling the exiles to return had generated a very limited response. What the mullahs needed was a high-profile endorsement. Shortly after that January 1987 meeting in Tehran, they got it.

Fereidoun Fesharaki, an energy adviser to the former shah, accepted Rafsanjani's invitation and returned to Iran in March 1987 after a seven-year exile. The Tehran regime paid all of his expenses, including round-trip airfare. While Fesharaki has denied that his 1987 trip involved nuclear matters, he published an op-ed upon his return to the United States designed to convince anyone sitting on the fence that it was now safe to return to Iran.

"Having held a senior government post under the shah in the late 1970s," Fesharaki wrote, "I was naturally worried about being detained. As it turned out, I was somewhat surprised by the pragmatism of the ruling regime in Iran. I had expected a bunch of fanatics running wild in the country." Instead, he found a country where "repression is not overt."

Iran was poised to win the patriotic war against Iraq, but the "pragmatic mullahs" had devised a system to allow the sons of well-to-do families to escape the horror of the battlefield. "For a fee, the government provides a one-time exit visa," Fesharaki revealed. "So if a young man does not want to fight, exile is the price that must be paid." This was major news to many Iranian families, who were terrified that if they returned to Iran, their teenage boys would be sent off to the front.

"The mullahs' only real loyalty is to themselves and their newfound power," he wrote. "They are not fools vying to destroy the world; they are pragmatists."

Fesharaki left the real kicker for the end. Despite rumors about internal instability, the ruling clerics were solidly in the saddle and were not likely to be removed. "The regime is using organized chaos, energy, and determination to maintain control. A major change in power in this century seems unlikely."[9]

Many Iranian Americans interpreted Fesharaki's commentary as a sweeping endorsement of the Tehran regime. If you care for your country, he was saying, go home and help it win the war with Iraq. You won't be persecuted. Your sons won't be sent off to the war. The mullahs have lost their radical edge and Iran is on the road to becoming a "normal" country once again. And by the way: if you had any hope that the regime was about to collapse, forget it.

Similar siren songs have been played by pro-regime lobbyists ever since. It was a powerful message, and it worked.

SERVING IRAN

Following Fesharaki's visit, the effort to lure the exiles home became more successful, and in 1988 the AEOI decided to hold nuclear conferences annually, moving the venue to a comfortable Caspian Sea resort at Ramsar. Exiles I interviewed in Europe at the time said they were being contacted by Iranian diplomats who offered them all-expenses-paid round-trip travel, including an exit visa stamped into their passports before they even arrived in Iran. When he addressed the Ramsar conference on October 29, 1988, Rafsanjani exhorted the 150 exiles in attendance to return home permanently. "If you do not serve Iran, whom will you serve?" he argued.

Many of the exiles had been trained in areas useful to Iran's effort to master the nuclear fuel cycle. They came from Germany, France, Britain, Sweden, Norway, and the United States.

Iran began sending young, "ideologically pure" students to perfect their skills at the best universities in the West so they could eventually replace the expatriates, whose loyalties would always remain suspect. Large numbers were sent to Australia; others went to Germany, France, and Britain. When they returned home, they were given jobs in the weapons complex or as instructors at Sharif Technical University, established by the Revolutionary Guards in the early 1980s. This allowed the regime to keep security tighter and to avoid contact between its nuclear workforce and foreigners.*

*Sharif University and its Physics Research Center became so notorious as a procurement front for Iran's clandestine nuclear programs that the German Economics Ministry eventually banned high-technology sales to it. Several other universities played similar roles in procurement and training for the nuclear weapons program, including the Engineering Faculty at the University of Mashad, the Amir Kabir Technical College, and the Tarbiat Modarres University.

According to an Israeli official who was tracking Iran's nuclear activities closely, Iran succeeded in training between fifteen thousand and seventeen thousand young people in this way—not an exaggerated figure when one considers that the Iraqi nuclear effort employed twenty thousand technicians. "Even if worse came to worst and Iran's nuclear facilities were destroyed, at least the basic know-how would remain, just as in Iraq," he said.[10]

While overseas, some of these students sought to obtain U.S. nuclear weapons secrets. A report prepared by the General Accounting Office (GAO) for Senator John Glenn in October 1988 revealed that Iranian students had gained access to America's top nuclear weapons labs, despite the lack of diplomatic ties between the two countries.

Although the Iranians were participating in unclassified research, the GAO warned that "unclassified visits are not without risk. Certain countries are known to be seeking U.S. weapons data, and [Department of Energy] studies have shown that it is possible to derive classified and sensitive information from unclassified access to these facilities." Worse, the Energy Department had not followed its own requirement to obtain background information on the visitors, the auditors found. "As a result, suspected foreign agents and individuals from facilities suspected of conducting nuclear weapons activities have obtained access to the laboratories without prior DOE knowledge."[11]

U.S. weapons labs were a treasure trove of information on enrichment and reprocessing technologies, with millions of documents that were unclassified and readily available to researchers. In a separate study, the GAO found that "foreign countries viewed by DOE as a proliferation risk routinely obtain these documents," many of which "provided information related to resolving operational reprocessing problems or improving the technology" involved in various phases of the nuclear fuel cycle.[12]

America's nuclear weapons labs were a sieve, open to virtually all comers. But U.S. government scientists resolutely refused to lock them down in the name of scientific "openness."

In yet another report, the GAO found that Iran had attempted to purchase computer codes initially developed to model and test various U.S. nuclear warheads. These simulation programs allowed users to model, in two and three dimensions, the effects of a nuclear blast on weapons components. It was critical technology that allowed countries seeking to keep their nuclear weapons program secret to design a warhead without extensive testing.[13]

"With the physics easily accessible on the public record," then UN weapons inspector David Kay told me in 1992, "making a bomb for a country like Iran or Iraq becomes an engineering problem, not a problem of physics. The important skills are in electronics, mechanical engineering, and metallurgy."[14]

Quietly, Iran was trying to train a new generation of engineers in precisely those skills, and to buy the physics and the technology from willfully blind suppliers in Europe and the United States.

By the time the West woke up to what Iran had been doing, nearly twenty years after the fact, it was way too late to stop it.

THE EXILES

This is doable.

—Former president Richard M. Nixon, reviewing a U.S. plan to overthrow the mullahs, early 1987

Marion Smoak was not the type of person one normally would imagine at the center of a clandestine intelligence operation aimed at one of America's most dedicated and dangerous enemies.

Originally from Aiken, South Carolina, home of world-famous polo ponies, Smoak was an equestrian and a gentleman. He was also a Republican, at a time when South Carolinean politics was dominated by the Democratic Party. When Smoak planned his first run for the state senate in 1966 as a Republican, he nevertheless went to U.S. senator Strom Thurmond—then a Democrat—for his blessing. Thurmond was immensely popular, and the two men hit it off. "He told me I'd never get anywhere as a Republican, but I ignored that particular piece of advice," Smoak recalls with a chuckle. Smoak won his election, and shortly afterward it was Thurmond who switched parties.

Smoak's real talent was not as a legislator, but at putting people together. Easygoing, cultivated, and impeccably polite, he helped the Nixon campaign win South Carolina in 1968, and in 1970 was appointed by Nixon as deputy chief and later chief of U.S. protocol. While serving in that position, he accompanied then governor Ronald Reagan of California on two trips to the Far East. "I don't remember where I first met Bill Casey, but we were both active in Republican politics during the Nixon years," Smoak told me. By the time Casey became Ronald Reagan's director of the Central Intelligence Agency, that relationship had deepened. "I knew him well enough that I could pick up the phone and call him and say, 'I need to see you,' and he'd clear his calendar."

That's what happened in early January 1983. Smoak had someone he wanted Casey to meet. He was no ordinary client, but someone Smoak was helping on the side, without remuneration. When he described the young man, Casey immediately agreed. And, as he often did for meetings off the CIA campus in McLean, Virginia, Casey came accompanied only by his wife.

The luncheon at the exclusive Chevy Chase Club on January 13, 1983, was nothing short of historic. And until now it has remained a closely guarded secret. Smoak's guest at the private country club, just off the Capital Beltway, was a twenty-two-year-old Iranian named Cyrus Reza Pahlavi, the eldest son of the former shah of Iran. Casey was about to launch a covert operation.

To his followers among the hundreds of thousands of monarchists who fled to the United States after the Islamic Revolution, he called himself the crown prince. But at that first meeting with CIA director Bill Casey, he was greeted as His Imperial Majesty. Reza's mother had conducted a secret coronation ceremony on his twenty-first birthday, in the Koubeh palace in Cairo, and he found the title suited him well.

Smoak had chosen his guests with care for this ultimate power lunch. Along with Casey and his wife came Michael Deaver, then President Reagan's chief of staff, who also brought his wife; former CIA director Richard Helms and his wife; Ed Djerejian, a senior State Department official who was close to the family of Vice President George Bush; Nancy Moore Thurmond, Senator Strom Thurmond's twenty-seven-year-old wife, a former Miss South Carolina; General and Mrs. William Quinn; three aides to Pahlavi; and a number of others.

Casey turned to Reza as soon as they were all seated and, in his gruff mumble, launched right into the subject. So tell me how we're going to get rid of these sons of bitches, he asked the young prince.

Reza was excited and launched into an elaborate monologue on how he perceived the weaknesses of the new Islamic government in Tehran. They were incompetent, Iran's economy was in shambles, and the war with Iraq was taking a deadly toll on Iranian families. We just need to be present and to encourage the people, he said. Reza always employed the royal "we" when referring to himself.

The people of Iran will carry His Majesty to Tehran on their shoulders, added an aide, Colonel Ahmad Oveissy.

So how can we help? Casey asked.

Reza laid out his plan. He wanted to organize a network of former SAVAK officers to gather intelligence from inside Iran that he would use in making his case for regime change to friendly Arab governments. Ultimately he expected the conservative Arab monarchies would finance his return to power. But for the present, he needed financial support.

Casey lifted his glass, and the entire table prepared to join him in a toast to freedom and to the future of U.S.-Iranian relations.

"Long live the shah!" Casey said.

As they were all getting ready to leave, Casey promised that someone from his shop would get back to the young prince shortly.

KEEPING THE BED WARM

The offer, when it came, would be far less than Reza had received from the king of Saudi Arabia, whose gift of $5 million had already been spent. According to court papers filed by a former aide, Ahmad Ansari, $700,000 of the Saudi money had gone to build and equip a private discotheque in the basement of Pahlavi's new residence just down the road from CIA headquarters in Virginia. Reza desperately needed the $150,000-per-month stipend Casey was proposing. He gave instructions to his assistant, Shahriar Ahy, to deliver one-third of the money to Parviz Sabati, a former SAVAK director general in charge of his intelligence-gathering network. The rest would go into the privy purse to pay his retainers.

Casey was so excited about the prospects of reviving the Iranian opposition that he had already dispatched a team of operations officers to Europe to prepare a new headquarters for the young shah. They would build his organization and massively fund it. The $150,000 per month was just key money to get in the door.

The CIA director had just one concern, he told Reza in front of witnesses when the two next met. You've got to fire that Ahy character.

Shahriar Ahy was Reza's top aide and political adviser, who had joined him in exile in Morocco and followed him when the young shah moved to Fairfield, Connecticut, in early 1984. A banker by trade, Ahy was a nephew of Housang Ram, the former shah's personal banker and head of the bank Omran, which handled royal assets in Iran and abroad.

Ram had recently been released by the regime in Tehran after three and a half years in jail. Some said his wife was close to Ayatollah Khalqali, the warden of Evin prison, and had paid the notoriously bloodthirsty cleric to arrange an amnesty for him. Other sources claimed he had negotiated his own release by offering the regime the codes to secret accounts he controlled on the former shah's behalf with the Darius Bank in Spain. Whatever the truth, Ram was out of jail and out of Iran, and he made Casey nervous. He didn't want the man's nephew anywhere near his operation.

Reza declined to heed the CIA director's advice. For one thing, Ahy had more financial expertise and certainly better contacts with world leaders than did Reza's financial adviser, Ahmad Ansari. Besides, if Casey was really worried that Ahy's family connection to Housang Ram would make him vulnerable to pressure from the regime, wouldn't that also affect Ahmad Oveissy, Reza's chief of staff, who was married to Ram's daughter?

There was no way Reza was going to get rid of Oveissy. The former Imperial Guards colonel was like a father to him.

Within weeks, Casey pulled his team of advance men back from Europe and broke off his meetings with the young shah, without explanation. However, the $150,000-per-month stipend continued for several years, as did lower-level contacts. Former agency officials called it Casey's way of "keeping the bed warm," without getting into it. They referred to Reza disparagingly as "shah-let" and "Baby Shah."

As for Ahy, Casey's suspicions were unfounded. Today he is a driving force behind the movement to hold an internationally monitored referendum on clerical rule.

CIA RADIO

Ahmad Oveissy opened the room at the Marriott Hotel in Arlington, Virginia, using a special cipher lock, not a key card. A slight man, Oveissy had recently undergone surgery for cancer and was missing a large chunk of his jaw. With him were Shahriar Ahy and the man the CIA hoped to recruit to take control of the operational arm of the pro-monarchist resistance, then headquartered in Paris.

It was a bleak November afternoon, with a hint of snow swirling across the Key Bridge outside. The newcomer had just come from Dallas, Texas, and shivered slightly from the cold. He was short, impeccably dressed in a woolen overcoat and dark gray suit, and looked more like a television newscaster than a guerrilla fighter.

Dr. Manoucher Ganji had been the former shah's minister of education from 1976 to 1979. He also became an influential adviser to the Shahbanou, the shah's wife, in the dark days leading up to the revolution. When he finally managed to escape from Iran after six months in hiding, he moved to Dallas, where he opened a chain of bakeries. But he had remained constantly in touch with Iran, working with former colleagues in the Ministry of Education who went back and forth to Iran clandestinely.

In 1981, Ganji penned a twenty-five-page memorandum on human rights violations in Iran that won the attention of William vanden Heuvel, a deputy U.S. representative to the United Nations. With Vanden Heuvel's support, Ganji managed to place the issue of the Islamic Republic's human rights record on the agenda of the UN Commission on Human Rights in 1981. Every year since then, UN delegates have been obliged to take up the question of Iran's torture of political prisoners, stoning of female adulterers, execution of dissidents, and other abuses.

By the time Ganji traveled to Washington, D.C., the situation inside Iran had deteriorated dramatically. Tens of thousands of teenage boys were being sent off to the war front with Iraq, armed with little more than a plastic key they were told would open the gates of heaven if they were martyred on the battlefield. Political opponents of the regime were being rounded up and brutally tortured. Thousands had been hanged in public; some were beheaded in secret prisons, their bodies dumped on deserted roadsides at night.

During the Republican National Convention in Dallas in 1984, Ganji had led a three-day protest against the clerics that received national news coverage. His excellent English transformed him overnight into a de facto spokesman for the opposition in exile.

With Oveissy hovering over him like a scarecrow, serving tea, the young shah launched into a long exposé of the sorry state of his CIA-funded operation in Paris. The Front for the Liberation of Iran (FLI) was led by former prime minister Ali Amini, a pro-Western technocrat now in his eighties. The CIA-backed broadcasting operation had become a shambles under his direction. They desperately needed a younger man, and Reza Pahlavi wanted the fifty-four-year-old Ganji to set it right.

He wanted more than just an exile radio; he wanted Ganji to transform the FLI into the backbone of a full-fledged resistance movement that could become the avant-garde of a counterrevolution. "Doctor, we need you," he said. "I pledge you my total support."

Ganji insisted that their priority had to be the freedom of Iran, not the restoration of the monarchy. The young shah agreed. They also agreed to maintain total secrecy when it came to the financial support the radio was receiving from the U.S. government.

THE BAKER

Ganji learned the details of that support during a follow-on meeting a few weeks later, after he sprang the news on his wife and two grown children. Returning to Washington, he took a taxi to the Bristol Hotel at 24th Street and Pennsylvania Avenue for lunch with a group of American officials. The leader of the group was an older man Ganji referred to only as "the professor."

John Kenneth Knaus was a legend inside the agency. An academic by training, he had "taught" foreign operatives at clandestine CIA training camps around the world. He took the plunge into the world of operations when a group of Tibetans showed up to hear him lecture in 1958 and has never looked back since.[1] Helping pro-freedom movements move their countries from dictatorship to democracy has been his specialty ever since. Only a handful of experts inside the U.S. government or in academia have mastered this black art.

Ganji and the balding academic with the owlish glasses hit it off immediately. "He had read every book that had ever been written on Iran, and everything you can imagine on civil disobedience and nonviolent struggle," Ganji recalled. "He was a master, absolutely."

After the cordial lunch, the small group adjourned upstairs to a small suite in the hotel, where they briefed Ganji in detail on the mess he was about to find in Paris. The eighty-one-year-old Ali Amini was absent-minded but a tyrant, who insisted on micromanaging everything in his small domain. Thanks in part to U.S. taxpayer subsidies, he lived like an aristocrat, with a large apartment in Paris, a cook, and other servants. On good days he worked four hours.

For Ganji, the frustration of his new partners—who never told him for which government agency they actually worked—barely registered. The former minister turned baker was brimming with enthusiasm.

"We have to do much more than just broadcasting," he said. "This regime is vulnerable; you know that better than I do. We can do a lot."

As Ganji laid out his vision of how they could set up a clandestine network of nonviolent resistance cells, the "professor" peppered him with questions about Iran and with encouragement from other operations he had led. But he was also careful not to raise false expectations. He had been chastened too many times in the past when his protégés believed he could deliver things that were beyond his power.

There were clear limits on what the U.S. government was trying to do, he said. He didn't want Ganji to do things that would get his people killed.

I may not have any choice in the matter, Ganji replied. The minute we raise the flag, they will be after us. These people are killers.

Ganji and Knaus bonded that afternoon. For the next eight years, they became a team.

GANJI GOES TO PARIS

Ganji arrived at Orly airport in Paris on a cold morning in January 1986, with three suitcases and six boxes of books. Among the possessions he had brought with him was a small box of Iranian soil he had taken out with him from hiding seven years earlier. It was a constant reminder of why he was fighting. He wanted to plant the seeds of freedom in that soil and to live long enough to see them grow.

After settling into a small Left Bank hotel on the rue Gregoire de Tours, Ganji took the subway to the western suburbs of Paris for his first face-to-face encounter with Amini and his operation.

It was not where he had expected a clandestine radio station would be based.

Le Vesinet was one of the wealthiest suburbs of Paris, where foreign diplomats and businessmen came to escape the pollution and the stress of the city. It was full of large, walled-in villas and parks, set around a meandering stream. He had been told that Amini's headquarters would be hard to find, but as soon as he flagged a cab in Le Vesinet and gave the address, the driver laughed. "You mean that place with the huge antenna?" So much for discretion.

The Front's office boasted a 15-meter-high antenna on the rooftop. Its purpose was to broadcast news and Persian music for Iranian expatriates in the greater Paris area, not to beam messages of freedom into Iran. As Ganji began to probe into the operations of Radio Sedaye Nejat-e Iran, he found that despite the $150,000 per month in salaries and overhead the CIA was providing, this was about all it was doing. The huge new studio had been equipped with state-of-the-art mixers and recording gear to make music for the exiles.

Empowered by Knaus and the Iran team back at Langley, Ganji quickly asserted his authority. His first move was to climb up on the roof and get a team of people to take down the antenna. Next, he fired more than half of the fifty people on Amini's staff. Ganji was impressed by how much tea they could consume during a four- to five-hour day and how little actual work they got done. A two-hour daily political program was produced at a separate studio in the center of Paris and shipped down to Cairo, where a vintage World War II shortwave transmitter beamed the message into Iran. Within months, Ganji expanded this program to six and a half hours per day, while cutting the overall budget by more than $40,000 per month.

Amini and his ousted colleagues were furious. In April, Amini filed a lawsuit against Ganji for theft of property but dropped it once he realized that his backers in Washington had switched horses. One of Amini's broadcasters dished to the press about CIA operatives paying employees of the radio with "bags of cash" in the Paris Metro. Others claimed that Ganji was shipping money off to Swiss bank accounts or back to Dallas to pay his debts. (In fact, Ganji was earning $5,500 per month, less than he had made running his bakeries, while supporting his family back in the States and his own two-room apartment in Paris.) While clandestine operations such as the one Ganji was now running always paid employees in cash, the CIA bean counters demanded written accounts and regularly visited Paris to meet with Ganji and his top aides, former deputy ministers Parviz Amouzegar and Manoucher Tehrani, to scrutinize how the taxpayers' money was being spent.

Amini also complained to Cyrus Reza Pahlavi in Connecticut, saying Ganji had "turned Paris upside down." After all the things he had done for the king, to be treated like this now was a humiliation, Amini said. He begged the young shah to do something. So did another aide, Hormooz Hekmat. He had two small children to take care of, and now, thanks to Ganji, he was out of a job.

Pahlavi came to Paris and confronted Ganji at the stylish Hotel Raphael just off the Champs Elysées. Can't you let Amini remain nominally in charge? he asked. You don't have to actually let him run anything—just give him an office and a secretary so he can tell people he's still important. You can't fire all these people. Doctor, you have upset the peace. It can't go on like this.

I'm not running an employment agency, Ganji replied icily. I'm trying to liberate my country.

Shahriar Ahy walked into the room, bringing the cigarettes Pahlavi had sent him out to buy. Pahlavi stood up and extended his hand. Doctor, I'm sorry it didn't work.

Ganji just looked at him incredulously. You don't have to be. Goodbye.

By this point, Ganji was fed up. He had packed his bags and was ready to return to Dallas. He had not come to Paris just to run a radio station. He needed dedicated people who were willing to risk their lives to bring freedom to Iran, not paper pushers and lackeys. So far, the CIA had given him total freedom. They hadn't imposed a single employee on him or told him what to broadcast. They had respected his reputation for independence—something Pahlavi did not.

Then he received a call from a friend in Washington, D.C., whom he had told about the encounter with Pahlavi.

I've made some calls, the friend said. I've spoken to people very high up in the administration, and they want you to know that you have their total support. Reza may think he controls this operation, but this is your baby, not his. It's your people whose lives are on the line, not his. So unpack your bags and let's get back to work.

We've got a regime to overthrow, he added.

The next day a CIA control officer showed up with two months' back salaries for all of Ganji's staff.

THE BIRTH OF IRAN-CONTRA

Once it was clear that he had won the power struggle in Paris, Ganji changed the name of the Front to the Flag of Freedom Organization (FFO), in reference to a famous Persian legend about a blacksmith named Kaveh who hoisted his leather apron on a pike in defiance of a murderous dictator.

He also began recruiting operatives among former students and acquaintances who were willing to hand-carry portable transmitters into Iran so they could defeat the regime's sophisticated jamming operation. During initial tests later that year, he achieved results that left Ken Knaus and the CIA's Paris station chief, Charles Galligan Cogan, speechless. Through local contacts in Europe, Ganji's people jury-rigged the backpack transmitters the CIA had provided to expand their range from around 1 kilometer to well over 7 kilometers. FFO operatives took the transmitters into Iran illegally, crossing the border from Turkey and Pakistan. To enhance the operatives' chances of survival, all contacts with the organization back in Paris were handled by courier.

Ganji's organization catapulted to fame in September 1986, when they managed to interrupt Iranian state television for eleven minutes to broadcast a videotaped appeal to the Iranian people by Reza Pahlavi. People all over Iran watched in awe as the crown prince, whose face was unknown to them at the time, appeared on their screens and read a patriotic speech, encouraging them in their struggle against the clerics. Pahlavi's feat was mentioned by *Time* magazine and ABC News, although no reporters asked the key question of how much assistance the young shah was receiving from the United States.

Inside Iran, top regime leaders watched the speech in fear. They were convinced the United States was going to launch an armed uprising against them. The broadcast was one of the events that decided a top Khomeini aide to leak news of the top-secret visit to Tehran by National Security Adviser Robert McFarland in October 1986, thus unleashing the chain of revelations that became the Iran-Contra scandal. The clerics wanted to show the Americans they were in control.

The broadcast also gave heart to Reza's aunt Ashraf, the former shah's twin sister. Known among Iranian exiles for her commitment to restoring the monarchy, Ashraf put together a plan to restore Reza to the throne. She enlisted the help of a former CIA operations officer and said she was ready to put up $2 million cash.

THE NIXON PLAN

A far more ambitious plan, which I can reveal here for the first time, was hatched by former treasury secretary John Connolly with the blessing of former president Richard Nixon.

Connolly and an Iranian investment banker named Bijan Kasraie took their idea to Nixon in early 1987, at the height of Iran-Contra. The idea was to establish a provisional government, with Reza as its titular head, on a parcel of liberated Iranian territory.

Even De Gaulle had needed to set up shop someplace, Nixon observed. As he chewed over the ideas Connolly and the Iranian banker had presented, he became increasingly enthusiastic.

This is doable, but it needs some refinement. Let me work this, he said. He started to get really excited. Now that CIA Director Bill Casey and Defense Secretary Caspar Weinberger and Navy Secretary John Lehman have all resigned, all the guys with guts are gone, he said.

Nixon made a bunch of calls and got back to them a few days later with some new ideas and contacts who could work the more technical parts. Over a period of several weeks, they put together a detailed planning document. When it was all ready, Kasraie and Connolly turned it over to the young shah's companion and financial adviser, Ahmad Ansari, and asked him to hand-carry it up to his boss.

It was a huge sheaf of documents. There were large maps, drawings, outlines, ship deployments, radio frequencies. Some of the maps were so large they folded out. The whole thing was larger than a coffee-table art book and weighed several pounds. Ansari had to carry it in a special portfolio.

When he spread out the documents on Reza's desk at his house in

Connecticut, the young shah was fascinated. He was going to become king after all! And the United States was going to help him! As he paged through the drawings and deployment schedules, his heart pounded, half in fear, half in anticipation.

The plan called for the U.S. Navy to land Reza and a small band of armed followers on Kish island, an oasis resort in the Persian Gulf, off the most barren and deserted part of Iran's southern coastline. This was the region where Alexander the Great's armies had given up hope as they marched home to Babylon after crossing the Hindu Kush mountains and conquering the Indus River valley. The region is almost totally devoid of water, trees, and habitation—even today.

But Kish itself was an island paradise. The shah used to bring family and friends to vacation on its sandy beaches and built a private airstrip on the island. For Reza, it was a place of happy memories. The airstrip still existed, and it would be Reza Pahlavi's lifeline to the outside world. Carrier-based F-14s would patrol the airspace, to keep the Iranian air force at bay. U.S. warships would patrol off the coasts.

During the first phase of the operation, he would set up radio and television transmitters, and announce that he was establishing a Free Iranian government on liberated Iranian territory. That would provide the fig leaf for the Arab monarchies on the other side of the Persian Gulf to recognize his provisional government.

Reza then would invite "all elements" of the patriotic Iranian armed forces to join him in restoring freedom to their homeland, including dissident Pasdaran officers who were fighting Iraq. With their help, he would begin the long march to Tehran, gathering supporters on his way, much as Napoleon had done when he returned from exile on the island of Elba to rule France briefly in 1815.

By the time their swelling ranks reached Tehran, the mullahs' regime would have collapsed, swept away by the people in anticipation of Reza's return.

When Ansari had finished briefing the plan, the young shah turned to him. How are we going to escape if things go wrong? he asked. It was the only question that he had.

The next day he discussed it with his closest advisers, Shahriar Ahy and Ahmad Oveissy, who agreed with his initial assessment. Where was the Tehran component of the plan? Where was the political piece?

Even though it had the backing of a former president of the United States and a former treasury secretary, it was the nuttiest thing they had ever heard.

THE MISSILE MAN

The bullets we manufacture are more effective than others, because they are coupled with the grace of God.

—Iranian Revolutionary Guards minister Mohsen Rafiq-Doust, speaking on Iranian television, March 10, 1988

Sabzevar Rezai was an unlikely candidate to become the military commander of the Islamic Republic Guards Corps and the man in charge of ballistic missile development. And yet, by the mid-1980s, in the midst of the brutal eight-year war with Iraq, the bearded, tough-talking Rezai became known as the regime's missile man.

Because his father worked for the National Iranian Oil Company under the shah, the young Sabzevar was able to attend the NIOC technical high school in Ahwaz in the early 1970s, near the southern border with Iraq. But as the winds of revolution blew across the oilfields, he lost interest in his studies. By 1973, after coming into contact with radical Islamists close to the exiled Ayatollah Khomeini, Rezai and a friend named Ali Shamkhani set up a small underground group called Mansouroun, to promote violent revolution against the shah. As yet unskilled in the techniques of violence, both men were picked up by SAVAK and briefly jailed.

After his release the young Rezai made his way to Tehran, where he enrolled at the University of Science and Technology to study mechanical engineering. By 1975, the Islamist underground was expanding, led mainly by Marxist groups such as the Soviet-backed Mujahedin-e Khalq. Undeterred by his arrest, Rezai threw himself into the struggle.

He also took time out to attend to his personal life. In Tehran, he frequented a mosque run by an influential cleric, Ayatollah Jalali-Khomeini, who was close to the clandestine revolutionary leadership and especially to Ayatollah Khomeini, then living in exile in Iraq. The young Rezai asked him if he knew any girls he could marry. That is how he met Nasren Khabang, who was studying religion with Jalali-Khomeini's wife. Under the mullah's watchful eyes, the two soon married. The first of their three children was born on September 22, 1976. As the revolutionary movement intensified,

Rezai moved his wife and their young children from safe house to safe house, always managing to stay one step ahead of the shah's secret police.

Not long before the revolution erupted in 1978, Rezai went to Lebanon to receive military training, leaving his wife and children in care of a brother-in-law. In a PLO camp in Lebanon's Bekaa Valley he learned how to shoot Soviet weaponry, from RPG-7 rocket launchers to handheld SAM missiles. He also learned about explosives, detonators, and how to build car bombs. An important part of his training as a professional revolutionary were the techniques of clandestine operations: how to forge identity papers and to alter his appearance, how to establish a safe house and communicate with a clandestine cell to escape detection by the shah's security services. The shah's men never arrested him again.

While in the Palestinian camps he became friends with a young mullah named Ahmad Khomeini, the son of the famous ayatollah. The flamboyant young Khomeini posed for Western photographers in his cleric's garb and turban, shouldering an RPG-7. But Rezai was more cautious. He was tough, low-key, and decisive.

Back in Iran, Rezai put to use the skills he had learned in Lebanon as the organized resistance to the shah's regime intensified. He became a professional terrorist and a key figure in the Mujahedin Engelab-e Eslam (Holy Warriors of the Islamic Revolution). He liked to refer to the clandestine group as the "secret hand of the revolution."

Once the shah was forced into exile, Rezai and his Mujahedin took to the streets with their machine guns and Palestinian keffiyehs, spearheading the putsch that brought Khomeini to power during the night of February 11–12, 1979. Rezai personally took part in the assault on air force headquarters, the first base that fell to the insurgents. In the ensuing weeks, Rezai's Mujahedin played a major role in rounding up remnants of the imperial regime and murdering them. Rezai boasts of these actions today.

Ayatollah Khomeini was pleased with his work and called him to his villa in the posh northern suburb of Jamaran, which he had transformed into his war room. Now that the revolution has won the first battles, we need to consolidate our victories, Khomeini said. He had a new job for the young revolutionary. But first the old man wanted him to get rid of his Persian name and adopt a proper Islamic one. From now on you will be called Mohsen, he said. Mohsen the beneficient, the charitable.

Khomeini had grown to trust and respect the hard young terrorist and put him in charge of organizing a new intelligence service for the fledgling organization that came to be known as the Islamic Republic Guards Corps, or Pasdaran. Khomeini's goal was to create an instrument of Islamic terror that would act as secret police and enforcer for the new regime, just as the Bolsheviks had done after the Russian Revolution in 1917. The key was keeping the new organization separate from the provisional government, which was run by the nationalist Mehdi Barzagan, who by mid-1979 was telling the revolutionaries their work was accomplished and it was time to go home. The Guards were the revolution's children and protectors, the tip of the spear.

Rezai was one of twelve original founders of the Guards, as was Rafsanjani, and helped write the charter that allowed the organization to become a formidable instrument of revolutionary terror. Even though Ayatollah Khomeini was plagued with heart trouble that prevented him from receiving visitors during this time, he asked young Mohsen Rezai to report back to him weekly on his progress in building the new intelligence service. Both men knew that the struggle was just beginning, and they needed a secret strike force capable of crippling the Marxists and counterrevolutionaries before they could regroup.

Then, in September 1980, Saddam Hussein launched his epic invasion of Iran, hammering Iranian units up and down the 1,200-kilometer border. Iranians watched in horror as the remnants of the shah's imperial army collapsed one after the other before the Iraqi onslaught. After a two-week siege, the Iraqis seized the city of Khorramshahr in the oil fields of southwestern Iran, and seemed poised to advance deeper into the country. Faced with imminent defeat, President Abolhassan Banisadr ordered air force pilots who had been jailed because of their loyalty to the shah to be released so they could fight Saddam.

In Iran's time of peril, Mohsen Rezai saw opportunity. In a private audience with the ayatollah at his villa in Jamaran, he urged Khomeini to allow him to throw his Pasdaran troops into the fray. We are not strong like the *artesh*, he said, referring to the remnants of the regular army. We don't have their weapons or their training, but we are burning to defend the Islamic revolution. The *artesh* are unwilling to die, because we killed off their generals. The Iraqis are coming. I beg you to give us a chance.

If you think you can do it, go ahead, the old man said. I give you my blessing. That's how the most sensitive and far-reaching orders were given in the new Islamic Republic. There was no executive order, not even a letter. Just a nod and a few words from the Supreme Leader. Only later would his underlings put it in writing to cover their actions.

With Khomeini's authority behind him, Rezai began transferring weaponry from the regular army to the fledging Pasdaran corps. He launched a massive recruitment drive among the youth, to bring in fanaticized supporters who were willing to die to defend Islam and the regime.

Soon he had assembled a force 100,000 strong. As Rezai threw increasingly large numbers of fighters into battle, his stature and his power grew.

But it took time to train the Pasdaran troops and to overcome the rivalry with the regular army. Confronted with massive Iraqi offensives in February 1982, Rezai's clerical masters made the decision to send virtually unarmed young boys into battle, their arms linked together, to clear the Iraqi minefields. Some of these new fighters were no older than twelve. But they broke through at Susengerd in Rezai's home province of Khuzestan, smashing Iraq's supply lines and causing Iraqi troops to flee in terror. Within a week, working side by side with regular army troops, they destroyed three Iraqi divisions, shifting the tide of the war. Thus began the era of the gruesome "human wave" offensives that captured headlines around the world.

To demonstrate his own fanatical belief in the justice of the ayatollah's war, Mohsen Rezai took helicopters and jeeps to the battlefield in the midst of the fighting, taking along with him his five-year-old son, Ahmad. Born on the run from the shah's secret police, young Ahmad was a true child of the revolution. Now Mohsen Rezai wanted to steel him with the brands of war.

FROM CORRUPTION TO REVOLUTIONARY VIRTUE

The formidable war machine built up by the former shah lay in tatters. At the start of the hostage crisis in November 1979, the United States had imposed a total arms embargo on the revolutionary regime. Helicopters sent to the United States for upgrading were impounded. Several billion dollars' worth of military spare parts Iran had already paid for were seized and put in storage in warehouses around the United States. Within weeks of the Iraqi invasion, Iran's air force was grounded, and its helicopter fleet severely impaired. The F-14s that could fly had no sophisticated Harpoon missiles to launch. The utter collapse of the Iranian army and air force during the early weeks of the war proved how impotent were armies in the developing world without the active support of their arms suppliers.

Rezai and other military leaders made a strategic decision early in the war to shift the entire Iranian armed forces to Soviet standard equipment. It was a momentous and difficult move. It didn't just mean different tanks and planes and guns. It meant going from inches and pounds to meters and kilograms. It meant a whole different set of tools and repair shops, with an entirely new logistics system and inventory of spare parts. It meant new networks of suppliers to master. Everyone from pilots and artillerymen down to mechanics and load handlers would have to learn their skills all over. But it was the only way out.

Secret arms contracts brokered by Soviet ambassador Vladimir Vinogradev in the opening days of the war led to an emergency airlift to Tehran of jet fuel from Soviet bases, followed by tank engines, 130-mm artillery pieces, and ammunition from Syria, Libya, Bulgaria, and North Korea. Cementing the deal was a military cooperation agreement between the Islamic Republic and the Soviet Union signed in July 1981. Iran had escaped the embrace of one superpower only to fall into the clutches of the other.

Rezai urged Ayatollah Khomeini to make a second strategic decision that was far more painful. Because of the arms embargo, Iran needed to revive the vast defense manufacturing base built up by the shah. It wasn't going to be easy, since most of the factories had been established as joint ventures with American defense companies that had severed relations with Iran. Under the ayatollah's own instructions, angry mobs had ransacked Military Industries Organization factories during the early days of the Islamic Revolution. Khomeini had derided the arms industry as a symbol of waste, greed, and personal ambition, and called Western technology a corrupting influence. Production machinery was trashed in the anti-Western orgy that gripped the country. Rezai urged the ayatollah to shift gears. Reluctantly, he agreed.

The first plants to reopen their doors after the revolution were the Parchin and Sultanatabad munitions factories, since these relied the least on American technology. By 1982, under the auspices of the Pasdaran's Defense Industries Organization, new contracts were signed with suppliers from West Germany, Great Britain, Sweden, Austria, Italy, and Switzerland. They sent lathes and special tooling, blueprints, and raw materials. Rezai's people called it the "self-sufficiency jihad." The arms industry had gone from corruption to revolutionary virtue under Mohsen Rezai's command. Islamic Iran was on the march.

By 1982 the Pasdaran had grown so large it became a government ministry, and Rezai was given a new political boss. Mohsen Rafiq-Doust was a former Khomeini bodyguard, who had driven the ayatollah from the airport into Tehran upon his triumphal return from exile in 1979. He was one of the original twelve founders of the Pasdaran, along with Rezai and Rafsanjani. Iranian exiles claim that he earned his nom de guerre (*Rafiq* means comrade, *Doust* means friend) after he was sent on a mission to northwestern Iran to assassinate four "comrades" whom Khomeini had declared enemies of the revolution. (Some jokingly refered to him as Rafiq-Khost—"enemy" of the comrades.) His meteoric rise was helped by a political marriage to Rafsanjani's sister. Rafiq-Doust tried to strike a popular chord when he explained why the Pasdaran had revived the shah's weapons industry. "The bullets we manufacture are more effective than others, because they are coupled with the grace of God," he told Iranian television. Rezai secretly detested his minister, whom he saw as greedy, cruel, and corrupt.

Rezai became the regime's chief procurement officer in addition to his duties as military commander of the Revolutionary Guards. Along with Rafiq-Doust, he began scouring the globe for weaponry. Syria and Libya contributed surplus Soviet weaponry from their stockpiles, as did others. But increasingly he turned to China and North Korea. By 1982 he had cut so many deals with Pyongyang that the Stockholm International Peace Research Institute (SIPRI) listed North Korea as Iran's single largest arms supplier in its annual review of the arms trade.

China frequently used North Korea as a conduit to disguise its own sales to Iran. But the North Koreans worked as a conduit for Soviet arms deliveries as well. Such was the case with an $18 million shipment of four hundred SAM-7 missiles and one hundred launchers, "sold" from a Soviet arsenal to North Korea to disguise its true recipient. This black-market deal was negotiated by Rafiq-Doust through a French arms dealer, who chartered an unmarked Israeli DC-9 to pick up the missiles in Poland and fly them directly to Iran. Such deals were more costly and less reliable than the government-to-government transactions Rezai preferred. Because the brokers risked serious jail time if they were caught, they padded the contracts with huge profits, as did their Iranian counterparts.

In June 1985, Rezai traveled to China to lay the groundwork for a massive, $1.6 billion weapons deal signed by Rafsanjani during an official visit to Beijing that July. Western military attachés tracking the war used to joke that the Chinese jets ran out of gas before they hit the end of the runway, but Rezai was deadly serious about his China connection. In addition to Silkworm anti-shipping missiles and F-7M fighters (an improved Chinese version of the venerable MiG-21), Rezai wanted the Chinese to help set up new weapons factories so the Pasdaran could assemble Chinese missiles and artillery rockets in Iran, instead of buying them off the shelf. It was a major step toward self-sufficiency. To Rezai's surprise and delight, the Chinese agreed.

By the end of the year, Chinese construction crews broke ground on a series of missile facilities near the city of Semnan, 175 kilometers east of Tehran, and in the Great Salt Desert near Shahroud, farther east. Iran's missile industry was born.

Although the Oghab missile had a range of just 40 kilometers, it was cheap and it carried a huge 300-kilogram warhead, making it an effective terror weapon against Iraqi border cities. It was just what Iran needed to break the morale of the Iraqi population, Rezai believed. The first three prototypes of the new missile rolled off the assembly line in Semnan in late 1986 and were immediately sent to a Revolutionary Guards missile batallion on the southern front. They launched them successfully on December 7, 1986, against Basra, the second-largest city in Iraq, beginning a new phase of the eight-year conflict known as the War of the Cities.

To propel the Oghab and other solid-fuel missiles it built with Chinese assistance, Iran was forced in the mid-1980s to import large quantities of ammonium perchlorate (AP) from Holland, Belgium, West Germany, Pakistan, and the United States. On a tip from the U.S. Customs Service, Belgian Customs intercepted one shipment en route to Iran via a West German front company. Subsequent seizures in January and February 1988 forced the Iranians to abandon direct purchases of the vital chemical. Instead, as missile designers told me later at an arms fair in Abu Dhabi, Iran established its own AP production plant, with Chinese help.

By 1988, nearly one thousand of these short, stubby, solid-fueled Oghab rockets had poured off the new Chinese assembly line near Semnan, beyond the range of Iraqi SCUDs. During the 1988 War of the Cities, Rezai's commanders fired 243 Oghabs into Iraqi border cities, prompting his mentor, Iranian defense minister Mohammad Hossein Jalali, to commend him on Iranian television. "Eighty percent of the missiles raining down on the Saddamists and sending them to hell are manufactured by our defense industries," he said with pride. In addition, the locally produced missiles cost "one-third what we would spend if purchasing from abroad."

At the same time, Rezai turned to North Korea for help with the liquid-fueled SCUD-B, a longer-range missile with a larger warhead that allowed Iran to hit Baghdad. In its base version, the Soviet-designed SCUD-B could fire a one-ton warhead at targets up to 300 kilometers distant. But it was notoriously inaccurate.

Like Iran, North Korea was a pariah state. This affinity persuaded Rezai and his political masters to throw in their lot with Pyongyang, which by 1985 had run out of funds to pursue its missile development programs. The Islamic Republic agreed to finance North Korea's effort to reverse-engineer the SCUD-B, in exchange for missiles and production technology. Iran also offered to help out in the clandestine acquisition of production equipment in the United States and Western Europe. Missile experts now recognize the North Korean SCUD program as a joint development project that mated North Korean engineers with Iranian cash.

The North Korean–Iranian connection surfaced in odd ways. In May

1984 a Soviet émigré, Yuri Geifman, was indicted in New York for unlicensed exports of sophisticated electronic components to North Korea, for use in ballistic missile guidance systems. In October of the same year, an Iranian businessman based in West Germany, Babak Seroush, was indicted on similar charges, following a U.S. Customs investigation. What North Korea could not obtain through the smugglers, it imported from China, including the entire liquid fuel rocket engine and key guidance components.

In January 1987 the first SCUD-B prototype was test-launched in North Korea. In June, North Korea and Iran signed a $500 million contract that covered the delivery of ninety to one hundred production SCUD-B missiles. Iran deployed its new missiles to a special Pasdaran unit under Rezai's direct control, and fired seventy-seven of them against Iraq during the War of the Cities.

Iran's largest ballistic missile plant was built by the North Koreans near Isfahan, where the Swedish firm Bofors had built a huge, state-of-the-art explosives factory. Production of the SCUD-B began in 1988.

Isfahan was a natural choice for strategic weapons manufacture. In addition to boasting a skilled workforce, it was close to iron mines, mineral resources, and refineries, and housed a gigantic Soviet-built steel plant. So great were the needs of the weapons complex that the Iranian government asked Danieli Spa of Italy to expand the Soviet plant in 1989, and built a second, even larger steel plant 70 kilometers away. The $4.7 billion Mobarakeh steel complex was contracted out to a consortium of Italian, Japanese, and Swiss companies. By common agreement they all referred to it as a "development" project.

Rezai traveled to Pyongyang in March and October 1989. On both occasions he met with North Korean leader Kim Il Sung to discuss new, longer-range missile projects. On November 29, 1990, a senior North Korean military delegation paid a return visit to Tehran to bring test results to Rezai and his Revolutionary Guards missile team. Together the two pariahs were going to build better and longer-range missiles.

The North Koreans referred to the new project as No-Dong. Western experts called it the SCUD-C. If deployed near Iran's borders, the new missile would give Iran the capability of launching strikes deep into central Turkey. To the south, if equipped with a chemical or nuclear warhead, the new missile could annihilate U.S. forces pre-positioned at the Dhahran air base in Saudi Arabia. But if Iran wanted to threaten its archrival, Israel, the SCUD-C was not enough.

Rezai knew there was yet more work to be done.

THE BLIND SWEDE

We should fully equip ourselves both in the offensive and defensive use of chemical, bacteriological, and radiological weapons. From now on, you should make use of the opportunity and perform this task.

—Ali Akbar Hashemi-Rafsanjani,
addressing the Islamic Republic Revolutionary Guards, October 6, 1988

On the twenty-eighth floor of the A Tower of the international center in Vienna, Director General Hans Blix pondered the request he had received from Iran's delegate to the International Atomic Energy Agency. Since his appointment to the cushy IAEA job in September 1981, the former Swedish politician had prided himself on his diplomatic skills. He knew that this particular request would not be well received by the agency's top funder, the United States. But he was inclined to honor it anyway.

Blix had always been a strong defender of the agency's cooperation with countries such as Iraq and Iran, despite fears that they were secretly developing nuclear weapons. Both countries were living up to their side of the nuclear bargain, and the international community had an obligation to live up to its side as well. After all, that's what the Nonproliferation Treaty (NPT) was about, Blix argued. The nuclear powers agreed to transfer nuclear technology to non-nuclear weapons states on condition that they not use that technology for anything other than peaceful ends. As the world's nuclear watchdog, it was the IAEA's job to ensure that *everyone* upheld his side of the bargain, starting with the nuclear weapons states. Blix took that responsibility seriously.

Like many technocrats from first-world countries, Hans Blix had a healthy skepticism regarding the technical capabilities of the developing world and great confidence in the ability of his inspectors. He seriously doubted that countries such as Iran or Iraq could work on nuclear weapons undetected. So when the Iranians requested that the IAEA provide assistance in rebuilding the bombed-out reactor at Busheir, Hans Blix was inclined to agree. After all, the KWU reactor was a light-water design that ran on 3 percent enriched uranium, totally unsuited as weapons fuel. No one had ever used such a reactor for a clandestine bomb program. Most of his colleagues at the agency agreed that the American fears were simply groundless.

Besides, Iran had a perfect right to nuclear power. It had signed and ratified the NPT under the shah, and regularly allowed IAEA inspectors to visit its one safeguarded nuclear research reactor in Tehran. Ironically, that small, 5-megawatt reactor had been supplied by the Americans in the 1960s and required fresh supplies of highly enriched uranium fuel. In 1987, after the Americans had refused to fulfill their commitments, Blix helped Iran work out a deal with Argentina to purchase fuel for the reactor. He considered it a double victory. Not only had he tweaked the noses of the Americans, who had reneged on their obligations under the NPT; he also had convinced the Iranians to make technical alterations so the reactor could be fueled with uranium enriched only to 20 percent, not the 93 percent weapons-grade mix required by the original U.S. design. There was no way the Iranians could transform those tiny shipments of fuel into weapons material without the IAEA knowing it. The system worked.

The sixty-one-year-old Blix stood before the broad windows of his office overlooking the imperial splendor of his beloved Vienna and felt a sense of destiny and power. In his own country, he had never been able to rise above his political rivals. Blix's former colleagues still recall his meekness when he attended interagency meetings in the 1970s as a cabinet undersecretary at the Ministry of Foreign Affairs. "Whenever someone would present a strong position, Blix would keep quiet and go along," one of his former colleagues told me. "We always knew we could get him to do whatever we wanted." Blix's former boss, Deputy Prime Minister Per Ahlmark, has a similar recollection. "I was responsible for helping Blix get where he is today, and I regret it," he told me. "I don't think the American government realizes just how bad he really is."

But here in Vienna, Blix was at home. He was perfectly suited for this job, and he liked it. As a UN bureaucrat who managed more than 1,100 employees, he earned a substantial salary that was protected from Sweden's outrageous socialist tax system. He had a decent housing allowance, an education allowance for his children, and always traveled first class. Once every three months, the world's nuclear powers came to him in Vienna to hear his quarterly report, and he managed to navigate the shoals of the Cold War between the United States and the Soviet Union with aplomb. The Soviets had recognized his evenhandedness in 1987 by awarding him an honorary doctorate from Moscow State University (something the Americans didn't have the grace to emulate, he thought ruefully).

As someone from a country that itself had once pursued a clandestine nuclear weapons program, only to abandon it as politically unfeasible, Blix felt a particular sense of self-righteousness when he scolded the Americans for their suspicions of countries such as Iraq and Iran. After all, in the 1960s Sweden had stockpiled dozens of reactor cores—thousands of kilograms of highly enriched uranium—in deep underground storage bunkers dug out of the cliffs of its rugged southern coast. If it had wanted, Sweden could have produced more than twenty nuclear weapons with that material, dramatically altering the world's nuclear balance at the height of the Cold War. But that never happened. Why? Because when rational men and women contemplated the abyss of nuclear devastation, they were naturally repelled, Blix believed. It was condescending on the part of the Americans to think that the Iraqis or the Iranians were any different. When the head of Iran's Atomic Energy Organization, Reza Amrollahi, told him that Iran was far too intimate with the horrors of war ever to contemplate developing nuclear weapons, Hans Blix believed him. After all, Amrollahi was a reasonable and intelligent man.

Of course he would go, Blix decided as he reread Amrollahi's letter asking him to visit Iran's bombed-out reactor at Busheir. Like Saddam Hussein's Iraq, Iran's clerical leaders had upheld their side of the nuclear bargain. It was up to him as the arbiter between the nuclear haves and have-nots to stand up for countries such as Iran who had legitimate rights that the Americans and their cronies sought to trample. Iran wanted assistance from the IAEA in developing its uranium mines and building nuclear power reactors? Hans Blix was about to become their champion. It was not the IAEA's business that Iran was making massive purchases of uranium yellowcake from South Africa and Namibia, as that pesky *Nucleonics Week* reporter had claimed. Sales of yellowcake were beyond the purview of his agency. Even journalists must know you can't make nuclear weapons from natural uranium, he huffed. As long as the Iranians kept to their safeguards agreement with the agency, it would be discriminatory not to help them.

BLIX LENDS A HAND

Blix traveled to Busheir on June 22, 1989, and was surprised by what he saw. Iraqi warplanes had devastated virtually the entire sprawling facility in systematic bombing attacks during the last two years of the Iran-Iraq war. The huge, reinforced-concrete reactor vessels abandoned by KWU ten years earlier were still standing, but their walls were severely fissured.

Storage hangars lay open to the sky, their roofs demolished by Iraqi bombs. Equipment lay rusting in the open air.

In Tehran, Blix told Iranian prime minister Mir Hossein Mousavi that the IAEA was willing to help Iran complete the reactors, but he cautioned that the work would almost have to begin again from scratch. Mousavi complained in front of Blix to the Iranian press that the West German government had been dragging its feet in negotiations to begin the work. While that was true—Foreign Minister Hans-Dietrich Genscher was insisting that Iran and Iraq sign a formal peace treaty before he would agree to allow German technicians back onto the site—there were plenty of other suppliers around capable of doing the job. Blix pledged he would formally query the West German government on its intentions as soon as he returned to Vienna.

It soon became apparent that the real sticking point was money. Just one week after Blix toured Busheir, a delegation of Iranian parliament members from the budget committee flew down to tour the site. Committee chairman Morteza Alviri later told the BBC they estimated Iran had already spent $3 billion to build a heap of ruins. Billions more would be required to finish the project.

To demonstrate his good faith, Blix agreed to have the IAEA host a one-week quality-assurance training session for nuclear power plant managers, with eighteen Iranian participants. He also sent a Radiation Protection Advisory Team (RAPAT) to survey the Busheir reactors, at Iran's request. According to the IAEA Annual Report for 1989, such missions "review infrastructure needs and define a long-term strategy for technical assistance and cooperation." Amrollahi told Blix that Iran was interested in building many more nuclear power plants and wanted IAEA assistance in doing seismic tests of various sites. From 1982 to 1989, Iran received some $2,452,900 in aid from the agency, IAEA reports show. This included $400,000 for a study of the Busheir nuclear power plant, and $312,000 in "procurement assistance." An additional $1,667,700 was received for nuclear research programs during the same period from the United Nations Development Program, UNDP.[1]

As this open cooperation between Iran and the IAEA began to take shape, Rafsanjani and his nuclear team quietly looked elsewhere to purchase special equipment and assistance. Two days before Blix arrived, Rafsanjani himself had gone to Moscow for long-awaited talks with Soviet leader Mikhail Gorbachev, seeking a broad range of nuclear technologies. He also floated the idea that Iran would entertain a Soviet bid for completing the reactors at Busheir. While in Moscow, Rafsanjani inked a deal to buy

$1.9 billion in Soviet weaponry, including a squadron of MiG-29 fighters. The arms deal brought the Soviet Union's previously covert sales to Iran out into the open and astonished many Middle East "experts," who had taken at face value Ayatollah Khomeini's famous slogan "Neither East nor West" and believed his public refusal to cooperate with the communists.

President Khamenei was dispatched to North Korea, where he concluded a secret $500 million trade agreement that included nuclear and missile technologies. Other senior officials were sent to Romania, Hungary, Libya, and Brazil in search of technology and equipment. Major deals to build new industrial plants and to purchase advanced machine tools were struck with Germany, France, and Italy.

Just as A. Q. Khan had told them, building a large nuclear power plant with IAEA assistance and safeguards provided Iran with a convenient cover story for acquiring the goods, technology, and know-how it needed to pursue a clandestine nuclear weapons program. As long as the Iranians never openly spoke about their intentions, greed kept suppliers from asking questions. Hans Blix made sure the IAEA played along.

Iran's goal was to acquire the capabilities that would allow it to produce weapons-grade plutonium or highly enriched uranium without being detected. While the Busheir plant could be used for that purpose, in late 1989 the Iranians lucked upon an even better solution when they struck uranium in the east.

Reza Amrollahi announced the finds in a September 1989 interview with the hard-line Tehran daily, *Resalaat.* Iranian mining engineers had discovered large deposits of natural uranium near Saghand, in the eastern province of Yazd, which Iran hoped eventually to export.[2] He told a Tehran radio interviewer soon afterward that uranium had been discovered "in ten areas" throughout Iran, and that Iran's Atomic Energy Organization planned to open a "high bleaching project" at one of the mines that would become operational by the end of the year. Bleaching is a well-known milling technique for processing uranium ore into yellowcake. One month later the budget committee of the Majles reported that Iran would open a "uranium bullion plant" near Yazd—presumably a milling plant—that would employ eight hundred workers. Funds for the plant were allocated within the 1989–94 Five-Year Plan.[3]

Amrollahi subsequently stated that Iran would open three such milling facilities at different locations. In addition to Saghand, the sites were identified as Bandar Abbas and Bandar-e Langeh, both of which are along the Persian Gulf coast, not far from the Strait of Hormuz. Iran turned for help in building these milling plants to an unlikely source.

In 1989 the Argentine National Institute for Applied Research, INVAP, signed an $18 million contract with Iran to build a series of unsafeguarded facilities for processing uranium ore. U.S. officials familiar with the deal told me that INVAP planned to build the milling plant and a separate facility for fabricating nuclear fuel that could be used in a 27-megawatt research reactor the Iranians were trying to purchase from China.[4]

With a domestic supply of uranium that was outside the scope of its safeguards agreement with the IAEA, Iran had opened a back door to the uranium fuel cycle. In total security it could build uranium conversion plants and even enrichment facilities using dual-use equipment imported from the West for legitimate civilian purposes, just as A. Q. Khan had done in Pakistan. Because none of these activities was being carried out in facilities Iran had declared to the IAEA, Hans Blix and his nuclear "watchdogs" would remain in the dark.

They just weren't looking.

THE AYATOLLAH DIES

Ayatollah Khomeini died on June 3, 1989, and was succeeded by President Ali Khamenei, a minor cleric who was viewed at the time as a temporary seat warmer. In August, Rafsanjani took Khamenei's place as president and announced a new government that publicly shunned radicals known for their involvement in the U.S. embassy takeover in 1979 and for creating Hezbollah and other international terrorist groups. He also kicked out left-wing prime minister Mir Hossein Mousavi, whose policies of nationalization and centralized state control had bankrupted the Iranian economy.

Behind the scenes, Rafsanjani and his team were negotiating with the United States, France, Germany, and South Korea to exact the highest possible price for their hostages then being held by Iranian surrogates in Lebanon. He wanted trade, aid, and clandestine technology deals for Iran, and cash bribes for the hostage takers. (In exchange for the French hostages, for example, he demanded shipments of enriched uranium in fulfillment of the 10 percent ownership stake purchased by the former shah in the Eurodif uranium enrichment consortium in France.) This nasty game of hardball was vintage Rafsanjani. On the one hand he issued orders to surrogates to take the hostages, while with his other hand on his heart he protested his innocence and negotiated their release.

And all the while he and his nuclear team were quietly working away.

GENERAL JIANG

On January 21, 1990, Rafsanjani and Defense Minister Ali Akbar Torkan received an important visitor in Tehran. He was the deputy director of China's Commission on Science, Technology and Industry for National Defense (COSTIND), General Jiang Xua. His all-powerful organization was in charge of the Chinese weapons establishment, including arms and technology exports. General Jiang had come to Tehran with the text of a ten-year nuclear cooperation treaty, which he signed with Torkan that same day.[5]

The Chinese agreed to expand the Isfahan nuclear research center, and signed a framework agreement for the 27-megawatt research reactor the Iranians had been seeking. The China Nuclear Energy Industry Corporation (CNEIC)—the export arm of China's Ministry of Energy Resources—was designated as the prime contractor. The heavy-water reactor design the Iranians wanted used easy-to-manufacture natural uranium. More important, it was a natural breeder of weapons-grade plutonium. In Iraq, such a reactor—supplied by the French—was openly referred to as a nuclear bomb factory.

The Chinese also pledged to provide an electromagnetic isotope separation (EMIS) machine, known in the West as a calutron, so the Iranians could carry out experiments in uranium enrichment, and to train Iranian technicians at Chinese nuclear research centers. U.S. satellite photographs, taken in September 1991, soon detected major construction work at the Isfahan reactor site. The United States also detected the presence of large numbers of Chinese technicians at the site.

More clear warnings, ignored.

THE GERMANY SYNDROME

Even though Iran has not acquired nuclear capability yet, it reserves the right to use any weapons—including nuclear—to try to combat the imposition of U.S. hegemony.

—**Salam** editorial, June 20, 1991

One dreary afternoon in late January 1991, when the news was full of allied bombing raids on Iraq, an alert German counterintelligence officer noticed unusual activity at the Iranian embassy in Bonn. An Iranian intelligence officer named Karim Ali Sobhani, working in Germany under non-official cover, arrived at 133 Godesberger Allee in the sleepy suburb of Bad Godesberg, not far from the Rhine river. Shortly after he arrived, a German businessman known to be in contact with Leybold AG, a prominent supplier of nuclear and missile production equipment, rang at the front gate of the embassy and was ushered inside.

Sobhani's activities had been flagged to the Germans by the CIA after a federal court in Maryland convicted him in July 1988 of illegally purchasing chemicals to make mustard gas for Iran. Under U.S. pressure, the Germans expelled Sobhani in 1989, despite the fact that he then enjoyed diplomatic status. But the seasoned intelligence officer continued to return to Germany after his expulsion, and the Germans let him in under an intelligence agreement they had negotiated with Tehran. Germany's relationship with Iran was a hall of mirrors. To placate the Americans, they automatically placed Sobhani under surveillance.

Leybold AG had earned a world-class reputation for its expertise in manufacturing state-of-the-art metallurgy and vacuum equipment for manufacturing missiles and uranium enrichment. It also had a long track record of selling this equipment to nations suspected of developing nuclear weapons on the sly, starting with the sale in 1979 of a large electron beam welder to Pakistan. Leybold sold similar machines to Iraq in the 1980s, which UN inspectors eventually found in Iraqi nuclear facilities. Although the Leybold equipment could be used to make automobile parts, it was essential for the high-precision task of manufacturing uranium enrichment centrifuges. The machines were licensed for "general military applications such as jet engine repair, rocket cases, etc."

To the German watchers who kept tabs on the Iranian embassy, the connection was clear. They had a known Iranian procurement agent meeting with an intermediary for a top German supplier of nuclear technology. It spelled trouble.

As the German gumshoes investigated, they came to believe that Sobhani and the German businessman were attempting to ship a Leybold vacuum melting furnace to Iran, via India. It was a key piece of equipment for anyone seeking to shape molten radioactive materials into the core of a nuclear weapon. When I asked them about the encounter not long afterward, Leybold denied any knowledge of these discussions.

Leybold earned a significant portion of its total revenue (some sources said 30 percent) from sales of high-technology furnaces, electron beam welders, and other nuclear-related equipment to countries of proliferation concern. The company hit the international spotlight in 1981, when a shipment to Pakistan of vacuum pumps worth 6 million DM was revealed in *The Islamic Bomb*. Authors Herb Krosney and Steve Weissman alleged that the Leybold equipment was used in Pakistan's clandestine uranium enrichment program. This was confirmed several years later by A. Q. Khan's biographer Zahid Malik, who noted that the pumps could be "purchased anywhere" and "did not require special permission" or an export license.[1]

In fact, Leybold had been a key supplier to Dr. Khan's clandestine procurement network ever since Khan first visited the company in 1979. Their activities were being monitored by intelligence agencies in a half-dozen countries.

In 1986 a pair of Leybold engineers came under investigation for having allegedly used their access to a uranium enrichment plant in Gronau, West Germany, operated by the Urenco consortium, to acquire secret production technology for Dr. Khan's network. The case began with a complaint for copyright infringement two years earlier from Uranit GmbH, which had hired Leybold to manufacture special machinery for the Gronau plant and had supplied them with blueprints. Leybold denied any involvement in the diversion of Urenco technology and was never charged.

Although the original Uranit complaint was dropped for lack of evidence, German prosecutors later alleged that the Leybold executives, Dr. Otto Heilinbruner and Gotthard Lerch, stole a complete set of blueprints for Urenco centrifuges and production gear, and transported them by car to Switzerland to a company called Metallwerke Buchs (MWB), which began producing "parts for a uranium enrichment facility." Lerch was on the MWB board, giving rise to suspicion that the Swiss company was being used as a conduit by Leybold for illicit foreign sales.

An investigative memo by a German federal prosecutor in Hamburg, dated March 16, 1989, exposed Leybold's critical importance as a clandestine nuclear supplier. The prosecutor based his findings on a thick stack of invoices, shipping documents, travel vouchers, and other documents seized during searches of company headquarters and private homes, and on the interrogation of numerous employees of Leybold and MWB.

What he sketched out in that memo was nothing less than the inner workings of the A. Q. Khan network. I obtained a copy of the investigative file, including this key memo, from officials at the IAEA in Vienna in the early 1990s. But despite this detailed knowledge, the IAEA never blew the whistle on the Khan network, and Western intelligence agencies never shut it down. It continued to operate until the United States intercepted the German-registered cargo ship *BBC China* in October 2003, loaded with virtually an entire uranium centrifuge plant crated up for delivery to Libya.

Prosecutors found that Leybold officials would take orders for uranium enrichment equipment and split them into smaller parts. They farmed out the work to suppliers in different countries, including a Leybold subsidiary in France, SOGEV SA. MWB then assembled the goods in Switzerland and shipped them to a Liechtenstein firm called Merimpex, which sent them on to the Middle East.

Other companies named in the documents as active participants in the network included Grant Trading, Inc., of Panama; Euro Asia Engineering Supplies Pte. Ltd., Singapore; Oceanic Trading Ltd., in Grand Turk and Caicos Islands; National Metal in Riyadh, Saudi Arabia; and SPA Mideast in Dubai. Payments were made through Habib Bank Limited of Singapore.

The Germans called on French Customs for help, since much of the equipment was either manufactured in France for Leybold or transshipped through various French ports en route to Merimpex. The French examined the shipping documents and technical specifications for four categories of equipment. They concluded that "the implication is strong that these parts are for the production of a nuclear plant, which supports your conclusion in your letter of September 14, 1987 that the final destination is Pakistan."[2]

The end-users—whoever they were—were picky. Merimpex rejected ten crates of equipment produced by Leybold's French subsidiary in December 1985 and "sent them back to Leybold for cleaning," according to the French Customs report.

Despite the wealth of documentary evidence, the prosecutors were forced to drop the charges against the former Leybold executives later in 1989 because of loopholes in German export laws. Unlike the United States, where *exporters* of high-technology goods had to demonstrate that their equipment would not contribute to banned weapons programs, in Germany the logic was reversed. Companies were free to export unless *the government* could prove that their goods were going to banned destinations, such as known ballistic missile plants or nuclear facilities. "As a country that sells a third of its GNP abroad," German commentator Josef Joffe said, "West Germany has export laws whose liberality is probably exceeded only by Hong Kong. Bonn is so impotent in the pursuit of malefactors precisely because government and business both want it that way."[3]

By 1991, Germany had become Iran's largest supplier of controlled technologies, with annual sales worth $1.8 billion that were licensed because of their applicability to a variety of weapons programs.

A Cologne court eventually brought a second indictment against Heilinbruner and Lerch on the very narrow charge that they had illegally exported proprietary technical information to Switzerland. The new charges no longer mentioned the sale of the centrifuge blueprints to Pakistan or to any other foreign destination.*

The second Leybold trial began on March 30, 1992, but Heilinbruner and Lerch were acquitted just one month later. "The problem was that everything happened in Switzerland," state prosecutor Veilhaber told me. "We could not prove beyond reasonable doubt to the court that Lerch or Heilinbruner were actually responsible for stealing the blueprints," even though the Swiss police had found the blueprints in Lerch's desk drawer when they raided the MWB offices in Switzerland.[4]

Meanwhile, Germany's foreign intelligence service, the BND, was conducting its own investigation of Leybold's sales to Iran, Iraq, Libya, and North Korea. Stamped "Top Secret," Report No. AZ:30-31c-0326-91

*Many years later, the head of Iraq's top-secret centrifuge program, Dr. Mahdi Obeidi, disclosed that he had invited a German centrifuge expert named Bruno Stemmler to Baghdad in August 1988. Dr. Mahdi couldn't believe his eyes when Stemmler pulled out of his briefcase an entire set of the Urenco centrifuge blueprints and offered to sell them as well as prototypes of key parts for just over $1 million. "I didn't ask how they came into his hands," Dr. Mahdi wrote. "As I eagerly thumbed through page after page, I felt my pulse quicken as the significance of these documents dawned on me. They were a virtual instruction manual." Dr. Mahdi added that without the blueprints and the help from Stemmler and other foreigners, Iraq would never have succeeded in building working centrifuges. Mahdi Obeidi and Kurt Pitzer, *The Bomb in My Garden: The Secrets of Saddam's Nuclear Mastermind* (Hoboken, NJ: John Wiley & Sons, 2004), 91.

revealed that Leybold was now disguising sales to questionable overseas customers as domestic transfers to other German companies, in order to foil German export control authorities. When the BND transmitted their report to Chancellor Helmut Kohl on October 23, 1991, the German leader already knew about Leybold's latest ruse. Indeed, it had become an embarrassment.

In July 1991, German customs inspectors seized a Leybold furnace in the port of Hamburg as it was being loaded on board the Libyan freighter *Jarif.* Leybold claimed it had not sold the furnace to the Libyans, who intended to use it for their Al-Fatah ballistic missile program. They had sold it to German weapons manufacturer Fritz Werner GmbH. Whatever they did with the furnace was their responsibility, Leybold claimed.

News of the seizure was leaked to *Der Spiegel* on September 6, 1991. Under mounting public pressure from opposition members of Parliament and from the United States, Kohl convened his cabinet five days later to enact emergency regulations that temporarily blocked any further shipments to Libya. Leybold eventually admitted it was aware that Fritz Werner intended to ship the induction furnace to the "Maktabl El Bahut Attacknia" in Libya but that it was intended to be used "for the production of spare parts, especially for automobiles."

A new export control law was drafted and approved by Parliament, which required German companies to seek an export license for sales to known weapons facilities in countries of proliferation concern. It also required German companies to designate a corporate board member who would be personally and legally responsible for any export control violation committed by the company. U.S. officials referred to it as the "Leybold law." It looked good on paper, but no corporate director was ever sent to jail under the new law.[5]

In the United States, Senator John Glenn published a list of Leybold sales of nuclear production equipment in his newsletter, *Proliferation Watch.* Leybold's clients included government entities in North Korea, India, Pakistan, Libya, Iraq, Iran, and South Africa—a veritable rogues' gallery of nuclear wannabes. The company protested that its sales were made in accordance with existing export control laws, which until then had been notoriously lax.

In December 1991, Glenn introduced legislation aiming to "take the profits out of proliferation" by forcing companies such as Leybold to choose between selling equipment to the United States or to rogue states. The Omnibus Nuclear Proliferation Control Act of 1991 passed with broad bipartisan support.

Leybold's record was so bad that its corporate parent, Degussa AG, fretted it would lose lucrative contracts with British and Japanese aerospace firms who subcontracted to U.S. companies. They hired a top U.S. public relations firm, Burson Martsteller, to improve the company's image. The company also announced a new set of "corporate principles," which it claimed would prevent such sales in the future.

But the damage had already been done.

DR. KHAN'S SPINNING MACHINES

Getting access to the centrifuge production blueprints was a critical success for Rafsanjani's men.

When Dr. Khan set up the Kahuta plant in the late 1970s, he was able to special-order parts from suppliers in Britain, France, Germany, and Switzerland from precise specifications. By the time Iran got around to building its own plant a decade later, European customs authorities were on the lookout for large orders of the maraging steel tubes, specialized magnets, bellows, power inverters, and vacuum equipment that had to be built to exacting specifications. So, instead of buying the actual components, Rafsanjani's men ordered the production machinery to make them, using the Urenco blueprints they had acquired from the Khan network.

Just as the Pakistani had discovered a decade earlier, willing suppliers lined up to provide the goods in Germany, Switzerland, France, and the United States.

"There are only two ways to build a centrifuge enrichment plant," a Western expert who worked for thirty years in the industry told me. "Either you buy it off the shelf, as some countries have tried to do, or you make it from scratch, starting with manufacturing all the components. That's a difficult road, because the components are all state of the art." And yet that was precisely what Iran was trying to do.

Natural uranium contains only 0.7 percent U-235, the fissile material needed to make an atomic bomb. The rest is U-238. Enriching uranium is the process of separating the two isotopes in order to increase the amount of U-235. Enriched to 4 percent, the uranium can be used in light-water power reactors to generate electricity. Enriched to around 90 percent, it can be used to make bombs. If a proliferator such as Iran started with reactor-grade fuel, it could reduce the size of its clandestine centrifuge enrichment plant "by a factor of five."[6]

Centrifuge enrichment was commercialized in Europe by Urenco in the 1970s, thanks in part to a $700 million investment from the U.S. government. It requires a number of industrial-scale facilities. The most critical—before the centrifuge plant itself—is the uranium conversion facility, known familiarly as a hex plant, where a fluoride compound is added to uranium yellowcake powder, transforming it into uranium hexafluoride (UF6). No hex plant, no enrichment.

Although UF6 is normally a solid, it becomes a gas when heated slightly above room temperature. This is what makes it possible to enrich uranium by centrifuge. When the uranium gas is spun at very high speeds in tall cylinders, or rotors, the heavier atoms of U-238 drop to the bottom and are scooped away as waste, called "tails." The lighter atoms of U-235 spin up to the top, where they are collected for further enrichment. It's a bit like making butter. The principle is simple, but applying it is not.

For starters, UF6 is highly corrosive, so the rotors must be made of exotic corrosive-resistant materials—special aluminum alloys, maraging steel, or more recently, carbon fiber-resin composites (CFRC). Next, the meter-high rotors must spin at speeds exceeding 60,000 rpm—over one thousand times per second—which generates incredible stress. If the rotor wall is too thick, it becomes unstable. If it's too thin, it bursts, so production tolerances must be incredibly precise. Only a handful of countries have mastered the process of producing centrifuge rotors, although many have tried.

As it spins like a top on a tiny spindle, the rotor is supported by a special ball bearing—not much larger than the tip of a ballpoint pen—and driven by special motors called high-frequency inverters. The top of the rotor is suspended between two axially opposed ring magnets, made of rare earth materials, that hold the rotor in place without physical contact and thus without causing friction. "Welding the micro-bearing to the centrifuge assembly is a black art," says James Swanson, a former Defense Department trade security analyst. "Only a handful of countries around the world are capable of doing it." A key piece of machinery for accomplishing this high-precision task is the electron-beam welder that Leybold makes.

While the centrifuge is spinning, the UF6 feedstock must be kept at just the right temperature. If it cools too much, it clumps and clogs the scoops, making a mess of the piping. But if the gas is overheated, corrosion increases, wearing out expensive parts. Most countries that have mastered the process began with a small pilot plant, or cascade, using some one hundred to two hundred centrifuges, before ramping up to an industrial-sized facility with fifty thousand centrifuges spinning all at once. "A centrifuge plant can be built stepwise and expanded as and when desired," wrote A. Q. Khan's admirative biographer. "However, the design and production of the centrifuges, and then to put up a functional industrial plant is a gigantic and Herculean task."[7]

The Department of Energy uses centrifuges at the Y2 enrichment plant in Oak Ridge, Tennessee, but they are huge machines, several stories high. If one of them breaks or needs maintenance, it shuts down the whole plant and is very expensive to replace. "Urenco's approach was to make rotors like toasters, and to throw them away if they broke," the Western centrifuge expert said. Such was the approach used by Pakistan. With equipment purchased in Germany and elsewhere, that was Iran's goal as well.

"LOOK, BUT DON'T TOUCH"

Germany was not the only country where the Iranians were shopping.

In Arlington, Virginia, just across the street from the Pentagon in a nondescript office building in Crystal City, a diverse team of intelligence analysts and armed services detailees pored over stacks of export licenses referred to them by the Department of Commerce. Their job was to identify militarily critical technologies and equipment that companies wanted to export to potential enemies of the United States, and to stop them from leaving the country. It was not always an easy task.

For most ordinary people, reading through the mounds of technical documentation and government forms would be a mind-numbing task. But for intelligence analysts such as James Swanson, a thirty-five-year-old U.S. Navy lieutenant commander, the dull prose and diagrams and numbers presented secret clues, which he decrypted like an Agatha Christie murder mystery for nerds. "By 1990–91, we were beginning to see a pattern in Iran of missiles and nukes," he recalls. Many of the trails Swanson first identified led back to the famous Dr. Khan.

One name that came up repeatedly was Leybold AG. Swanson noted that its U.S. subsidiary, Leybold Inficom, Inc., was trying to sell a gas chromatography unit to the plasma physics laboratory of Sharif University.

Now, that's cute, Swanson thought. Just what Dr. Khan ordered. Gas chromatography was used to measure the isotopic content of substances such as uranium hexafluoride. And nobody even blinked at Sharif University as the end-user? That was where the Revolutionary Guards were training their very own Doctor Khans. They were even importing ring magnets, although not from the United States. The United States had sent a not-so-diplomatic little note to the Germans warning them about Sharif University.

Swanson took out a large stamp from his desk drawer, carefully rolled it back and forth on the ink pad, then smashed it onto the front page of the Leybold application: Case No. D101465. "Bingo!" he sang out. He had just given them the bureaucratic equivalent of the finger by marking the application "RWA"—Return Without Action. It meant the government would not grant a license and would not provide the company with any justification for its decision. They'll try again, Swanson guessed.

And the Germans had let another one of Dr. Khan's favorite suppliers, Carl Schenck AG, ship a balancing machine to Iran. That little piece of exotic gear was absolutely critical to a successful centrifuge effort. Procuring such machines was a sure sign of Iran's intentions, Swanson believed. Now Schenck was trying to buy a fancy computer in the U.S. for Iran Aircraft Industries, which, as everyone knows, is only interested in maintaining Boeing 747s for Iran Air, even though it's managed by the Revolutionary Guards' Defense Industries Organization. Swanson stamped that one "Returned." He requested that Schenck provide more information on how the computer would really be used.

Sometimes, Swanson's counterparts at the Commerce Department's Bureau of Export Administration (BXA) approved licenses to Iran without ever referring them to the Defense Trade Security Administration (DTSA) or the Department of Energy. In 1990–91, Commerce approved high-technology exports to Iran worth $59 million. While that was a trickle compared to what was going out the door in Germany, nevertheless it included some astonishing items—such as mainframe computers from the Digital Equipment Corporation and NCR worth several million dollars each to the Revolutionary Guards' Sharif University of Technology, or similar mainframes from Sun Microsystems to the Amir Kabir University of Technology, the renamed Nuclear Research Center of Tehran University.

Swanson regularly went to experts' meetings of the Coordinating Committee on Multilateral Export Controls (COCOM), revived by President Reagan in the early 1980s to prevent NATO allies from shipping military technology to the Soviet Union. With the fall of the Berlin Wall, there was tremendous pressure to loosen the COCOM controls. And nobody wanted to apply them to countries such as Iran, perceived by virtually all COCOM members as a huge potential market.

During a negotiating session in London, a friend in British Customs took him deep into the bowels of Heathrow airport where Her Majesty's Customs and Excise impounded goods, to look at a crate being held there. From the destination marked on the shipping documents attached to the crate, both of them knew that the milling machine it contained was headed to an Iranian missile plant.

Look, but don't touch, the Customs officer said. Swanson grunted as he noted the manufacturer and the high-precision tolerances of the machine.

"A milling machine doesn't know what it is machining," he said later. "The same machine can make missile parts on Monday and Tuesday, nuclear weapons parts on Wednesday and Thursday, and washing machines on Friday. It just depends on how you program it." Of course, the Iranians knew exactly how to program it for all three uses, but on their export license request they only mentioned that it would be used to make washing machines. There was no legal way the British government could prevent it from reaching Iran.

That was how the Iranians assembled their capability, machine by machine, Swanson said.

The United States was beginning to pick up signs that the Iranians were building clandestine facilities that they failed to declare to the IAEA. "We had intel that they had secret facilities, but the intelligence community refused to release the information so we could act on it and warn exporters," recalls Michael Maloof, an operations officer who worked with Swanson at DTSA. "We felt there was a clear pattern that showed Iran's interest in developing nuclear weapons. But when we tried to block exports to undeclared facilities and procurement fronts, the intelligence community pushed back because it was their assessment that Iran was at least a decade away from a nuclear weapons capability."

In this instance, the CIA was right. But now it is more than ten years later, and virtually nothing has been done to slow them down.

Sometimes Iran brazenly purchased extraordinary things, such as computers worth more than $170 million that were considered to have a potential nuclear "end-use." When I went through licensing records released by the Commerce Department in 1991, it became apparent that 60 percent of all Iranian license applications over the previous three years in the United States were for items on the "Nuclear Referral List," which covers equipment, technologies, and materials COCOM members considered particularly useful to weapons production. While a majority of those licenses were denied, some managed to slip through the net. Typically this happened when the Commerce Department failed to notify other government agencies such as DTSA.

Now that its eight-year war with Iraq was over, Iran began making massive high-tech purchases in the West. In the United States, the Iranians expanded purchases sevenfold, from $131,589,535 in 1989 to over $871 million the following year. Swanson and his colleagues at DTSA tried to hold the line, but they were required by the Department of Commerce to justify on a case-by-case basis why they were refusing licenses for equipment the Europeans were shipping to Iran on a regular basis. It was time for the government to "get smart" on Iran, lobbyists for the exporting community argued.

If the United States and Europe had been more diligent in denying technology during the early stages of Iran's nuclear weapons program, they could have delayed it almost indefinitely. Instead, Iran was granted access to the developed world's premier high-technology suppliers. Much of their equipment is now being found by IAEA inspectors in Iranian nuclear plants.

The names of Iran's suppliers are among the Agency's best-kept secrets. But they have been known to export control authorities for years.

PEANUT BUTTER PUMPS

When U.S. Customs officers working at the port of Newark, New Jersey, saw the eight crates with the strange markings, at first they didn't know what to think. Only one word was written clearly in English. It was "Chemical."

Once they realized that the address on the crates was written in Farsi, they called in an Iranian translator who decrypted the destination. The inscription read, "Sazemane Sanaye Defae Jomhouri Islami Iran (Chemical)." That translated to Defense Industries Organization of the Islamic Republic of Iran (Chemical).

Upon opening the eight wooden crates, they found industrial pumps, specially designed to handle a very thick material called nitrocellulose lacquer. Dr. Stephen Bryen—Jim Swanson's boss at DTSA during the Reagan administration—revealed the customs seizure in testimony before the House Ways and Means Committee on April 19, 1991.

Nitrocellulose lacquer was used to make ball powder and gun propellants, or when dissolved in nitroglycerine, it formed a thick explosive paste used to make double-based propellants for rocket motors. It could also be used to make plastic explosives such as C4 or Semtex, the compound that brought down Pan Am 103, he said. It wasn't the first shipment of such pumps the company had made to Iran. And unless Congress reformed U.S. export controls, it wouldn't be the last, Bryen warned.

The same company—Warren Pumps Inc., of Warren, Massachusetts, a division of Imo Industries, Inc., of Lawrenceville, New Jersey—had made two earlier shipments to Iran in the 1980s, Bryen said. When the company asked Commerce whether it should submit an individual license for the sales, they received a form letter informing them that the pumps were G-DEST—"general destination"—meaning that no license was needed and they could be shipped anywhere.

After Bryen revealed the sale to Congress, Imo lawyers called the equipment "a general purpose pump," but said the company had no clue why they had been purchased by an Iranian military plant. "We manufacture pumps. We don't manufacture weapons systems," they protested. In fact, they argued, the expensive, nickel-plated devices had been "designed to pump thick materials such as peanut butter."[8]

The Chemical Industries Group of Iran's Defense Industries Organization was the backbone of the Iranian weapons industry, and it certainly wasn't making peanut butter. It operated two giant military explosives factories that had been modernized and expanded in the 1980s by Western firms, despite the arms embargo then in place on Iran.

The Parchin facility was the oldest gunpowder plant in the Middle East. Built with German help in the 1920s by Reza Shah, it was expanded and modernized in the 1970s by his son, Mohammad Reza Pahlavi, with help from the Societé Nationale des Poudres et Explosifs (SNPE), the French national explosives and propellant maker. SNPE delivered hundreds of tons of the explosive HMX during the 1980s, ostensibly for naval mines, and set up a specialized production line to cast solid-propellant rocket motors. Casting the motors required special pumps that could move materials that were "thick as peanut butter."

Today the United States believes Parchin is being used to mold HMX into the high-explosive lenses needed to trigger a nuclear device.

Iran's main partner in Parchin was Fritz Werner GmbH, the formerly state-owned German weapons manufacturer. Despite the European Union arms embargo on Iran, they built fully automated production lines at Parchin for the production of nitrocellulose, chemical cotton, and other explosive products in the late 1980s. They were not alone. Virtually every European government was authorizing arms sales to Iran and Iraq during the 1980s.

The Iranians were so proud of the new state-of-the-art facility the Germans had built that they showed off a three-by-five-foot electronic wall chart of the various process lines at the plant to foreign customers. Using moving colored lights, it showed how the same raw materials could be transformed into a variety of different explosives, all based on a central computer that controlled the process flow lines. The DIO salesmen hadn't bothered to translate the captions from the original German or to take off the Fritz Werner company logo.*

Iran was on the march.

RICHARD CLARKE

Not everyone agreed with Stephen Bryen's somber assessment of how Iran and other proliferators were gaming U.S. export controls.

Richard Clarke, a career bureaucrat who then headed the State Department's Bureau of Political and Military Affairs, painted a glowing picture of success in testimony before Congress just four days later.

The old export control system worked so well, Clarke said, that missile projects "in several countries" had been thwarted, starting with Iraq's Condor, a solid-fuel missile under development jointly with Egypt, Argentina, and Germany. "Through coordinated use of intelligence and information-sharing, political demarches to several governments, vigorous pursuit of illegal U.S. exports, and visits to several involved countries, we have made great progress toward assuring that Condor will not be a proliferation threat in the future," Clarke said. Everyone was pledging cooperation to limit missile exports, including the Soviet Union, he intoned.

He never apologized to the American people, or acknowledged "I have failed you," when Russia helped build missiles in Iran four years later.

. . . AND THE FRENCH

On May 4, 1991, French foreign minister Roland Dumas was in Tehran for talks intended to bury a decade-long dispute over Iran's participation in the Eurodif uranium enrichment consortium. He also came to give an official blessing to the dramatic expansion already under way of French technology sales to Iran. "Iran is a market of 55 million inhabitants," a Dumas aide said. "Compared to that, Kuwait is peanuts."

---

*I photographed the flow chart at the DIO stand at the International Defense Exhibition (IDEX) in Abu Dhabi in February 1993. A second, state-of-the-art plant was built in Isfahan by Chematur, the engineering consulting division of peaceful Sweden's state-owned arms manufacturer, Bofors. Rafsanjani inaugurated the Bofors plant in 1989, and it began making large quantities of TNT, RDX, and propellants for solid-fuel rockets. "That damned plant in Isfahan put us out of business in Iran," a former Bofors salesman who handled the Iranian account told me.

This was just after the first Gulf War, and the French were still smarting from having lost a great ally in Saddam and a great market in Iraq. "Peanuts" was French for saying "sour grapes."

Everything was on the table during Dumas's visit to Tehran—even sales of enriched uranium from the Eurodif plant. Iran had been demanding that France either repay the $1 billion loan to the consortium from the former shah or make good on the uranium deliveries. When negotiations broke down, they ordered Hezbollah to take French citizens hostage in Lebanon to gain leverage.

Dumas had long favored Iran over Saddam Hussein's Iraq anyway. For one thing, the carpets were better; for another, the women were more beautiful. He was all smiles when he met with his "old friend," foreign minister Ali Akbar Velayati, and touted the growing commercial ties between their two countries. France had been nineteenth among Iran's suppliers Dumas told reporters. "Today, she ranks fifth. But that should improve even more," he beamed.

He had good reason to be optimistic. French banks had recently pledged $5 billion in fresh credits to the Iranian Central Bank to finance purchases of French equipment for Iranian industrial projects, and major French companies were beginning to sign major new contracts in oil, telecommunications, and petrochemicals. Alcatel's space division contracted to build satellite receiving stations in Iran. Satellite data and large computers to process it were essential to predict weather patterns, especially if one wanted to send a ballistic missile to an enemy hundreds of miles away.

A subsidiary of Spie-Batignolles, a French construction giant, was awarded a $290 million contract to expand the Arak petrochemicals plant. The sprawling Arak complex produced chemicals that could be used to make mustard gas, and had an air separation unit, built by Air Liquide of France, that produced large quantities of nitrogen, which Iran needed as fuel for various missiles. When these contracts were signed, the French government did not require a license for manufacturing equipment that could be used to make chemical weapons or rocket fuel. When I inquired what had been shipped, French licensing officials said they "wouldn't even hazard a guess." They simply had no clue.

And the French were gung-ho to do much more. The National Confederation of Employers (CNPF), the main industrial association of France, was frenetically sending delegations to Tehran and receiving top-level Iranians in Paris, including Velayati. French industrial leaders "have all agreed on the importance of exploiting the new economic openness the

Iranians are now showing," the CNPF said, especially now that Baghdad had been declared off limits.

The billion-dollar question was, Would the French turn to Iran to replace Iraq as their premier arms market? "So far, there have been no government authorizations delivered to companies seeking to sell arms to Iran," the Quai d'Orsay said. "We still have an embargo here, and we are enforcing it."

Now that Saddam had flown twenty-four of his French-built Mirage F1 fighter-bombers to Iran for safety, someone had to maintain the planes.

BETRAYAL

It wasn't just the sultry heat of the Persian Gulf that was making Ahmad Ansari sweat. By the time his Iran Air flight from Dubai began its descent into Tehran's Mehrebad airport that afternoon in early July 1991, Ansari's heart was throbbing with a mixture of fear and anticipation.

He hadn't been back to Iran since the revolution. For most of the intervening years he had worked for Reza Pahlavi, self-styled heir to the imperial throne. In the eyes of the Islamic revolutionary leaders, Ansari was a living example of *corruption on earth*, the vile scum of the former regime that the revolution was dedicated to stamping out. Indeed, that's what the official at the Iranian Interests Section in Washington, D.C., had told him when he had applied for a new Iranian passport. If you ever get into the country, they're going to kill you. You're completely out of your mind.

Maybe he was out of his mind, he thought as the gold-domed minarets and broad avenues of Tehran came into view. He was about to betray Reza to his mortal enemies. And yet he felt curiously blameless. He had abandoned himself to God's mercy. If they kill me, that is my destiny. I am already dead.

Ahmad Ali Masood Ansari was not just any employee of Reza Pahlavi. He was his confidant, mentor, and second cousin. They had prayed together, and he had accompanied the young shah during his first escapades, although Ansari didn't drink. They had been constant companions since 1981, when the young shah turned twenty-one and left his mother to become an international playboy.

More important, as far as his survival was now concerned, Ahmad Ansari was also Reza Pahlavi's money man.

The former shah had named Ansari a trustee of his will, which distributed a modest inheritance to his five children and his mother. Reza had entrusted his share to Ansari to invest. Ansari knew where the offshore bank and the Liechtenstein trading companies were located that controlled those assets, because he personally had set them up on Reza's behalf. It was priceless knowledge, and if it became necessary, he was prepared to trade it for his life.

But Ahmad Ansari knew much more. He knew about the young shah's $4 million mansion, just down the road from CIA headquarters in Langley, Virginia. He knew about the $700,000 they had spent to equip the basement with a full-blown discotheque. He knew about the eighteen cars Reza owned through Medina Development Company, one of many companies Ansari had set up for him. He knew about the payments to retainers, former SAVAK officers, flunkies, and hangers-on, because he personally had signed the checks. He knew the young shah intimately, and it wasn't a pretty sight.

By March 1989, Reza was broke—so broke, in fact, that he instructed Ansari to get a $200,000 bridge loan to pay his retainers and his expenses for the next few months. He had gone through his inheritance, spending $34 million over the past seven years, according to an accounting Ansari provided to a northern Virginia court. He had lost another $10 million when a currency trader in London leveraged their million-dollar investment and kept borrowing money to cover his losses. They were suing the trader, but Ansari had no idea when they might see that money again. Reza's advisers placed the blame for the financial mess squarely on Ansari's shoulders. "One day he told Reza he was worth $40 million, and the next day he told him he was broke," recalls Shahriar Ahy.

But Reza told Ansari there was light at the end of the tunnel. He was going to Geneva to meet with the Swiss lawyer in charge of the trust funds his father had established and hoped to persuade him to release $200 million to him now. I know you've done everything you can, he told Ansari shortly before leaving in April. But you've got to get that bridge loan. Just get me through the next three months and we're going to be rich. Ansari was so close to him that Reza had named him the executor of his own will.

Reza might have been broke, but he knew there was much more. His father had hidden his immense wealth while he was in Nassau and Mexico in 1979, shortly before he was admitted to the United States for a gall bladder operation. One set of funds, which Ansari referred to as the "public will," was managed by a Swiss lawyer named Jean Patry. In a letter dated May 28, 1979, the shah had instructed Patry to set up three foundations in Liechtenstein called Niversa, Zarima, and Rukam. The foundations were controlled by Pallerga SA, a fiduciary in Geneva, which opened accounts under its own name on their behalf in four Swiss banks: the Union de Banques Suisses

(Geneva Branch), the Credit Suisse (Geneva Branch), the Chase Manhattan Bank (Suisse) SA, and the Banque Gutzwiller Kurz Bungener S.A.

The complicated ownership scheme had been designed to foil the best attorneys the Islamic Republic could hire in its worldwide effort—aided by President Jimmy Carter and the United Nations—to freeze and seize the former shah's assets. And it worked. The revolutionary regime never uncovered the names of the foundations or their beneficial owner, for the simple reason that Patry controlled them through bearer shares as the former shah's nominee. There was not a single public document or registration certificate that showed a link between the Niversa Foundation of Liechtenstein and the former shah of Iran.

These funds contained over $100 million. Reza's 20 percent share came to roughly $24 million, half of which he had received at the age of twenty-one. But even if he received the second installment as scheduled on his thirtieth birthday, it would barely suffice to dig him out of the financial hole into which profligate spending, bad luck, and the currency losses had plunged him. Besides, he had already borrowed against that money when he bought his first house in Fairfield, Connecticut, in 1984.

The $200 million Reza had referred to was part of a second trust fund the former shah had established to benefit the next monarch. Under the terms of his will, the money would go to Reza should he succeed in restoring the Pahlavi dynasty, but it could just as easily go to his younger brother Ali Reza, should Reza decide the fight was too difficult to pursue. (Ali Reza was respected and feared by the Islamic Republic for his courage, while Reza was not). Alternatively, the funds could be distributed to the family, but only if they collectively renounced the Peacock throne. Such was the catch-22 the former shah had set for his eldest son. Pursue the throne and the tremendous wealth that went with it and possibly get killed in the process by the Islamic Republic—or renounce the throne in favor of his younger brother and lose all.

In a letter dated July 2, 1979, Patry described how he had implemented the shah's plan. An estimated $22 billion was held by two nominee corporations, the Lutecia Foundation and Establishment Daletze, with the Union de Banques Suisses. After cashing in various bonds, Patry transferred some of the assets to the new foundations in Liechtenstein—the "public" will. But the immense bulk of the money was headed for the secret trust fund. "We remitted to Maitre Jean-Pierre Cottier, attorney in Lausanne, a beige envelope, a brown packet and various documents," Patry wrote. Among the documents were bearer shares denominated in Spanish pesetas for two companies, Bahia Las Rocas and Marbe S.A., and the shares of Establishment Daletze. This was the jackpot the Islamic Republic was ready to kill for. By the time Reza went to Geneva seeking an advance, Ansari says Cottier—the Swiss lawyer—had informed him that the secret funds were now worth $35 billion.*

Ansari never heard from Reza while he was in Switzerland or when he got back a few weeks later. Instead he received a phone call from the Kredit Banque Suisse in Geneva in mid-April 1989, informing him that the accounts of the corporations he had set up for Reza had been sequestered—frozen—by order of the Debt Collection Agency of Geneva.

His first thought was that the Islamic Republic had finally pierced the corporate veil he had so carefully woven to protect Reza and his money from exposure. But it made no sense. Just as the former shah had done, Ansari had established a series of shell companies controlled by bearer shares that he had deposited in a safe-deposit box in Geneva. He had given the companies anodyne names and registered them in the British Virgin Islands, Anguilla, and the Netherlands Antilles, where crooks, con men, drug dealers, and tax evaders found safe haven. Who would ever connect the Don Patrick Establishment, the Donogal Establishment, Ile Investments Ltd., Obcess, or Idalio Corporation with the family of the former shah of Iran? Who would ever think that the Mid-Continental Bank and Trust, of the West Indies republic of Anguilla, had been established by Ansari for Reza Pahlavi's benefit to facilitate currency trading in Switzerland? And who would ever think that a safe-deposit box registered in the name of a seemingly anonymous company called Banbane in a Swiss bank vault would contain the bearer shares for all of these companies?

Ansari was pretty proud of his scheme. He was especially perplexed by the alleged debt of 24 million Swiss francs (approximately $12 million) the Swiss government agency was seeking to recover.

It was only later, once the lawsuits had begun, that he learned exactly what had happened. When Reza went to the Kredit Banque Suisse in Geneva, he asked to examine the contents of the safe deposit box Ansari had set up for him. He presented the key Ansari had given him to a bank officer. His signature matched the signature card Ansari had sent the bank. As he later told the court, everything he expected to find was there. But as he was going through the documents, Jean-Pierre Cottier—the Swiss

*There were many other bearer-share corporations that the former shah set up through his Swiss lawyers in the Netherlands, Antilles, and other offshore financial havens, with names like Fawn Incorporated N.V., Namont N.V., Aurora Overseas Ltd., Orell Ltd., Willemstad N.V., Allenpoe N.V., Excelibur N.V., Stonestar Ltd., and so on.

lawyer in charge of his father's secret trust fund—approached and said he was not sure that Reza was authorized to view the contents of the box. The young shah was understandably furious.

Reza filed his first complaint in Switzerland and got a Swiss court on April 19, 1989, to sequester all banking documents and accounts that Ansari had controlled on his behalf. Then he sued Ansari in Virginia and got a court order summoning him to deliver the documents that Reza had gotten frozen in Switzerland. When Ansari protested that he could not comply, the court pronounced summary judgment in Reza's favor and ordered Ansari to pay Reza $7.2 million in damages. To this day, Ansari believes that Cottier instigated the dispute between him and Reza, to prevent Reza from withdrawing money from the trust funds under his management and giving it to Ansari instead. After all, management fees on $35 billion were no small beer.

The lawsuits became public, and the Persian-language media in exile smelled blood in the water. The former shah's lawyer in New York, Robert Armao, attempted to mediate; so did a prominent Persian broadcaster in Los Angeles, and a confidant of the former shah, Housang Ansary (no relation to Ahmad Ansari). At one point Reza's lawyers offered to drop the suits and pay Ansari $500,000, but Ansari insisted that Reza use the proceeds of the sale of his McLean, Virginia, house to reimburse $1.7 million to the small investors and household employees who had lost money in Reza's offshore bank. Reza refused, arguing that they had invested their money at risk and deserved to share the risk with the royals, who were not depending on his investment schemes for their retirement. The almost daily subpoenas, the hearings, and the legal fees broke Ansari both financially and in spirit.

In late 1990, Ansari ran into Mohsen Kangarloo while traveling to Frankfurt, Germany. Kangarloo, whose name surfaced during the Iran-Contra hearings as the Tehran contact of arms broker Manucher Ghorbanifar, knew Ansari from before the revolution, when Ansari had taught economics at Melli University in Tehran. Now he was plugged in at the highest levels of the government in Tehran, and was a personal friend of President Ali Akbar Hashemi-Rafsanjani. He canceled his flight to Tehran and spent two days with Ansari at his Frankfurt hotel.

Leave all this, Kangarloo said. Come back to Iran. I'll take care of you. You have nothing to fear.

As the lawsuit took its toll, Ansari began to seriously consider Kangarloo's offer, and in late spring 1991 he phoned him in Tehran. Okay, he said, I'm finished here. I'm coming. But you've got to get me in. I have to travel on my U.S. passport.

Everyone had heard stories of friends and relatives who had been arrested at Tehran's Mehrebad airport. Some were arrested just as they were about to board a plane to leave; others were taken as they tried to return to Iran, in hopes that the revolutionary regime would welcome their return. A hint of nervousness, a sideward glance arousing the suspicion of a Revolutionary Guards officer, and his life could end in an instant. But Ahmad Ansari was ready. He had come with God. He had always tried to live a moral life. He had never lied to Reza. He had never lied to the U.S. courts. Indeed, that is why the shah had appointed him a trustee of his will. But they had nailed him to a cross. He had even stood up to Reza's mother, the former empress, during the final months of the shah's regime, when he felt she had betrayed the Imperial Army and SAVAK to the revolutionaries. He was no supporter of the mullahs, but neither did he believe Reza was fit to rule. He had come to make his peace with the regime.

In a few minutes he was going to find out if Kangarloo was as important as he pretended to be.

MURDERING THE OPPOSITION

Ali Fallahian was a key Rafsanjani ally on the Supreme National Security Council. As Minister of Information and Security (MOIS) since Rafsanjani assumed the presidency in 1989, he was the president's top intelligence officer. Like Mohsen Rezai and foreign minister Ali Akbar Velayati, he came from Khouzestan, the oil-rich province bordering Iraq and the Persian Gulf in the southwest. The Khouzestanis formed a clique within the regime, who helped each other informally across the bureaucracy.

When Rafsanjani took office, he instructed Fallahian to finish off the opposition once and for all. The wily intelligence minister called on his network of fellow Khouzestanis to contribute assets and facilities for this task. Foreign Minister Ali Akbar Velayati provided freshly minted service passports for the teams of killers Fallahian sent out to Europe. Post and Telegraph Minister Mohammad Gharazzi allowed Fallahian's men to use his ministry as the logistics hub for various hit teams, so that killers and support officers in different countries could coordinate their operations by calling a central number in Tehran, without ever contacting each other in the field.

They murdered Kurdish leader Abdelrahman Qassemlou on July 13, 1989, after pretending to negotiate a truce with him during two days of secret talks in Vienna. Qassemlou's Kurdish Democratic Party of Iran revolted against the Islamic regime right after the revolution, and had been a thorn in the regime's side ever since, pinning down several Revolutionary Guards divisions in northern Iran during most of the eight-year war with Iraq. Killing Qassemlou had been sweet revenge. His murderer, Mohammed Jaafari Sahraroudi, was promoted to brigadier general in the Pasdaran Corps when he returned to Tehran after the hit.

Next came the brother of Mujahedin-e Khalq leader Massoud Radjavi, gunned down by killers riding a motorbike in Geneva on April 24, 1990. An Islamic Marxist group that allied with Khomeini to overthrow the shah, the MEK tried to grab power from the mullahs in 1981 to establish a Soviet-style dictatorship. As former allies, their defection was particularly galling. The regime referred to them as the Monafaqeen—the "hypocrites"—and murdered MEK members wherever they could find them. In 1986 the regime cut a deal with French prime minister Jacques Chirac to expel Radjavi and the group's leadership from France in exchange for French hostages in Lebanon. When Radjavi relocated to Iraq and openly sided with Saddam Hussein during the war, his treason alienated the vast majority of Iranians. But the Mujahedin continued to find new recruits, and for Rafsanjani and Fallahian, they were the main enemy.

In Paris, Fallahian's killers got Cyrus Elahi as he was leaving his apartment on October 23, 1990. Elahi was a key aid to Dr. Manoucher Ganji, who was running the CIA-funded Flag of Freedom organization and broadcasting daily into Iran. Although the Agency considered Ganji's instructional programs in the techniques of civil disobedience to be of marginal value, the regime took Ganji and his organization so seriously that they hunted down his operatives all over the world.

The following year, Fallahian's men struck again in Paris, this time hitting a key aide to National Front leader Shahpour Bakhtiar. Bakhtiar was widely considered to be the only Iranian capable of rallying the diverse factions of the opposition, from the center-left to the Constitutionalists on the center-right. If anyone posed a serious threat to the regime, it was Bakhtiar. As the last prime minister of the shah who desperately tried to reform the monarchy, no one else had his legitimacy.

The assassination campaign paid off. One by one, the regime picked off the leaders of the main opposition groups in exile. And neither the Austrians, the Swiss, nor the French really complained. They understood that these killings were an "internal affair," as Rafsanjani pretended.

As he looked over the folder on Ahmad Ansari that Kangarloo had given him, Fallahian smiled to himself. He got his start as a revolutionary prosecutor in his home town of Abadan right after the revolution, where he led the fight to track down members of the MEK. By the early 1980s, he moved on to other prey. Mullahs were being assassinated all over Iran by the anticlerical "Forghan" group, whose slogan was "Islam Without Mullahs." Ayatollah Khomeini personally ordered Fallahian to set up a top-secret assassination squad to counter the Forghan. In the mid-1980s he coordinated the revolutionary courts and the intelligence office of Mohsen Rezai's Pasdaran.

There were many ways to crush the opposition, he thought as he prepared to charm Ansari. Sometimes using a bullet was the least deadly.

ANSARI IN TEHRAN

Ahmad Ansari was about to reach into his shirt pocket for his American passport, when Kangarloo's assistant spotted him. He shook his finger and rushed toward him the minute Ansari stepped off the plane. Put that away, he said. He flashed a plasticized identity card to the two Pasdaran officers in their green khaki uniforms who stood guard on the tarmac, and they waved to a side door. Ansari began silently praying as they entered an empty corridor. No other passengers or officials were in sight.

When Kangarloo's assistant opened the door at the end, a rush of hot air poured over them and they were out in the light. Welcome to Tehran, the man said, loosening up once they'd reached his waiting car. He took Ansari to the majestic Esteqlal hotel, the old Hilton, off a grand boulevard overlooking Tehran. You are not allowed to leave the hotel, he warned. You must not try to see anyone. When it's time, I will come for you.

He waited five days, a golden bird in a golden cage, as the state-run television broadcast footage of visiting Chinese premier Li Peng. But finally it was time. Kangarloo phoned and said Fallahian was ready to meet him.

Ahmad Ansari had rehearsed his lines many times. He would not lie. But neither would he offer the whole truth. He had a plan, and only God knew if it would work.

PERSIAN CHESS

Fallahian welcomed him into the familiar reception room in Sultanatabad, where he had been interrogated many years earlier by his predecessor at SAVAK, Parviz Sabati. It was Thursday, and most ministry employees were home or at mosque. Fallahian was dressed informally, in a loose-fitting robe and a turban, and his young children scampered about in the hallways. Ansari found their presence reassuring, an innocence that belied the sinister nature of their interview.

He told the intelligence chief about Reza's lawsuits. He told him about Reza's lifestyle, his cowardice, his indecision. And he told him of his wish, which was to publish a book that would simply describe what he had experienced over the past decade. *Me and the Pahlavis*, he said. That would be the title.

Ansari said he was willing to help the Islamic Republic recover the assets of the former shah, if they would help him to defend himself against Reza's lawsuit.

Fallahian just smiled. We have to keep this boy Reza in the game, he thought. Much better than sending a hit team to dispatch him. Keep him in the game and let him neutralize the others. Besides, we have our sources.

Don't ever forget, he reminded Ansari. We Persians invented the game of chess.

LIFTING THE STONE

Because the enemy has nuclear facilities, the Muslim states, too, should be equipped with the same capacity.

—Iranian vice president Ata'ollah Mohajerani, *Abrar* daily, October 23, 1991

David Kay did not realize he was about to change history when he led a team of a half-dozen weapons inspectors into the desert west of Baghdad for the third day straight, on June 26, 1991. A brash Texan political scientist who had been working for the U.S. government before he went to the IAEA several years earlier, Kay had visited the military base at Abu Gharaib on the two previous days, but irate Iraqi officers had refused to allow his team to enter. At one point, when Kay climbed on top of his Land Rover to take pictures of movement beyond the electrified perimeter fence, he found himself surrounded by Iraqi soldiers who ordered him down at gunpoint. That night Kay gathered his top advisers in Baghdad's Palestine Meridien hotel and told them to follow him for a walk in the *souk*. Everyone knew what that meant. With Iraqi minders and electronic surveillance covering every nook of the French chain hotel, it was the only way they could prepare an actual game plan in secret.

They had to find a way to get inside the base, Kay said. The CIA had just tipped him off that U.S. spy satellites showed the Iraqis were loading some kind of heavy equipment onto flatbed trucks and getting ready to move them. If they could elude their Iraqi minders just long enough, they could bluff their way onto the base and start taking pictures, Kay argued. Catch 'em in the act.

The next morning they put the plan into action. Armed with fresh coordinates that his CIA contact transmitted to him using a code keyed to a biography of President George H. W. Bush, which Kay had happened to bring with him, Kay and his small team set off in two Land Rovers and a bus into the 120-degree heat. As they neared the base, Kay ordered his New Zealand driver to speed past it—and to pass their Iraqi escort. The Iraqis were torn whether to chase Kay down the sand-strewn highway beyond the base, or stay with the other two vehicles. When they eventually gave chase, Kay had his driver jump the divider and swerve in front of the on-coming traffic, so they could double back to the main entrance. Arriving alone and unaccompanied, Kay ordered the stunned Iraqi guard at the first gate to let them onto the base.

From the far end of the base, Kay could hear the roar of truck engines and heavy machinery, just as the CIA had said. "If you deny me entry to this site," Kay shouted at the sentry, "I will report you to the United Nations Security Council." Kay made it actually sound like a threat.

One of his team members, Mike Baker, spotted a nearby water tower and climbed up to get a better view. "There are loads of tank transporters starting to move and kicking up dust," he shouted. "They look like dinosaurs in heat. They are heading for the back exit."[1]

Kay leaped back into his Land Rover and roared around the dirt perimeter road until they caught up with eight huge tank transporters carrying large objects hastily covered with tarpaulins. Another team member, Rick Lally, snapped pictures as they bounced along the wrong side of the road, trying to overtake the convoy. Just then, shots rang out as their Iraqi minders roared up behind them. Not wanting to endanger the lives of his men, Kay ordered his driver to abandon the chase. Lally quickly ejected the digital memory card from his camera and hid it on his body. Surrounded by angry Iraqis carrying AK-47s, Kay got out of the Land Rover and set up his bulky satellite telephone in the dirt on the side of the road to call for backup. His bosses were IAEA director general Hans Blix in Vienna, and UN Special Commission chairman Rolf Ekeus, who worked out of UN headquarters in New York.

The two Swedes were as different as oil and vinegar, and cordially detested each other. Kay told them he had been fired upon when he tried to enter a suspicious site. Both Swedes told him to withdraw and pledged to take the next plane to Baghdad to resolve the issue. Ekeus lodged a protest with top Iraqi officials the next day, who merely laughed and dismissed Kay's allegation that Iraq had a secret uranium enrichment program. Blix took care of Kay. In fact, as Kay set out to correct the brazen lies of an Iraqi scientist who tried to explain that they had never worked with enriched uranium, Blix turned on him icily. "Don't you *ever* contradict a government official again," he said.[2]

Blix had brought IAEA legal adviser Mohammad El Baradei along with him to Baghdad. The mild-mannered Egyptian was tasked with soothing Iraqi ruffled feathers and working out enhanced access arrangements for the inspectors. As he was traveling back to Baghdad with the inspectors on their bus, his conversation was recorded by several of Kay's colleagues.

"I know you haven't seen what you think you've seen," Baradei said, "because the Iraqis have told me they never had a nuclear weapons program. I'm an Arab and one Arab would not lie to another."[3] Today Baradei has replaced Blix at the IAEA, where he has tried to avoid a nuclear showdown with Iran.

Although Blix and Baradei were still in denial, the pictures taken by Baker and Lally blew the lid off of Iraq's clandestine nuclear weapons program. What they had photographed, unbeknownst to themselves at the time, were huge magnet assemblies known as calutrons, which Iraq was using to secretly enrich uranium through electromagnetic isotope separation (EMIS).

The EMIS program took the IAEA by surprise, since no nation was known to have used this method of enrichment since the Manhattan Project, when an energy-gobbling plant in Tennessee nearly caused a power outage along the entire East Coast of the United States. To avoid detection, the Iraqis had removed the calutrons from the enrichment plant at Tarmiya just ahead of an earlier IAEA visit, and were hoping to bury them at Abu Gharaib—at least until David Kay showed up unexpectedly.

As Kay and his teams of inspectors confronted the Iraqis and discovered new documents, it soon became apparent that at the time of the U.S.-led invasion of Iraq in February 1991, Iraq did not have just one nuclear program that was ten years from achieving weapons status, but at least three separate programs that were mere months from making the bomb. Blix never forgave David Kay for showing that the emperor had no clothes and fired him unceremoniously a few months later. (Kay left Vienna to become director of the Uranium Institute in London, a position he lost in April 1993, again thanks to Hans Blix.)[4]

David Kay's discovery shook the world. It was the first concrete evidence that Saddam Hussein had broken all the rules. Virtually overnight, the underlying mythology of the IAEA that Hans Blix and others were so intent to preserve was shown to be a self-serving lie. In their desire to pursue lucrative export markets, the nuclear "haves" were willing to turn a blind eye to proliferators such as Iraq or Iran. And the nuclear "have nots" were willing to play the same game, declaring what amounted to Potemkin nuclear sites and allowing IAEA accountants to visit them regularly to make sure that declared stockpiles of nuclear materials were still present, while they carried out the real nuclear weapons research at other, undeclared facilities.

Once the news of Iraq's subterfuge sank in, IAEA spokesman Hans Maier called the Iraqi situation "totally new for us. Our board made a statement to the Security Council yesterday [July 21, 1991] that Iraq had broken the NPT and arguing that we could have done better and will do better in the future under three conditions: we have better information from Security Council members on proliferation programs, including satellite photographs; we have better access to nuclear sites during inspections; and [we have] better political backing from the Security Council." The reason the IAEA had failed to detect Iraq's clandestine nuclear weapons program was because "no other NPT signatory had ever delivered information to us, only to the media," he whined.

It was a litany Hans Blix would repeat for years to come. Don't leak to the press; leak to the IAEA and we'll handle things quietly. The IAEA never mentioned that the trade it was trying to protect ultimately led to mass murder.

Maier speculated that the Iraqi experience "could lead to challenge inspections elsewhere if the NPT parties agree to it." The first target that immediately came to mind was North Korea, he said.

No one breathed a word about Iran.

KARRUBI TO PAKISTAN

Rafsanjani and his nuclear team were closely following events in Iraq—indeed, they could hardly avoid them. Saddam had flown his air force to safety in Iran, and U.S. cruise missiles were flying over Iranian territory; one even crashed into a group of houses near the Iranian city of Ahwaz, killing a number of villagers. The United States presented its apologies for the accident, which Rafsanjani promptly accepted. Better that than to have them "miss" closer to Tehran!

For all his bluster, Saddam Hussein had shown himself powerless to prevent the U.S. attack. The fifth-largest army in the world had been cut to shreds. The Americans had warned Saddam not to use his chemical or biological weapons, or else they would retaliate with a nuclear strike. But Rafsanjani felt sure the Americans would think twice if Iraq had nuclear weapons. That was Saddam's big mistake: going into Kuwait before the weapons were ready.

The presence of 500,000 U.S. troops and some two thousand warplanes within easy striking distance made Rafsanjani and his army commanders nervous. For years they had played a dangerous game, tickling the

American tiger with terrorist strikes in Lebanon and in the Gulf. So far, the Americans had never really struck back. They had knocked out a few oil platforms but never targeted the heart of the regime itself. With so many U.S. troops sitting on Iran's doorstep, Rafsanjani was less willing to take a chance. Iran couldn't afford to make the same mistake Saddam had made. They needed nuclear weapons. They had to go faster. And that meant spending more money, Rafsanjani knew.

Pakistan's military was equally worried by the U.S. willingness to use force against a Muslim country. Because Pakistan was much closer to acquiring an actual nuclear arsenal than Iran was at the time, Pakistani leaders used more direct language in their public statements.* Rafsanjani decided to send his ally, Mehdi Karrubi—the one the Americans found so "moderate" during the Iran-Contra affair—to sound out Pakistan's new prime minister, Nawaz Sharif, on expanding nuclear and military cooperation.

Karrubi was coming to play a major role in relations with Pakistan, China, and North Korea now that Rafsanjani had become president. "No country has the right to come here and make decisions about the future of Islamic countries," Karrubi huffed when he arrived in Islamabad on February 25, 1991. Speaking to the local press, he emphasized "the need to increase cooperation between Pakistan and Iran . . . for the defense of this region." He advocated joint education programs for nuclear scientists—"joint syllabus, joint instructions, and joint laboratories."

Most important, he came with a down payment of $50 million to thank Pakistan in advance for its contribution to Iran's nuclear programs.

THE NEW NUCLEAR CENTER

Another lesson Rafsanjani and his advisers learned from the war in Iraq was that Iran must brazenly assert its right to acquire nuclear technology and nuclear power under the NPT. In part, it was because Saddam Hussein never made a credible claim for nuclear power that Iraq's clandestine

*"Pakistan needs credible 'nuclear deterrence' to avoid the dangers of war," an editorial in the Karachi daily *Nawa-I-Waqt* advised on January 25, 1991. "The United States just cannot bear any Arab or Islamic country to develop nuclear capability" and was "forcing itself on Pakistan's nuclear program," the same paper complained one week later. The U.S. reluctantly cut off military aide to Pakistan and suspended deliveries of nuclear-capable F-16s to the Pakistani air force in 1990, when the State Department could no longer certify that Pakistan had *not* become a nuclear weapons state, as required under the Presslar amendment.

weapons program now lay so exposed. Rafsanjani had no doubt it was going to be taken apart piece by piece by David Kay and the cowboys from the UN Special Commission. Even though Kay nominally reported to Hans Blix and the IAEA, it was clear he did not come from the same culture as the international bureaucrats.

With this in mind, Rafsanjani dispatched First Vice President Hassan Habibi to inaugurate, with great fanfare, a nuclear medical research center in Karaj, just north of Tehran, on May 11, 1991. The new center was devoted to producing radioactive isotopes for medical and agricultural research. It was funded by the Atomic Energy Organization of Iran, which Rafsanjani had decided to put in charge of those aspects of Iran's nuclear program that were "declared" to the IAEA in Vienna, isolating it increasingly from the clandestine weapons work.

Located near an air force base and a large military-industrial complex, the new center was staffed with Chinese and Russian technicians, according to Western intelligence reports. Earlier that year Iran had purchased a small experimental cyclotron from Ion Beam Applications in Belgium that was installed in Karaj. Because it was similar to Iraq's enrichment calutrons, the cyclotron purchase—which became public—led French intelligence officials I consulted to suspect the beginnings of uranium enrichment research, although still on a laboratory scale.

At the ceremony, Habibi swept aside allegations that Iran was conducting military nuclear research at Karaj or at any other site. Iran's nuclear program was "exclusively" for peaceful purposes and fully transparent to the nuclear "watchdogs" of the IAEA. "Such propaganda is aimed at defaming the Islamic Republic and it has no truth at all," he said.[5]

THE VISITORS

We should like to acquire the technical know-how and the industrial facilities required to manufacture nuclear weapons, just in case we need them. This does not mean that we currently want to build them or that we have changed our defense strategy to include a nuclear program.

—Rafsanjani scientific adviser Homayoun Vahdati, quoted in **Die Welt**, January 27, 1992

Everything that we have seen is for the peaceful application of nuclear energy and ionizing radiation.

—IAEA safeguards director Jon Jennekins, after an inspection tour in Iran, February 14, 1992

Because the United States is the most powerful nation on earth, most Americans don't pay much attention when foreign leaders visit Washington. The visits are so numerous that the *Washington Times* publishes a weekly calendar of them every Monday. If it's Tuesday, it must be the prime minister of Belgium or the president of Kazakhstan. And so on. Even to veteran Washington-watchers, it's mostly ho-hum.

But in most other countries of the world, visiting dignitaries get big headlines. They get especially big headlines if the country suffers from semi-pariah status, as does Iran. Each foreign visitor is paraded about as a vote of confidence for Iran's system and Iran's leaders.

The prime minister of the People's Republic of China was a big catch. Like the United States, China was a permanent member of the UN Security Council and a declared nuclear weapons state. Its voice counted in world affairs. So, on July 7, 1991, when Li Peng began a three-day stopover in Iran during an extensive Middle East tour, he was given the silk carpet and caviar treatment—especially when it became clear that he had come prepared to make large decisions about the future of nuclear cooperation with Iran. Iran's state-run media covered his every meeting and utterance.

The Chinese had been watching the Iranians closely for some time. They worked side by side with Iranian nuclear technicians at the Isfahan nuclear research center and were impressed by their knowledge and their seriousness. They worked with the Iranians in the harsh desert conditions of central Iran, where they were jointly prospecting for uranium. And in Pakistan, Chinese nuclear experts taught classes to visiting Iranian researchers. Li made an unprecedented tour of Iranian nuclear and missile facilities in Isfahan and took time to speak personally with the Chinese team leaders. How were their working conditions? Were the Iranians treating them well? Did they miss their families? What did they think of the Iranians' capabilities? He had so many questions.

At the culmination of the trip, the two leaders signed a series of military, industrial, and economic agreements, potentially worth as much as $5 billion. They discussed potential Chinese assistance in completing the Busheir reactors, now that companies in Sweden, Argentina, France, and Germany had all turned down Iran's request to bid on completing the project. Referring to Busheir, Li told the press that China had agreed to provide Iran with "the necessary expertise and technology for the completion of an Iranian nuclear reactor."

Li gave Rafsanjani a long list of sensitive nuclear production equipment China was now able to provide so Iran wouldn't have to resort to expensive middlemen. "Chinese nuclear technology is as good as it comes," a nuclear expert working for Senator John Glenn told me when we discussed this list shortly after Li's visit. "They have the technological expertise that would allow them to create major disruptions in the global game if they were willing to take the political risks to do so."[1]

But Li also brought bad news about the big 27-megawatt heavy-water reactor Iran wanted China to build. The American administration was simply pressing China too hard, he said. It was a large, visible project and there was no way they could hide construction or operation of the reactor from American spy satellites. Even if they moved it from Isfahan to Qazvin—an undeclared site—the Americans would figure out sooner or later what was going on, and China was not willing to pay that price. The Americans were threatening to cut off China's Most Favored Nation status if the deal went through. That could bankrupt the Chinese economy.

His experts had told him there was an even better solution than building the big visible reactor, Li said. China could build a working model, so that Iran could understand the principles of the real reactor and run miniature breeding and reprocessing experiments that no one could see. Although the scale model was just 1 percent of the size of the actual reactor, it contained all the systems of the real thing. Scale models of this sort were not just toys. As an added incentive, China would provide the blueprints for the reactor, so the Iranians could build their own full-scale plant later on, when they were ready to produce plutonium.

Li Peng also expressed concerns about Iran's relations with Pakistan. Pakistan was an old friend of China. After India had tested an atomic device in 1974, China had provided assistance to Pakistan for its own weapons program. Because China already had invested so much in Pakistan's nuclear infrastructure, in some sensitive areas it was easier for China to operate through Pakistan than deal directly with Iran.

But Li's experts had been telling him that Iran could never achieve a good level of cooperation with Pakistan because of their religious differences. He had received disturbing reports about clashes between Shiite and Sunni militias in Pakistan, the bombing of mosques, and murders and kidnappings of prominent religious leaders on both sides. He understood that Iran could not remain indifferent to the sufferings of fellow Shiites in Pakistan. But it would be unfortunate if Iran got involved in any way in Pakistan's domestic affairs. That would make it much more difficult for China to press its friends in Pakistan to help Iran in these sensitive areas.

As they sat side by side in Rafsanjani's ceremonial office, with an enormous bouquet of fresh flowers behind them, Rafsanjani gave a little smile. Of course Iran had extensive ties to Pakistan's Shiite minority, primarily through the Beit al-Rahbari, the Leader's office, and a number of charitable foundations, he said. But Iran's efforts had always aimed at promoting better ties between the two communities, not stirring ancestral hatred. Besides, said the Fox: Iran was committed to developing strategic cooperation with Pakistan, and was pleased to have China's blessing in this endeavor.

On July 9, the day after Li Peng returned home from Tehran, Rafsanjani dispatched Pasdaran commander Major General Mohsen Rezai to Islamabad to meet with Prime Minister Nawaz Sharif and the entire Pakistani high command. Rezai was responding to the invitation of Pakistan's outspoken army chief of staff, General Mirza Aslam Beg, a radical Islamist who openly advocated nuclear cooperation between Pakistan and other Muslim countries, including Iran. (Beg was so open about his views, recalls former assistant secretary of defense Henry S. Rowen, that he warned Rowen during a January 1990 visit to Islamabad that Pakistan would transfer nuclear weapons to Iran outright if the United States insisted on cutting off military aid to Pakistan.) "There was no particular reason to think it was a bluff, but on the other hand, we didn't know," Rowen said.[2]

Rezai and his team of defense industry experts were given the grand tour of Pakistani defense plants in Islamabad and Lahore, where Pakistan was producing new weapons with Chinese help. On July 13, at the end of

Rezai's four-day tour, the Pakistani chairman of the joint staff, Admiral Iftkhar Ahmad Sirohey, revealed that Pakistan was prepared to conclude a defense treaty with Iran. Echoing his colleague General Beg, he called for unity among Muslims and added that the Islamic world was facing serious threats that required Muslim states to close ranks. Back in Tehran, the state-run press presented the trip as a "strategic milestone in the effort to rejuvenate the Muslim world."[3]

From the nuclear Stop & Shop in Islamabad, Rezai took his bleary-eyed procurement team to China and on to North Korea, where he was becoming a frequent visitor. It was a far cry from the buying missions the Iranians used to send to Geneva to bargain with international arms merchants in the 1980s, who sat for months in gigantic suites at the Hotel Metropole, eating roast lamb on the carpet. Rezai was a quick study. He was businesslike. And he had options.

Iran, Pakistan, China, North Korea: it was a deadly nexus. By 1991 their strategic goals were identical and their cooperation was running full-bore.

WHAC-A-MOLE

As he looked at the list of export license requests from Iran that his analysts had flagged, Deputy Assistant Secretary of Defense for Nonproliferation Policy Henry Sokolski knew there was a problem. A former defense staffer for Dan Quayle before the Indiana senator was tapped to be vice president, Sokolski was the top civilian in charge of the Pentagon's nonproliferation effort. It was his job to coordinate export control policies with America's defense needs, and this was just not working.

He fired off an anxious memo to Paul Wolfowitz, who ran the Pentagon's policy shop under Defense Secretary Dick Cheney, asking him to weigh in. Our guys are getting ripped to shreds when they try to stop this stuff at interagency meetings, Sokolski said. It's missiles, it's nukes, it's enrichment. If we don't start taking these exports seriously, we're headed for another Iraq. Has no one learned a thing? We're being asked to prove that stuff is going to a known nuclear or missile facility for it to be denied. It's absurd! Are there no grown-ups around? And this is what they called an *Enhanced* Proliferation Control Initiative? It's a joke!*

*The Enhanced Proliferation Control Initiative (EPCI) was President George H. W. Bush's response to the mounting scandals caused by Western assistance to Saddam Hussein's weapons programs.

For Sokolski, the kicker had been learning that Iran was trying to buy a heavy-water research reactor. It came across the intel wire in early 1991, just as the war in Iraq went hot. But then it was all over the place. The Iranians went to Argentina for heavy water and a hex plant to convert yellowcake into uranium hexafluoride for enrichment. Then they went to China to buy the reactor itself. And when that didn't work, they sent new teams to India to try to purchase a 10-megawatt Russian-designed reactor from New Delhi. At least the State Department sent Reggie Bartholomew to Delhi to put out that fire. It was like playing Whac-A-Mole, Sokolski thought. Hit one supplier, and another one just pops up.

A heavy-water reactor had but two real uses: it produced inordinate amounts of weapons-grade plutonium, and it could produce tritium, which was used to boost the yield of nuclear weapons. And that was it. The Iranians wanted to buy a freakin' bomb plant, for chrissake. Game over. We don't need to know any more. That's proof, but nobody seemed to care, Sokolski thought. The more excited he became at the interagency brawls, the greater the indifference he encountered.

On October 31, 1991, Chinese president Yang Shangkun arrived in Tehran for a three-day official visit. Like Prime Minister Li, he also took the Isfahan tour and questioned Chinese technicians at the nuclear research center. In addition, he visited Darkovin, a site most analysts believed had been abandoned for years, where the French had planned to build a 935-megawatt power reactor along the Karoun River near Ahwaz during the time of the shah. Yang told the Iranian press he had come to "meet old friends and make new ones and to expand mutual ties and cooperation." The Chinese were calling it a "courtesy call."

But Yang met repeatedly with Rafsanjani and was accompanied everywhere he went by Finance Minister Mohsen Nourkhbaksh, the man with Rafsanjani's checkbook. As Sokolski followed the reporting, it was clear that this trip was all about the money. If you're the president of the People's Republic of China, you don't schlep around Iran for three days without a drop of alcohol just to play nice. He wanted to know if the Iranians were going to pay.

And then Yang flew to Pakistan—Pakistan, for crying out loud, land of the Islamic bomb! Sokolski recalled how troubled Harry Rowen had been after his encounter in Islamabad with General Beg. Clearly, Yang had flown in to give the Pakistanis the green light, because they dispatched ground forces commander General Asif Nawaz back to Tehran just hours later, on November 2, to sign the nuclear deal with Rafsanjani and Mohsen Rezai. China gives Pakistan bomb designs, equipment, and technical assistance.

Pakistan turns around and sells it to Iran. It was not complicated. Everyone knew the Pakistanis and the Chinese were up to no good. What was it going to take to get people's attention? This is getting real serious, folks.

Wolfowitz sent Sokolski's complaints up the food chain and got Defense Secretary Cheney's attention. But then something happened as the 1992 presidential elections approached. They got rolled at the last minute, at a deputies' meeting. Sokolski was hauled on the carpet and told to stop getting in the way of U.S. exporters. The sales to Iran were going to be made whether he liked it or not. That was White House policy. Get with the program.

Sokolski remembers having a faithless moment, and calling his old friend and mentor Albert Wohlstetter, a farsighted strategist revered by the American Enterprise Institute. Maybe the Democrats really will be better on this stuff than we are, he said. After all, Clinton was saying all the right things about refusing to coddle dictators in Beijing and Baghdad. Perhaps, if he's elected, he'll put the system to rights.

Fat chance, Wohlstetter replied.

TOO LITTLE, TOO LATE

CIA Director Robert M. Gates was unequivocal when he appeared before Chairman John Glenn and the Senate Governmental Affairs Committee on January 15, 1992. "Today," he told the senators, "over twenty countries have, are suspected of having, or are developing, nuclear, biological, or chemical weapons and the means to deliver them."

At the top of the list of potential troublemakers, of course, was Saddam Hussein's Iraq. Then came Iran, Syria, Libya, and Algeria. North Korea occupied a category all by itself, since the United States believed it was on the verge of going nuclear at any moment. India and Pakistan were de facto nuclear powers already.

The threat of unpredictable, radical regimes acquiring weapons of mass destruction was so imminent, Gates argued, that the U.S. intelligence community had to reorient its collection priorities. After the Iraqi war, he had instructed the CIA to set up a nonproliferation center staffed with over one hundred officers from several agencies "to better formulate and coordinate intelligence actions" in support of government policy, he said.

But the CIA's efforts came too late. Ever wary of potential embargoes by supplying governments, Rafsanjani and his weapons development team had learned another vital lesson from Iraq's experience: build your own.

Iran's military industries were growing at a phenomenal rate, to the point where they would soon be able to export a broad variety of conventional munitions and even missiles. German companies had built a dedicated chemical weapons plant at Qazvin, which the German government had never managed to shut down, and were supplying billions of dollars' worth of dual-use production equipment for all varieties of weaponry.

Just as V. I. Lenin had predicted seventy years earlier, the Western capitalist nations were selling the rope that later would be used to hang them. Iran's suppliers became its best lobbyists, persuading their national export control authorities to approve such sales because they *might* be used in legitimate civilian projects.

Iraq's success should have provided an object lesson in the need to establish meaningful export controls, but it did not. Iraq also should have demonstrated the cultural blindness of Western governments and suppliers, who continued to believe that the brown-skinned peoples of the world were simply incapable of serious scientific and technological accomplishments.

That arrogance blinded them to A. Q. Khan, and it blinded them to Saddam. Now it was blinding them to Iran.

"WHITE-KNUCKLE MODE"

Pierre Villaros was not your ordinary nuclear inspector. Unlike IAEA director general Hans Blix, a Swedish-trained lawyer, Villaros had cut his teeth as a physicist designing nuclear weapons for the French military. He had a good understanding of how a country seeking to keep its nuclear intentions secret went about its business. After all, that was what France did in the 1960s, when it was stealing technology left and right from the United States for its nuclear weapons program.

In Washington, Blix was being subjected to increasingly bitter criticism. U.S. officials told reporters that Blix was "part of the problem, not part of the solution." Blix was being made to take the blame for the IAEA's high-profile failure to detect Iraq's secret nuclear weapons program in the 1980s. The plodding Swede's pride had been hurt, even though he tried hard to bury his emotions from view.

Villaros knew his assignment to the special inspection of Iranian nuclear facilities in February 1992 was all about Blix and his pride. Blix intended to show those Americans that the agency knew better than they did when they screamed about a clandestine nuclear weapons program in

Iran. He intended to prove that their "best source of information"—the Mujahedin-e Khalq—was nothing more than a band of forgers and fabricators, intent on substituting their own dictatorship of the hooded and the veiled for the fist-in-velvet-glove rule of the clerics.

Since June 1991, Mujahedin representatives had been holding press conferences in Paris, London, and Washington, alleging a vast, secret Iranian nuclear weapons program. They claimed three thousand people were working at a secret research center near Isfahan, never declared to the IAEA. They claimed the Revolutionary Guards were using Sharif University of Technology as a procurement front and as a research establishment for nuclear weapons work. They claimed that the Guards had a special "atomic weapons" branch that had established a secret nuclear weapons center near the city of Qazvin at a place called Moallem Kalayeh (also written Ma'allem Kelayeh), disguised as an "industrial unit." And they claimed that the regime, which everyone knew was strapped for cash after the economic collapse caused by eight years of war with Iraq, had allocated $240 million to the Atomic Energy Organization of Iran for 1991–92 (the Iranian fiscal year began on the Persian New Year, March 21, and ran through the following March 20). Well, Blix was going to call their bluff, and Villaros had been chosen to lend credibility to the exercise.

Some of the MEK allegations were patently absurd, Blix said. They claimed, for instance, that the regime had purchased a cyclotron from Belgium, and that Guards Corps officials had noted in a "secret report" to Rafsanjani, "To our disbelief, what we were unable to acquire anywhere else was readily provided to us by the Belgians."

That was ridiculous, Blix said. The Belgians didn't even make such equipment, let alone export it.

Villaros quietly corrected his boss and said that his sources in French intelligence had identified the sale by Ion Beam Applications to a new, undeclared nuclear site in Karaj, near Tehran.

Make sure you go there, Blix said curtly. But remember: this is not a challenge inspection, as we are doing in Iraq. He instructed Villaros and the inspection team leader, Deputy Director General Jon Jennekins, a Canadian who doubled as head of the secretive Safeguards division, to clear everything with him ahead of time, then with the Iranians. He didn't want any surprises.

Villaros and Jennekins culled the information they had received from the Mujahedin, the press, and what they had heard from their own sources, since none of the five declared nuclear powers was providing any intelligence officially. The Russians and the Chinese refused because their own technicians and companies were involved. The Brits and the Americans refused because they didn't trust Blix. And the French refused because if the Americans didn't think it was important enough to reveal intelligence sources and methods, why should they?

They came up with a list of eight sites they wanted to inspect, but Blix told them to narrow it down further—no more than six. He reminded them once again that they were going on a "familiarization tour," not a challenge inspection. He told them to submit the list of sites to the Iranian authorities through their Vienna-based delegate to the IAEA, well ahead of their departure for Tehran. The Iranians, predictably, made no objections. Instead, they prepared.

Once the agency team arrived in Tehran on February 7, 1992, Jennekins gave operational control over their movements for the next five days to the Iranian government, asking them as a courtesy to handle travel to the agreed sites. It was an invitation to failure.

Most of the "familiarization tour" was a piece of cake. The team flew down to Busheir to examine the vast amount of material the Iranians had stockpiled on site, including row after row of equipment for the reactor vessels in special airtight storerooms filled with argon gas to prevent contamination by the hot, humid, salty air of the Persian Gulf. It was impressive. After such a costly investment, no one had any doubt that Iran fully intended to complete the project and build the huge nuclear power reactors, no matter whom they eventually chose as their new contractor. It was just the type of project the IAEA had been created to promote. The inspectors loved it.

They also went to the Tehran Nuclear Research Center to inspect the 1960s-generation U.S. research reactor. Nothing of interest there, especially given Iran's problems in getting new supplies of enriched uranium to power up the reactor.

The newly opened Karaj research center was a no-brainer. Contrary to what the Mujahedin had alleged, it was a classic medical isotope research and production site. Even the Belgian-supplied equipment appeared to be used for perfectly legitimate purposes. The cyclotron, too small to be used for serious uranium enrichment, was useful only for tabletop experiments.

Isfahan was more dicey. The Iranians took them to a newly built research site near the university, where the Chinese had delivered a tiny heavy-water reactor, a light-water subcritical reactor, and a graphite subcritical reactor. None of the equipment or materials had been declared to the IAEA. But, as Jennekins pointed out, the Iranians were not obliged to do so under the terms of their safeguards agreement. They were scale-model research machines, not production or power reactors, and used infinitesimal amounts of nuclear fuels. There was no way they could be used to produce significant quantities of weapons-grade uranium or plutonium.*

In the spirit of completeness, Jennekins and his team insisted the Iranians take them to Yazd province to inspect a uranium mine and possible milling plant, which this writer and others had described more than three years earlier, when Iran originally announced it had discovered uranium deposits. Although Iran was not obliged under the NPT to declare uranium mines or even milling facilities, they graciously agreed to chaperone the IAEA team to the mine.

Jennekins and his team found no milling plant or any other conversion facilities. Indeed, there was not much besides earth-moving equipment, crushers, conveyor belts, and trucks near the small, open-pit mine at the edge of the desert. They did not ask to see any of the other nine uranium mines the Iranians claimed they were operating, or inquire where the Argentinean milling plant was located. Iran's Great Salt Desert was not the most hospitable place in the world, and they were happy to fly back to Tehran that same day.

Of the six sites they visited, only one presented the slightest problem at all: Moallem Kalayeh. This is where the Mujahedin claimed the regime had headquartered its secret nuclear weapons program, the "Alamout Plan," named after the mountain hideout of the legendary Hassan Sabbah and his eleventh-century cult of assassins.

The Mujahedin claimed that the Revolutionary Guards had spent more than $300 million to build secret uranium-enrichment labs at the site since 1987, and that it was chockablock with equipment imported from France, Germany, and Italy. Other sources said it was the site the Iranians had chosen to install the 10-megawatt heavy-water reactor they now were trying to buy from India, and that laser enrichment equipment, obtained in the United States in 1978 and previously located at Tehran University, had been installed there.

Villaros, Jennekins, and their team of inspectors were naturally apprehensive when they assembled at Doshan Tapeh airbase in Tehran that snowy February morning, for the short helicopter ride into the Elburz mountains to the north. They were even more apprehensive after they had strapped in and the army helicopter rotors began to kick up snow, when a

*"Significant quantity" was a term of art used by the IAEA. It meant the amount of fissile material needed to make a nuclear explosive device. By IAEA standards, this was around 25 kilograms of highly enriched uranium, or 5 kilograms of plutonium.

loud blast erupted directly overhead and the pilot quickly cut power. One of the two engines had just exploded.

An hour and a half later, after they had changed helicopters, they went into white-knuckle mode as they were tossed about by blizzard-force winds. The driving snow was so thick they could see nothing, and they could only imagine what their pilots must be seeing as they attempted to find the landing pad. Despite the cold, they were sweating by the time the pilots finally put down.

Outside, the craggy mountains and the tiny hollow where they had landed were covered in 6 feet of snow. Everyone was glad when their Iranian army guides bustled them into a group of waiting jeeps and drove them to a nearby building to warm up.

Welcome to Moallem Kalayeh, the base commander said.

Once they had warmed up, he took them on a tour of the facility, which their guide described as a "proposed training and recreation center" for staff members of the Atomic Energy Organization of Iran. When completed, it would be able to handle conferences with up to four hundred people. The complex was built in a 10-acre clearing in the mountains and comprised six storage buildings, four dormitories, a large collective kitchen, and a dining hall, all in various stages of construction. Work had begun in 1989. There was not a scrap of nuclear equipment anywhere in sight, not a single machine or any sign of hastily cleared installations. It appeared to be exactly what the Iranians said it was.

When they went back into the reception area to warm up before returning to Tehran, one of the team members pulled out a map and gave Villaros a nudge. How can we be sure this is really Moallem Kalayeh? he whispered. With all the snow, we can't see a thing!

Villaros had brought a portable GPS receiver and read out the coordinates. They matched the coordinates the Mujahedin had given for the site: 36 degrees 60 minutes north, 50 degrees east. This is it, all right, he said.

Their Iranian guide overheard them and pulled out a detailed map to show them their location and the nearby village of the same name as the site described by the Mujahedin. He apologized for the weather and for the rough ride but explained that no one had ever intended the facility for winter use. It was just a summer retreat, a resort motel for government employees and their families.

As the IAEA team was preparing to return to Vienna on February 12, 1992, Jennekins met with the local press in Tehran. He was furious that he had been forced to risk his life in a wild-goose chase, and he intended to put a stop to this kind of thing in the future. "There doesn't seem to be a shred of evidence of any of these misleading misrepresentations," he said, alluding to the Mujahedin's charges of a secret Iranian nuclear weapons program. "Everything that we have seen is for the peaceful application of nuclear energy and ionizing radiation."

They had visited six sites, he revealed. "There was absolutely no restriction, no limitations on access." When asked if the IAEA had information on any other potential nuclear sites, he cut his questioner short. "We saw all of them," he said.

Villaros bit his tongue and kept quiet. Jennekins was well aware that Blix had vetoed two other sites—a new nuclear laboratory called Ibn Haytham, and a suspected reactor site at Gorgan. They could discuss it later.

On February 14, 1992, back in Vienna, the IAEA issued an official statement that marked a dramatic and unmistakable turning point in Iran's nuclear development.

The agency had gone to Iran at the invitation of the president of the Atomic Energy Organization of Iran, and not because of any international concern over Iran's nuclear research, it stated. The purpose of the four-member team that Jennekins headed was "to familiarize itself with the current status of the Iranian nuclear research and development program and in particular to discuss with Iranian officials present and possible future technical assistance and cooperation projects, the state of the Busheir nuclear power project, on which construction ceased in 1979, and the scope and objectives of research and development activities under way at the Isfahan Nuclear Technology Center, the Tehran Nuclear Research Center, and the Karaj Agricultural and Medical Research Center." The team had visited a "uranium exploration project," as well as "a facility under construction in the mountains north of Tehran near Ma'allem Kelayeh. All of the facilities and sites selected by the IAEA for inclusion in the visit were accepted by the Iranian Authorities."

The ever-wary Blix made sure that this glowing report included a word of caution to cover potential discoveries later on. The activities reviewed by the inspection team "were found to be consistent with the peaceful application of nuclear energy and ionizing radiation. It should be clear that the Team's conclusions are limited to facilities and sites visited by it and are of relevance only to the time of the Team's visit."[4]

But, in discussions with reporters, IAEA officials made clear they had no plans to renew their adventures in Iran anytime soon. Once bitten, twice shy.

So, had the IAEA been fooled yet again? Members of Jennekins's inspection team hotly contest that conclusion. But Yossef Bodansky, research director of the House Republican Research Committee Task Force on Terrorism and Unconventional Warfare, in Washington, D.C., immediately took issue with the IAEA's self-satisfied claims. Bodansky had written frequently on Iran's clandestine nuclear weapons program, and claimed to have sources inside Iran as well as within the U.S. and Israeli intelligence communities.

The IAEA inspectors had been taken to a place called "Moallem Kalayeh," he wrote in an after-action report for members of Congress, "but the Ma'allem Kelayah identified as part of Iran's military nuclear program is not the name of a place, but the name of a cluster of facilities located in Qazvin. . . . Simply put, the IAEA inspectors were taken to the wrong place."[5]

One explanation given for the mixup were the GPS coordinates. The Mujahedin later said they had made a mistake, and the correct location was 36.16 north, not 36.60. The site the IAEA visited was deep in the mountains north of Qazvin, whereas the correct coordinates indicated a location 40 kilometers *south* of Qazvin, in a valley well beyond the mountain range (and out of the snow). But just as it's hard for a regular reader of the *New York Times* to appreciate how often the paper retracts its own news, corrections after the fact involving Iran's clandestine nuclear program went unnoticed. Iran had stood accused, and its accusers had been wrong. End of story.

The failed IAEA inspection in 1992 made things easier for Iran's clandestine bomb program. Because Hans Blix had cleverly forced the issue using faulty intelligence, there was no way the inspection could have been a success. By failing, the IAEA essentially gave Iran another ten years to develop their nuclear capabilities without fear of being called on the carpet.

The IAEA failure encouraged Rafsanjani and his nuclear team to go on buying, building, training, and planning. Even in the wake of Iraq, they had managed to successfully hide their clandestine program from UN inspectors. Nothing could stop them now.

Besides, they knew they were more clever than Saddam Hussein. They weren't about to invade another country or confront the United States openly before their arsenal was ready.

BLIX AGAIN

I had breakfast with an unrepentant Hans Blix in Paris some months later, and asked him about the February 1992 inspection in Iran.

"We get lots of disinformation," he began, referring to the Mujahedin report. "So if we receive some alarming report we won't immediately ask for a special inspection. We will first analyze the so-called information to see if there is any reason to believe it is safeguards-relevant. We don't have a right to go anytime, anywhere."

But wasn't there a problem with an IAEA culture that sought to promote nuclear exports instead of preventing proliferation? Hadn't that kept the IAEA from asking tough questions, from knocking on closed doors?

Ridiculous! Blix stormed. It simply was not true that the risk of proliferation was increasing. "Show me the problem areas! So far, there is no evidence of problem areas in Iran. And even if we get satellite photographs—which we have been asking Washington to provide to us—we will analyze them before acting."

Besides, Blix added, what about U.S. nuclear cooperation with Iran under the shah? Don't forget it was the United States that transferred Iran's only nuclear research reactor and gave the Iranians access to all kinds of nuclear technology during the 1960s and 1970s. "Isn't the United States demonstrating a double standard, that it's all right to spread nuclear technology to one regime, but bad with another?" That would never be the IAEA culture, he added with a note of self-righteousness.

The important thing was not verification, but political guarantees by the nuclear powers. "They must first reduce the motivation for states to acquire nuclear arms," he said. That meant real disarmament by the nuclear states, and a nuclear-free zone in the Middle East, which Israel did not seem ready to accept.

FAIRY TALES

I recently asked an old friend who has been working for a European government, tracking Iran's nuclear program for the past fifteen years, if the 1992 incident made any more sense today than it did at the time.

"The IAEA went to the wrong place. It's as simple as that," she said. "Moallem Kelayeh *was* important. We have verified everything and it all checks out." The IAEA no longer evokes the failed 1992 inspection but frequently refers to the uranium enrichment site initially identified by the MEK. They now call it Lashkar Ab'ad and situate the facility some 40 kilometers *south* of Qazvin—precisely where the Mujahedin said it was, once they corrected their coordinates.

As a final poke in the eye to the IAEA inspectors, Rafsanjani sent First Vice President Hassan Habibi to officially inaugurate a new laboratory of the Atomic Energy Organization's Laser Research Center in Tehran on October 15, 1992. The Iranian press identified it as "Ibn Haytham"—the same facility that Villaros had wanted to inspect—and said it included a "semiconductor furnace for making lasers" that had been purchased from a European country.

But, as far as Hans Blix was concerned, it didn't exist, because the Iranians hadn't declared it.

Scheherazade—the ancient courtesan whose *Thousand and One Nights* were the Persian equivalent of *Alice in Wonderland*—was spinning her tales again.

LEGACY OF THE IAEA'S FAILURE

The failed 1992 IAEA inspection was like a gale-force wind that drove away the clouds that had been hovering over Iran. European exporters and government delegations flocked to Iran to do business now that suspicions over Iran's nuclear intentions had been dispelled. Not even the gangland-style murder of the new secretary general of the Kurdish Democratic Party of Iran and three associates, in the Mykonos restaurant in Berlin on September 17, 1992, could dampen the enthusiasm for the export bonanza. Iran was opening up, it had a skilled workforce, and it needed everything.

Trade with Europe was brisk. From Germany alone, Iran imported $5 billion worth of dual-use goods in 1992 for large-scale projects, including its military industries. Italy's Daniela SpA expanded the gigantic Soviet-built steel plant in Isfahan. So great were the needs of the missile and defense plants clustered around the city that the Iranian government decided to build a second, even larger steel plant 70 kilometers away to feed the hungry metal-benders. The $4.7 billion Mobarakeh steel complex brought together a consortium of top-drawer companies from Italy, Japan, and Switzerland. Iran wanted nothing less than the best and was willing to pay for it.

Mannesman Demag, of Germany, was selected to rebuild the Ahwaz steel plant, badly battered during the war with Iraq. Production was initially restored to the prerevolutionary capacity of 300,000 tons and later raised to 860,000 tons per year. Mannesman machine tools were found in no fewer than seven Iraqi weapons plants after the first Gulf War, according to UNSCOM inspection reports.

As I looked at these and other industrial sales to Iran for the Simon

Wiesenthal Center in Los Angeles in late 1992, a pattern began to emerge. Iran was building basic industries that could go either way. The steel plants, for example, could produce rolled steel sheet for manufacturing cars and trucks or that could be used to produce ballistic missiles, artillery rockets, and the like. Petrochemical plants produced large quantities of ethylene, used to make everything from plastics to explosives and chemical warfare agents. A fertilizer plant in Khorasan designed by M.W. Kellogg, a major supplier of nerve gas to the U.S. Army in the 1950s, incorporated an ammonia production line that could be used to produce heavy water, company officials told me. Because of the legitimate civilian use, no European supplier turned them down.[6]

From their debriefings of French businessmen traveling back and forth to Iran during this time, French intelligence noticed a curious development. It used be that the businessmen were taken directly to the factories they were to supply. Then that changed—even for petrochemical projects. "The Iranians are now making generic demands, for example, pumps, and refuse to give the intended use or the end-user," a French counterintelligence officer told me. It was a lesson they had learned from the inimitable Dr. Khan.

In late 1992 a front company working on behalf of the Ministry of Sepah, Iran's Revolutionary Guards, approached the Ayres Corporation of Albany, Georgia, with a $6.7 million offer to purchase crop-dusting aircraft. The company applied for an export license and was turned down, because similar aircraft had been used by Iraq to spray civilians with chemical warfare agents.

But the sale was almost approved, I learned later from General Brent Scowcroft, national security adviser to President George H. W. Bush.

During the final months of the Bush administration, a debate raged on whether to open the floodgates to U.S. exporters seeking to cash in on Iran's buying spree. Boeing wanted to sell several billion dollars' worth of civilian airliners. Caterpillar had requests for hundreds of millions of dollars' worth of earth-moving equipment. Chrysler was talking with Iran about building a truck plant. The list was long, and it was worth billions of dollars. "Because it was politically sensitive, we decided to leave those decisions to the next administration," Scowcroft said. "The Iranians came up to us with offers to talk, but when it came right down to it, they could never decide to go ahead."

That caution eventually saved them from political embarrassment.

12

LOOSE NUKES

Today the slogan "Death to America" belongs to each and every Iranian.

—Iranian Supreme Leader Ayatollah Ali Khamenei, July 14, 1993

The Chinese were bending over backward.

Everywhere Major General Mohsen Rezai and his buying delegation went, the Chinese received them with full military honors. At the Beijing airport, when he landed in early January 1993 in Rafsanjani's executive jetliner, they hauled out a military marching band. As a token of his appreciation, Rezai presented his hosts with a handcrafted Mauser pistol from the original Parchin munitions works. In Shanghai, where the Chinese flew Rezai and his fifty-man purchasing team aboard a government aircraft, sailors piped him on board the flagship of the Chinese navy as if he were a visiting naval commander.

They certainly were eager to make a sale. They showed him destroyers and frigates, missile boats and gunships. They had new systems on offer, especially a longer-range version of the Silkworm anti-shipping missile that the Pasdaran were already assembling in a Chinese-built factory near Bandar Abbas. No one had seen a presentation of the C-802 before, they said. It flew at supersonic speeds, just 10 meters above the waves. The secret was a TRI-60 turbojet engine the Chinese were buying from Microturbo SA in France, and a radar guidance system. Not even the U.S. Navy was able to detect it, let alone defend against it. Once these new missiles went operational, Iran would become the absolute master of the Persian Gulf. They could hit targets up to 60 miles away.

It turned out that the C-802 was an upgraded version of the French Exocet, which the China Precision Machinery Import-Export Corporation (CPMIEC) had not only copied but improved.

How did they manage to import the engines from France when China was still subject to a European Union arms embargo, Rezai wondered. The man from China Precision just gave him a blank stare. Embargo? No embargo on engines. Engines are not weapons. Rezai and the Pasdaran missile technicians who accompanied him took note.

In Shanghai, Rezai presented a ceremonial sword to the Chinese admiral who hosted them, and signed a number of smaller deals. Ali Shamkhani, who headed the Pasdaran navy, was eager to order the latest Hega-class fast-attack craft, equipped with the C-802. Rezai agreed. The first five missile boats arrived in July 1994. The Pasdaran dubbed them Tondar ("swift-flying"), after the Persian name they had given to the C-802 missiles they carried. The U.S. Navy referred to them as Huodong-class boats, and watched with trepidation as they began patrols in the Persian Gulf. Vice Admiral J. Scott Redd, commander of U.S. naval forces in the region, called them "a new dimension . . . of the Iranian threat to shipping."[1]

In addition to the Chinese boats, the Iranians retrofitted a number of the Combattante II (Kaman class) missile boats they had purchased from France in the early 1980s with C-802 launchers, and installed other missiles in coastal batteries in the Strait of Hormuz and on the island of Hengham, which lies off the coast of Qeshm island. For U.S. commanders in the Gulf, the C-802s were a serious headache.

Rezai was closer to Shamkhani than to any other officer on his fifty-man delegation. They liked and respected each other, and had brought up their children together, sending them to the same elite government schools. During the early days of the revolution, they lived close to each other in a special housing development reserved for senior Pasdaran officers on the grounds of the Firouzeh Palace, the hunting estate of the former shah on the southern outskirts of Tehran. Enclosed by high walls and gates, access to the area was tightly controlled by armed security guards. The revolutionaries had renamed it Shah'rak Koladouz. More recently, they had moved to a new housing development in Lavizan park in north Tehran, near the vast Lavizan-Shian missile and nuclear complex.

Rezai brought his eldest son, Ahmad, along on the buying mission to expand on his military education. From the time the boy was just five years old, Rezai had taken him with him on official trips. Now the boy had turned sixteen and Rezai was grooming him for a career with the Pasdaran. He reckoned young Ahmad needed to learn how to deal with people like the CPMIEC and China Great Wall salesmen, who would always be trying to buy him off. The Chinese were getting pricey, he said. Perhaps they are starting to take our business for granted.

He hadn't originally planned to go to North Korea, especially in the dead of winter. But the North Koreans had insisted, calling him repeatedly while he was in China. They had something new to show him and asked that he come immediately. He phoned his contact in Rafsanjani's office, the Nahad. They were already aware of the North Korean request and ordered him to make the trip. Then he called his wife in Tehran. Something unexpected had come up, he said. He had to keep the boy out of classes for another week or ten days. He would make up the work when he came back, but Dad would make sure that he read ahead in the physics and math books he had brought with him.

When they arrived at the airport in Pyongyang on January 12, 1993, they were greeted by Defense Minister O Jin-u, a deputy to Great Leader Kim Il Sung. As expected, Rezai made a brief statement for the government cameras. He had come to strengthen military ties, he said. Iran and North Korea had much in common. Both nations were the victims of "U.S. plots," whether in the Persian Gulf or in the Korean Peninsula. The U.S. military presence in both regions was "an indication of the U.S. animosity against the two nations."

Before the real business of his visit began, they were taken to the military cemetery, where Rezai composed a long anti-American message in Persian in the guest book. We salute the courage of the brave people of Korea who lost their lives defending their homeland against American aggression, he wrote. The people of Iran are your brothers in courage and steadfastness, and hope to equal your feats of bravery in expelling the aggressor Americans.

For nearly an entire week, the North Koreans escorted Rezai and his delegation to military bases all over the country. They split them into two groups. Rezai and the men who had already taken the tour plunged directly into negotiations. His deputy, Mohammad Baqr Zolqadr, the dark-skinned fanatic who had just come back from training Osama bin Laden's terrorists in Sudan, led the second group, including his boss's son.

Young Ahmad marveled when they were taken to a top-secret air base, carved out of the rock inside a mountain. As they entered, their North Korean hosts pointed out the thickness of the special blast doors, designed to withstand a direct nuclear hit. Deep inside the mountain they came to a huge cavern, where two dozen aircraft were parked like ducks in a row, nestled into each other's wings. In separate storerooms carved out of the rock, the North Koreans had stockpiled missiles, fuel, and all the necessary maintenance equipment. They managed the entire complex from a modern control room, where flight officers surveyed the buried runway through a giant glass window, a bit like the control tower on an aircraft carrier. But most amazing of all was the underground runway, pitched at a steep upward slant. As the jets cycled up their engines, the jet wash was deflected by a blast wall and vented through a series of long tunnels to the surface to reduce the heat signature. The jets hurtled upward using a catapult, similar to those on an aircraft carrier. At the end of the runway, doors opened onto the sky. The jets shot out, afterburners lit, like missiles emerging from a launch tube buried halfway up the mountainside.

At one missile test range the elder Rezai visited, Iranian engineers were working side by side with the North Koreans, preparing telemetry equipment for a test. They were working to extend the range of the missile known in the West as the No-Dong.

In fact, it was a joint development project, which the Iranians then referred to as Zelzal-3. (*Zelzal* is Persian for "earthquake.") The Self-Sufficiency Department of the Revolutionary Guards was in charge of the project. For greater security, they jobbed out work to small R&D facilities spread across Iran, including a computer research center in the Lavizan military district in north Tehran, not far from Rezai's house. Propellant, payload, and design work in Iran was being carried out by the DIO's Defense Technology and Science Research Center in Karaj. North Korean technicians and Russian ballistic missile experts were now working at both sites to upgrade the missile.

With a greater range than the SCUD-Cs North Korea had been shipping to Iran since the late 1980s, the Zelzal-3 would bring Israel within range of Iran for the first time.

Rafsanjani and Defense Minister Akbar Torkan—who had headed the DIO before Rafsanjani appointed him to defense in 1989—were more concerned with range and payload than with accuracy. The original specifications called for a Circular Error Probable (CEP) from between 1,500 to 4,000 meters, an unheard-of margin of error in the West. This meant that just half of the missiles would fall within 1,500 to 4,000 meters of a target area. The key was making sure the new missile could carry a warhead large enough for the Chinese bomb design Iran is believed to have purchased from Dr. A. Q. Khan. Given the density of Israel's population, it didn't much matter where it fell.

We need a nuclear missile to deal with Israel, Rafsanjani told Rezai repeatedly. We need to show other Muslim states that Iran is the only Muslim nation capable of defeating Israel.

The missile Rezai and his team inspected during this January 1993 trip to North Korea has been modified significantly and is today known as the

Shahab-3. Displayed repeatedly at military parades in Tehran on huge mobile launch vehicles, today it is deployed with special Revolutionary Guards missile units and is aimed at Israel.

As Rezai was heading for Pyongyang, a member of the Majles back in Tehran was publicly criticizing the government for caving in to North Korean "extortion." The North Korean government was demanding cash payments of between $2.4 billion and $2.7 billion for the SCUD-B and Silkworm missiles they had delivered to Iran during the 1980–88 Iran-Iraq war. It was scandalous, the deputy complained. Iran had been making regular payments to North Korea in oil. Why this sudden demand for cash? The Rafsanjani government should refuse to pay and stop buying inferior weapons from such a backward regime, he said.

When reports of the deputy's complaint reached him in Pyongyang, Mohsen Rezai laughed outright. That would help to confuse the Americans, he remarked to his son. The North Koreans were now supplying much of the same missile production gear the Islamic Republic had been buying previously from China, and at much cheaper prices.

While Rezai and his buying team were out touring, guards from the Pasdaran's Herasat department, responsible for his protection but also for ensuring the political purity of government officials, hung around the guesthouse in Pyongyang playing billiards. At one point Rezai thought to take them to task, since it was forbidden in Islam—*haram*—to play billiards, and they of all people should know it. (While not himself a cleric, Rezai was very observant of Islamic rules.) But he knew it was a futile complaint, since they all knew that Khamenei had made a great show of playing billiards with his North Korean hosts every time he had visited the country as president.

He was glad when the week was over and the visits and the toasts and the meals and the backslapping were coming to an end. It had all been for show, he knew. The real reason for the trip was about to be revealed to him by the Great Leader himself.

Rezai met with Kim Il Sung alone. No aides, no note-takers, not even his own translator were allowed in the room in the Great Leader's palace. Just the two of them, and Kim's personal interpreter.

The aging Kim was terminally ill, although Rezai didn't know that at the time. He still appeared robust, jovial, and keenly aware of his visitor. Look how much we have accomplished together, he said, as they reviewed work on the new joint missile project. Neither man had any doubt as to the missile's purpose as a nuclear delivery vehicle. And that was when Rezai told Kim about the bombs.

The stories about Iran's attempts to purchase nuclear warheads from Kazakhstan and other Central Asian republics were true, he said. Rafsanjani had sent buying teams all over the place. But there had been problems. To avoid detection, the weapons had been disassembled and transported piece by piece in separate trucks. They had put a nonprofessional in charge of the operation, and the results were predictable. When the bombs arrived in Tehran in late 1991 and early 1992, key parts were missing. Iran could hardly go to the Russians and ask them for assistance, since Yeltsin's intelligence people had raised a public stink about the missing bombs.

Iran needed Kim's help to get those weapons operational. The aging North Korean leader agreed immediately.[2]

After the hour-long meeting, Kim welcomed Rezai's delegation into the ceremonial banquet hall, and posed for photographs with each one individually before lunch.

On the plane back to Tehran, Rezai was ecstatic. His lifelong dream of making Iran an independent nuclear power capable of defending itself against aggression—even by a superpower!—was about to come true. As he mulled over his meeting with Kim in the executive cabin of the Boeing 707, a close adviser asked him how they would ever manage to ship atomic weapons from North Korea to Iran.

We don't need to, Rezai said. We have all the parts but one. And now North Korea has agreed to supply us what we are missing.

Once we have the complete warheads, it's very easy, he explained. It's no more complicated than a conventional warhead. We can just swap them out.

Fitting a nuclear warhead onto an existing missile was far more complicated than Rezai let on, as Iran would find out (see chapter 26). But Rezai's adviser was not a technician and was struck by Rezai's broad-brush vision of Iran's future. For sure, a few nuclear warheads did not make an arsenal. But it was a start, and it would provide an insurance policy should the Americans ever decide to attack. Now Iran's leaders had to do some hard thinking about the new strategic situation the warheads had created.

As was their way, there would be no announcement, at least not now. There would be no dramatic increase in Iran's aggressive behavior. But small steps previously unthinkable—such as deploying anti-shipping missiles on the three islands at the entry of the Persian Gulf they had seized from the UAE in September 1992—could now be ventured, without fear of U.S. intervention. (Iran insisted the islands were its sovereign territory, illegally transferred to the Emirates by British occupation forces in the

1970s. Seizing the islands had been a tremendously popular move in Iran, since it appealed to the latent nationalism of most Iranians).

The adviser, who later defected to the West, was stunned as he listened to Rezai explain these things. Only a handful of Iran's inner leadership circle had any clue what had taken place in that closed-door meeting with Kim. These were the regime's most closely guarded secrets, and they were stunning indeed. When he related this story to me, he said that he assumed the missing bomb part Rezai had referred to was the fissile material core. But Clinton administration officials with whom I have shared this anecdote believe that the North Koreans did not have enough fissile material at the time, or the inclination to share it, even with Iran.

"Our worst-case estimate—really, worst case," said Gary Samore, a National Security Council official who handled nonproliferation issues, "was that the North Koreans might have had 12 kilograms of plutonium. In theory, you could make a bomb or two with that amount. But the question is, would the North Koreans be willing to give up their only strategic asset? My guess is it would be highly unlikely."

Others believe Samore and his former colleagues who missed the Iran–North Korea nuclear connection—just as they missed the A. Q. Khan network—were just plain wrong.

A State Department official working to counter the Iranian nuclear program told me in December 2004 that the North Koreans had a secret uranium enrichment program that was up and running all during the 1980s, at sites they never had declared to the IAEA and that had never been inspected. While their stockpile of weapons-grade plutonium may have been limited, to this day no one knows how much uranium they managed to enrich in secret. Like Iran, they had tapped into the A. Q. Khan network and were using undeclared supplies of natural uranium as well as imported uranium for enrichment.

A former Pentagon intelligence officer, Robert W. Gaskin, who tracked North Korea's clandestine programs until he left the military in January 1992, delivered a report to then undersecretary of defense Paul Wolfowitz in 1990 saying that North Korea would have two nuclear weapons by 1995. "I missed it by a year," he told me in 1994, at the peak of the Clinton administration's nuclear negotiations with North Korea.

Gaskin said the Pentagon had cataloged several dozen undeclared uranium processing sites in North Korea, some of them potential enrichment plants, that could have given North Korea the capability of making weapons-grade fuel without detection. But the Clinton White House chose to ignore this information, in its quest to find a "solution" for the red-hot North Korean nuclear crisis that would avoid a military showdown.*

"The idea that the North Koreans signed the Agreed Framework [that required them to abandon their plutonium-based facilities] only *after* they had an enrichment program in place to provide an alternative uranium route to the bomb would be in character," the State Department official told me. "So if they are collaborating with Iran and Pakistan on missiles, why not collaborate on nukes?" he added. "One of the big reasons you want missiles is to deliver nuclear weapons. They're basically terror weapons. The real payola is to put a nuke on top of the damn thing. If you're collaborating on all this stuff, and have a worldwide collaborative weapons laboratory with a network of collaborative rogue states when it comes to missiles, why would you leave off the agenda the really big thing, the reason you all want the missiles?"

But in 1993 and 1994, when these transfers took place, the U.S. intelligence community was still wearing blinders. Except for a few enlightened visionaries at DTSA, who were sidelined by Clinton administration political appointees, it took countries and programs one at a time and failed to see the connections between them.

HOLOCAUST SURVIVOR

As Mohsen Rezai was negotiating with Kim Il Sung in Pyongyang, Holocaust survivor Tom Lantos was in Strasbourg, France, looking for ways to stop Iran, North Korea, and other "rogue regimes" from getting access to nuclear weapons technology.

Congress is full of unusual characters, but Lantos would stand out at a circus. A California economics professor who hosted a popular TV talk show, Lantos had a shock of silver hair, an acid tongue, and an anti-government populist streak. Elected to the House as a Democrat in 1980 from the Bay Area, Lantos made waves during the late 1980s for investigating fraud and abuse at the Health and Urban Development agency, HUD.

*At Kusong, the North Koreans had a milling plant capable of refining 300 kilograms per day of uranium ore into yellowcake. At Pyongsan, they had a second plant, completed in 1984, which Gaskin said the Pentagon believed was a clandestine enrichment site. Other uranium-related facilities were identified at Pakch'on (an underground uranium conversion facility and a suspected bomb assembly plant), Unggi (a uranium mine, identified in 1993), Sonchon (a uranium mine), and Hungnam (a uranium mine first identified in 1992).

After the Clinton-Gore election victory, Lantos lobbied hard for new responsibilities. He convinced Foreign Affairs Committee chairman Lee Hamilton to give him a subcommittee that thrust him to the forefront of the sexiest foreign policy issue of the day: weapons of mass destruction and the arms trade. With the good looks and sharp wit to become a star, Lantos wanted to become the "adult" in the Clinton administration's foreign policy stable, perhaps even—who knows?—secretary of state.

In 1944, Lantos was sixteen years old when the Nazis invaded his native Hungary and deported him and hundreds of thousands of Jews to work camps in the countryside. Fooling his guards, he managed to escape and made his way back to Budapest, where he met Swedish diplomat Raoul Wallenberg, who hid him in a three-room safe house with fifty others. Wallenberg tapped Lantos as a courier because his blond hair and blue eyes helped him avoid suspicion from Nazi troops. By the time the Soviets swarmed into Budapest in January 1945, Wallenberg had saved tends of thousands of Jews from the death camps by handing out Swedish passports. One of them, Annette Tillemann, returned to Budapest after the war and married the young man with the blue eyes and blond hair who had helped her to escape. Shortly afterward, Lantos and his new bride came to America.

Wallenberg was not so lucky. He was arrested by the Red Army and disappeared into the Soviet gulag, where he is believed to have died in 1947. Working with President Reagan, Lantos helped persuade Congress to make Wallenberg an honorary U.S. citizen in October 1981, a recognition shared only with one other foreigner—Sir Winston Churchill. Even today, the California congressman continues to press the Russian government to reveal the full truth about Wallenberg's fate.

Tom Lantos wanted to create a legacy. His new subcommittee gave him the vehicle to promote a new vision of world affairs after the collapse of the Soviet empire, and a new role for America as the guarantor of freedom and internationally recognized standards of behavior. He called it "collective security." He believed it was essential to prevent rogue states from getting their hands on weapons and technologies that would allow them to threaten world peace. Now he needed a detail person, someone who knew the complex issues involved in weapons proliferation. He turned to an old friend and former Reagan administration hand, Richard Perle, who gave him a name and a phone number in France. That's when my phone rang and Lantos asked me to meet him in Strasbourg, where he was attending a European parliament session. He wanted to offer me a job.

"ROGUE REGIMES"

Just two months into the Clinton administration, as I was shuttling back and forth between Washington and Paris in late March 1993, I discovered that preventing the export of critical technologies to rogue regimes such as Iran was going to be more complicated than I had thought. I was prepared for the industry lobbyists and their congressional backers, who argued that controlling U.S. exports for reasons of national security merely handed lucrative overseas markets to foreign competitors. But I had not been prepared for the secret policies President Clinton brought into the Oval Office regarding one of Iran's largest suppliers: the People's Republic of China.

With Congressman Lantos's approval, I requested licensing records of U.S. high-tech exports to China from the Department of Commerce. Our goal was to determine whether U.S. companies had been selling equipment to China that was used to produce weapons for export to Iran and other rogue states. We hoped to identify a few egregious cases to win broader support for tightening licensing procedures codified in the Export Administration Act (EAA).

When the Commerce Department finally delivered the several-thousand-page printout to the Rayburn House Office Building, Rep. Sam Gejdenson (D-Conn.) kept me from looking at it for three full weeks, ostensibly on jurisdictional grounds. (Gejdenson chaired the House Foreign Affairs subcommittee with legislative oversight over the Commerce Department.) When his office finally turned over the documents, I was told to drop my plan for analyzing the records and to work on other assignments.

I didn't realize at the time that China figured prominently in a plan devised by top Clinton administration appointees to recompense Silicon Valley executives for their financial support during the 1992 election campaign. Nor was I then aware of Bill Clinton's long-standing ties to major campaign contributors Mochtar Riady and Lippo Group who sought to influence U.S. policy toward Communist China. My work for Lantos could have led to greater restrictions on the sale of military technology to Communist China, so it had to be stopped.[3]

Lantos directed me to work on Iran, and so for several months I pored over Shippers Export Declarations (SEDs) we had requested from the Census Bureau, along with two interns. These forms must be filed by all exporters and provide information on the equipment shipped and the foreign end-user. Our interest was to determine whether the Enhanced Proliferation Control Initiative (EPCI), established by President Bush in 1990, was effective in preventing military technologies from reaching Iran. Under EPCI, U.S. exporters were required to obtain a license to export any goods—even a pencil or a screwdriver—to foreign entities or projects of "proliferation concern."

The regulations called on Commerce to develop a "blacklist" of such projects and to make it available to exporters. But Commerce told us they never published a blacklist, for fear that identifying projects and entities of concern would jeopardize U.S. intelligence sources and methods. Instead they said they had worked out an ad hoc arrangement so exporters could ask them informally whether a particular end-user was okay. If the answer was no, then Commerce issued what they called an "informed" notice, requiring the exporter to apply for a license.

We asked Commerce how many "informed" notices they had sent out. "One would think this would be an easy question to answer," Lantos said. "After all, EPCI was enacted because of our failed export-control policy toward Iraq. The Commerce Department was under a lot of public pressure to improve its performance. One would have thought that Commerce would want to keep very close track of this information." But they did not. Lantos wrote Commerce Secretary Ron Brown on August 31, 1993, asking for a detailed report on EPCI cases and informed notices. He never received a reply.[4]

New trade restrictions signed into law by President Bush in October 1992 prohibited high-technology sales to Iran altogether. Despite this, U.S. exports to Iran actually increased in the ensuing months. We uncovered dozens of cases where U.S. high-technology gear normally subject to licensing was simply shipped to Iran without a license, with the full approval of Ron Brown's Commerce Department. The goods went under so-called G-DEST authority, approved for general destinations, including Iran.

In 1992, fully 60 percent of the $750 million worth of U.S. goods and equipment shipped to Iran was subjected to Commerce Department licensing because of the sophistication of the technology involved. Since the new restrictions were signed into law by President Bush on October 23, 1992, however, the percentage of licensed goods dropped to a mere 2.5 percent of total exports. But there was no corresponding decline in the sophistication of the equipment exported.

Among the equipment shipped under G-DEST authority were toxins and microorganisms, turbojet engines, vacuum pumps, centrifuges, machine tools, gas separation equipment, large hydraulic presses for metal forming, gas chromatagraphs, and mass spectrometers. Also included were a series of high-powered computers, worth close to $1 million each. All of this equipment normally required a license. But the Commerce Department allowed it to go to Iran without scrutiny.

One of the exports in question was shipped directly to the Atomic Energy Organization of Iran; two went to a suspected chemical weapons plant. Toxins, which can be used in medical research or for biological weapons, were shipped without explanation to a Tehran bank. Once again, as happened with Iraq, the Commerce Department had apparently decided to adopt a "don't ask, don't tell" policy. Commerce rejoined by calling it "low-level equipment."

In a September 14, 1993, hearing on "rogue regimes," Lantos named more than 230 companies that were selling technology and equipment to Iran that could be used for weapons of mass destruction. And then he hit a raw nerve: he accused China of serving as a transit point for suppliers who otherwise would not export directly to the rogues. "Advanced electronics, computers, and sensing devices sold legally to China are incorporated into ballistic missiles systems and re-exported to countries such as Syria and Iran," he said. "I believe the Commerce Department would discover a massive diversion of U.S. goods to Chinese ballistic missile exports if they carried out their statutory duty and conducted pre-license and post-shipment inspections in China."

There was no way the Clinton administration was going down that route. Just two hours after this hearing, Lantos received a call from the White House and was told to get with the program. And I was told to look for another job.

"WE WANT THE DIRT ON BUSH"

The Intermediary was not surprised when he heard this story. He knew what was going on behind the scenes because he was carrying the messages from the Clinton White House to Rafsanjani's Nahad, the presidential office in Tehran.

An Iranian exile who made his peace with the regime and was devoutly religious, the Intermediary was contacted by the White House just weeks after President Clinton took office in January 1993. They knew about his contacts in Tehran, and they wanted his help. To his astonishment, the Clinton people asked him to fly to Tehran to ask Rafsanjani for information on the so-called October Surprise.

In a 1991 book by the same name, former Carter administration official Gary Sick alleged that as a vice-presidential candidate in 1980, George H. W. Bush had initiated secret contacts with the Khomeini government aimed at delaying the release of U.S. hostages until after the 1980 elections. Sick's allegations triggered a massive investigation by congressional Democrats in 1992 aimed at damaging President Bush's reelection chances.

The final report of the Task Force to Investigate Certain Allegations Concerning the Holding of American Hostages by Iran in 1980 was released on January 3, 1993. Task-force lawyers had flown to Algeria, Britain, Belgium, France, Germany, Italy, Portugal, Spain, Switzerland, and South Africa to interview more than 230 people. They examined "over 21,000 recorded conversations on 548 tapes" from one key witness, and pored through "thousands of raw, unredacted documents from the CIA, NSC, and the National Security Agency (NSA)." In their quest for dirt on Bush, congressional Democrats left no stone unturned. Despite these exhaustive efforts, the task force's report concluded: "There is no credible evidence supporting any attempt or proposal to attempt, by the Reagan Presidential Campaign—or persons representing or associated with the campaign—to delay the release of the American hostages in Iran." They had come up empty-handed.

The partisan Democrats who arrived in the White House with President Clinton were hoping the Intermediary could finally get them the goods. They wanted the information by March 1993, the Intermediary told me—just in time to embarrass the former president before a scheduled "private" visit to Kuwait in April, which the Kuwaitis had planned as a multimillion-dollar celebration of Bush's victory in the Gulf War over Saddam Hussein.

Rafsanjani was not sure how to respond to the request, or how to evaluate the new U.S. president. After several weeks of waiting in a Tehran hotel, the Intermediary's contact at the Nahad, a Rafsanjani adviser, finally summoned him to his office. If this was part of a more broad-based U.S. initiative to renew ties and expand trade with Iran, then the Iranian president would have much information to communicate, he said. But first he needed to know that the new U.S. president was sincere. As a sign of goodwill, Rafsanjani wanted Clinton to release some $2 billion worth of military spare parts paid for by the shah that were being held in a warehouse outside of Washington's Dulles International Airport in Sterling, Virginia. The United States was still holding $17 billion in Iranian assets frozen during the 1979–81 hostage crisis, he said. It was a lot of money, and Iran wanted it back. (The U.S. never acknowledged the $17 billion figure; the real amount, they said, was closer to one or two billion.)

Returning to Washington, he duly communicated Rafsanjani's reply to his NSC contacts, but they were already distracted by Inside the Beltway politics. Clinton was getting roasted in the press over his "don't ask, don't tell" policy toward gays in the military. As a gesture to Tehran (and to the U.S. business community), the administration made a halfhearted effort to back Boeing plans to sell civilian airliners to Iran. But the billion-dollar deal ran into a buzz-saw on Capitol Hill, when Senator Jesse Helms and others angrily questioned the wisdom of allowing a huge aircraft deal with a country on the State Department's terrorism list. In June the new administration backed down.

That experience convinced the president and National Security Adviser Tony Lake to carefully balance any secret overture to Tehran that would open trade and please Clinton campaign contributors, with a public policy of sanctions and containment. It was Lake and his top Middle East adviser, Martin Indyk, who crafted the new theoretical approach toward rogue states that became known as "dual containment."

PROJECT SAPPHIRE

In late February 1994, Elwood Gift, a nuclear engineer from the Y-12 plant at Oak Ridge National Laboratory in Tennessee, was told to pack winter clothing for a long and possibly dangerous trip to the former Soviet republic of Kazakhstan. He was about to venture into the Wild East, where the CIA believed nuclear smugglers, former KGB officers, and corrupt government officials were working hand-in-glove with Iranian agents to transfer nuclear materials and possibly nuclear weapons to Iran.

His destination was the Ulba Metallurgy Plant, twenty miles outside the Kazakh city of Ust-Kamenogorsk. The CIA had evidence that a team of Iranian nuclear scientists had visited the Ulba plant in August 1992 and suspected they had purchased low-enriched uranium and beryllium, a material used to boost the yield of nuclear weapons. Recently a stockpile of over 600 kilograms of weapons-grade uranium had been discovered in a neglected storage site at the plant. After extensive negotiations carried out by the U.S. ambassador to Kazakhstan, William Courtney, the Kazakh government asked for U.S. assistance in making sure it was secure from nuclear smugglers. The era of "loose nukes" had dawned.

Ulba had been shrouded in secrecy until very recently. Built in 1949, for many years it was known only as "Mailbox 10," a dark island in the top-secret Soviet nuclear archipelago. According to Monterey Institute non-proliferation expert William C. Potter, the plant was known to produce uranium fuel pellets, beryllium, and tantalum. Discovering that it was also making highly enriched uranium fuel for Soviet nuclear submarine reactors had shocked Gift and his colleagues at Oak Ridge. The stockpile of highly enriched uranium discovered at Ulba was apparently left over from the Alfa-class nuclear attack submarines, forgotten by Soviet officials when the disaster-ridden Alfa project, with its liquid-metal-cooled reactors was finally abandoned in the late 1980s.[5]

Gift was given free rein to examine the entire plant and was given fifteen samples of the nuclear materials stored in three different vaults. Kazakh officials put one sample into a mass spectrometer to analyze its isotopic content. It turned out to be U-235 enriched to approximately 90 percent.

When Gift returned home with the samples, the news sank in. Six hundred kilograms of weapons-grade uranium was enough to make at least fifty bombs. It was a huge stockpile, and from what Gift could tell, it was just sitting there, ripe for the plundering. National Security Council official Rose Gottemoeller convened a high-level interagency meeting at the White House on March 25, 1994, where it was decided to do everything possible to secure the Kazakh weapons material, before the Iranians could get it. The mission was given the name "Project Sapphire."

There were loads of stories of loose nuclear materials from the former Soviet Union, many of them obvious scams. Dealers offering to sell a mysterious substance they called "red mercury" were popping up everywhere. According to some reports, red mercury dramatically increased the yield of nuclear weapons, making it possible to make bombs that would fit into a suitcase. But, according to others, it was little more than an expensive red herring. "We erred on the side of caution," recalls former Clinton national security council expert Daniel Poneman, one of the rare holdovers from the administration of George H. W. Bush. "We worked our butts off and tried to get everything we could."

Despite the urgency of preventing the Iranians from acquiring the huge stockpile of nuclear material at Ust-Kamenogorsk, it took another seven months before President Bill Clinton authorized the operation to airlift the material out of Kazakhstan. In utmost secrecy, twenty-nine men and two women headed for Kazakhstan on board a giant U.S. Air Force C-5 transport plane on October 7, 1994. The extraction team was led by thirty-six-year-old Alex Riedy, who worked for Martin Marietta, the civilian contractor in charge of the Oak Ridge nuclear storage facility. Riedy knew they had only a few weeks to transform and repack the 1,050 containers full of nuclear material, some of which had corroded and were leaking radioactive sludge. Once the harsh Central Asian winter arrived, it would be difficult to fly out of the isolated airstrip, where snow-clearing equipment was an unknown luxury. As Riedy and his team began to assemble the containers, they made an alarming discovery that confirmed their worst fears. Just next door to the main storage site where the bomb-grade material had been kept, they found empty shipping canisters with Tehran addresses. They had arrived not a moment too soon.

When the team finally finished their work and loaded up the C-5s ready to head home, snow and bad weather shut down the airport for two days. Finally, late on the afternoon of November 20, 1994, the two C-5s that had managed to land before the storm took off for the twenty-hour nonstop trip to Dover Air Force Base in Delaware. The cargo was offloaded and trucked down to Oak Ridge in four unmarked convoys with a heavily armed escort. As the last convoy arrived in Oak Ridge, Defense Secretary William Perry gave the administration a pat on the back. "We have put this bomb-grade nuclear material forever out of the reach of potential black marketers, terrorists, or new nuclear regimes," he said. "This is defense by other means and in a big way."

Perry was right—up to a point. Everyone was on the lookout for loose nukes. As a senior intelligence analyst at the State Department's tiny bureau of intelligence and research confided to me more than eight months before Mohsen Rezai's trip to North Korea, you couldn't spend a full day on the job without tracking some new story: a warhead missing here, radioactive material discovered there. And many of these reports—especially those suggesting that authorities in Kazakhstan had been the conduit for Iran's purchase of nuclear artillery shells—were taken very, very seriously by intelligence agencics from the former Czech Republic to Germany, Britain, France, and the United States.

The problem was, with all eyes looking out for loose nukes, no one was focusing on the real proliferators who were Iran's partners in crime: the governments of North Korea, China, and the Russian Federation, not to mention the harder-to-track network of the elusive Dr. Khan.

13

RED LIGHT, GREEN LIGHT

CIA Director Jim Woolsey was disturbed. The satellite photograph the European division chief had just handed him seemed to corroborate his worst fears. It showed an Iran Air cargo jet sitting on the tarmac at Zagreb airport in Croatia, its nose raised, surrounded by what appeared to be Croatian Interior Ministry troops. Although the picture had been taken from space, the Iran Air lettering and the winged-Pegasus insignia were crystal clear, and there could be no doubt what was going on. The locals were offloading crates of weapons and ammunition. From CIA reporting in the field, it was clear that the weapons were intended to help the Bosnian Muslims, who recently had entered into a confederation with the Croatians.

I thought we had a policy to oppose this type of thing, Woolsey remarked. We did, the division chief said. Someone was undoing that policy.

Bosnian Muslim leader Alija Izetbegovic opened the Iranian arms pipeline in May 1991, when he made the first of several trips to Tehran asking for aid. Rafsanjani and Supreme Leader Ali Khamenei welcomed his approach, championing Bosnia's plight as a "Muslim" cause. Iran became the first Muslim nation to recognize Bosnia as an independent state, just one year later. Iranian military advisers, along with several hundred Mujahedin fighters from various nations, soon began flowing into Bosnia. Many of them were veterans of the Afghan war, trained in camps managed by Osama bin Laden.

To the befuddlement of the CIA and American academics, the fighters were all Sunni Muslims, but the Iranians were Shias. The analysts insisted that Sunnis and Shias could barely talk to one another, let alone cooperate in waging war. This view was supported by Muslim activists such as Abdelrahman Alamoudi, chairman of the American Muslim Council. Alamoudi and his assistant, Khaled Saffuri, became prominent lobbyists on behalf of arming the Bosnian Muslims through an organization called the American Task Force for Bosnia. Whenever someone mentioned the Iran-Bosnia link-up, they went ballistic. Ironically, they felt no stigma at supporting the Mujahedin fighters, whereas Iran was clearly off limits.*

Despite the efforts of these Muslim activists, opposing the arms deliveries by Iran was standing U.S. policy. In September 1992, the Bush administration received the first intelligence reports of an Iran Air cargo jet landing in Croatia with a shipment of arms for the Bosnian Muslims. "We raised hell," said Secretary of State Lawrence Eagleburger. U.S. protests to Croatia succeeded in shutting it down.

As a candidate for president, Bill Clinton had promised to reverse that policy. But when he dispatched Secretary of State Warren Christopher to Europe in 1993 to win support for lifting the arms embargo, Christopher was given the cold shoulder. In fact, the French were arming the Serbs, and the Germans were backing the Croatians. None of the Europeans wanted to see the Bosnian Muslims armed and able to defend themselves. At best, they hoped the United States would agree to spearhead a UN peacekeeping force that would cover their tracks.

In April 1994 the European division chief at the CIA Directorate of Operations received a cable from the CIA station chief in Zagreb, asking Langley for guidance on a peculiar situation. The U.S. ambassador to Croatia, Peter Galbraith, had summoned the station chief to his office, asking for assistance in convincing the Croatian government that it was U.S. policy to wink and nod at the Iranian arms shipments to the Muslims. The station chief replied that he couldn't take any action unless a presidential finding authorized him to do so, and Galbraith went away. Disturbed by the encounter, the station chief reported the contact to headquarters and asked for guidance.

As he reread the memo, Woolsey felt the station chief had acted appropriately, but he wanted more information. First, he called National Security Adviser Tony Lake, asking him if such a finding had been signed by the president without his knowledge. Lake said no. Then he called Secretary of State Warren Christopher and asked if he was aware of what Galbraith was doing. Christopher said no. Finally he called Deputy Secretary of

*They tried to get the House Republican Task Force on Terrorism and Unconventional Warfare to fire research director Yossef Bodansky after he issued a report detailing Iranian cooperation with the Bosnian Muslims in 1992. When that failed, prominent members of the task force who were close to Saffuri and Alamoudi resigned, including deputy task force chairman Dana Rohrabacher (R-Calif.). Alamoudi is now serving a life sentence in a U.S. federal pen on terrorism-related charges.

State Strobe Talbott, whom Christopher said was the point man on Bosnia. Talbott fudged. "Galbraith has no instructions," he told the Senate Select Intelligence Committee, in closed-door hearings on these exchanges. "If he's doing more than that, he should stand down."

But in fact it was a lie. There *was* a secret policy to allow the Iranians to arm the Bosnian Muslims. It had been approved by Tony Lake at the White House as part of a larger initiative to open Iran to U.S. businesses. Talbott was the point man at State. Galbraith had promised them he could communicate the "green light" to Croatian president Franjo Tudjman "without any fingerprints." As a former senior editor of *Time* magazine, Talbott had lived through the Iran-Contra scandal and appreciated the dangers of leaving behind evidence that could be discovered by congressional or media investigators if things went wrong. He insisted that only verbal orders be transmitted to Galbraith in the field.

As Woolsey raised questions, the Intelligence Oversight Board launched an official investigation to determine whether U.S. laws governing covert action had been breached. If the administration wanted to arm the Bosnians covertly, there was an entire branch of the government that had been set up to do that type of thing. The proper procedure was for the president to sign a covert-action finding, and for the director of Central Intelligence to brief it to the congressional oversight committees. Then the CIA could get down to the business of secretly moving the weapons. But that never happened. The Clinton people apparently trusted the Iranians more than they trusted the American political system and used the Iranians to implement their secret policy. Woolsey felt he had been rolled once again.

President Clinton's disdain for his CIA director and for the U.S. intelligence community was legendary. Fifteen minutes before the president-elect announced Woolsey's nomination in December 1992, Press Secretary Dee Dee Myers came up to him in Little Rock. "Admiral, I didn't know you served in the Bush administration as well," she said. Woolsey informed her that he was not an admiral. In fact, he'd never gotten above captain in the army. "Whoops, we'd better change the press release," she said. Woolsey later quipped that someone in the Clinton personnel office must have thought they were reappointing retired Admiral Stansfield Turner, a man held in derision by Agency old-timers after he gutted the CIA operations directorate under Jimmy Carter. In the fall of 1994, when someone crashed a single-engine Cessna into the White House lawn, jokes circulated that it was Woolsey trying to get an appointment with the president. During his entire tenure, he had just two face-to-face meetings with Clinton, outside of the regular NSC meetings. "I didn't have a bad relationship with the president. I just didn't have one at all," Woolsey said.

Neither Woolsey nor his station chief was kept informed when the "green light" was delivered by Galbraith and U.S. negotiator Charles Redman to Croatian president Franjo Tudjman on April 29, 1994. But within days Iranian arms began to flow, and that was what caught Woolsey's attention.

Not long afterward, the Iranians began sending a different sort of "adviser" to the Bosnian Muslims, and the CIA station chief nervously reported their activities back to headquarters. The new arrivals included MOIS officers and members of the Revolutionary Guards' "Qods Force," the overseas action arm responsible for terrorist attacks and assassinations. "We saw the Iranians equipped with all sorts of sophisticated electronic eavesdropping equipment, casing out U.S. military positions in the region," a highly placed U.S. intelligence source told me. The United States already had troops in Macedonia and elsewhere in the former Yugoslavia, as part of a UN-led peacekeeping force, and feared they were about to become targets of Iranian terrorists.

"The Administration's Iranian green-light policy gave Iran an unprecedented foothold in Europe and has recklessly endangered American lives and U.S. strategic interests," a House select subcommittee investigating the covert policy concluded. "Iranian Revolutionary Guards accompanied Iranian weapons into Bosnia and soon were integrated in the Bosnian military structure from top to bottom as well as operating in independent units throughout Bosnia. The Iranian intelligence service [VEVAK] ran wild through the area developing intelligence networks, setting up terrorist support systems, recruiting terrorist 'sleeper' agents and agents of influence, and insinuating itself with the Bosnian political leadership to a remarkable degree. The Iranians effectively annexed large portions of the Bosnian security apparatus [known as the Agency for Information and Documentation (AID)] to act as their intelligence and terrorist surrogates. This extended to the point of jointly planning terrorist activities. The Iranian embassy became the largest in Bosnia and its officers were given unparalleled privileges and access at every level of the Bosnian government."[1]

Woolsey resigned in disgust in January 1995, frozen out by the White House. He was unhappy about the cavalier attitude the administration demonstrated toward the intelligence community and did not want to become the fall guy for failed backdoor deals with rogue states such as Iran to which he had not been privy and of which he did not approve. It was bad policy to allow the Iranians into Bosnia, and it would ultimately come around to bite us, he felt. But he never really knew how far the secret overture had gone. The CIA had been cut out of the loop.

In February 1995, NATO troops raided a "terrorist training school" where they arrested eight Bosnians and three Iranian Pasdaran officers, who invoked diplomatic immunity and were allowed to fly back to Iran. Items seized in the raid included "bomb devices within shampoo bottles and children's toys and a training video showing how to ambush a car on an open highway and to kill its occupants," the House select subcommittee report found. The secret overture to Iran backfired so dramatically that the U.S. had to evacuate key operatives, diplomats, and family members from the U.S. embassy in Zagreb in order to reduce the number of targets available to Iranian terrorist teams who were shadowing them.

When the neighborhood got rough, President Clinton's response was to abandon the streets to the thugs.

GANJI AND THE CIA

Dr. Manoucher Ganji was unaware of the secret negotiations between emissaries of the Clinton White House, directed by National Security Adviser Tony Lake, and the mullahs in Tehran. But in February 1994, just two months before Lake gave the green light to allow Iran to arm the Bosnian Muslims, Ganji received an envoy in Paris from Washington, D.C., who delivered a curious message. The visitor was a senior U.S. government official deeply involved with Ganji's program, who had become a trusted friend. Along with a young deputy and a robust French government security detail, they dined at a famous restaurant in the Bois de Boulogne, then went for a walk after dinner along the lake.

Manoucher, he said finally, why don't you think about other sources of funding? What you've done so far has been magnificent. No one doubts your courage or what you've accomplished. We could help you. What do you say?

The younger deputy turned to his boss. Why are you telling him this?

I've got to be honest with him, the older man said. This administration isn't serious about this operation, and people are getting killed.

As they paced around the leaf-speckled water on the chilly night, Ganji drifted away. He thought of men such as Hamid Amid-Ansari, a patriot with a wife and children in his early forties, who'd lost his life when regime intelligence agents found him in possession with one of Ganji's secret transmitters inside Iran. He thought of his closest friend, Cyrus Elahi, gunned down in front of his Paris apartment by an MOIS killer. He thought of Abbas Gholitzadeh, kidnapped by Turkish Islamists and turned over to an Iranian hit team, who murdered him and left his mutilated body by the side of a road to rot. He thought of Attaollah Bay-Ahmadi, head of Flag of Freedom military operations, who was tracked down by regime killers and murdered in his room in the Hotel Astoria just hours after arriving in Dubai on a mission to establish contact with an opposition network inside Iran. He thought of the eighty or so other top members of his organization who had been arrested inside Iran and never heard of again.

My God, what is going to happen to all of them? Ganji wondered. Has all of this been in vain?

Ganji's relationship with his American backers had been rocky for several years. At one point toward the end of the Bush administration, when National Security Adviser General Brent Scowcroft was considering a new overture toward Iran, the CIA considered dropping the program altogether. "Their guys were getting killed," a former operations officer who worked with Ganji said. "Our support was mainly lip service, so you had to wonder if it was worth it for what they accomplished. Paris was crawling with MOIS assassins. My guys were also at risk, just meeting with him in Paris. Compared to what we did with the Soviets, this was a halfhearted effort."

The motto among these Paris-based officers backstopping Ganji's operation tells it all. "No risk was too small to avoid," the former operations officer said.

As Washington cooled, Tehran raged and began gunning for Ganji more seriously than ever. On March 16, 1993, Supreme Leader Ali Khamenei issued a fatwa, or religious ruling, condemning Ganji to death and ordering Iranian hit teams to murder him. Ganji obtained a copy and gave it to *Paris Match*, along with a dramatic inside glimpse into the life of a stalked man who was working day and night to bring freedom to his country. "When Dr. Ganji wants to go to a restaurant, he takes his armored car and is escorted by six French policeman, who eat at two adjoining tables," *Match* wrote breathlessly. The seven-page feature story called him "the most hunted man in France."

A prime-time French television magazine ran an hour-long documentary on Ganji and his operation. They showed video footage of the normally dapper Ganji being taught by French special forces trainers to jump off a bridge outside of Paris and rappel 25 meters to the ground below. They showed him on the shooting range and practicing how to escape from his fifth-floor studio apartment using a rope. It was serious stuff. And the risks were very real.

When the decision finally came to defund Ganji's operation—which cost U.S. taxpayers less than $2 million a year—Ganji had already lined up financial support from another government. He was extremely proud of his success. Unlike many opposition groups, he had not turned to Iran's traditional enemy—Saddam Hussein's Iraq—nor had he gone to Israel. When the CIA and his supporters in Congress learned of his feat, they were amazed. Word quickly reached the State Department, and U.S. diplomats took Ganji's new foreign backers aside, urging them to sever the relationship. It was Washington politics at its worst.

Putting an end to the only serious CIA operation designed to undermine the clerical regime in Tehran was a political decision, made at the highest levels of government, aimed at encouraging the mullahs in Tehran to cut a deal. People died as a result.

"It wasn't because of the budget; it was much more fundamental," a former operations officer told me. "We couldn't go beyond what our government was prepared to do, and there was no use leading people into false expectations and hopes that we were not going to be able to fulfill." It simply wasn't U.S. policy to overthrow the government of Iran, despite what Ganji hoped and Tehran thought and feared. "Keep the bed warm, keep your hand in—whatever cliché you want to use—but that was it. Nobody was prepared to invade Iran or fly C-130s full of exiles into the country."

Previously, Ganji and his people had been working on the fringes of what U.S. policy makers were going to tolerate. But with the Bosnia green-light policy, that had changed dramatically. "We couldn't ask them to commit to things that were going to endanger their lives that we knew were not going to be supported and backed up by Washington," the former operations officer said.

Ganji returned to Dallas in July 1995, to visit his wife, who was dying of cancer. He felt guilty having been away so often, but as always, Soroya consoled him. You have done the right thing, she said. Without this, our children would have no future.

While he was in Dallas, a senior U.S. government official flew from Washington to meet him. The broadcasting operations are being closed down effective September 30, 1995, he said. But we want you to remain in Paris as head of the Flag of Freedom organization. You're a brave man and we respect what you have done and the risks you have taken. We want to show that the flag is still flying. The United States was willing to give him

$28,000 per month—no strings attached—as long as he remained in Paris and disbanded the organization.

Ganji shook his head in disgust. I can't do anything real with that, he said. This flag has been taken down.

Ganji requested a final meeting with the director of Central Intelligence—at that time, John Deutsch. When he was ushered into the executive suite on the seventh floor of CIA headquarters on August 14, 1995, Deutsch was unavailable to see him. Instead he was greeted by deputy director George Tenet and the head of Middle East operations.

I've come to thank the United States of America for all you have done for the cause of freedom in Iran, Ganji said. History will remember this. And you will see the results.

The head of the Middle East operations directorate told Tenet what Ganji had been doing. It had been an honor for the Agency to work with him. Now, of course, Dr. Ganji was moving on. His wife was ill, and he wanted to devote more time to her. Although the words weren't spoken, the CIA men made clear they wanted to keep Ganji on the reservation, keep him from talking, and were willing to pay hard cash to gain that favor. Tenet sat back in the sofa, waiting for Ganji to name his price.

Ganji took a long sip of coffee and let the silence thicken across the coffee table. I haven't come here to ask for anything, he said finally. I have come to say thank you, that's all. Tenet was nonplussed.

When he got back to Paris, Ganji announced he was forming a new group, the Organization for Human Rights and Fundamental Freedoms for Iran (OHRFFI), and held a three-day conference in the Paris suburb of Barbizon to strategize with the top members of his organization, some forty of whom attended. The emphasis from now on was on rallying opposition forces in the struggle against the Tehran regime, he announced. Losing the CIA money was also a liberation, since he was no longer bound by the restrictions barring activity inside the United States.

From being a hands-on leader running agents into a hostile country, Ganji was about to become a politician.

LUBRANI CROSSES SWORDS

Uri Lubrani was a living legend. A warrior diplomat, intelligence operative, and hard-nosed policy driver for Labor and Likud governments alike, Lubrani was no pink-skinned warrior when he came to Washington in November 1994 to openly join battle with the Clinton administration over Iran.

In the late 1960s he had been Israel's ambassador to Ethiopia, at a time when the young Jewish state had few friends around the world. He was stunned to learn about the existence of a tribe of "black Jews," called Falasha, who had lived quietly at the headwaters of the Nile for perhaps as long as three thousand years. When a revolutionary Communist junta threatened to wipe them out twenty-five years later, Lubrani helped organization "Operation Solomon," the top-secret airlift deep in the desert that brought the entire Falasha community to Israel.

After Ethiopia, Lubrani was posted to Uganda under Idi Amin, and quietly built up security cooperation between the two countries before Amin went off on his killing spree. In part, it was Lubrani's detailed knowledge of the African despot and his security establishment that allowed Israeli commandos led by Jonathan Netanyahu to rescue the passengers of an El Al airliner hijacked to Entebbe airport in 1976.

During the mid-1970s, Lubrani was posted to Iran as Israel's unofficial ambassador. It was the heyday of the shah's reign. But as Lubrani deepened his contacts within the shah's court and the military, he began to hear disturbing rumblings of discontent. The kicker, he told me, was a dinner party he attended at the home of a top adviser to the shah in late 1977.

The shah had jetted down to the private beach resort he had built for his court on Kish Island in the Persian Gulf. With the shah safely out of town, his top advisers began talking out of school, mocking his gestures, his habits, his every decision. "It wasn't just the criticism; it was the tone of the criticism," Lubrani said. "It was personal. It was vicious. These were his top advisers, people who, whenever I saw them at court, were falling all over themselves to praise His Imperial Majesty. I realized at that moment that they no longer feared him, and that if things went bad, they wouldn't lift a finger to defend him."

Just as President Jimmy Carter flew to Tehran in December 1977 and called the shah's Iran an "island of stability," Lubrani sent a cable back to the Foreign Ministry in Tel Aviv predicting the imminent demise of the shah's regime. It is a tribute to his political bosses that they heeded his warning and began making contact with the entourage of a dissident cleric named Ruhollah Khomeini, who had set up shop in a Paris suburb. Those contacts helped Lubrani negotiate the escape of nearly three-quarters of Iran's 80,000-strong Jewish population during the early months of Khomeini's reign.

As word of Lubrani's famous Tehran cable spread within diplomatic circles after the revolution, so did his reputation for analytical wizardry grow.

But Lubrani was not just a desk warrior. In 1983 the Defense Ministry put him in charge of its Lebanon-Syria desk, and for the next two years, as Israel took daily losses from suicide bombers and a newly minted militia called Hezbollah, he combed the Lebanese countryside and mountain passes by helicopter and car, and on foot. Once, during the winter of 1984, he was visiting a Christian militia leader in the mountains outside of Zahle in central Lebanon when a sudden snowstorm stranded him and a Lebanese-born aide, Jacques Neriah, for several days. Unlike other Israeli officials, who had locked Israel into an alliance with the Christian Maronites, Lubrani sought broader contacts and periodically courted a variety of Muslim leaders, at times playing them off one another.

Playing Lebanon is like playing the piano, he liked to say. You've got to learn to use all the keys.

He watched with alarm as Iran's Revolutionary Guards Corps built up forces in Baalbek, in Lebanon's Bekaa Valley, and trained Hezbollah operatives in the use of explosives, detonators, and bomb-making electronics. By the time he came to Washington in November 1994, Iran was providing some $60 million to $70 million per year to Hezbollah—small beer for the Iranians, but a deadly threat to Israel. They had taken Israeli soldiers and a downed air force navigator named Ron Arad hostage. In retaliation, Lubrani ordered a crack Israeli commando to kidnap a prominent Hezbollah kingpin in south Lebanon named Sheikh Abdul Karim Obeid and to bring him to Israel. When negotiations for a prisoner exchange collapsed, he ordered the kidnapping of the lead kidnapper, Mustafa Dirani. Dirani and his ilk were the dregs of humanity, who would sell their own children for the right price. Lubrani had no second thoughts in ordering his capture. Israel eventually got most of their soldiers back, but the pilot Ron Arad is still missing. Lubrani today believes he is in Iran.

Lubrani and other Israeli policy makers were worried that the Clinton administration had "gone soft" on Iran, despite the declared policy of "dual containment" that, in theory, sought to restrain Iran's bad behavior. As Lubrani and his team of Iran-watchers saw it, the only restraint they saw was coming from Washington.

In Bosnia, Iran's Revolutionary Guards were busily spending money and expanding their presence, as the United States calmly looked on.

In Argentina, the Pasdaran sent their top terrorist operative, Imad Mugniyeh, to lead the operational commando that blew up the AMIA Jewish Community Center in Buenos Aires in July 1994.

The murderous truck-bombing killed eighty-six Jews and devastated the Jewish community for years. Investigative judge Juan José Galeano fingered Iran for the bombing and recommended the expulsion of Iran's ambassador to Argentina and three other Iranian diplomats whom he believed were top Pasdaran officers. By the time warrants were issued for their expulsion, however, all four had fled the country. So had Mugniyeh and ninety-three Iranian students who had not been named in the investigation.

As Galeano told me later, the White House refused an appeal from the FBI to send forensic teams to Argentina to help with the investigation. The Clinton people simply didn't want to hear that Iran could be involved, Galeano said.

Rafsanjani was not housebroken, despite the friendly overtures he was making to U.S. oil companies, inviting them to invest in Iran. American companies, led by Exxon and Coastal, had become the largest purchasers of Iranian oil, accounting for fully 25 percent of all Iranian oil exports. This had thrown an economic lifeline to the regime, which was struggling under a mountain of debt, most of it to European suppliers. In the meantime, Iran was turning increasingly for supplies of hard-to-get nuclear and missile production gear to countries in Asia where the U.S. intelligence community found it difficult to operate. Lubrani had decided to toss his hat into the ring, to go public with Israel's concerns, even if it meant a public spat with the Clinton administration.

Iran had become the capital of an Islamic Comintern, he told a forum at a Washington think tank. Their first priority was to obtain nuclear and other WMD capabilities, and America's policy of "dual containment" had achieved next to nothing when it came to curbing their excesses. There were no moderates within the regime, and no amount of inducements would get them to change their behavior. "How can you change a regime that takes its cue from God?" he said.

By not cracking down, the United States was only encouraging Iran to continue its worst behavior. "Let me make it absolutely clear," Lubrani said. "The Iranis have no doubt in their mind that when some of the largest U.S. companies seek a working or trading relationship with Iran, even if this is done indirectly, it cannot be done without the knowledge and explicit approval and authorization by the highest quarters in Washington. This is so because it would be unthinkable to an Irani mind, which has no understanding of the inner workings of a democracy, that such activities are at all possible without being sanctioned from above."

The red light/green light approach had not been lost on the Iranians themselves. Ali Sabzalian headed the Iranian Interest Section in Washington before moving to New York at the beginning of the Clinton administration to launch the Center for Iranian Trade and Development. As its name suggests, CITAD aimed to promote U.S. trade and investment in Iran. Sabzalian dismissed the harsh U.S. rhetoric against Tehran as mere politics intended "for public consumption." His group was actively canvassing U.S. companies who wanted to do business in Iran.

"We want to trade with the U.S. and they want to do business with us." Sabzalian's Center issued a press release on December 2, noting that "U.S. trade figures do not include an estimated tens of millions of dollars in U.S.-made goods purchased by Iran from third countries." Iranian diversion of U.S. products through third countries was becoming a prime concern to government investigators.

Facing Lubrani was Martin Indyk, the coauthor with National Securitiy Adviser Anthony Lake, of the administration's dual-containment strategy. An Australian Jew who had led a prominent Washington think tank before he was tapped to spearhead the Clinton administration's Middle East policy in 1993, Indyk had no patience for contrary views. He stuck out his square jaw and turned on Lubrani with icy contempt.

"The United States is not seeking the overthrow of the regime in Tehran; you are," he said. A nearly audible gasp erupted from the well-heeled audience of policy wonks, pundits, and scholars. The administration had made tough decisions on Iran and was sending a clear message to its partners in Europe and elsewhere. Early on, the U.S. decided to forgo a lucrative $3 billion to $5 billion contract to sell Boeing airliners to Iran, out of concern this could enhance Iran's military capabilities. "Whatever Iran is able to purchase from us today is a net benefit to the U.S.," he said. "Nothing strategic is going out. If Iran wants to buy U.S. goods, why not? It merely weakens them economically."

To the astonishment of a senior U.S. intelligence analyst who attended the forum, Indyk then claimed financial difficulties caused by U.S. pressure on Iran's creditors had caused Iran to suspend cooperation with North Korea on the No-Dong missile program earlier that year. "Our policies have had the effect of making Iran less capable today of creating problems for the United States than before," he said.

Without calling Indyk a bald-faced liar, the analyst turned to me later and remarked that the U.S. had satellite photographs taken just weeks earlier, in October 1994, that showed No-Dong missiles being assembled at a site located 25 miles north of Isfahan. The Iranians were gearing up for full-scale production and deployment of a No-Dong equivalent missile, he said. The only thing that had changed recently was the schedule, which slowed somewhat because Iran was behind in its payments to North Korea.

Lubrani realized that he had crossed a red line. The battle was now engaged. Over the next six months he became a frequent traveler to Washington, New York, and Los Angeles. He met with journalists, members of Congress, Jewish leaders, and think-tankers, calling in every chit he had accumulated in his long career.

Iran's mullahs were determined to get the bomb, and only the United States could stop them. They had to persuade the Clinton White House to change course on Iran before it was too late.

THE $3 MILLION SUITCASE

Buhary Seyed Abu Tahir was something of a playboy. The son of a Sri Lankan businessman who lived in Dubai, the handsome young Tahir drove a Rolls-Royce and wore well-cut European suits, and jetted around the world to make deals. Despite the trappings of Western decadence, he worked hard for his money. When his father died in 1985, the young Tahir inherited his SMB Group and traveled to Pakistan to sell air-conditioning equipment. There he met up with Pakistani industrialist Abdul Qadeer Khan. It was the beginning of a beautiful friendship.

The A. Q. Khan Research Laboratories in Rawalpindi were expanding. Dr. Khan needed much more than just air conditioners. The first phase of the secret uranium enrichment plant he had built for the Pakistani government had been completed and now he was ready for other challenges. But after all the publicity he had received as father of the Islamic bomb—and especially with criminal charges filed against him in Europe—Dr. Khan was no longer free to travel as he liked. Indeed, he liked to tell his supporters, "I am now one of the most wanted scientists in the world." B. S. A. Tahir was just the type of enterprising young contact he needed, who fit perfectly into Dr. Khan's far-flung network of middlemen, technology brokers, and shadowy financiers. The Sri Lankan from Dubai was equally at home in Europe, Asia, or the Middle East.

Dr. Khan had convinced his master's at Pakistan's general staff to let him develop new conventional weapons systems for export. There was no reason to allow Europe and America to dominate the arms markets in the Arab and Islamic world, he argued. Pakistan had developed many new capabilities and was able to compete with the best. Although many of his "new" weapons appeared to be knockoffs of Chinese or North Korean designs (his Baktar Shikan antitank missile was cloned from the Chinese Red Arrow), he was also selling "special" equipment to select customers.

Sometimes the eagerness of Dr. Khan to compete on the world market took on comic overtones. When I visited his stand at the International Defense Exhibition in Abu Dhabi in 1997, a salesman handed me a stout gray shopping bag full of trinkets emblazoned with Dr. Khan's name and the Pakistani government seal. (I still have the bag hanging on my office wall.) The Pakistani government seal also appeared prominently on brochures for the defense products the A. Q. Khan Research laboratories were offering for export.

The commingling of government with his private business network was a sleight-of-hand he shared with his friend and financial backer Agha Hasan Abedi, the elusive chairman of the Bank of Credit and Commerce International (BCCI). Shortly before the spectacular crash of BCCI in 1991, Abedi very publicly donated 1.5 billion rupees (around $25 million) to Dr. Khan to build a new nuclear research center in the wilds of the Northwest Frontier province bordering the Afghan terrorist training camps of Osama bin Laden.[2] Today the Pakistani government of Defense Chief General Pervez Musharraf claims that Dr. Khan was operating on his own. But at the time he had the backing of Musharraf's predecessors, including General Aslam Beg and General Hamid Gul, powerful supporters of bin Laden's jihadis and proponents of sharing Pakistan's nuclear technologies with rogue states, including Iran and North Korea.

One place Dr. Khan could still visit unmolested was Dubai, where the Dubai government maintained a lavish apartment as a guesthouse for his personal and business use. In late 1994 he called on his young friend, asking for help. Tahir had just turned thirty-five years old. Dr. Khan had a very special transport he needed for Tahir to arrange through his company. Pakistan had decided to upgrade some of his factories, so he had surplus equipment for sale. Dr. Khan had found a buyer in Iran. It wasn't a huge order, he said, but he needed Tahir to organize the transhipment of two containers of used parts on board a merchant ship owned by a company in Iran. Included in the shipment were five hundred aluminum centrifuge rotors of the P1 design, and the critical maraging steel bellows that connected them. These parts were so hard to make, and required such sophisticated technology, even Japan reportedly had been unable to manufacture them. But the ever-resourceful Dr. Khan had obtained classified blueprints to make the bellows, which he had jobbed out to a manufacturer in Switzerland.

The Iranians also felt comfortable doing business in Dubai, whose thriving port was a smuggler's paradise. On a clear day, if you drive down to the town of Sash on the northern tip of the Arabian peninsula facing the

Persian Gulf, you can make out the low, dark shadows of the Iranian mainland across the leaden Strait of Hormuz. Iran is a brooding presence in the lives of the Emirates. Smugglers and traders in speedboats and dhows, the ancient cargo vessels whose sails clog the Dubai creek, regularly ply the short crossing. A scant 30 miles of water separate the two countries.

Dr. Khan knew that Tahir and his local company could simply melt into the woodwork in Dubai, whereas his own company's activities were being tracked by the U.S. Customs office that the UAE government had been forced to accept. Dubai was the trading capital of the entire Middle East. Although it manufactured little, the United Arab Emirates was a major re-exporter of goods imported from other countries, including the United States. It was one of the dirty secrets of the trade, known to the U.S. government and to U.S. companies. Oilfield equipment manufacturers, computer makers, high-technology firms, whatever: if you can't sell to Iran, sell to Dubai and your local agent will handle the rest. According to the UAE's own Central Bank, 36 percent of all re-export trade from the UAE went to Iran in 1994. It was a billion-dollar-per-year business.

Just down the coast from Dubai was the Djebel Ali Free Trade Zone, which was packed with Iranian offshore companies that traded regularly with Dubai. The Iranian government's Mostazafan and Janbazan Foundation (also known as the Foundation of the Oppressed, or the Bonyad-e Mostazafan va Janbazan) maintained a small office suite at Djebel Ali. Running it was an itinerant Iranian named Ali Sobhani—possibly the same Sobhani who was indicted in the United States in 1988 on WMD-related charges and who reportedly contacted Leybold in Germany for key uranium enrichment equipment in 1991. Sobhani rarely used the office, which cost the foundation an annual rent of just $9,500. Neighbors I spoke with shortly after Dr. Khan made this shipment told me that Sobhani showed up only when he had a major deal to close. "We will see him here day in and day out for some weeks, then he will disappear for weeks on end," one merchant said. "They never mix with non-Iranians. They are very secretive." The Iranian government used the foundation for high-tech procurement and to funnel money to Iran's secret overseas operations.

By the time Dr. Khan's shipment reached Iran in early 1995, the Iranians had been buying centrifuge components and production equipment through the network in Europe for almost a decade. In 1991, Sharif University placed an order for ring magnets with the Austrian firm Triebacher, according to a European intelligence service, the same company that had supplied the specially designed magnets to Iraq. As the IAEA discovered later, Dr. Khan sold Iran the first set of centrifuge blueprints in 1987. Iran installed its imports in a workshop at Amir Kabir University in Tehran, later moving them to a "watch factory" to prevent discovery.

But they purchased most of the equipment in Germany, where the government had been unable—or unwilling—to crack down on the high-technology trade. By the time Dr. Khan's latest shipment arrived, Iran had purchased large quantities of high-strength aluminum as well as flow-forming machines, so it could produce the centrifuge rotors on its own. Now it was hoping to upgrade those machines using more exotic maraging steel 360, a lightweight, high-tensile material whose export was closely controlled. They had also purchased electron beam welders, balancing machines, numerically controlled lathes, and masses of vacuum pumps and special piping to handle the flow of uranium hexafluoride into the cascade, says David Albright, a former UN arms inspector who has been tracking Iran's programs for over a decade for the Institute for Science and International Security in Washington, D.C.

Albright estimates that a clandestine Iranian cascade built with Dr. Khan's components could have produced somewhere between 6 and 10 kilograms of weapons-grade uranium per year. That would have given Iran enough fissile material for its first domestically produced bomb by 1997—*if* all went as planned. But the P1 design was deeply flawed, Albright and other scientists contend. U.S. intelligence analysts joked that the waste heaps around the Pakistani enrichment plant in Kahuta were piled high with rejects—P1 centrifuge tubes that had exploded when spun up to high speed, or cracked from various production defects. Making centrifuges and balancing the rotors so they could spin at more than 1,000 revolutions per second without wobbling was a black art.

To this day, no one knows with certainty whether Iran managed to get the Khan centrifuges working. If they did, Iran could have made enough fissile material by the time serious IAEA inspections began in 2003 to produce four or five nuclear weapons. If they had used 4 percent uranium as feedstock, they could have between twenty and twenty-five bombs today.[3]

The delivery of Dr. Khan's centrifuges in 1995 "was the type of thing that would make your hair stand up on your head," a former U.S. government official who tracked Iran's black-market procurement told me. It was important "because it shows beyond any doubt that the designs of the [Iranian] program were serious."

But it is not clear whether the Clinton administration ever saw it. "We didn't see procurement for a large-scale enrichment program in the 1980s and the 1990s," says Gary Samore, who tracked proliferation and the black market at the State Department and, starting in 1997, at the National Security Council under Sandy Berger. "We saw bits and pieces, reports of interest in centrifuges and lasers. But we never had a comprehensive understanding of their procurement system."

Dr. Khan's subterfuge of having B. S. A. Tahir handle the shipments through his UAE company had apparently worked. Not long after the containers with the Pakistani centrifuges arrived at the Iranian port of Bandar Abbas, an Iranian government emissary showed up at Dr. Khan's guesthouse in Dubai, carrying two suitcases that he handed over to Tahir. Inside was the equivalent of $3 million in UAE dirhams for Tahir and his partner, Dr. Khan.

Not bad for a few days' work, Tahir thought.

14

THE PARTNERS

It is true that the contract does contain components of civilian and military nuclear energy. . . . Now we have agreed to separate those two.

—Russian president Boris Yeltsin, May 10, 1995, commenting on a new Russian-Iranian nuclear cooperation agreement

The Indonesian lounge on the second floor of UN headquarters in New York was flooded with sunlight and bodyguards when Bob Einhorn sat down for coffee with his counterpart from the Russian Foreign Ministry. The two men had agreed to meet in the gaudy delegates' lounge with its brightly colored wall hangings, since it was normally closed to the press. Einhorn was the top arms-control specialist at the State Department, a career diplomat, not a political appointee. He could tell by the relaxed manner of his counterpart that the Russian didn't have a clue what he was about to spring on him. It was the type of moment that comes rarely, and Einhorn savored the pleasure, gently leading his quarry into the trap.

We are very concerned about the nuclear cooperation agreement Minatom has signed with the government of Iran, he began. Einhorn was referring to the $800 million deal signed in Tehran on January 8, 1995, by the visiting Russian minister of atomic energy, Viktor Mikhailov. Thrilled that they had negotiated a bargain-basement price and eager to thumb their noses at the Germans, who had caved in to American pressure not to finish the heavily damaged plants, the Iranians had announced the deal to complete the first reactor at the Busheir nuclear power complex even before the final protocol was actually signed.

Einhorn used all the customary diplo-speak to lay out his case. The United States has worked hard to persuade other governments not to provide precisely this technology to Iran. We have worked not only with Germany, but with Siemens licensees in Argentina, Spain, and Sweden, because we believe the reactor project could serve as a front for clandestine nuclear weapons procurement and training, he said. The United States was disappointed that Russia had leapt into the breach. We hope that your government will reconsider.

The words were clear but familiar. Like the body language, they were designed to reassure his counterpart, to convey the impression that none of this was personal. They were both doing their jobs and would have to report back to their bosses. After all, it's what they did for a living.

My government will uphold all its commitments under the Nonproliferation Treaty, the Russian replied. I can assure you that there is nothing in this contract that will be of concern to America, unless of course your intention is to prevent any kind of technical cooperation between Russia and Iran.

Well, actually . . . Einhorn replied. He made a show of shuffling through papers in the black leatherbound folder, crested with a gold eagle, on his lap. I have something I'd like you to look at.

He passed the document to the Russian and watched him carefully. This is going to be a treat, he thought. It began when the Russian noticed that the document was not in English, but in Cyrillic letters. That caused him to raise his eyebrows. Einhorn allowed him a minute to leaf through the many pages of text, watching as his lips pursed and the furrows in his brow deepened.

I think you might want to turn to the last page, Einhorn said finally. Recognize the signature?

The Russian sighed, shaking his head. I do indeed. I won't ask you how you got this—you probably don't know. (That was true.) But I can tell you that this is the first time I've heard anything about this. Nobody at my ministry is aware of this.

I'm sure that's right, Einhorn replied. But I'd appreciate it if you would express our concern to Moscow.

I cannot believe President Yeltsin is aware of this, the Russian said. You know, Minatom has become almost a government unto itself. This will help us cut them down to size. I thank you.

The document Einhorn passed to the Russian was a secret protocol attached to the reactor contract signed in Tehran. According to my sources, it was delivered to the CIA by a spectacular stroke of luck when a member of the Revolutionary Guards technical team sent to Moscow to pursue the follow-on negotations, Sardar Shafagh, walked into the U.S. embassy carrying a briefcase crammed with documents, and said he wanted to defect.

Getting the Revolutionary Guards brigadier general out of Moscow was no mean feat. Even when he was safely in the United States, the CIA was reluctant to show the actual document to the Russians, since it would confirm what they must by now suspect about the missing Iranian. But

Einhorn and his colleagues felt the secret protocol was such a critical piece of evidence, and so startling, that the benefits of releasing it far outweighed the costs. An English-language translation of the secret protocol made its way to the nonprofit Natural Resources Defense Council in Washington a few months later.

It's no wonder the Russian was surprised when he saw the actual text Viktor Mikhailov had signed in Tehran. The secret protocol baldly contradicted the reassurances of peaceful nuclear cooperation Mikhailov and the Iranians had uttered at the signing ceremony.

The Russians had agreed to supply Iran with a broad range of nuclear technologies, not just to install a 1,000-megawatt light-water power reactor at Busheir. The secret agreement stipulated that within three months the two parties would sign a contract to build a 30–50-megawatt research reactor that could be used to breed weapons-grade plutonium. By the end of March 1995 they were to finalize terms for the secret delivery of 2,000 tons of natural uranium to Iran, a sale that would greatly expedite Iranian enrichment plans. Minatom also agreed to provide assistance with uranium mining and to train Iranian nuclear technicians at Russian nuclear research centers. That worried the Americans, because they understood that exposure to Russia's top weapons design institutes could bring inestimable benefits to the Iranians. "The broader Iran's nuclear technology base," one U.S. official tracking the Russian-Iranian exchanges told me at the time, "the better chance the Iranians have of growing that key individual to a successful nuclear program: the weapons designer."

The Americans were also worried that expanding contacts with the Russian nuclear establishment through a broad-based official relationship would give the Iranians the opportunity to identify disgruntled Russian scientists and hire them on private contracts. "The Iranian Intelligence Ministry is orchestrating these attempts to procure nuclear materials, dual-use technology, and nuclear expertise," the official said, "and this is a worldwide effort. We are seeing a pattern of activity."

According to an August 1994 report by the BND, the German federal intelligence agency, fourteen nuclear scientists from former Soviet nuclear weapons plants had been working in Iran on private contracts since 1991. Now that number could expand exponentially, the Americans feared.

But by far the most worrisome thing to the United States was a pledge by Mikhailov to offer Iran a full-blown centrifuge enrichment plant, the same capability the Iranians had been trying to piece together themselves using A. Q. Khan's blueprints and a worldwide network of clandestine nuclear suppliers. Buying a centrifuge plant was an unmistakable sign of

Iran's nuclear intentions, the Americans believed. Even if Iran really did intend to build a nuclear power plant—which the Americans were not sure was the case—the Russians had agreed to supply the fuel. Iran had no need to spend billions more to develop its own enrichment capability. Building a centrifuge plant meant only one thing: Iran was after the bomb.

U.S. Ambassador Thomas Graham referred obliquely to the Russian deal at a January 27, 1995, news conference in New York during a meeting to prepare the five-year NPT review conference. "The United States believes that Iran has taken a decision to pursue a nuclear weapons option, even though they are a party to the Nuclear Non-Proliferation Treaty," he said.

Einhorn's Russian counterpart delivered the document and the stiffly worded message back to Foreign Minister Andrei Kozyrev. But instead of finding a diplomatic excuse for canceling the agreement with Iran, the Russians thumbed their noses at the United States.

Kozyrev's deputy, Georgy Mamedov, flew to Washington in mid-February 1995 to meet Deputy Secretary of State Strobe Talbott, Undersecretary Lynn Davis, Einhorn, and others. After telling the Americans that Russia had no intentions of canceling the deal, Mamedov flew to Tehran, where he delivered a similar message from his boss to Iranian Foreign Minister Velayati. "Kozyrev said in his message that certain powers, through their policies, were supporting injustice in the world and that the independent states would react because there was nothing more significant than national sovereignty and freedom," the Islamic Republic News Agency reported on February 25.

Clearly the United States had only one option left, Talbott and others argued after meeting Mamedov. Take it directly to the top. Engage the headman himself—that is, if Boris Yeltsin could be found sober.

THE IRANIAN AIRPORT . . . IN GERMANY!

In Germany, Iranian buying teams were following A. Q. Khan's procurement blueprint. They worked through lists of suppliers who had willingly sold Dr. Khan critical production machinery and components for Pakistan's uranium enrichment program more than a decade earlier. Without ever revealing their intentions, they bought vacuum equipment from one company, valves from another, specialized computerized numerical control equipment from a third, and so on. They were also purchasing advanced machine tools for missile manufacturing.

They brazenly used the official office of the Defense Industries Organization in Dusseldorf for many of these purchases. For years the Germans watched, but did nothing.

The Iranian purchases reached such high volume and intensity that two of Ayatollah Khomeini's former government ministers acquired a private airfield at Hartenholm, 35 miles north of Hamburg, to accommodate the traffic.

Mousa Khajer Habibollahi and his business partner, arms dealer Mehdi Kashani, purchased the airport for $6.5 million, doubling the price the previous owners had paid for it just a few years earlier. With a single 2,000-foot runway, Hartenholm was too small to accommodate commercial jets and had no control tower. It was useless for direct flights to Tehran. But its small size also kept it discreet. Under European regulations, planes weighing less than 7.5 metric tons (16,500 pounds) were not required to report their ultimate destinations. There were no passport or customs controls at Hartenholm.

By March 1995, German intelligence officials were telling reporters that the airport was being used by Iran as a transit point for military spare parts and dual-use technology purchased on the black market by Iranian agents in Austria, Germany, Poland, the Czech Republic, and elsewhere. The equipment was flown in on small planes from around Europe, then transferred to cargo ships in nearby Hamburg for the onward trip to Iran. Small consignments of critical equipment were flown directly from Hartenholm to Poland, where they were loaded onto Iran Air cargo jets. The Iranians were careful to break down the shipments into small, unrelated components to escape controls, just as Dr. Khan had done. The Germans claimed there was nothing they could do to stop it.

A former Oil Ministry engineer and foreign trade minister, the fifty-two-year-old Kashani had a rap sheet a mile long. U.S. Customs case files identified him as "a known diverter . . . dealing in Hawk missile parts, electronics parts, and munitions to Iran via Belgium." In March 1992, Spanish police arrested Kashani and five others for attempting to purchase Stinger missiles and radar gear. The arrest came after undercover U.S. Customs officers personally handed Hawk missile klystron tubes to Kashani in Spain, but Kashani was soon out on the streets again.

Kashani and Habibollahi had established a far-flung procurement network with companies in Britain, Spain, Ireland, Panama, France, and Germany. Their Darya Pey company had branches in Iran and throughout Europe, and at one point even did construction work through a subsidiary at the giant U.S. naval base at Diego Garcia in the Indian Ocean. To facilitate shipments, Kashani also purchased a small German airline, Nordair Hamburg GmbH, which he based at Hartenholm. It kept the business tight.

U.S. Customs officials I asked about the pair were not convinced that the German government was serious about cracking down on the arms and technology traffic. Even when an Iranian and a Dane were arrested at the airport in 1994 carrying illegal drugs, the Germans allowed the operation to continue. They pointed out that Chancellor Kohl's intelligence coordinator, Berndt Schmidbauer, had cultivated a close personal relationship with Iranian intelligence minister Ali Fallahian, officially inviting him to Germany in October 1993 despite Fallahian's personal involvement in the assassination of Iranian dissidents on German soil.*

When Kashani and Habibollahi were forced to sell Hartenholm after a series of news articles in March and April 1995 exposed their operation, they simply shifted their operations to a different airport.

At the Pentagon's Technology Security Administration, operations officer Mike Maloof was tracking the network. He had identified some two dozen German and Swiss suppliers who were feeding Iran's missile and nuclear programs. Along with his "techie," Jim Swanson, he plugged the information into a gigantic flow chart and took it over to the chief operations officer at the CIA's nonproliferation center, veteran operative Jim Pavitt.

Before Maloof even finished his presentation, Pavitt blew up. What do you think you're doing? he shouted. You're going to f—k us royally.

Maloof said he wanted to get the information scrubbed of classified sources and methods so he could present it officially to the Germans. They can stop some of this stuff from ever getting to Iran, he said.

No way I'm going to clear anything for the Germans, Pavitt said. Schmidbauer will just turn around and hand it over to MOIS. And then people are going to get killed.

THE CHINESE HEX PLANT

And then there was China. The U.S. intelligence community was beginning to pick up clear indicators that China was expanding nuclear cooperation

*Fallahian was so elated by the attention that he called a press conference at the Iranian embassy in Bonn on October 7, 1993, where he announced that Schmidbauer had pledged to provide Iran with sophisticated communications gear and other assistance. Schmidbauer was hauled before the German parliament the next day, and explained that in exchange for two personal computers—one for Rafsanjani, one for Fallahian—and a course in the history of the German intelligence service, Iran had pledged to forgo terrorist attacks on German soil.

with Iran well beyond the limits of purely civilian research and technology. Chinese nuclear technicians had been observed at the recently opened nuclear research center in Karaj, and were crawling all over Isfahan, where Rafsanjani had inaugurated a small Chinese research reactor the year before. They were delivering calutron enrichment devices—in "massive quantities," according to one intelligence official—similar to those used with success by Iraq. There was concern that Iran was using the calutrons as an alternate method of enrichment in a brand-new nuclear center in Bonab, in Iran's West Azerbaijan province. When ground was broken at Bonab on September 11, 1994, IAEO chief Reza Amrollahi claimed it was solely dedicated to isotope research for agricultural purposes. Iranian press accounts referred to it as a "cyclotron center." (The enrichment calutrons were frequently referred to as a form of cyclotron.) Since 1986 the city had been represented in the Majles by Seddiqi Bonabi, an AEOI physicist who specialized in laser enrichment.

Most troubling of all were indications picked up by the CIA that China and Iran were finalizing an agreement to build a uranium hexafluoride (UF6) plant in Isfahan, and that China recently had shipped UF6 to Iran. For years, the absence of a "hex plant" was considered the missing link in Iran's uranium enrichment program. They had the mines and a few milling plants that allowed them to transform the ore into yellowcake. At the far end of the fuel cycle, Western intelligence agencies had been detecting procurement efforts since the late 1980s of centrifuge parts and technology. But without an industrial-scale uranium conversion facility to produce the vital feedstock, there could be no significant enrichment. Now the CIA believed that was about to change.

In early April 1995, Einhorn passed scrubbed intelligence on the hex plant negotiations to a visiting Chinese foreign ministry official in Washington. As he had with the Russians, Einhorn made clear that the United States hoped China would refrain from making the sale. But the Chinese were even less cooperative than the Russians had been. They asked for more details. They wanted to know if the information was authentic.

Two years later, at a public forum in Washington well after the deal had become the centerpiece of extensive U.S.-Chinese wrangling, I asked Chinese foreign ministry arms control expert Dr. Wang Xiaoyu about the status of the deal with Iran. "Hex plant? What hex plant?" he said. "I am not familiar with that specific case. When was that?" The Chinese would repeat the same rote denial for years.

Secretary of State Warren Christopher decided to up the ante personally during a joint photo op with Chinese foreign minister Qian Qichen in

New York, on the fringes of another preparatory meeting for the NPT renewal conference. "Our position is one that Iran . . . is simply too dangerous with its intentions and its motives and its designs to justify nuclear cooperation of an allegedly peaceful character," Christopher said. "We think that cooperation and the techniques that would be developed there, the expertise that would be developed, the scientists [that] would be there, lend themselves to such great possibilities of misuse and abuse that we think that cooperation should not [be] begun."

Qian replied through an interpreter that any agreements China had with Iran had been placed under IAEA safeguards. It was a bald-faced lie, but that didn't stop Qian from hammering home his point. "There is no international law or international regulation or international agreement that prohibits such cooperation on the peaceful use of nuclear energy," he said.

It was the diplomatic equivalent of a middle-finger salute.

Over the next two years Einhorn and his NSC counterparts would make twenty trips to China in an effort to get the Chinese to back off from building the hex plant in Iran. The Chinese eventually agreed to cancel the deal as part of a comprehensive U.S.-China nuclear agreement signed in October 1997, in exchange for U.S. commercial reactor technology. The U.S. announced it as a great nonproliferation victory.

But it was already too late, and the U.S. negotiators knew it. "We knew by that point that the Chinese had already transferred drawings, blueprints, and design information to the Iranians," says Einhorn. "But our feeling was that if all foreign cooperation ceased, the Iranians might not be able to complete it, or at least, it would take a lot longer."

Wrong again.

MISSING THE TARGET

The deal with China to build a hex plant raised other questions as well. Didn't the construction of an industrial-scale facility mean that the Iranians had already built a pilot plant to master the various chemical processes it required?

Even more fundamentally, why buy a hex plant if you had no use for the product?

Didn't the fact that Iran was preparing to make a major cash investment to produce UF6 suggest that they already had—or were about to acquire—the centrifuges to enrich it? Ten years after the fact, the correct answer to these questions means the difference between a nuclear-armed Iran, and an Iran that only dreams of getting the bomb.

To Einhorn and NSC nonproliferation boss Dan Poneman, the answer was crystal clear: Iran's expensive black-market procurement of centrifuge components had failed, so Iran was now planning to buy a turnkey enrichment plant from Russia; the secret protocol the CIA had acquired showed that. So they focused their energies on shutting down the Russian deals with Iran. As America's Cold War superpower adversary, Russia had an entire archipelago of previously secret nuclear cities, choked with underpaid weapons designers, technology, and materials. Compared with Russia, the rest of the world was a nuclear desert.

Getting the intelligence community to concentrate their resources on Russia—and, to a lesser extent, on China—was a perfectly rational approach on the part of the Clinton administration nonproliferation team. And it would have disastrous consequences.

Even Gordon Oehler, the straight-shooting boss of the CIA's nonproliferation center, would later admit that the Agency completely missed the real story going on behind the scenes with A. Q. Khan. Those great big contracts with Russia and China were not a nuclear program but a fraud program, he believed. Reza Amrollahi, the Rafsanjani relative in charge of the program, was corrupt, incompetent, and a lousy manager, Oehler and other former U.S. officials told me.

That didn't mean the Iranians didn't have bad intentions. It just meant that they were unlikely to turn their dreams into a real threat anytime soon. That was the meaning of those recurring CIA estimates that Iran "could" acquire nuclear weapons capability in five to ten years.

Five to ten years was not a measure of time; it was merely another way of saying "eventually."

SUMMIT IN MOSCOW

The May 9–10, 1995, summit between Presidents Bill Clinton and Boris Yeltsin in Moscow began like a bad rerun of the Cold War. No sooner had Clinton arrived in Moscow for the formal opening ceremony than Russian security agents formed a line behind him, preventing his top advisers, Secret Service detail, and even the aides carrying the suitcase with his secure communications link from following him into the Kremlin. Clinton shrugged and plowed ahead, until the shouting behind him grew intense.

It wasn't his own men who were making all the fuss, but the Western correspondents and photographers who also had been barred by the KGB men from covering the opening event. He took Yeltsin aside and asked him to let them all through. White House spokesman Mike McCurry later said the Kremlin considered their acquiescence to Clinton's request a "major concession."

The two leaders had a lot to discuss, and Iran was by no means at the top of the agenda.

- In Chechnya, Russia was engaged in a murderous war against separatists and was massively deploying troops and armor in flagrant violation of the 1990 Conventional Forces in Europe (CFE) treaty;
- In Bosnia, the United States wanted Russia to participate in a multilateral peacekeeping force aimed at thwarting the ambitions of Russia's traditional allies, the Serbs;
- In Europe, the administration was seeking to expand NATO eastward right up to Russia's doorstep, a move that angered and alarmed the Russian military. As a sop, Clinton was offering Russia membership in an ill-defined "Partnership for Peace" pact that included the NATO allies;
- Clinton was seeking Yeltsin's agreement to deactivate strategic nuclear delivery systems to be reduced by START II by removing their nuclear warheads or otherwise removing them from hair-trigger alert.

According to *Washington Post* columnist Jim Hoagland, Clinton also handed Yeltsin "a five-page, single-spaced U.S. intelligence report summarizing Iran's nuclear weapons program" that drew on "sensitive HUMINT [human intelligence] and SIGINT [signals intelligence] reporting." Undersecretary of State Lynn Davis told reporters in Washington that Iran had a "crash program" to acquire nuclear weapons. Just before the summit, Secretary of State Warren Christopher announced that Clinton planned to demand that Yeltsin cancel the $800 million agreement to build nuclear power plants in Iran. "We will not be satisfied by anything other than the end of the nuclear program," the outspoken Christopher announced.

Yeltsin rebuffed that demand outright, insisting that Russia had a perfect right to sell light-water power reactors to Iran. After all, this was the same technology the Americans had offered to North Korea just the year before, calling the deal a "victory" for nonproliferation! Yeltsin's refusal to entertain the U.S. demand, and the administration's unwillingness to press the Russians further, had dramatic consequences. As time wore on, the reactor deal and all the training that went with it provided the "legend" Iran used with great success to expand its nuclear infrastructure and to mask procurement and research cooperation with Russian nuclear labs. And that was precisely what worried the U.S. intelligence community. The United States believed Iran had some two thousand nuclear technicians, of whom only 220 were trained scientists. Russian assistance could change all that.

When the two leaders emerged from the two days of tense talk, Yeltsin made a curious announcement. The January 8 agreement with Iran had been "concluded legitimately and in accordance with international law," he said. "But it is true that the contract does contain components of civilian and military nuclear energy. . . . Now we have agreed to separate those two. Inasmuch as they relate to the military component and the potential for creating weapons-grade fuel and other matters—the centrifuge, the construction of shafts—we have decided to exclude those aspects from the contract."

What was "military" nuclear assistance, if not bombs? Not even Clinton's own advisers had suggested that Russia was consciously planning to help Iran acquire nuclear weapons. Yeltsin's statement was a remarkable admission that the January 8 protocol was not as innocent as the Russians and the Iranians tried to make out. And what was that mysterious "uranium shaft," translated variously as "mineshaft" or "vault"? Some sources I spoke with at the time believed it could be a reference to a nuclear weapons test shaft, which must be dug several hundred meters below the earth and equipped with a variety of electronic sensors. Others insisted it was just a uranium mine. But no one could explain why Yeltsin called it a "military component" of the sale.

Nonproliferation adviser Daniel Poneman touted the summit as a great success. "We did not believe Iran was purely interested in a light-water reactor (LWR) for energy," he told me. "We further believed that if we were able to lop off the proliferation-prone aspects of the Russia-Iran cooperation, then Iran's interest in the LWR would evaporate. All roads led to Moscow. So the brunt of our effort was to persuade the Russians to stop the things we were most worried about, and that was the deal we got. We went at it with great vigor as a high priority."

In response to U.S. concerns, Yeltsin appointed Prime Minister Viktor Chernomyrdin as his point man to handle detailed discussions with the Americans over Iran. Clinton appointed Vice President Al Gore. The creation of the so-called Gore-Chernomyrdin Commission was a great victory for the process-oriented bureaucrats. It soon became clear that it was a catastrophe for America's long-term strategic interests.

Speaking to the ITAR-TASS news agency just one day after the summit, Viktor Mikhailov pooh-poohed the whole idea. Gore and Chernomyrdin would only be discussing "technical details" such as the disposition of spent fuel from the Russian-built reactors in Iran. Meanwhile, Mikhailov and Minatom would aggressively pursue new nuclear contracts in Iran. For example, he said, there was nothing to prevent Minatom from finalizing the contract to build a centrifuge plant in Iran at a later date, since there was nothing "military" about enriching uranium. Training of Iranian experts at Russian nuclear facilities would continue apace. And he expected a contract to build a 40-megawatt research reactor to be signed soon.

So much for the great U.S. victory in Moscow.

THE INTERMEDIARY RETURNS

Behind the scenes, Deputy Secretary of State Strobe Talbott, National Security Adviser Tony Lake, and Ambassador Richard Schifter, a former assistant secretary of state for human rights and humanitarian affairs during the Reagan and George H. W. Bush administrations, were conducting secret, parallel talks in an effort to head off the Russia-Iran nuclear deal, as I first reported in October 2000. Talbott was working the Russians, Lake coordinated within the administration, while Schifter was asked to use his contacts with U.S.-based intermediaries with close ties to Tehran. The initiative also had the "active backing of Vice President Al Gore," several sources involved in the negotiations said.

"The problem was how to hold a dialogue and reach an agreement, all without appearing to talk," the Intermediary who shuttled back and forth between Washington and Tehran told me. "Neither side wanted to be seen publicly as taking the first step toward the other." Both sides had staked out public positions of such mutual hostility it was difficult to back down.

For the second time since Clinton took office in 1993, the Intermediary was tapped to carry messages and position papers between the two governments. But this time he felt their efforts would be crowned with success. "We got to the point where lawyers on both sides were involved," he said. The lawyers were tasked with drawing up a bill of Iranian assets blocked in the United States, and with crafting a global settlement that would resolve all outstanding cases at the Iran-U.S. Claims Tribunal in The Hague, Netherlands. Tens of billions of dollars were at stake.*

The asset agreement was the sweetener. The core of the deal was a U.S. gambit to persuade Iran to build a natural-gas-fired power plant at Busheir instead of a nuclear one. To make the deal "irresistible," the White House even offered at one point to help finance the project, to be completed entirely by Russian firms. It was nonproliferation by bribery—not necessarily a bad or even an expensive proposal, considering the alternatives a nuclear Iran would present. "The final U.S. proposal was on Rafsanjani's desk in early May 1995, just before Clinton's Moscow summit with Yeltsin," the Intermediary recalls. But the deal fell through when neither side could agree on who would be seen as taking the first step. Then, on May 6, 1995, President Clinton issued Executive Order 12959, banning all trade with Iran.

Rafsanjani and his advisers felt they had been tricked. In addition to the secret negotiations with the White House, for nearly two years they had been working to lure U.S. oil firms back to Iran. In March they had signed an unprecedented agreement that committed Texas-based Conoco to invest $600 million in an offshore oil field, in exchange for a share of the production. It was the first time since the revolution that Iran had agreed to allow a foreign firm to exploit Iran's oil. Rafsanjani was willing to brave the revolutionary orthodoxy because his country was desperate for foreign capital and technology. Iran's largest oil fields were old, and the equipment was rusting away. Estimates published by the Oil Ministry called for $15 billion in foreign investment just to maintain Iran's production at current levels. The key to bringing the foreigners back was to get a major U.S. firm to lead the way.

But Rafsanjani's advisers had failed to read the political tea leaves in Washington. The trade embargo was no double-cross. It was a desperate political balancing act, in direct contradiction to stated administration policy up to that point. That policy was spelled out in briefing documents, talking points, and diplomatic "demarches" delivered by U.S. embassies to governments in Europe, which I obtained from the State Department under the Freedom of Information Act.

"We have not attempted to cut off exports to Iran of ordinary, nonsensitive goods," Washington instructed State Department officials to tell

*The Hague tribunal provided a forum to resolve financial disputes resulting from the 1979 Iranian revolution, but it was mired in bureaucracy and political ill will. It was established by the Algiers Accords of January 19, 1981, that ended the hostage crisis in Tehran.

their European counterparts in February 1995. "It is our judgment that other countries would not cooperate with such an initiative, and unilateral U.S. trade restrictions will not affect the Iranian economy when the same goods are available elsewhere," the declassified portion of the cable states. "We have closely examined U.S. trade policy toward Iran. We see no clear benefit—in terms of our policy objective of pressuring Iran—in pursuing unilateral prohibitions that would have no meaningful impact on Iran's revenues or policies."[1]

But when the Conoco deal was announced, on March 4, 1995, Congress reacted with stunned fury. Senate banking committee chairman Alfonse D'Amato (R-N.Y.) summoned Conoco and the State Department to explain their lapse of judgment and immediately introduced legislation to sever all U.S.-Iran trade. Conoco was just as surprised at the embargo as Rafsanjani, since top company officials had briefed the State Department from the start and had never been told to break off negotiations.[2]

Clinton issued the executive order banning trade with Iran to prevent congressional Republicans from claiming victory over the administration. It was a partisan political gesture, not national security policy.

THE PENETRATION

My government is keeping its nuclear options open.
—Iranian arms control official Hassan Mashadi, September 1995

To this day I am not sure whether President Clinton's meeting at a Washington restaurant with Crown Prince Reza Pahlavi was a chance event, or was scripted and planned in advance. When I called the White House for an official comment a few days later, spokeswoman Mary Ellen Glynn termed it "a chance meeting." And yet, the way it occurred, the words that were spoken, and the reception within the Iranian community all suggested that the "chance meeting" was part of a carefully orchestrated Kabuki dance, aimed at sending another message to Tehran. This time the message was quite different from the conciliatory gestures delivered to Rafsanjani by the Intermediary.

It was a splendid Sunday afternoon in early July, relatively dry by Washington standards. Reza had invited me and his top political aide, Shahriar Ahy, to lunch at the Sequoia restaurant in the Washington harbor at Georgetown. Sailboats and motor launches plied the Potomac. From time to time a rowing crew from the nearby Georgetown University boat slip pushed by. From the topmost tier of the broad terrace, we had a magnificent view. The tables all around us were packed.

Suddenly an athletic-looking man in a dark suit leaned toward me and asked if we would mind changing tables. It was not really a question, but a polite order. He was wearing an earpiece, and when I looked up, I noticed several other men like him flowing out through the doorway from the dining room. Bill Clinton's taste for eating out was well known in Washington, but I had never yet experienced the sudden rush and thrill of the Secret Service detail locking down a public restaurant for the president's pleasure.

We were ushered to a new table, freshly laid by the restaurant staff, and took our seats without question. Even our wineglasses were brought to us, without our having to lift a finger. Later, as I reflected back on these events, the questions began. Our original table was located a good 30 or 40 feet from the dining room doors, on an isolated part of the terrace, far from where the president would eventually sit. The table to which they moved us was directly below the dining room doors, so that anyone coming out onto the terrace from inside would have to pass right in front of us.

The next instant was a blur of activity. Dark suits began rushing through the doorway, forming a protective phalanx, and then Clinton appeared, nonchalantly engaged in conversation with his wife and U.S. Trade Representative Mickey Kantor and his wife, who trailed just slightly behind him. Instinctively we stood up as the president approached. Reza had asked me to lunch to help devise a strategy for persuading the U.S. administration to take a tougher line against the mullahs in Tehran, and here was the man himself we were seeking to influence. Reza's jaw dropped and he just stared at the president, struck dumb.

When it became clear Reza was going to let the president pass by our table without saying a word, I took a step forward, smiled, and extended my hand. "Mr. President," I said, "I'd like you to meet Crown Prince Reza Pahlavi, the oldest son of the former shah. He's one of the leaders of the Iranian opposition, and he wanted to commend you for your recent decision to ban trade with Iran."

With that, Ahy must have given Reza a kick, for he lurched forward with his hand extended and mumbled a few words of greeting to the president.

Without skipping a beat, Clinton locked Reza in his gaze, all the while pumping his hand. "I'd like to see our two countries become friends again," he said, oozing sincerity. "You know, I tried it the other way for two years, and that didn't work. Now we're going to try it this way and hope we will have greater success."

It was the first time any U.S. official had acknowledged, even in such an offhand way, the secret overtures to Tehran that had recently collapsed. No one yet knew about the Bosnia green light or about the messages the Intermediary had taken to Tehran.

Reza commended him for the trade ban, calling it a "very courageous move," and assured the president of his support. "We have been waiting for something like this for the past sixteen years," Pahlavi said. "The Iranian community is absolutely thrilled with what you are doing."

Clinton seemed to forget about the rest of his entourage. It was his gift as a politician to draw you into his aura and make you feel as if you were the most important person in the world. He talked about the sanctions and about the difficulty the administration was having getting allies in Europe and elsewhere to see things the way we did. "I want you to know that we're working very hard to get our allies on board to put more pressure on the government in Tehran," he said.

At one point Clinton asked Reza what more he would like the United States to do. "You know, Mr. President, in the end it must be up to the Iranian people to decide the form of government they want. We would like to see free and fair elections under international supervision."

"I'll remember that," Clinton said.

The president and his party strolled down to a large table just below ours, protected by a ring of Secret Service guards. Over the next hour, a dozen or more diners came over to our table to say hello to Reza, most of them speaking first in English, then in Persian. Some of them asked to pose for photographs with him, along with family members. Was it possible that so many Iranian Americans had chosen that particular afternoon in mid-July to take their families to the Sequoia restaurant in the Washington harbor? Was their goal to send a message to Clinton about Reza's popularity? And why had the Secret Service not moved us out of the president's path, but into it? There were just too many coincidences.

I wrote up the encounter, with Reza's approval, for my *Iran Brief* fax service, and the news spread like wildfire through the Iranian American community. In Tehran the meeting was viewed as a part of a U.S. government conspiracy. The opposition Mujahedin-e Khalq issued a statement violently condemning the encounter, claiming that it proved "the enmity of the United States to the Iranian people's revolution." When challenged, that democracy allowed for strong differences of opinion and respect for different viewpoints, an MEK spokeswoman in Washington sneered. "We do not want that type of democracy. Your type of democracy is not for Iran," she said.

Whether planned or just chance encounter, the meeting energized Reza. Over the next few weeks he sought to become active in the Iranian opposition again, and debated precisely what role he should play.

Advisers such as Ahmad Oveissy, whose father-in-law, Housang Ram, recently had returned to Tehran in an attempt to get his property holdings returned by the regime, urged Reza not to get involved in exile politics. "You are the king," he argued. "You are above politics. Everyone should come to you."

Shahriar Ahy agreed. "Reza's role is like that of Juan Carlos in Spain," he said. He was there to establish legitimacy and stability during the transition period after the people swept the mullahs from power. Neither Ahy nor Oveissy mentioned that Housang Ram had phoned them in distress from Tehran, because the regime was not allowing him to leave the country.

EXILE BICKERING

A few weeks later, on July 27, Dr. Ganji came through Washington on his way to Dallas and invited Reza to lunch at the Four Seasons hotel, a posh but discreet watering hole overlooking the C&O Canal in Georgetown. Outside of the MEK, Ganji had become the most vocal exile leader in Washington and had just come from meetings with the chairman of the House International Relations Committee, New York Republican Benjamin Gilman, and other members of Congress.

Ganji and Reza hadn't spoken since their bitter encounter at the Hotel Raphael in Paris many years earlier, and any semblance of unity among the various Iranian opposition movements in exile was long gone. Most of the groups were led by aging dinosaurs from the previous regime, who bitterly detested one another. Ganji asked me to attend the lunch as a guarantee that the tone would remain cordial.

I was stunned when the two men greeted each other like long-separated family, warmly kissing each other on both cheeks.

"Don't look so surprised," Reza said, catching my look. "Dr. Ganji and I have been through a lot together. I have greatly admired all the good work he has done over the years."

As we dined heartily, Reza described at length his vision for the future of Iran. "Americans imagine George III whenever they say monarchy," he said. "They don't understand that in today's Iran, even to non-monarchists, this institution carries tremendous weight. It's a guarantee against the disintegration of Iran."

He and Ganji agreed that it was important to break down the psychological barriers that so fractured the opposition. Together they composed in longhand a joint declaration, which they both signed in my presence, calling on all groups in favor of pluralistic democracy in Iran to "set aside their differences and unite around a core of shared values."

"It's important when you write about this, Ken, that you emphasize that this is not a new deal or a tactical alliance," Reza said. "This is a long-term strategic alliance that we have shared with Dr. Bakhtiar for many years.* My goal is not the restoration of the monarchy, but the freedom of Iran."

One of the weaknesses of the regime, I pointed out, was its inability to integrate non-Persian minorities—Kurds, Azeris, Balouchis, and others—who dominated the nation's borders. Until now the monarchist groups have refused even to talk to the minorities. Any wiggle room there, I asked.

Reza waxed enthusiastic as he laid out the details of his decentralization plan, which included local autonomy for the Kurds within the framework of a united Iran. He sounded like a college freshman after his first day in Government 101.

"Local autonomy clearly means a local elected government and administration," Dr. Ganji pointed out, "and the use of Kurdish in addition to the national language." Reza agreed, then added, "We are not just talking about Kurdistan, but full civil rights for all Iranians. What makes our country rich is our diversity."

It was these remarks that set off the firestorm.

Later that afternoon I faxed a copy of the dispatch I was preparing to release to Reza's office for any last-minute comments. Minutes later, Reza phoned and patched me into a conference call with Oveissy and Hormuz Hekmat, his new political adviser. Hekmat began shouting the minute he came onto the line. There was no way the king was going to advocate Kurdish autonomy. It was political suicide! Instinctively, I turned on the tape recorder I used for telephone interviews.

"Who is this Ganji, anyway?" Hekmat went on. "He does not represent any significant group among Iranians. He has no following. He has had a budget—I don't care about the source. For you to meet with him, Your Majesty, is disastrous."

Hekmat forgot to remind Reza that he had worked for Ganji when Ganji first came to Paris, and that he had been one of the first supernumeraries Ganji had let go.

"It would not be appropriate for me to issue a joint statement with Dr. Ganji, given his particular situation," Reza said. Apparently he had already forgotten that he had written the statement himself and signed it.

"Your Majesty," Hekmat said, "this might help Dr. Ganji, elevate his status, but it will weaken you. In fact, it will be the kiss of death for you."

*Dr. Shahpour Bakhtiar, the last prime minister of the former shah, was a central figure in the National Front, the broadly popular center-left movement of Mohammad Mossadeq. After fleeing Iran in 1979, Bakhtiar surfaced in Paris. Following a failed assassination attempt in 1980, regime agents finally murdered him in his home outside Paris on August 6, 1991.

"Dr. Hekmat," I said, "what do you think the opposition has accomplished in sixteen years with this kind of backbiting and bickering and name-calling?"

"Mr. Timmerman, I am not calling Dr. Ganji names. What I am telling you is that he cannot set up a meeting in any town of the world with more than fifty people, and those fifty people will not even want to have their names published. That is something I know. I have known the opposition forces abroad for fifteen years. He is not a political force. He has had certain means at his disposal to criticize the Iranian regime—radio, media, writers, and salaried people—but he does not represent a political force. He is not the head of a political organization; he is the head of a bureaucratic setup. Or was, I don't know what his situation is today. For the king to make a joint statement with Dr. Ganji is absolutely beyond belief. If he signed a statement with me, it would have been better than signing a statement with Dr. Ganji."

Ganji was disgusted when I spoke with him later. "At 3:00 p.m., Reza agrees to one thing, and by six he goes back on it. And we're not even in Iran!"

Unaware of the furor my dispatch had unleashed in the exile community, CIA deputy director George Tenet told Ganji when the two met soon afterward that the joint declaration was the "greatest thing" Reza Pahlavi had ever done.

REZA'S "TOUGH CALL"

Senator Alfonse D'Amato was also unaware of how Reza Pahlavi was allowing himself to be manipulated by his advisers when he sent him an invitation to testify before the Senate Banking Committee. D'Amato was introducing new legislation in September 1995 that would extend the U.S. trade embargo on Iran to include secondary sanctions on foreign companies that invested more than $40 million in the Iranian oil and gas ministry.

The D'Amato bill was prompted by news that the French oil company CFP-Total had been awarded the $600 million oil and gas field development project Conoco had been forced to renounce because of the president's trade embargo. "The rationale for targeting oilfield development projects is to tighten the financial noose around the Tehran regime's neck," a D'Amato aide said. "This will cut into the amount of money available to Iran to pursue its nuclear program."

Tehran was desperate to head off the D'Amato sanctions bill, which it feared would significantly deter foreign investment. Already it was waging an extensive propaganda campaign against the trade ban through front organizations it helped establish in the United States. Some masqueraded as legitimate Iranian American interest groups.*

The trade ban was having far greater impact on the Iranian economy than even its most hard-line advocates had hoped. The Iranian government responded by banning foreign currency trading, which made the Iranian currency virtually inconvertible overnight. This prompted Iranian exporters, who normally got paid in dollars and changed them with local currency brokers, to scale back exports. (The alternative was huge losses when the government forced them to convert their dollar earnings into rials at the artificially low official rate of 3,000 rials to the dollar.) Without ever figuring into the calculus of U.S. policy makers, the sanctions had sent the Iranian economy into a steep downward spiral, giving the United States tremendous potential leverage against the regime.

D'Amato turned to Reza because he wanted to show that the sanctions had been embraced enthusiastically by the Iranian opposition as a means of weakening the regime. He sent an official letter of invitation to Reza's office in mid-August 1995. On August 26, Reza wrote back that he would have to decline.

"This is the first time I've had to make a tough call like this in years," he said. But after extensive meetings with his supporters, he had detected a lot of opposition to his appearing as a witness before a U.S. Senate committee. "I don't want to be seen as favoring the sanctions," he told me. "The problem is how this will play inside Iran."

---

*Among the groups lobbying against sanctions and promoting U.S. trade with Iran were the Center for Iranian Trade and Development (CITAD), established by Ali Sabzalian, a former head of the Iranian Interest Section in Washington, D.C.; the Iranian American Cultural Council, set up by Ali Mohammadi, who was listed by the State Department as a "dependent" of the Iranian Interest Section; *Iran Khabar*, a Persian-language newspaper in Gaithersburg, Maryland, whose founder, Hossein Sarfaraz, acknowledged getting startup funds from Tehran; and the Forum for American-Iranian Relations (FAIR), established by Bijan Sepasy, who acknowledged in a Justice Department filing that the organization was established with a $120,000 "loan" from the Tehran government. The regime also had its own television network in the United States, Aftab TV, set up by foreign minister Kamal Kharrazi when he was still Iran's Permanent Representative to the United Nations in New York. Another network, Peyk TV, was based in Virginia.

As these groups were exposed, they were replaced by more-sophisticated organizations that maintained a hands-off relationship to Tehran and raised their money mainly from U.S. corporations seeking to do business in Iran. The most notorious of these was the American-Iranian Council (AIC), run by former Communist Party activist Housang Amirahmadi; and SiliconIran, a San Francisco Bay Area group that promoted investment in Iran and was run by a former Iranian government journalist, Susan Akbarpour, who claimed political asylum when she came to this country in 1997.

In fact, I learned from discussions with several of his supporters who attended those meetings, everyone was urging Reza to take advantage of the Senate banking hearing. They believed that the nationally televised hearing would provide him an unhoped-for opportunity to make the case for freedom in Iran to the American people. But two advisers urged him not to go: Shahriar Ahy and Ahmad Oveissy.

"It will be very dangerous for His Majesty to testify," Oveissy said. "Look at all the people who have been assassinated. The shah will be placing a target on his back."

Oveissy's two brothers had been gunned down by the regime in Paris in 1984, when word leaked out they were plotting a coup. That experience, family members said, had marked him indelibly.

To D'Amato's staff, Oveissy gave a different excuse. Their letter, he said, showed disrespect because it was addressed to "Mr. Reza Pahlavi," not to his Imperial Majesty.

GOOD NEWS FOR FALLAHIAN

For intelligence minister Ali Fallahian, the news had been all bad for some time.

Riots had been breaking out across the country for over a year. The unrest began in the Balouchi city of Zahedan, but soon spread to the Persian heartland. The first real test came on August 3, 1994, when the regular army defied direct orders to open fire on rioters in Qazvin. The regime called in an elite division of the Revolutionary Guards based in Tehran, who turned their machine guns on the crowds. Government media acknowledged fifty dead. In an interview with a German newspaper shortly before his death in December 1994, former prime minister Mehdi Bazargan said there were between three thousand and four thousand casualties.

By November, as the rioting spread, the Majles adopted a bill that authorized law-enforcement forces to "shoot to kill" anyone demonstrating against the regime. The Associated Press reported that the move "follow[ed] a string of riots in nearly every major Iranian city over the past two years." The law protected officers who killed or wounded protesters from civil or criminal charges.

On January 21, 1995, riots erupted after a soccer match in Tehran featuring two of the nation's leading teams. More than 100,000 fans poured out of the stadium into nearby streets, where they clashed with Pasdaran riot-control units. Tehran newspapers carried pictures of the stadium in flames, and called the event "Iran Soccer's Black Friday." Several hundred demonstrators were wounded, and more than one thousand arrested.

In April, things got worse. Riots erupted over the rising price of water and basic services in Eslamshahr and Akbarabad, poor suburbs to the south of Tehran that were bastions of support for the regime. The state-run media acknowledged that one person was killed. But Agence France-Presse put the death toll at between ten and fifty, and opposition groups put the casualties at 144. Some reports said the rioters were dispersed by helicopter gunships.

One of Fallahian's jobs was to infiltrate, decapitate, and otherwise disrupt the opposition. Since taking office in 1989, he had murdered the leaders of every major opposition group in exile. But the almost hysterical crackdown by the regime in response to uncoordinated disturbances betrayed their fear that they were losing their grip inside the country. Senior MOIS and Revolutionary Guards intelligence officers were beginning to defect to the United States. One of the most damaging, Manoucher Moatamer, was Fallahian's relative. He said that he and Fallahian were given the same fake patronymic to disguise their true identity. (Moatamer said he was known as Abbas Fallahian within the ministry.) That relationship led Iranian exiles who first heard of the defection through word of mouth to announce erroneously that Fallahian himself had defected to the United States.

After a momentous escape from Iranian government agents, Moatamer surfaced in Venezuela in July 1994, warning that the Iranian government was planning a series of attacks against Jewish and Israeli targets in Buenos Aires and London.

Just hours after he first gave the information to the Venezualan authorities, a massive car bomb demolished the AMIA Jewish Community Center in Buenos Aires, killing eighty-six persons. One week later the Israeli embassy in London was hit, well after he had warned of the attack.

Investigating Judge Juan José Galeano flew to Caracas and was so startled by Moatamer's information that he recommended the immediate expulsion of Iran's ambassador to Argentina and three other Iranian diplomats.

"I told [the judge] that the bombing was planned by Mr. Ali Akbar Parvaresh, a deputy speaker of the Majles and the representative of Imam Khamene'i to the Supreme Defense Council," Moatamer said. "I was present at the meeting where these decisions were made and the bombing was planned. . . . One person [involved] was the ambassador of Iran to Argentina, Mr. [Hadi] Soleimanpour, who was one of the student Followers of the Imam's Line who was involved in the hostage taking at the American embassy in Tehran. I knew him well. He had been kicked out of Spain as a diplomat, but Argentina had accepted him."

But the most startling information was contained in microfilmed documents from internal regime planning sessions Moatamer brought with him from Tehran. The minutes from the meetings demonstrated unequivocally that Iran's government ordered and planned the attacks in Buenos Aires and London. They also revealed that the regime was planning a terror campaign against the Saudi royal family, using a Sunni Muslim proxy named Osama bin Laden and Saudi Shiite groups, a campaign that actually began in November 1995. "Since the 1987 massacre of Iranian pilgrims in Mecca," Moatamer told me, "the Iranians have asked bin Laden not to come to Iran. But they keep in contact with him through the Iranian embassy in London. . . . Bin Laden is one of the very few people who can pick up the phone and speak directly with the Supreme Leader, Ayatollah Khamenei, in Tehran."*

In late April 1995, Fallahian's agents had arrested five foreign spies, including a Russian named Makarov, said to be an officer in Russia's Foreign Intelligence Service. They also arrested three Iranians he believed had delivered nuclear secrets to the United States.

As a precaution, the Atomic Energy Organization of Iran was ordered to dismantle the main centrifuge plant at the Amir Kabir nuclear center at Tehran University and move the equipment to a new facility in the Revolutionary Guards military production compound at Lavizan-Shian in northern Tehran. (They needn't have worried. The International Atomic Energy Organization had inspected the small research reactor at Amir Kabir earlier that year and had never realized that a centrifuge plant was operating next door.)

---

*Moatamer made this statement to me in late 1998. (See "Iran Organizing U.S. Networks," *The Iran Brief*, Serial 5201, Nov. 2, 1998.) But he provided the same information to his FBI debriefers three years earlier—well before the Saudi terror campaign began. I spoke to one of his debriefers in May 1995. He was remarkably "underwhelmed," as he put it. "We got great material from Moatamer about the Buenos Aires bombings at first, and absolute trash ever since. Problem is, we have to go and verify everything, even if we know it's false." Because of the "wall" created between law enforcement and intelligence gathering that was institutionalized by a 1995 memo by Deputy Attorney General Jamie S. Gorelick, the FBI was forbidden to share this information with the CIA, where bin Laden was well known. The Clinton administration insisted on treating terrorism as a simple law-enforcement problem to be handled through the courts, not as a threat to national security.

The only good news was the note on his desk from one of his agents in the United States. Thanks to his sources, Fallahian knew about Reza Pahlavi's refusal to testify before the D'Amato committee before the unwitting senator even received his letter.

His advisers had been right, he realized. There was no point in killing the young shah. He was much more useful to them like this. As long as he kept one toe in the game, no other leader could pretend to unify the exiles.

HOUSANG RAM

Housang Ram, the former shah's private banker, was distressed. He had returned to Iran in 1994, after his contacts in Fallahian's office had promised him—promised!—they would leave him alone. He had been pardoned by Ayatollah Khomeini himself a decade earlier and had fled Iran, setting up house in an expensive villa in the spa of Evian, France, that he could hardly afford. As the bills piled up, he decided to return to Tehran to die. He could live like a king in Iran on $2,000 a month.

Not long after he returned, he received a visit from an MOIS officer. We know all about the holding company in the Caribbean, he said. Why have you been lying to us about this?

Ram protested that he knew nothing about a holding company and that he had provided the regime all the information he possessed when they put him in jail the first time, fifteen years before.

After that visit, Ram applied for an exit visa, but his application was denied. He was now well over seventy and didn't think he would survive another spell in Evin Prison. He called around desperately, trying to get former colleagues from Bank Omran—now called Bank Mellat—to locate the other directors of the Caribbean holding company. He also sent a handwritten fax to the directors of Firstar Bank of Milwaukee saying that he was under duress, and that no one claiming to represent him, even bearing his shares, was legitimate.

The regime had never given up its effort to seize the former shah's assets. During the early days of the revolution they'd won judgments in Germany that gave them control of the shah's 25 percent shareholding in Krupp AG, the huge industrial and weapons-manufacturing conglomerate. They had also seized smaller holdings in Deutsche Babcock, a heavy industrial and construction company, and in Thyssen, the German steel company.

But despite all the money they'd spent on lawsuits, they'd never recovered any significant property in the United States, with the exception of a Fifth Avenue office building that belonged to the Pahlavi Foundation.*

Now that was about to change. The holding company in the Caribbean controlled shares purchased by the shah in the First Wisconsin Bank—now called Firstar Milwaukee—worth an estimated $50 million. In mid-1995, without notifying the U.S. government, the regime quietly took possession of the holding company that controlled the shares. Ram's ruse with the fax hadn't worked.

They also learned that under Housang Ram's leadership, the Bank Omran had been in the process of establishing a joint venture, Omran Financière, with Bank Pictet in Geneva, the oldest private bank in Switzerland. Using $500 million in assets transferred by the shah, the new joint venture was planning to make overseas investments. What happened to all that money, the MOIS man wanted to know.

At the same time, the Iranian government relaunched a long-dormant effort to seize the Villa Suvretto, a former luxury hotel in St. Moritz, which the shah had transformed into a ski chalet for his family and entourage. A Swiss appeals court ultimately rejected the Iranian government claim, and notified the Shahbanou on July 17, 1995, that she could take possession of the property. The tenant for the past fifteen years, media magnate and, since 1994, Italian prime minister Silvio Berlusconi, was ordered to pay back rent of more than $4 million. The Iranian government valued the villa at $10 million. It wasn't much, but it was a start.

They also had their eyes on three enormous tracts of land—over 738 acres!—that the shah had purchased in the 1960s on the outskirts of Marbella, Spain through Daletze and Bahia Las Rocas, two of his bearer-share corporations. With the massive development that had taken place as Marbella became a favorite summer stop for Saudi royals and jet-setting hangers-on, the property was now worth close to a half-billion dollars.

MOIS PENETRATION

Ed Ball was no Eliot Ness. Overweight, bald, dressed in well-worn suits of a style that was coming back in fashion, he was the head of the Iran

*Like the vast holdings of the Pahlavi Foundation in Iran, the New York foundation was rolled into a conglomerate called the Bonyad-e Mostazafan va Janbazan—Foundation of the Oppressed and Disabled—that was controlled by Iran's Supreme Leader in person. To disguise its relationship to the Tehran regime, the New York foundation was renamed the Alavi Foundation in 1992 and operates as a legally distinct entity.

section at the FBI's Washington, D.C., field office. His main beat was keeping tabs on the MEK, which had set up a vast influence operation in Washington. Through sympathizers spread around the country, the Mujahedin had given more than $138,000 to congressman (and future Democratic senator from New Jersey) Robert Toricelli, their biggest supporter on the Hill. The FBI got involved because the group was on the State Department's list of international terrorist organizations.

During the 1970s, MEK hit teams murdered Americans working in Iran. During the revolution, they worked hand-in-glove with Khomeini's thugs to assassinate senior officers of the shah's regime. Mujahedin leader Massoud Rajavi actively supported the takeover of the U.S. embassy in Tehran. The MEK was run like an underground military organization, its members traveling under assumed identities and living in communal safe houses rented by wealthy supporters. Ed Ball's job was to make sure that MEK operations in the United States never got out of hand.

He was also watching the activities of the Iranian regime. He kept tabs on the twenty-two employees of the Iranian interests section in Washington. The justification for maintaining so many employees was to issue new passports to Iranians living in the United States, but, as Ball had learned, they used the passports to terrorize the community. People who wanted to return to Iran after years in exile to bury Grandma were required to submit to extensive interviews. They were probed on family members still living in Iran, family members in Europe and the United States, friends, acquaintances. Why didn't they return to Iran permanently? Were they sympathizers of the MEK? Of Reza Pahlavi? Did they know So-and-So? The endless questions were humiliating and intimidating.

The FBI's New York field office and attorneys working for Manhattan district attorney Robert Morganthau were conducting separate investigations into the operations of the Alavi Foundation in New York. On April 27, 1992, they had arrested foundation president Manoucher Shafie as he stepped out of a car in front of Iran's permanent mission to the United Nations in New York, carrying a box containing a polygraph machine. The case was taken very seriously by the U.S. intelligence community, since they used the lie detectors extensively to determine the bona fides of defectors. For Iran to acquire one would give them a leg up on how to train their agents to defeat the device. Nevertheless, a New York judge ruled that Shafie could not be prosecuted because the federal agents who arrested him could not prove that he actually knew what was inside the box, since it was sealed, ready for shipment to Iran, at the time of his arrest.[1]

Shafie's successor as Alavi president, Mohammad Hossein Mahallati, was investigated by the Feds in 1993 for allegedly trying to buy botulinum toxin to ship to Iran, which the government believed would be used to produce biological weapons. Mahallati operated a series of trading companies out of an office suite located at 516 Fifth Avenue in New York. One of those companies, Al Makasseb General Trading, was implicated in a deal to illegally export mainframe computers to Iran. Another, Elmi Inc., was the exporter of record for the botulinum strains and also shipped $11,260 worth of centrifugal drying equipment to Iran that could be used for drying anthrax spores—a necessary step for weaponizing anthrax.

Mahallati's brother, Mohammad Jaafar Mahallati, was Iran's ambassador to the United Nations in the 1980s. Such ties are no accident. When Kamal Kharrazi took over as Iran's UN rep, his brother, Sadez Kharrazi, was a regular visitor to the foundation's Fifth Avenue headquarters. Alavi had also subsidized mosques in Brooklyn and Jersey City, where, unbeknownst to the FBI, Osama bin Laden's Afghan-Arab networks were raising funds and recruiting for jihad. (There is no evidence to suggest that Alavi knew about these activities.)

Ed Ball was on Alavi's case because the foundation spread money for propaganda and other purposes to groups in the Washington area. The foundation was funding an Islamic Education Center in Potomac, Maryland, whose prayer leader, Iranian-born Bahram Nahidian, acknowledged to a U.S. court that he had sheltered the assassin of a former diplomat turned opponent of the clerical regime.* The FBI feared the regime was using the center to spot and recruit other terrorists.

The FBI's Iran unit was also responsible for protecting prominent dissidents from potential threats to their security and kept a number of individuals under surveillance who they believed were undercover MOIS operatives. The Iranian government had not assassinated anyone in the United States since 1980, but that could always change, and Ed Ball didn't want to be caught flat-footed.

As Reza Pahlavi became more active in exile politics in early 1995, Ed Ball and his watchers detected a dramatic increase in the activity of those operatives. Even more alarming was the fact that Ahmad Oveissy, Reza's faithful retainer and closest confidant, had been talking to them.

---

*The assassin—American-born David Belfield—disguised himself as a postman and gunned down former Iranian diplomat Ali Tabatabai when he answered his door. Nahidian told the FBI that he had converted Belfield to Islam while the latter was serving a prison sentence at Lorton Reformatory in Fairfax County, Virginia. Belfield changed his name to Daoud Salhuddin and fled to Iran after the assassination, where the regime granted him political asylum.

Most of the five individuals the watchers had identified had longstanding friendships with Oveissy. Two were former officers in the Imperial Army. Another was a relative of Reza's wife. One was a former secretary. As Reza's eyes and ears, Oveissy naturally would want to keep tabs on them to make sure they posed no threat. Just to make sure, Ball contacted Reza's secretary and asked her to set up a meeting for him with Reza outside of the office, without Oveissy present. After she relayed the request to Reza, Oveissy called her into his tiny office to schedule the meeting—and fired her the same day.

Ball had to swallow his surprise when Oveissy greeted him at Reza's mansion in McLean, Virginia. They all sat down in the glass-enclosed veranda where Reza received visitors. Oveissy served them coffee. Ball cleared his throat. We believe you have a security problem, he said. We've identified five individuals known to you who may be working for the Islamic Republic.

Ahmad, what do you know about this? Reza asked.

I have looked into everything, Your Majesty, Oveissy replied. There is nothing to this.

There is your answer, Reza said.

Ball left, quietly steaming. Any respect he had had for the son of the former monarch evaporated in that instant. What was the point of spending taxpayer dollars to carry out clandestine surveillance if the target you were trying to protect refused to acknowledge the danger?

THE ADVISER

Hassan Mashadi was Iran's delegate to the Chemical Weapons Convention in The Hague. Although he was not yet forty years old, he was authorized to speak publicly on sensitive issues. I met him at the Italian Riviera resort town of Castiglioncello in late September 1995, at a conference on nuclear proliferation sponsored by the Union of Scientists for Disarmament.[2]

One would not normally think of an academic conference as a place where dramatic revelations would be made. But Mashadi's statements left his audience stunned.

"While I do not believe Iran is actively seeking nuclear weapons," Mashadi told the conference, "at the same time Iran is not going to renounce that option."

I almost did a double-take when I heard him say that. Here was clear language very unlike the standard denials one was used to hearing. Looking around the room at some of the world's most respected experts on nuclear strategy and weapons proliferation, I saw that others were just as surprised as I was.

Did that mean that Iran intended to withdraw from the NPT if it felt an imminent threat to its security? I asked. Again, his answer was direct: "Iran does not believe it should renounce that option if its survival is at stake."

Clearly the technology Iran was acquiring from Russia, China, and others could be used in a weapons program as well as for civilian applications, I said.

That was intentional, he acknowledged. His government was "keeping its nuclear options open."

Iran was not being treated fairly by the international community, he complained, especially when compared with Israel. "Iran has signed all the treaties—the NPT, the Chemical Weapons Convention, the Biological Weapons convention—and Israel has not. We are respecting all our treaty obligations while Israel is not. If you cannot assure Iran it will be treated equally, then you shouldn't be surprised if we turn to other weapons."

Fear of Israel was driving Iran to develop long-range missiles "to deter an Israeli attack" on Iran's nuclear facilities or leadership, he said. "You cannot expect a nation with legitimate security concerns to sit idly by in the face of a threat. If you tell them not to go nuclear, then what option do you leave open for them?"

The United States was "blowing out of all proportion" Iran's recent behavior, when it accused Iran of sponsoring terrorism or commiting aggression against its neighbors. "Iran has never been an aggressor against any of its neighbors." Referring to the disputed islands in the Strait of Hormuz and Iran's diplomatic sparring with the UAE over their sovereignty, he said, "Iran is merely trying to claim its natural position in the region, and some countries are trying to deny it that role. Iran is not a country to be ignored."

After that afternoon's session, I pressed some of the international arms control experts attending the conference for their reaction to what Mashadi had said.

The United States had long ago come to the same conclusion about Iran's nuclear weapons program, said Brookings Institution fellow Bruce Blair, a former strategic nuclear planner with the government. The United States has been targeting suspected Iranian weapons plants—in particular, nuclear facilities—since the mid-1980s, he revealed. The Iranian facilities were part of the nuclear weapons target set for the U.S. strategic reserves, as were some eight hundred similar targets in China, North Korea, India, and Pakistan. "They call it 'active counterproliferation,' " he said.

Alexander Konovalov was a top expert on nuclear strategy at the Russian Academy of Science Institute for the United States and Canada. "Iran is saying that the NPT does not prevent it from developing nuclear weapons design or research," he noted.

Jack Mendelson, president of the Arms Control Association in Washington, D.C., called Mashadi's interpretation of the NPT "a significant statement showing that Iran has not given up nuclear arms."

"If you are a piano player," a German foreign ministry analyst said, "keeping your options open means you are practicing."

That evening, Mashadi and I went for a long walk through the resort town, whose restaurants and bars were crowded with young people come for the weekend from nearby Livorno and Pisa. We talked politics, but also about ourselves. Prior to being assigned to the Permanent Directorate of the Chemical Weapons Convention in The Hague, Mashadi represented Iran for five years to the Council for Disarmament in Geneva. He doubled as an adviser to Foreign Minister Ali Akbar Velayati for International Organizations, including the International Atomic Energy Agency. He was arguably the regime's top expert on arms control and one of just a handful of strategic defense planners.

Mashadi identified with the "moderates" who surrounded President Ali Akbar Hashemi-Rafsanjani, who he insisted were sincere in seeking a rapprochement with Washington.

What is it the U.S. wants from Iran? he asked me point-blank. It was well past midnight by this time, but we were both charged with energy by our encounter.

"I certainly can't speak for the U.S. government," I ventured.

"Oh, come on, Ken," he said, giving me a nudge in the ribs.

Iran has changed, he said. The hard-liners have been kicked out of government, and whatever excesses may have been commited in the past are now definitely over. It's time to make a deal.

As I mulled over his comments later on, I could see how many would find his line of reasoning attractive, especially in Europe. The revolution was now more than fifteen years old, and its leaders had matured. Iran wanted to be treated as an ordinary country again, not as an international pariah. And it was a rich potential market for Western exporters.

But Tehran's leaders could never quite renounce doing the things that had earned them pariah status, just when relations appeared to be on the mend.

16

THUNDER

If America continues its plots against the Islamic Republic, we will strike against the United States in the region with all conventional and unconventional means. We will not observe any type of law or moderation in our operations against the Americans in the region.

—Iranian Revolutionary Guards commander Major General Mohsen Rezai, September 24, 1996

On the evening of June 25, 1996, the most powerful officials of the Islamic Republic of Iran gathered solemnly at the home of president Ali Akbar Hashemi-Rafsanjani in the posh Jamaran district in north Tehran. Ali Fallahian, his minister of intelligence, was there. So was the chief of staff of Supreme Leader Ali Khamenei, Hojjat-ol eslam Mohammadi-Golpayegani, and his top deputy, Mohammad Mir-Hijazi. These two personally vetted all plans for carrying out overseas terrorist operations on Khamenei's behalf. The head of intelligence for the Iranian Revolutionary Guards, Brigadier General Morteza Rezai, was also present, as was Deputy Commander Rahim Safavi, a Khamenei protégé.

In the West, academics, journalists, and think-tank "experts" hyped the differences between Rafsanjani and Khamenei. Rafsanjani's faction had just won a major victory in Majles elections and appeared poised to open the country to foreign investment, which Khamenei and the hard-liners fiercely rejected. During the election campaign, Revolutionary Guards commander Mohsen Rezai (no relation to Morteza Rezai) had clashed openly with Rafsanjani and with his own deputy, Safavi. In an unprecedented speech on April 15, only four days before the elections, Mohsen Rezai called Rafsanjani's "liberals" a "cancerous tumor."

But as the informal gathering at Rafsanjani's house showed, the only real difference among Iran's clerical leaders was on the degree of violence they believed should be used to achieve their goals of preserving the revolution. And on that critical question, Rafsanjani and Khamenei were united.

Rafsanjani was sitting next to the telephone, clicking his prayer beads. His guests made small talk, and seemed to be waiting for something to happen.

At a few minutes past 10:00 p.m. the telephone rang, and Rafsanjani snatched it up. A hush fell over the room. Rafsanjani listened, nodding his head. Then a great smile spread across his face. "The package has been delivered," he said, repeating the words the person at the other end had just spoken. The room broke out into cheers before he could replace the receiver. Rafsanjani signaled a servant, and silver trays of chocolates were passed around. It was the equivalent of popping champagne corks in the West.

While the National Security Agency has never publicly identified who was on the other end of the phone that night, that telephone call was described in closed-door hearings before the Senate Select Intelligence Committee later that year. Rafsanjani's informer had phoned to tell him of the successful attack against the Khobar Towers military residence in Dhahran, Saudi Arabia, that killed nineteen U.S. servicemen. It was an Iranian government operation from start to finish. That explained the chocolates and the cheers.

I can reveal here that the person on the other end of the phone with Rafsanjani was Mustafa Hadadian, who later became head of intelligence operations in Khamenei's office. Hadadian phoned him from an underground bunker in Parchin that was being used as the operations center for the Khobar Towers bombing. Sitting with him were the head of MOIS terrorist operations, Mustafa Pourghanad; the head of the Revolutionary Guards Qods Force, Ahmad Vahidi; and his star terrorist planner, Imad Mugniyeh. They received the news from a Revolutionary Guards liaison officer in Canada. It was just the opposite direction the Americans and the Saudis were looking.

Ahmad Rezai, the son of Revolutionary Guards commander Mohsen Rezai, remembers that his father was also eating chocolates that night, but at home. When news of the attack on Khobar Towers was announced on the radio, he asked his father if Iran could do such a thing. He just laughed. "He told me Iran could do much more than this, but never acted out in the open. Instead they used other contacts, such as the Hezbollah of the Arabian Peninsula."

His father said he believed that attacks on U.S. troops in the Persian Gulf would force the Americans to withdraw. "He said that if we killed just one U.S. soldier, the others would withdraw," the younger Rezai said. The Iranians saw that such attacks had worked in Lebanon, under Reagan, and believed they would work again. Osama bin Laden shared that belief, according to the 9/11 Commission Report.

The U.S. intelligence community had been warning of the impending attack for months, but no one in the Clinton administration wanted to hear of the danger. They believed that conciliatory gestures, including a renewed offer from the president to hold a "full and frank dialogue" with the Tehran regime, would calm Tehran's leaders. The last thing the president wanted was an open conflict with Iran to erupt just as his reelection campaign got under way.*

"From April 1995 until the time of the Khobar Towers bombing in June 1996, the analytic community published more than 100 products on the topic of terrorism on the Arabian peninsula," a classified Senate report issued on September 12, 1996, revealed. That included specific intelligence warnings that the Khobar Towers residential complex was under surveillance by Iranian intelligence agents and their local surrogates, in an effort "to target American servicemen in the eastern province of Saudi Arabia for terrorist acts," the report stated.

CIA director Jim Woolsey had traveled to Saudi Arabia in December 1994 to discuss the threat from Iran with his Saudi counterparts. Since he had discovered the secret green light the Clinton White House had given to Iran to arm the Bosnian Muslims earlier that year, his concerns of impending Iranian terrorist attacks had been growing daily. "By March 1995," the Senate report went on, "the Intelligence Community had determined that Iranian operations in Saudi Arabia were no longer simply intelligence gathering activities but contained the potential for the execution of terrorist acts." The report concluded that the bombing had not resulted from an intelligence failure, "but a failure to use intelligence" by America's political leaders.

Some of the intelligence reporting was premonitory. An April 3, 1995, a cable from the CIA station in Saudi Arabia stated that "U.S. military commanders here are very/very concerned about the Iranian efforts in Saudi Arabia." These concerns led to a high-level intelligence briefing for U.S. military commanders in the region "on the Iranian plotting against U.S. military personnel in Saudi Arabia." Other Western intelligence agencies detected a new, Iranian-run camp in Lebanon's Bekaa Valley where

---

*In Tehran, Clinton's offer was met with scorn. CLINTON REQUESTS NEGOTIATIONS WITH TEHRAN, ran the banner headline in *Keyhan*. The state-run paper commented that Clinton was behaving "like a drunk bastard shouting in the streeet. . . . He should be treated like a thug." Clinton made the offer in an interview with an Arabic-language weekly in London just three days after the House of Representatives unanimously passed its version of Senator D'Amato's Iran Sanctions Act. Despite multiple requests, the White House refused to release an English-language text of the interview. See Kenneth R. Timmerman, "Clinton Offers Iran a 'Frank Dialogue,' " *Washington Times*, June 24, 1996.

Saudi dissidents were being trained in intelligence work and bomb-making techniques.

Then on March 28, 1996, a Saudi guard at the al-Haditha border crossing intercepted a car arriving from Jordan that was carrying 38 kilograms of plastic explosives. The driver, a Saudi Shiite named Fadel al-Alawi, admitted under questioning that he was part of an Iranian-sponsored plot to bomb U.S. troops in Dhahran. Like the other participants, he had been recruited while on a pilgrimage to the Sayyeda Zeinab shrine in Damascus, and had been sent to Lebanon for military and intelligence training by Iranian Revolutionary Guards specialists. Over the next week the Saudis arrested three of al-Alawi's co-conspirators, who provided additional details of the plot. But the Saudis apparently never informed U.S. military commanders at Dhahran so they could improve security.

Revolutionary Guards Brigadier General Ahmad Sherafi worked under Ahmad Vahidi and Hossein Mosleh in the Qods Force, the quasi-independent branch of the Revolutionary Guards established by Rafsanjani that carried out foreign terrorist attacks. When he learned that four of his operatives had been arrested, he contacted the head of the Saudi terrorist group he had put in charge of the bombing, Ahmed al-Mughassil, and ordered him to take charge of the plot personally.

Al-Mughassil returned to Saudi Arabia in late April 1996, activating members of the group living undercover in Qatif, a farming area not far from Dhahran. He provided them with Iranian passports, money, timers, and explosives, and told them that their target was to be the Khobar Towers complex.

In early June they bought a tanker truck for 75,000 Saudi riyals (around $20,000), and began constructing the bomb, using the plans Sherafi had given them. The RDX/hexalite explosives they used were later traced back to a military factory in Iran.*

Shortly before 10:00 p.m. on the evening of June 25, 1996, a young Saudi Shiite named Hani al-Sayegh drove a Datsun into the parking lot adjoining Khobar Towers building 131 and parked in a corner. His task was to give the all-clear sign for the bombers. A few minutes later, another member of the plot drove into the parking lot in a white four-door Chevrolet Caprice and parked. Al-Sayegh surveyed the main gate of the housing complex, but no one seemed to take notice of the arrival of the two cars, so he flashed his lights once to give the all-clear sign.

---

*According to one unconfirmed report, the truck was shipped on a barge to a small, IRGC-controlled port near Bandar Abbas where Qods Force explosives experts rigged the bomb then shipped it back to Saudi Arabia.

Ahmed al-Mughassil drove the truck with the bomb himself, with another young Saudi named Ali al-Houri in the passenger seat. These professionally trained bombers were not candidates for a suicide attack. Al-Mughassil backed the truck along the fence until it sat just in front of building 131. Then he set the timer for the bomb and, along with al-Houri, jumped into the waiting white Caprice and sped away. Hani al-Sayyegh followed close behind in the Datsun. Just minutes later the truck exploded, ripping into the north side of the building where the Americans were housed. Al-Mughassil phoned his Revolutionary Guards contact in Canada, who then placed the confirmation call to the operations center in Iran.[1]

LOUIS FREEH'S MISSION

News of the Dhahran attack was met with gloating by the state-controlled press in Tehran. *Abrar*, close to hard-line elements in the Revolutionary Guards, warned the next morning that Saudi Arabia "will be the second country in which an Islamic Republic will be established" after Iran. *Keyhan*, published by Iran's Intelligence Ministry, said the bombing was "revenge" for the execution of four Saudis on May 31 for their involvement in the November bombing in Riyadh. The four executed men had professed loyalty to Osama bin Laden.

Ayatollah Ahmad Jannati, the hard-line secretary general of the powerful Council of Guardians, had returned from the annual pilgrimage to Mecca one month earlier and predicted during a Friday prayer sermon that "the ruling dynasty in Saudi Arabia will soon be toppled by an Islamic Revolution."

Just days before the bombing, the Revolutionary Guards intelligence service and MOIS hosted a conclave of the world's top terrorists in Tehran. Among the invitees for the June 21–22 coordination meeting were Imad Mugniyeh, the regime's widely traveled operations master, who was believed to have participated in planning sessions with the Khobar Towers bombers; Ahmed Jibril, secretary general of the Popular Front for the Liberation of Palestine—General Command; Ahmed Salem, a leader of Egypt's Islamic Jihad movement; and Ali Mohamed, a former U.S. Special Forces adviser who became the bodyguard and confidant of Osama bin Laden.* It was yet another sign of the Iran's willingness to flaunt the

*Mohamed was later arrested in the U.S. and pleaded guilty to five counts, including conspiracy to murder in the African embassy bombings case in October 2000.

conventional wisdom that Sunni and Shiite fundamentalists could not work together.

The rumor of Iranian government responsibility surfaced within days of the attack, as did calls for military retaliation. The White House replied that they would respond "appropriately" once the investigation had reached a final conclusion. They hinted, however, that the FBI was having difficulty operating in Saudi Arabia, and that the Saudis weren't cooperating with the investigation.

The FBI certainly committed its share of errors. The forensics team it sent to assist the Saudis in combing through the rubble was led by a five-foot-ten blonde female, who strutted out in the hot Saudi sun wearing a tanktop and close-fitting shorts. Stopped by the *mutawwa* religious police when she ventured into the Saudi capital similarly unclad, the FBI special agent was forced to wear Islamic *hijjab*, covering herself from head to foot. She left Saudi Arabi in protest.

As a former marine, FBI director Louis Freeh was determined to discover the identity of those responsible for murdering nineteen U.S. servicemen and to bring them to justice, one way or another. He made the first of many trips to Saudi Arabia in November 1996, and persuaded the Saudi interior minister, Prince Nayef ibn Abdul Aziz, to give him a copy of the videotaped interrogation of the six suspects the Saudis had taken into custody.

He also discovered that the Saudi resistance to allowing the FBI to interview the suspects directly had nothing to do with the niceties of Islamic law, as the American press had been reporting. It came from the Clinton White House. Freeh eventually disclosed in an opinion piece that appeared in the *Wall Street Journal* on May 21, 2003, that he had had to appeal to former president George H. W. Bush to use his influence with the Saudi government to break the log jam, because the Clinton people were trying to keep the truth from coming out.

It took Freeh two and a half years, but eventually the FBI was able to interview all six Saudi Hezbollah suspects, without the presence of Saudi officials. They described in detail how the attack was planned, funded, and executed under the control of the Qods Force. "The information we learned," Freeh told a U.S. district court in December 2003, "was that the attack was organized and sponsored by the IRGC . . . with participation in the planning and the funding by MOIS and other senior officials. They [the Iranians] provided funding, training, travel, and other support." Saudi Hezbollah provided the people on the ground. "But all the training and the funding was done by the IRGC with support from senior leaders of the government of Iran." At one point, Freeh said, MOIS director Ali Fallahian personally took part in planning sessions with al-Mughassil and other Saudi Hezbollah members.[2]

In 2000, Freeh went to the White House to brief President Clinton on the conclusions of the investigation, which showed beyond any possible doubt that the Iranian government had ordered, planned, and managed the attack. But Clinton refused to even consider retaliation. "Louie was so pissed off by the president's reaction that he stormed out and handed in his White House badge," a former deputy told me.

Freeh never returned to the Clinton White House after that. But he resisted White House pressure on him to resign so he could bring the Khobar Towers case to closure, despite his own growing financial needs with children about to enter college. A federal grand jury finally handed down an indictment that named Iran in June 2001. Freeh left government shortly afterward.

To family members of the Khobar Towers victims, Louis Freeh had become a hero. "He was the only man in Washington during this whole thing who gave a damn," said Katherine Adams, mother of U.S. Air Force Captain Christopher Adams, a pilot who had been taking someone else's tour of duty in Saudi Arabia so he could stay home with his wife while she was having a baby. "He was the only man who kept his word to the families, who cared, who met with us. [President] Clinton never did anything, except to show up for a photo op," Mrs. Adams told me and *Insight* magazine reporter Scott Wheeler during the December 2003 court hearings in Washington.

Asked in the corridor if there was any al-Qaeda role in the attack, Freeh responded categorically, "Absolutely not."

As the 9/11 Commission would later discover, multiple intelligence reports detailed the operational ties between Saudi Hezbollah and al-Qaeda. But no one had ever thought to tell Louis Freeh. Another failure.

THE RAAD PLAN

Sixty-six-year-old Darioush Forouhar was a member of the old guard, but not the old regime. Jailed repeatedly under the shah because of his alliance with Bakhtiar's National Front, Forouhar was the founder and leader of Iran's oldest political party, the Hezb-e Mellat-e Iran, or Iran People's Party (IPP), which he formed in the 1950s. The IPP was a secular, center-right party that believed Iran should be independent of all foreign influence. He denounced American influence during the 1970s and accompanied Ayatollah Khomeini on his triumphal return from exile in February 1979. After a brief stint as labor minister during the first post-revolutionary government, Forouhar fell out with the new regime and went into hiding in 1981. He was jailed for a year in 1982.

With his dramatic upswept mustaches and military bearing, Forouhar reminded Iranians of a traditional Persian father figure. Stern but just. Crafty but true. After several years of quietly rebuilding the IPP's grass-roots network and recruiting senior members of the Revolutionary Guards who had become disenchanted with the regime, Forouhar crossed his own Rubicon in April 1996 when he called on Iranians to boycott the Majles elections and demand a referendum on regime change instead. That action made him a target of the regime.

Among his top aides was his son-in-law, a brilliant veteran of the Iran-Iraq war who became a journalist and, after fleeing Iran in the late 1980s, the European spokesman for the party. Homayoun Moghadam claimed to have recruited fellow Revolutionary Guards volunteers who went on to occupy senior positions within Revolutionary Guards intelligence. He also claimed to have family members and other sources with access to the internal workings of the Supreme National Security Council.

Unlike Moatamer or Zakeri, he was not a defector. Homayoun Moghadam was an agent-runner, with live sources inside Iran. As the spokesman for a political party, part of what he said was clearly aimed at enhancing the image of the IPP. But with that caveat, he demonstrated to me and to intelligence analysts in several governments with whom he had contact that he had a unique understanding of Iranian intelligence organizations and real access to their secrets.

Khobar Towers was no accident, he insisted. It was part of a plan that had been developed by Rafsanjani and approved by Khamenei to launch a wave of terrorist attacks against the United States and Israel.

Homayoun claimed that his sources in Tehran had seen internal memos referring to a debate within the supreme National Security Council, chaired by Rafsanjani, which referred to the plan using the code name RAAD, or "Thunder." One memo called for a campaign of "strike" operations against the United States, "to create maximum chaos and instability among the U.S. leadership during the four months before the U.S. presidential elections." Iran was hoping that these actions would prompt both Republicans and Democrats to offer substantial concessions to the Islamic Republic.

Motivating the Iranian plan, the memo stated, was a belief in Tehran that the United States had embarked on an "imperialist assault on Iran" in close cooperation with Israel. Proof of that assault was the continued U.S. military presence in the Gulf, which Iran opposed, and the recent U.S. trade embargo and sanctions legislation on Iran. The memo also called for "put[ting] an end to Israeli aggression in the Arab-Moslem world," Homayoun said.

How much of this was true? I quizzed my own sources in the FBI, the DIA, and elsewhere who had come in contact with Homayoun. They agreed that his insights were "invaluable" and that his contacts within the regime were genuine. However, they warned that some of his sources might be feeding him false information mixed with 24-karat gold, in an effort to distract and disorient the Western intelligence agencies who were listening to him. As ever, the game was a hall of mirrors. I compared what he said with what I knew and could learn from other sources.

President Clinton himself seemed to understand the danger of Iran overreacting to U.S. actions. A senior aide to Secretary of State Warren Christopher told me that when Clinton met with the Emir of Kuwait in Washington in March 1996—not long before he gave the interview offering a renewed dialogue with the regime—he asked the emir to convey a message to the mullahs in Tehran. Tell them we are doing this (the trade embargo and the sanctions) not with the intention of toppling the regime. The United States isn't picking a fight or seeking a military confrontation with Iran. It's just their behavior we find objectionable, not the regime, Clinton said. Tell them we want to be friends eventually. It was the same thing he had told Reza Pahlavi.

The RAAD memo also mentioned aid to "Palestinian allies" to create a new terrorist organization to launch "limited but effective" suicide attacks against civilian and military targets in Israel.

That effort had already begun. Iran's opposition to the Middle East peace process turned violent on April 9, 1995, when an Iranian-trained bomber drove an explosives-rigged van into an Israeli bus in the Gaza Strip, killing seven Israelis and a visiting American student named Alisa Flatow.

In March 1996, as Israeli elections for prime minister approached, Iran ordered its Palestinian proxies into high gear. Suicide bombers struck a bus in Jerusalem on March 3, killing eighteen persons. The next day they struck crowded Ditzengoff street in Tel Aviv, killing twenty and wounding seventy-five others. Dozens more were murdered in suicide attacks that spring. "Israel, the only state in the world to be created by terrorism and brutal use of force, is now tasting its own medicine," the Iranian government news agency gloated. "The divine retribution on those who spread corruption and injustice on the earth will be severe."

On April 12, 1996, the Israelis arrested Hussein Mohammed Mikdad, a Lebanese Shiite who subsequently admitted that his Iranian handlers had instructed him to hand-carry a bomb onto an El Al flight originating in Tel Aviv. The only reason the Israelis caught up with Mikdad was his own incompetence. While preparing the bomb in his East Jerusalem hotel room, he had the misfortune of setting it off in his own lap. Mikdad had entered Israel on a forged British passport provided him by Iranian intelligence.

In May, Arafat deputy Mohammed Dahlan told reporters that his security forces had uncovered a new terrorist network known as the "Secret Apparatus" that was being controlled by Hamas operatives living in Jordan. "Our investigations have revealed that the responsibility for these groups lies within Hamas but they were being financed by Iran. This became clear from the interrogations," he said.

Iran had become a player in the Israeli-Palestinian political arena through proxy organizations that used suicide bombers as their main tool of persuasion. Their goal was to prevent any rapprochement between Israel and the Palestinians. It was a deadly new development.

But there was more to the RAAD plan, according to Homayoun.

On June 10, 1996—two weeks before Dhahran—Homayoun told me he had received information from a source he called "Elvis" within the Revolutionary Guards Protection and Intelligence Department. Iran was planning to hijack a U.S. civilian airliner.

Homayoun's source said the attack would be carried out by Lebanese surrogates—not directly by Iranians—and had been approved by Rafsanjani in person as a "warning" to the U.S. government. Elvis believed the operation would originate in Greece or somewhere else in the Mediterranean.

I phoned a former U.S. intelligence officer I knew who gave me the name of a contact at the State Department's Office of Counterterrorism. I did not feel qualified to judge whether the threat was serious but felt that as a citizen I had a duty to pass it on to the government—even if it meant missing a "story." He agreed to meet with me the following afternoon.

The details of Homayoun's warning were sketchy. My contact had asked the Federal Aviation Administration intelligence liaison officer to sit in on our meeting. I handed them a one-page summary of the information Homayoun had provided me, titled "Plan to Hijack U.S. Airliner," and briefed them in detail on what I knew.

Both officials were clearly concerned by the warning. However, because it was "not airline specific" and contained no precise date or location, they told me that "by law" they could not communicate it to the airlines or require the airlines to take action. "Nonspecific threats that cannot be countered cannot be passed along," the FAA man said, because of the overwhelming cost to the airlines and to the federal government. The information was "not actionable."

Homayoun's source had included an unrelated detail, which he insisted be included as a proof of his bona fides. He referred to "the recent joint military exercise" between U.S. and British forces off the East Coast of the United States, which the Iranian government believed was aimed at "testing the operating capabilities" of the United States and Britain to launch an amphibious strike against Iran's Persian Gulf coast.

I had no idea what he was referring to, I said. Although I had searched through a variety of public sources, I could find no trace of any such military maneuvers. We exchanged cards and agreed to stay in touch.

A few days later I spoke with a friend at the Pentagon and relayed the same information. He nearly exploded on the phone when I added the detail about the joint U.S.-British operation.

U.S. and British forces had held a joint amphibious exercise at Camp Lejeune shortly before the Elvis report, he said. The exercise had been classified until two helicopters collided, killing several servicemen. In a brief statement acknowledging the deaths, the Pentagon alluded vaguely to a joint exercise with British forces but provided no hint as to the nature of the training.

The FBI interviewed Homayoun on June 20, 1996. While they couldn't confirm his source in Iran, other information he provided them made them believe he was a legitimate opposition activist, not a disinformation agent planted by the regime.

On June 24, I communicated the same information to the head of the Defense Intelligence Agency's Middle East and terrorism policy support unit at the Pentagon, with whom I had been in contact. He did not follow up on the information. Two days later came the bombing of Khobar Towers. Within days, U.S. officials I interviewed were already talking about communications intercepts that clearly indicated Iran's responsibility for that attack.

On July 11, Homayoun phoned me, all excited. He had just received an urgent communication from Elvis, saying that the attack on a U.S. civilian airliner was "imminent." The Khobar Towers bombing was "just the start of a series" of attacks against the United States, Elvis said. He reiterated that the attack on the airliner would involve a plane that originated in a Mediterranean capital, probably Athens.

I phoned my contact at the State Department, and he asked me to fax the report to him immediately. I never heard from him again.

Six days later, in the early evening of July 17, TWA Flight 800 exploded twenty minutes after taking off from JFK airport and crashed off the coast of Long Island, killing all 230 persons on board. The plane had just arrived in New York from Athens and was heading back to Paris. I was stunned when I heard the news.

On July 19, I swapped information on the attack with a former CIA counterterrorism analyst. When I told him about the threat to a U.S. plane originating in Athens, he mentioned the possibility of a "double-timer." A standard chronometer would delay activation of the bomb for a certain number of hours, to allow the aircraft to land safely in New York. The second timer would incorporate a barometric trigger of the type used by al-Qaeda terrorist Ramzi Yousef not long before in a Japan Air jetliner in the Far East. The bomb blew up after he disembarked at a stopover, killing a Japanese businessman during the next leg of the trip. It was a tried-and-true technique, the analyst said.

That same day, July 19, National Security Council adviser Richard Clarke convened a White House meeting of the interagency Coordinating Security Group on terrorism to discuss the crash and its consequences. Present were representatives from the State Department's Counterterrorism office, the FBI, the DIA, the NTSB, and the Deputy National Intelligence Officer for Warning, John Pulsinelli.

At the meeting, a skeptical NTSB investigator said there was a remote possibility the crash might have been caused by an exploding center fuel tank. "We were all cautiously encouraged," Clarke wrote in his account of the meeting. Until then, the intelligence community and the White House had been convinced they were dealing with a terrorist attack. Now Clarke instructed the intelligence community representatives to "back off" their investigations of possible foreign terrorist involvement in the crash until the NTSB had thoroughly investigated the center fuel tank theory.

I learned of this meeting and what happened from three separate sources. A Pentagon contact said the DIA had received a "specific warning" about a threat to the TWA flight two days before the crash. This was clearly separate from the warnings I had passed along, which never mentioned TWA by name. This specific warning was distributed to the White House—where it was read by Richard Clarke—as well as to the top civilian leadership at DoD. "But it was buried among fifty or so other warnings, making it difficult to distinguish," my source said. It was reminiscent of the 1983 intercept from the Iranian embassy in Damascus, warning of the marine barracks bombing.

Another source told me that the warnings I had delivered to the State Department had been "scotched by a high level Middle East officer," who called the reports "bogus."

On July 20, I sent the two warnings to another DoD intelligence officer, who had not taken part in the White House meetings. He told me that he'd shared them with the Deputy National Intelligence Officer for Warning, John Pulsinelli, who "hit the roof" when he read them. The Elvis warnings supported reporting from a controlled intelligence source that the CIA had briefed to Clarke's White House group on May 31. There was no way we were dealing with circular reporting, he said.

It was now clear there had been multiple, independent streams of reporting into the intelligence community prior to the information from Elvis that all provided forewarning of an imminent Iranian terrorist attack against a U.S. civilian airliner.

By July 22—just one week after the TWA 800 crash—my DoD contacts were talking about a "systematic intelligence failure" and were trying to craft a work-around to better coordinate indicators of warning that were being pushed aside by politically correct bureaucrats such as Mr. Clarke. The word within the intelligence community was clear: it was an election year, and President Clinton did not want foreign terrorism to become the focus of his reelection campaign. Smother the fires, but do it without making visible smoke.

A great deal of information—much of it false—has been written about the crash of TWA 800. There was a major, highly classified presence of U.S. warships in the immediate vicinity of the crash site out at sea. The NTSB acknowledges that surface radar picked up an unidentified ship fleeing the vicinity of the crash at 40 knots. Despite more than two hundred eyewitnesses who reported seeing the vapor trail of a missile arcing up from the sea toward the aircraft from the precise location of the unidentified ship, the CIA went to great expense after that July 19 meeting at the White House to produce a video simulation, which it released to the media, arguing that what the eyewitnesses had seen was an optical illusion, creating by flaming jet fuel descending from the wreckage after the accidental explosion of the center fuel tank. If Hollywood had produced it, the CIA video would have been dismissed as pure fantasy.

I cannot affirm here with certainty that agents of the government of the Islamic Republic of Iran attacked TWA 800. However, the existence of multiple warnings of an Iranian attack against a U.S. civilian airliner—including a CIA source report that specifically named Flight 800 as the target—has never been properly aired in any of the public reports.

In the wake of 9/11, it is no longer tolerable for the U.S. government to cover up knowledge of threats to America. I believe Congress should demand that the intelligence community reopen its books on TWA 800 to a blue ribbon panel, and let the chips—and the responsibilities—fall where they may.

THE COUNTDOWN BEGINS

The Shahab-3 is an entirely Iranian missile.
There could be some adaptations from foreign makes,
but it is not similar to any foreign missile.
—Ali Akbar Hashemi-Rafsanjani, July 29, 1998

In early April 1997, workers of Iran's Shahid Hemat Industrial Group, a branch of the Defense Industries Organization, strapped a Russian-built rocket motor onto a test stand at an R&D facility just east of Tehran, and attached a series of measuring devices to its metal skin. Helping them were engineers from Kutznetzov, one of Russia's largest state-run weapons companies. Formerly known as NPO Trud, this company built rocket motors for deadly intercontinental ballistic missiles that had targeted the West during the Cold War.

When the R-214 motor was fired, the roar echoed off the Zagros mountains and could be heard by residents in nearby Bagh-e Melli, where the Shahid Hemat plant was located. A trail of fire shot back several hundred feet from the rocket test bed. It was clearly visible to the U.S. spy satellite orbiting overhead.

One thousand miles away in Tel Aviv, in his spacious office in the Kirya, Israel's equivalent of the Pentagon, Uzi Rubin pondered a satellite photograph of that obscure piece of desert on the outskirts of Tehran one week later. He didn't know where his bosses at the Israeli Ministry of Defense had gotten the picture, although he could guess; they just wanted his technical analysis. As he measured the long burn marks on the sand and rock, and compared them with the signatures of known rocket motors around the world, he came to a stunning conclusion: the Iranians had just test-fired the engine from a Russian intermediate-range nuclear missile—an SS-4—missiles that were supposed to have been destroyed under the 1987 INF treaty.

CIA analysts back at Langley, Virginia, had come to the same conclusion, using more precise environmental sampling techniques that allowed them to determine what type of liquid rocket fuel had been used and the amount of thrust the motor had generated. The hard data from the April 1997 rocket motor test convinced them that the story the Israelis had been telling them was true.

It was disturbing and embarrassing all at once.

ISRAELI INTELLIGENCE

Major General Amos Gilad was the research director at Israel's military intelligence department, known in Israel and in the West by its Hebrew acronym, AMAN. The April 1997 test data was only the latest piece in the puzzle that had been taking shape before his eyes for over a year.

Six months earlier he had traveled to Washington to present a preliminary briefing to U.S. officials on Russian assistance to the Iranian missile programs. Israel had sensitive human intelligence that Russian rocket scientists were traveling back and forth to Iran, he said. Some of them had been involved in major Cold War ballistic missile programs.

Iran turned to Russia in 1994, after a failed test of the No-Dong/Zelzal 3 missile they had jointly developed with the North Koreans. The missile fell well short of the target zone in the Sea of Japan, traveling less than 500 kilometers from the North Korean launch site. The failed test convinced the Iranians that they had reached a technological dead end, so they turned to Russia for help.

They began by inviting Russian technicians to visit the top-secret Defense Technology and Science Research Center near Karaj, 50 miles northwest of Tehran. They showed them the North Korean missile design, and asked if they could improve on it. Technical colleges run by the Revolutionary Guards began hiring "teachers" from Russian missile plants and technical institutes, paying salaries nearly ten times what they could earn in Russia. Russian advisers showed up at Iran's missile plants in Isfahan and Semnan, as well as at design centers in Sultanatabad, Lavizan-Shian, and Kuh-e Bagh-e-Melli on the eastern outskirts of the capital.

As they got better acquainted with the Russian systems, the Iranians realized there were better options available to them than the original North Korean design. In a very systematic and sophisticated fashion, we saw them sinking roots into the heart of the missile production industry in Russia, Gilad told the Americans. We can't say for sure who initiated the longer-range options. But we believe that Iran will soon test a missile capable of launching an unconventional warhead on Israel.

The Iranians called the new missile Shahab-3. The change of name was significant, he said. *Zelzal* was a Koranic name, used by the Revolutionary Guards; *shahab* was a Persian word, meaning "meteor" or "shooting star." The shift to a traditional Persian name suggested that Iran's national defense establishment had taken over the project.*

Russian companies are involved in every stage of the development process, from the rocket motors to the guidance fit, Gilad said. We don't think the Russian transfers are an accident. We believe that Foreign Minister Yevgeny Primakov sees the missile cooperation with Iran as a strategic opportunity for Russia. We also believe, however, that he will back down under pressure. That's why we need your help.

The senior American official at General Gilad's initial briefing in October 1996 was Deputy Secretary of State Strobe Talbott, the administration's point man for Russia policy.

Don't worry, he told the Israeli when he had finished the briefing. We've got everything under control. We have a huge agenda with the Russians that gives us tremendous leverage. We'll take care of this.

GORE-CHERNOMYRDIN

Gilad returned home thinking the problem was about to be resolved. He and his political bosses expected the contracts to be shut down, the Russians to go home. They expected to see Iran turn once again to the European black market. Instead their sources began telling them about new contracts between Russian and Iranian missile companies, more Russian advisers, new shipments of components.

Prime Minister Benjamin Netanyahu viewed with alarm the progress of Russia's missile cooperation with Iran. "Israel is on the receiving end of these missiles, whereas Strobe Talbott views this issue in the broader context of U.S.-Russian relations," a top Netanyahu adviser told me in Tel Aviv. Netanyahu decided it was time to escalate.

In late January 1997, General Gilad was sent back to Washington. This time he went directly to the White House, where he gave the entire "dog and pony show" briefing to Leon Fuerth, national security adviser to Vice President Al Gore.

It was critical to get Gore's attention, since he chaired the restricted

---

*Most Israeli briefings transliterated the Persian name as Shihab, taking into account the initial short vowel.

committee for U.S.-Russian intelligence exchanges on proliferation issues with Russian Premier Viktor Chernomyrdin.

This time Gilad added more specifics. He mentioned the names of Russian companies that had signed contracts with Iran. He mentioned specific missile components, dates of shipments, even the names of engineers. For the first time he cited Israeli concerns that Russia was preparing as a matter of state policy to transfer rocket boosters from dismantled SS-4 medium-range ballistic missiles, for a longer-range Shahab-4 missile still under development. The Shahab-4 could reach deep into Saudi Arabia, Egypt, and Europe, well beyond Israel. If successfully developed, it would give Iran the ability to exert subtle pressure on America's main trading and diplomatic partners. The countdown to nuclear blackmail had begun, he warned.

Russia's missile cooperation with Iran accelerated when former KGB boss Yevgeny Primakov was named foreign minister in January 1996, he added. For three decades Primakov had sought to counter U.S. influence in the Persian Gulf. He believed Russia stood to gain from a stronger Iran, capable of challenging U.S. interests in the region. The Israelis believed Primakov might be reaping a personal benefit from the missile transfers to Iran, as was Chernomyrdin.

Fuerth was sufficiently impressed by the quality of the Israeli intelligence that he brought it to the attention of the vice president. Gore turned to the CIA and was informed that the United States was aware of Russia's assistance to the Iranian missile programs but did not share Israel's concern over the urgency of the problem. The Agency had become wary of requests from Gore involving Russia ever since he had sent back an analytical paper on Chernomyrdin's corruption with a dismissive handwritten comment, politely described by the press as a "barnyard epithet."

Nevertheless, Gore raised the Israeli concerns with Chernomyrdin when the two met in Washington on February 6, 1997. The Russian premier told him it was "impossible" that Russian state-owned firms were involved in Iran's missile projects, and demanded that Gore supply him with more-specific information so he could investigate the matter back in Moscow.

That same day, acting CIA director George Tenet testified to Congress that the Iranian effort to acquire long-range missiles would "probably" succeed "in less than ten years," but not earlier. There was no way he was going to hitch his wagon to the Israelis without independent sources of information. So far, the vast U.S. national technical infrastructure of satellites had picked up nothing to corroborate what the Israelis were saying. It was all just "chatter," rumors from exiles and unreliable human sources.

STROBE TALBOTT

In August 1997 the Iranians carried out a second rocket motor test at the Shahid Hemat facility outside of Tehran, and it was a clear success. By this point the CIA had confirmed not only the general outlines of the Israeli thesis but had also identified other Russian entities that were cooperating with the Iranians to design and build the new missiles. They also identified Yuri Koptev, the head of the Russian Space Agency (RSA), as a key official involved in the transfers to Iran.

To placate Congress, which was threatening to draft legislation to sanction the Russian companies, President Clinton appointed veteran diplomat Frank Wisner to conduct a "joint investigation" with the Russians of the missile transfers. His Russian counterpart was none other than Yuri Koptev. "He was a good choice for the Russians," an Israeli official quipped. "He knows where all the bodies are buried and what secrets to really protect."

While the Russians and the Americans kept talking, Russian technicians kept traveling to Iran, the Iranians continued to work in Russian weapons labs, and shipments of vital missile components continued to reach Iran. "Whenever the U.S. provides more information to Russia about the missile programs," General David Ivry told me in Tel Aviv, "we see the Russians seeking to identify the sources of that information and to close them off. Meanwhile, the project is continuing, the testing is continuing—even accelerating."

In late September 1997, Israel's top arms-control official, Shimon Shtein, provided new information to Talbott during a visit to Washington. This time Talbott blew up. He warned Shtein that if Israel didn't stop leaking intelligence about the Russian missile sales to Iran, it would "seriously undermine" U.S.-Israeli relations.

Using four-letter expletives, he said the administration would cut back aid to Israel if the Israelis didn't stop going behind his back to Congress and the media. We are engaged in serious negotiations at the highest levels with the Russians about things that go way beyond a few missiles, he told the Israeli.

I spoke with Shimon Shtein in Tel Aviv shortly after this encounter. He confirmed the meeting with Talbott but would not comment on what had occurred. Talbott's angry threats were read to me from a cable by a top adviser to Prime Minister Benjamin Netanyahu. Talbott's office refused to comment.

As the months wore on, the Israelis saw the opportunity to choke off Russian aid to Iran slipping away. They could hear the countdown as the Iranians prepared the Shahab-3 for launch.

RUSSIAN STRATEGY

Congressman Curt Weldon (R-Pa.) was watching the Russian missile transfers to Iran with mounting unease. A student of Russian history who spoke fluent Russian, he believed the Clinton administration had bet too heavily on President Boris Yeltsin and had neglected the rising influence of Yeltsin's hard-line security advisers.

From sources in Moscow, Weldon learned that Yeltsin had adopted a new security doctrine for the Russian Federation that was a radical throwback to the Cold War. In some ways it was even worse. Weldon obtained a copy of a key strategy paper used to prepare the new doctrine and asked the CIA to translate it.

This chilling document, excerpts of which I've included in the appendix, confirms in black and white the suspicions the Israelis expressed about Russia's missile transfers to Iran. There was nothing arbitrary or accidental about the sales; they were Russian state policy.

The study was prepared by Prof. Anton M. Surikov, the head of the Russian Defense Ministry's in-house think tank, INOBIS. Surikov briefed it to Defense Minister Pavel Grachev and his deputy, Andrei Kokoshkin, in September 1995. (Kokoshkin went on to become Yeltsin's national security adviser two years later.) The copy obtained by Weldon bears the stamp "Approved." The main findings regarding the Persian Gulf were put into practice almost immediately.

The broad-ranging study proposed a new strategy for countering the "main external threats" to the Russian Federation. Despite the end of the Cold War, the study identified the United States as "the main external force potentially capable of creating a threat to Russian Federation military security and to Russia's economic and political interests. . . ."

The study reassessed Russia's commitments to START and the Conventional Forces in Europe (CFE) Treaty, and urged Russian leaders to form a strategic alliance with Iraq and Iran, as a means of countering U.S. encroachment in the oil-rich Caspian region.

It suggested that Yeltsin use the threat of selling nuclear and missile technologies as a "trading card" with the United States.

"And in case Russia is persistently driven into a corner, then it will be possible to undertake to sell military nuclear and missile technologies to such countries as Iran and Iraq, and to Algeria after Islamic forces arrive in power there," the study went on. "Moreover, Russia's direct military alliance with some of the countries mentioned also should not be excluded, above all with Iran, within the framework of which a Russian troop contingent and tactical nuclear weapons could be stationed on the shores of the Persian Gulf and the Strait of Hormuz." The study also advocated selling nuclear missile technology to Iran.

Just one month after he was briefed on the study, Defense Minister Pavel Grachev went to Iran to discuss military cooperation. His visit paved the way for a sweeping Ten Year Cooperation Agreement the two countries signed on December 28, 1995.[1] Two months after the briefing, Russia began shipping to Iraq gyroscopes scavenged from dismantled SS-18 strategic nuclear missiles. Within four months, the Russian government authorized Russian missile experts to travel to Iran, to work on jointly developing a new generation of nuclear missiles for Iran.

The Russians wasted no time in implementing their dangerous new strategy, but the Clinton team never connected the dots.

THE ARROW

In Tel Aviv, Uzi Rubin was hard at work on Plan B.

From his office in the Kirya, he shuttled back and forth to a top-secret factory near the town of Beer Yaacov, close to Ben Gurion International Airport, where engineers from Israeli Aircraft Industries and designers from the Israel Missile Defense Organization were putting the finishing touches on the free world's first antimissile system, the Arrow.

The location of the plant—known only by its initials, MLM—was so secret that each engineer who worked there had to be cleared by the minister of defense in person. The Iranian missiles posed an "existential threat" to Israel, Prime Minister Netanyahu and his top advisers believed.

"Any future war will involve long-range missiles, capable of striking targets throughout Israel, so we are building a national missile defense," Rubin told me in an interview at his office in the Kirya. The Arrow was partially funded by the United States, even though the Clinton administration adamantly refused to pursue a national missile shield for the United States.

As the Iranians began to test-launch the first Shahab-3 missiles, the Israelis announced their own tests of the Arrow. "We live in the Bronx of the Middle East," Rubin said. "But we have one advantage over our neighbors: the jet streams all flow east. So anyone sending nasty stuff on us is going to have to worry about it coming back on them."

Just in case Israel couldn't afford to deploy enough Arrow batteries to handle the hundreds of missiles its Arab neighbors and Iran had arrayed against them, the authorities instituted a nationwide civil defense program to distribute gas masks to every person in Israel.

"Every baby born in Israel is issued a gas mask at birth," Major General Yaacov Amit-Dror told me, "and they are regularly tracked by our civil defense teams to make sure they get new ones as they grow."

But the Iranians had something else in mind, not just a chemical or biological warhead. They were going nuclear.

FIRST FLIGHT

On July 21, 1998, Mohsen Rezai's dream became a reality.

Zelzal—the earthquake—sounded. Shahab—the Shooting Star—burned.

Under the watchful eyes of Russian technicians and Revolutionary Guards officers from the newly formed Missile Corps, the first Shahab-3 prototype was hoisted into a vertical position on its Mercedes launch vehicle, and the huge, liquid-fueled engine fired. First came a billowing cloud of white smoke from the ultra-cool nitric acid fuel, then the dust. There was so much dust, he didn't see the missile loose the chains of gravity until it was already well into the sky, streaking out toward the Shahroud test range in the Dasht-e Kavir, the vast salt desert east of Tehran.

Seconds later a warning flashed on the giant video screen in the war room inside Cheyenne Mountain, when U.S. Air Force Space Command early-warning satellites and long-range phased array radar picked up the launch. Later that day, photo analysts at the National Reconnaissance Office poured over the imagery. The CIA's Nonproliferation Center compiled the data.

CIA director George Tenet was stunned. And angry. Just months earlier he had told a congressional panel that Iran was still "five to ten years away" from developing medium-range missiles capable of reaching Israel and would not be capable of building a missile that could threaten the United States before 2010.

The DIA's top missile analyst, Dr. David Osias, had promised him there had been no increase in the threat. He cast that judgment in stone in the now-infamous National Intelligence Estimate on the ballistic missile threat (NIE 95-19), an assessment crafted by the intelligence community to support the political decision by the Clinton administration not to deploy a national missile-defense system.

The Shahab-3 prototype flew 620 miles southeast from Shahroud toward the Persian Gulf. The Russian-designed liquid-fueled engines completed their full 100-second burn, and then ground control engineers destroyed the missile in midair, presumably to prevent it from reaching populated areas along Iran's Persian Gulf coast.

The CIA analysts concluded that Iran's intent was to demonstrate the rocket's full range of 800 miles, not its accuracy. As they examined the imagery, they concluded that the ballistic arc described during the test demonstrated that the Shahab-3 could reach targets as far away as Tel Aviv and possibly Cairo.

Iranian defense minister Admiral Ali Shamkhani confirmed the test in a televised interview on July 26. "Perhaps many observers are surprised that Iran . . . freely confirms information on testing of a defensive weapon," he wrote three days later in a commentary that appeared in *Iran* daily. "If others observed such clarity, too, there would not have been such deceit and ambiguity regarding the nuclear capability of the Zionist regime."

Always Israel.

Rafsanjani told state radio on July 29 that such missiles were a basic component of any nation's defense forces and that Iran had developed the Shahab-3 on its own. "The Shahab-3 is an entirely Iranian missile. There could be some adaptations from foreign makes, but it is not similar to any foreign missile," he said.

Judiciary chief Ayatollah Mohammad Yazdi told a Friday prayer audience at Tehran University on July 31 that Iran had developed the Shahab-3 to counter Israel's nuclear deterrent. Iran intended to produce an arsenal of the missiles with the intent of "creating a military balance."

With typical bravado, Mohsen Rezai told a gathering of Revolutionary Guards recruits that Iran planned to make so many of the new missiles that "if any country fires even one missile at Iran, then we will definitely respond by firing ten."

The Iranians were so pleased with the new missile that they paraded it through the streets of Tehran on September 25, on its gigantic wheeled launcher. Just in case any ambiguity remained as to why Iran had developed the missile, the Revolutionary Guards Missile Corps festooned it with gigantic banners that read, "Israel must be wiped off the map" in both

Farsi and English. The banners were photographed by newsmen and broadcast worldwide.

Defense Minister Shamkhani was defiant. If Israel attacked now, Iran would retaliate "in a way the Israelis cannot imagine," he said. "Of course," he added, "this program will be pursued and we will have the Shahab-4 and even the Shahab-5 to respond to our defense needs."

In Tel Aviv, Israeli chief of staff Shaul Mofaz (who happened to be Iranian-born), responded the next day by telling IDF radio that Israel "must be ready to launch a preventive strike if this becomes necessary. The arming of an extremist country like Iran with long-range missiles capable of carrying nonconventional weapons in the long-term may even pose a threat to our very existence."*

NORTH KOREA

Quietly, one month after the successful test in Iran, a team of IRGC missile experts flew to North Korea in a specially equipped Boeing 707, carrying monitoring and telemetry equipment. U.S. satellites picked up their arrival at a North Korean airport, and followed them to a known missile test site.

On August 31, 1998, the unthinkable occurred. With the Iranians present, North Korea test-fired a multi-stage missile called the Taepo-Dong—an event the U.S. intelligence community said could never happen. The missile flew so far—well over a thousand miles—that it overshot Japan, U.S. officials said later.

The National Intelligence Officer for Strategic Systems, Robert Walpole, went into overdrive to redraft the missile threat briefing he gave Congress to include the new threats the DIA's David Osias had been saying didn't exist. Until now, he said, Iran and North Korea have been importing technology for their missile programs. But these latest missile tests show they have been sharing information and technology among them-

*In initial comments on the test, White House officials called the Shahab-3 "an Iranian version of a North Korean model called the No-Dong." Apparently they figured that no one would remember they had boasted of having shut down North Korean missile cooperation with Iran in 1994. And at any rate, getting caught up in that detail was better than pointing the finger at the Russian and Chinese state-owned firms that provided key components for the new missile.

selves—and with others. “Clearly proliferation is not going to stop with the first holders of the technology, but will go on,” he added.[2]

The rogues were hanging together, and the United States was so far behind the curve there was no way they could be stopped.

All of a sudden, Iran’s boast of producing missiles capable of reaching the American heartland no longer seemed far-fetched.

18

THE PRESIDENT, THE LEADER, AND THE MURDERERS

The legitimacy of the regime does not lie with the people. Those who say the legitimacy of the leader depends on his popularity do not understand. . . . Our regime gets its legitimacy from God.

—Hojjat-ol eslam Ali Akbar Nateq-Nouri, speaking before October 23, 1998, elections to the Assembly of Experts

Some called it "Tehran Spring," a reference to the brief explosion of freedom that erupted in Prague in 1968 before Soviet tanks crushed the hopes of an enslaved people.

The overwhelming election of Hojjat-ol eslam Mohammad Khatami on May 23, 1997, to replace Rafsanjani as president took Iran's ruling hard-line clerics by surprise. Their hand-picked candidate, Majles speaker Ali Akbar Nateq-Nouri, won less than 30 percent of the vote, despite being portrayed as the overwhelming favorite before the election.

In the West, Khatami was portrayed as a "moderate," just as Rafsanjani had been when he became president eight years earlier. Khatami's election was seen as a triumph of democracy over tyranny. Great expectations were born of renewed dialogue between Tehran and the West.

Pro-Tehran advocate Housang Amirahmadi set up a new lobbying group, the American-Iranian Council (AIC), with money from Conoco and other businesses eager to see U.S. sanctions lifted. The business lobbies were thrilled and shoveled money to think tanks and groups such as AIC to hold conferences to promote Khatami and renewed U.S.-Iranian relations. Their message was simple and compelling: Khatami is seeking to turn the page on terrorism. Iran is not a threat but an opportunity.

In Paris, the dissident Ayatollah Mehdi Rouhani sounded a more careful note. "The Iranian people did not know Khatami, and Khatami did not know the Iranian people," he said. "But by voting for Khatami, Iranians were voting against the regime, against Khamenei, against the system of *Velayat-e Faqih*."

Rouhani's caution was widely ignored by Western leaders, who embraced Khatami with a passion normally reserved for movie stars. Khatami promised reform, economic and social liberalization, Islam with a smiling face. It would have been churlish to remind people that as minister of Culture and Islamic Guidance in 1984, Khatami had presided over the creation of Hezbollah as the international terrorist wing of the Islamic Republic.[1]

CNN's Christiane Amanpour, daughter of an Iranian exile, gushed that Khatami's election presented a "new opening" for the U.S.-Iran relationship. In a much-acclaimed CNN interview broadcast on January 7, 1998, Khatami encouraged the expansion of cultural and economic exchanges between the two countries as an example of the "dialogue between civilizations" he had been advocating since his election.

To those who listened, Khatami insisted that his goal was not better relations with the United States but an end to U.S. economic sanctions, which he said were a U.S. effort "to inflict economic damage upon us." He also dismissed U.S. charges that the Islamic Republic was supporting terrorism. "Supporting peoples who fight for the liberation of their land is not, in my opinion, supporting terrorism," he said.*

Nevertheless, Khatami's statements "suggest he is trying to play a more constructive role in the international community," CIA director George Tenet told Congress on January 28, 1998. "[A] genuine struggle is now under way between hard-line conservatives and more-moderate elements represented by Iran's new President Khatami. And so the challenge is how to cope with a still dangerous state in which some positive changes may be taking place."

Khatami's interior minister, Abdallah Nouri, lifted restrictions on the press and allowed hundreds of new publications to appear, many of them critical of the government. But as Nouri handed out permits to newspaper publishers, Khatami's intelligence minister, Qorbanali Dori-Najafabadi, shut down the papers and jailed reporters, editors, and writers.†

*Khatami never wavered in his support for Palestinian violence against Israel, a view he shared with the hard-liners. On May 2, 1998, for instance, Hamas leader Sheikh Ahmed Yassin paid an official visit to Iran, seeking renewed financial support. Instead of urging Yassin to seek a negotiated settlement with Israel that would benefit Palestinians, Khatami joined Khamenei and others in condemning the U.S.-backed peace process. In comments reported in the Tehran press but ignored in the West, he called Israel "an extention of fascism." With Khatami's approval, the Majles continued to earmark $55 million per year in its official budget to terrorist groups that opposed the peace process, including Hamas.

†Dori-Najafabadi replaced Ali Fallahian at the head of MOIS after a German court accused Fallahian in 1996 of having organized the murder of dissident Kurdish leader Sharafkindi at the Mykonos restaurant in Berlin, on orders from Rafsanjani, Khamenei, and foreign minister Ali Velayati.

Opposition leaders who have since fled Iran believe Khatami's "liberalism" was an orchestrated effort to encourage opponents of the regime to come out in the open, where they could be identified and neutralized. Several of Iran's most prominent dissident writers disappeared in 1998 and were found dead weeks later. Others were jailed and accused of crimes against the state. Judiciary chief Ayatollah Mohammad Yazdi, an unelected official who reported only to the Supreme Leader, made sure they received harsh sentences from the Islamic courts. Some, such as *Iran News* editor Morteza Firoozi, were sentenced to death.

After killing the most prominent political dissidents in exile, the regime was now turning to those who dared raise their voices inside.

TEHRAN SPRING

On April 30, 1998, the Defense Intelligence Agency held an all-day seminar at Bolling Air Force Base, to listen to outside experts opine on events in Iran.

Former U.S. chargé d'affaires in Tehran Bruce Laingen, who spent 444 days as a hostage, was convinced it was time for the U.S. to launch a "substantive dialogue with Iran." Khatami's election brought "the hope of change in Iran," he said. "We have seen the apogee of clerical control."

Others argued for a resumption of economic ties, so U.S. businesses could cash in on the "bonanza" of new oil- and gas-field development in the Caspian Sea basin. Former national security advisers Zbigniew Brzezinski and Brent Scowcroft were the most prominent public supporters of this view.

The senior DoD intelligence analyst who was our host opened the day-long conference, which I addressed, on a note of awe. A "Prague Spring" had broken out in Tehran, he said. "However you look at it, something is clearly happening, both in Iran and here."

Azar Nafisi, a former Tehran University literature teacher, was more skeptical.

Just two days before the conference, she said, the regime had passed a new law making it illegal for a woman to leave Iran without the formal consent of her husband. "Since Khatami has taken office, government newspapers have reported six cases where individuals have been stoned to death for adultery. If a woman does not wear her veil properly, or is caught wearing 'vulgar' shoes or sunglasses, she is sentenced to seventy-six lashes. This is something Iranian youths live with every day."

"Under the shah," she added, "human rights groups such as Amnesty

International used to ask the Iranian government to enforce the law. The paradox is that today, under the Islamic Republic, the law itself is in violation of human rights, making a mockery of President Khatami's call for the rule of law."

Nafisi went on to write a best-selling account of life under the mullahs, *Reading Lolita in Tehran*. After years of hoping for change, she left Iran shortly after Khatami's election when the authorities canceled her lectures on American and British literature at the university because of their popularity. "In today's Iran, Jane Austen is subversive. So is lipstick," she said.

She thought the "Prague Spring" in Tehran was just the calm before the storm.

She was right.

HEZBOLLAH'S HELPERS

Fighting spilled into the streets of Tehran and Isfahan just one month later, as Khatami supporters clashed with an organized group of street terrorists known as Ansar-e Hezbollah (literally "Hezbollah's Helpers").

Over the preceding three years these armed thugs had attacked movie theaters and persons wearing Western clothing. They had broken up student meetings at universities and prevented "anti-Islamic" lectures by faculty members. They even physically assaulted Rafsanjani's daughter—a member of the Majles—after they caught her riding a bicycle in a public park outside of Tehran.

The regime claimed it knew nothing about Hezbollah's Helpers. But in fact the group was well organized and well funded. It had even taken out full-page ads in prominent Tehran dailies to publish a manifesto.

The group's aim was "to help the Islamic Revolution preserve its values," it wrote. "Our main goal is to counter those who want an Islam which does not govern, those who want to send Islam back to the graveyards and the mosques. This [type of Islam] is American Islam."

Their main supporter was Ayatollah Ahmad Jannati, secretary of the powerful Council of Guardians and a key member of the Supreme Leader's inner circle. Jannati believed the "reform" movement presented a vital threat to the regime, since its ultimate goal was to end absolute clerical rule.[2]

The most violent clashes that spring occurred on May 25 in Tehran's Laleh Park, where some two thousand students rallied under the banner of the Islamic Students Association (ISA). The students were calling for nonclerics and women to be allowed to run for the Assembly of Experts, the eighty-member body that selects the Supreme Leader, in elections scheduled for October. They were also seeking to end the power of the hard-line Council of Guardians to determine the eligibility of candidates running for public office. The council regularly disqualified prominent political figures from running for office because of factional squabbles. It was out of the question that they would allow open opponents of the regime to appear on the ballot.

Suddenly, scores of young men who had mingled with the crowd took metal bars from beneath their clothing and began swinging. They smashed the sound equipment and beat students until blood began to flow. When ISA president Heshmatollah Tabarzadi attempted to shout over the din, one of the attackers shouted back at him, "We don't want freedom. Freedom will lead to a day when the chador will be dropped and the Americans will return to Iran." Hezbollah's Helpers had struck again.

The day after the clashes, Interior Minister Abdallah Nouri announced that Khatami intended to embrace the students' demands and would ask the Majles to limit the powers of the Council of Guardians.

That was too much for the hard-liners. Before Khatami could make his move, the Majles simply removed Abdallah Nouri from office. Majles speaker Nateq-Nouri, a key Khamenei ally, scoffed at the demands for reform. "Our regime gets its legitimacy from God," he said. "The legitimacy of the regime does not lie with the people. Those who say the legitimacy of the leader depends on his popularity do not understand."

These essential reforms, which would impose clear limits on the political powers of the clergy, are still being demanded by pro-democracy groups in Iran today. But hope that the regime was capable of reforming itself—a hope Khatami helped kindle—was about to come to an end.

THE FOROUHAR MURDERS

For fifty-eight-year-old Khosrow Seif, the waiting was the worst.

A friend had phoned him with the news. It was around four-thirty on the afternoon of Saturday, November 21, 1998, and the friend had just come from the house of Darious and Parvaneh Forouhar, where he had an appointment to meet with the leaders of the opposition Iran People's Party. His voice was shaking from what he had seen.

You've got to come quickly, he said. It's happened.

Both of them?

Both, his friend said. They've finally done it.

Seif was Forouhar's top deputy. He wanted to know more.

The friend, a prominent businessman from the Tehran bazaar, had gone to meet Forouhar at the office he maintained in his home. When no one answered, he tried the door and found it unlocked. Inside, he found the seventy-year-old Forouhar slumped on the floor. Then he rushed upstairs and found Parvaneh, his wife. She was sixteen years younger and had clearly struggled with her assailants. Her body was a mess.

Seif lived around 5 kilometers across town and rushed outside to get a taxi. By the time he arrived at the two-story house in the cul-de-sac at the end of Hedayat Street, the police had sealed the area.

They knew who he was, but wouldn't let him into the house. They were looking for evidence, talking into their handheld radios. This is a crime scene, one of them said.

For hours, Seif waited outside in the cold. Finally he called friends at KRSI, the twenty-four-hour radio station in Los Angeles. They broadcast the news that Forouhar and his wife had been murdered, and asked their listeners to call friends and family in Tehran. Within minutes people began trickling into the street. Before an hour had gone by, a small crowd had gathered, surrounding the house. They were angry. Some shouted at the police. It was at least some comfort.

From the small yard they could see into the front room of the house through the open door. Forouhar was wearing a suit now, propped in his chair, head back, his hands on the chair arms as the policemen milled about. They've clearly repositioned the body, Seif remarked. Cleaned it up.

It was past midnight when the police finally let him into the house, along with Dr. Behrouz Boroumand, the family doctor, who was also on the leadership council of the IPP. He examined Forouhar's body and found twelve knife wounds. His assailants had also broken both his hands.

Go up and check the wife, one of the policemen said. We want to take the bodies to the morgue.

Dr. Boroumand demurred. I've seen too many murders, he said. I know what she's going to look like, and I don't want to see her like that.

It had taken the eleven men twenty-four thrusts with their knives to extinguish Mrs. Forouhar's screams.

KHATAMI CAVES

Seif's phone call to the Los Angeles radio station forced the issue, and the next day the regime announced that the Forouhars had been killed.

The initial version claimed that the couple had been murdered by their own bodyguards. Later an official government inquiry announced that the killers had been let into the Forouhar house by a "trusted friend" of the family and had presented themselves as filmmakers who sought to portray the modest lifestyle of the dissidents. The killers followed Mrs. Forouhar upstairs, where she had gone to change, and killed her there. Then they returned downstairs and killed her husband at his desk, where they had set up cameras for the photo shoot, leaving knives thrust in both victims' hearts.

Neither version had a shred of truth to it.

Just hours before the regime announced the deaths, President Khatami gave a speech in Bonab on his interpretation of Iran's "civil society." He blasted the regime's secular opponents and warned that dissidents who rejected the doctrine of absolute clerical rule would no longer be tolerated. That description fit the Forouhars to a tee.

When a funeral procession turned into a massive anti-regime demonstration on November 26, Khatami had second thoughts and announced that he was appointing a special panel to investigate the murders, which he now condemned.

And then the leaks began.

On December 3, an unsigned article appeared in the opposition *Keyhan*, published in London, carrying a Tehran dateline. It claimed the Forouhar murders were ordered by a secret Special Operations Committee run by former intelligence minister Ali Fallahian, now a top adviser to the Supreme Leader. The regime feared that Forouhar was on the verge of uniting opposition forces inside the country and linking them to exiles who had backing from foreign governments. It was the regime's nightmare scenario.

On January 5, 1999, MOIS released an unprecedented statement, claiming that "renegade government agents" were responsible for the "serial murders" of political dissidents and intellectuals. MOIS pledged to bring them to justice.

Shortly after the Forouhar murders, dissident writers Mohammad Mokhtari and Mohammad Jafar Pouyandeh were found murdered, along with a journalist, Majid Sharif. Two other dissidents were still missing and believed dead, one since August.

The MOIS statement called the murders "horrendous acts," and placed the blame on "irresponsible colleagues of this ministry with deviatory thoughts" who were "acting on their own and without doubt as surreptitious agents of foreigners." Supreme Leader Ayatollah Khamenei accused the United States and Israel of having plotted the assassinations to create instability in Iran.

The pro-Khatami daily *Salam* called for the resignation of Intelligence Minister Dori-Najafabadi, claiming that he had not been Khatami's choice to head the ministry but had been forced on the president by hardliners. "The least that must be done now is to replace him and probe his performance," *Salam* urged.

In the meantime, Khatami had learned the truth, thanks to tapes from video surveillance cameras placed by MOIS in the Forouhar residence.

The eleven-man hit team that murdered the Forouhars were careful to remove the recording devices before they left, taking with them—or so they thought—all trace of their dirty work. Unknown to them, however, cameras placed by a rival section of MOIS in charge of counterintelligence continued to roll, capturing their faces and the gruesome details of the murders. Counterintelligence agents entered the Forouhar house thirty-six hours after the killings and retrieved the second set of tapes. Once they had identified the killers, they presented their evidence to Khatami.

Khatami's first reaction was to keep quiet, until he was told that a copy of the videotape had been sent to Parastou and Arash Forouhar, the slain couple's surviving daughter and son, then living in Germany. Audio versions of the tape began circulating among Iranian exiles, including a segment where one of the killers could be heard talking to a superior by telephone, asking what to do with Mrs. Forouhar because she was making so much noise. The superior was identified as Mohammad Pourmohammadi, a deputy minister of intelligence. He was also the Supreme Leader's "personal representative" to MOIS. The link was clear.

As more information on the Special Operations Committee began to leak out—presumably from Khatami's office—Ayatollah Khamenei summoned the president to an extraordinary meeting at his residence in Tehran. I learned what took place behind those closed doors from a trusted Iranian source who provided me with handwritten minutes of the meetings.

Thirteen people attended the first meeting, which began at 3:30 p.m., after Friday prayers on January 15, 1999. Ayatollah Khamenei was accompanied by four top advisers, including chief of staff Hojjat-ol eslam Mohammadi-Golpayegani. Also attending were Rafsanjani, now head of the Expediency Council, Majles speaker Nateq-Nouri, Ayatollah Mahdavi Kani, Ayatollah Mohammad Yazdi, Intelligence Minister Dori-Najafabadi, and the new head of the Revolutionary Guards Corps, Major General Rahim Safavi.

Rafsanjani launched into a tirade against Khatami, accusing him of jeopardizing the very existence of the regime. An ocean of stability has been changed during the last fourteen months into a stormy sea, he said. Khatami had done more damage to the Islamic Republic than Gorbachev did to the Soviet Union. During the past twenty years the policies of Imam Khomeini and the revolutionary forces had succeeded in creating a well-knotted rope to serve as a lifeline of security and stability for the Islamic Republic. Your policies are unraveling that rope, he said.

Khatami's reforms had encouraged open defiance of the regime. People were not afraid any longer. This had given the opposition new energy.

The Ministry of Intelligence was the very backbone of the regime, he said. Khatami's accusations had damanged the morale of all revolutionary forces, including the Pasdaran. Fear was spreading that Khatami would order investigations there as well.

What you have done is worse than the actions of the shah, Rafsanjani said, turning to Khatami directly. The shah arrested politicians who had worked with him, but he never jailed members of the security forces as you have started to do. How dare you put on trial members of the security forces and highly placed members of the Intelligence Ministry! For long years they have worked for us and under our leadership. What will they answer in court? That they have executed our orders?

Ayatollah Yazdi said that the investigation into the Forouhar murders had led to an unbearable situation, and that the Judiciary was completely at a loss how to handle the case. Given that the minister of intelligence is a member of the religious establishment with a long background in the Majles, his indictment would be a blow to the whole establishment. For that reason we must close the file now, without wasting any more time, Yazdi argued.

As it was getting late, they agreed to continue their meeting the next day.

When Khatami arrived at Ayatollah Khamenei's residence the following afternoon, January 16, the compound was full of people, including a large number of security forces. There was a palpable tension in the air.

Khatami reitereated his demand for the resignation of the minister of intelligence and for the removal of Khamenei's personal representative to the MOIS, Pourmohammadi, the man the killers had called for orders from the Forouhar house.

You'd better look at this, said Majles speaker Nateq-Nouri. He waved a petition that bore the signatures of eighty-six members of the Majles, requesting that he convene a special session of parliament to remove Khatami and his government.

I've got another 106 Majles members who have agreed to sign on tomorrow if we don't reach a conclusion tonight, he added.

You have a choice, Khamenei said. He nodded to judiciary chief Mohammad Yazdi, who read out the alternatives.

Either you have the investigative committee you set up issue a statement declarating that the killings were the work of a small group of renegades, or we remove your government and declare a state of emergency.

Khatami requested a recess, so he could consult with his advisers, former interior minister Abdallah Nouri, and former prime minister Mir Hossein Mousavi, who had not been allowed to attend the meeting.

When he returned to Khamenei's residence that evening, he accepted the lie about the "renegade" officers. But, as a concession, he got Khamenei and the others to agree to get rid of the intelligence minister after a two-month cooling-off period. After all, he pointed out, one of the killers has already admitted that the decision to kill the Forouhars was made at Dori-Najafabadi's house.

Later that same evening, the presidential investigating committee released its findings, which were read aloud on state-run radio and television. "None of the [regime's] political groups or factions are in any way involved" in the Forouhar murders, the committee concluded. Knowing that MOIS "could not accept such a hateful, dirty crime, [the killers] acted on their own, without referring to their superiors."

Khatami had caved. Described by close associates as "weak-willed," "indecisive," and "nonconfrontational," he was constitutionally unsuited for the tough confrontations of the weeks and months ahead.

19

THE STUDENTS

On the second anniversary of his election, Khatami tried desperately to put the genie of freedom back into the bottle. As he lectured a crowd of 100,000 supporters at Tehran's Azadi (Freedom) Stadium on May 23, 1999, on the virtues of civil political discourse and the rule of Islamic law, thousands of demonstrators gathered elsewhere in the city, calling for greater freedom and an end to clerical rule.

Spearheading the most radical demonstrations were two former hezbollahis named Manuchehr Mohammadi and Heshmatollah Tabarzadi, the head of the Islamic Students Association. They led protesters in chants of "Death to Khamenei" and "Death to mullahs." Wherever they appeared and jinned up a crowd, Hezbollah's Helpers were never far behind. Neither were MOIS undercover cameramen, who methodically filmed the crowds.

Tabarzadi was well known in Iran as the former publisher of a pro-Hezbollah scandal sheet, *Payam-e Daneshjoo-ye Basiji* (*Message of the Militia Students*). In 1996 the *Message* was closed several times after Tabarzadi published breathless attacks, crammed with insider information, on the alleged corruption of key Rafsanjani allies, including Bonyad-e Mostazafan leader Mohsen Rafiqdoust. The *Message* ridiculed Rafsanjani and his pistachio empire, and claimed his relatives had created a "Mafia-style rule" over Rafsanjan city. It was widely believed at the time that Tabarzadi's sources were regime hard-liners, close to Supreme Leader Khamenei.

When other publications were struggling, the *Message* operated out of a three-story office building on Vesalle Shirazi street, close to Tehran University, and was printed on the government presses of the hard-line *Keyhan* daily whose publisher, Hossein Shariatmandari, was a Revolutionary Guards general and a close Khamenei adviser. Tabarzadi's trademark was a green camo army jacket, left over from his time in the Basij militia, and a full beard, which he trimmed with a razor rather than scissors, according to

Koranic prescriptions. He was so religious that he refused to shake hands with unbearded students, calling them *najess*—impure.

Mohammadi was "abducted" by Hezbollah's Helpers during a May 25 rally at Tehran University and handed over to MOIS interrogators. He told KRSI radio in Los Angeles after his release five days later that he had been forced to sign a written confession that he had received money from foreign sources and from Iranian opposition groups. He said he had been freed on bail pending trial by an Islamic court.

While Mohammadi was being held, Tabarzadi led rallies demanding his release. MOIS operatives arrested another 250 to 300 demonstrators, including charismatic student leader Gholamreza Mohajeri-Nejad. They held them for three days, then let them go.

For now, they were just playing.

Although Khatami had named a new head of MOIS, the Intelligence Ministry continued to play mind games with the dissidents. First they lured them into the open. Then they crushed them like gnats.

But the real leaders had yet to emerge.

"KILL HIM!"

The gathering storm broke on a late Thursday night in July 1999, when law-enforcement officers and Hezbollah's Helpers burst into student dormitories after midnight and went on a rampage of destruction. In their fury they punched holes through doors, ripped curtains from the walls, and dragged students from the beds and beat them silly. They went from building to building like a barbarian horde, setting fires as they left.

By 2:00 a.m., nearly everyone at the Tehran University campus in Amirabad was awake. Many fled, fearing for their lives.

Tabarzadi had been picked up by the police and thrown in jail two weeks before the attacks, and was nowhere to be seen. His detractors claimed he'd been placed in protective custody.

Mohajeri-Nejad was in building 19 when the horde struck. He was stunned to recognize General Nazeri, the head of the Law Enforcement Forces, the national paramilitary police. "He pointed to a student named Ezat Ebrahim Nejad, who had taken part in the demonstrations that day, and shouted to his people, 'Kill him!' A plainclothesman shot him dead right in front of my eyes," Mohajeri-Nejad told me. It all happened so fast no one had any time to react. Ebrahim Nejad had been identified by the MOIS cameramen, who followed the demonstrators wherever they went.

At another building the horde stormed up to the third floor and hurled two students off the balcony, after binding their hands and their feet. One of them died when he hit the ground.

Despite the hour, alert students snapped pictures of the confrontation and zapped them to friends and relatives in the United States via the Internet. I received some of those pictures through the Web site of the Foundation for Democracy in Iran (www.iran.org), a human rights monitoring group I worked for in my spare time. Soon the news was all over the exile radios in Los Angeles, and was picked up by the Persian-language services of Radio Israel, Voice of America, and the BBC.

On Friday morning, July 9, President Khatami sent prominent allies to the university, hoping to calm the storm. Rafsanjani's daughter Faezeh Hashemi came with the interior minister, but they were hooted off campus. As they jostled him, the students tore off the interior minister's turban and trampled it underfoot.

And that's when the uprising began.

THE JULY 1999 UPRISING

Later that day, groups of students gathered at the university, screaming their rage. By Saturday the ranks of protesters swelled into the thousands, with the students now calling for the resignation of hard-line clerics from the government. A long-haired youth named Ahmed Batebi held up the bloody T-shirt of one of the victims. His photograph made the front cover of *The Economist* and became the icon of the uprising. For that sin, Batebi was later arrested and tortured. He remains in prison today.

The murders at Tehran University acted like a spark, igniting protests in eighteen cities and towns across Iran. In Tabriz, a theology student was shot dead during clashes on July 11. Overseas Iranians marched in support of the pro-democracy demonstrators in Los Angeles, Houston, Dallas, New York, and a dozen European cities.

Khosrow Seif, the new leader of the Iran People's Party, ordered party activists to mobilize around the country. So did Roozbeh Farahanipour, a twenty-seven-year-old journalist identified in regime newspapers as "second in command" of the uprising. Farahanipour was secretary general of Marz-e Por Gohar ("Our Great Homeland"), a secular party that adopted the name of Iran's pre-Islamic national anthem.

Along with Seif, he believed it was essential to expand the protests beyond the university gates, but the pro-Khatami student leaders refused. On the third day of the uprising, Farahanipour and others broke down the university gates and the protesters swept into the streets of Tehran, where they were joined by thousands of ordinary city dwellers.

On July 12, an estimated ten thousand protesters clashed with police in Tehran. Another five thousand, including two thousand faculty members, staged a sit-in at Tehran University.

President Khatami, the "reformer," was under intense pressure. Viewing the chaos on Tehran's streets, a group of twenty-four senior Revolutionary Guards commanders warned him of dire consequences if he failed to put down the protests. It was time to choose, again.

"Mr. President, if you don't make a revolutionary decision today, and fail to abide by your Islamic and nationalistic duty, tomorrow will be too late and the damage done will be irreparable and beyond imagination," the commanders warned in a letter that was printed by *Keyhan.* "Our patience has reached its limits."

The letter was signed by the commanders of the IRGC land, sea, and air forces, the Qods Force, the head of the Basij (militia), three deputy commanders, six division commanders, two base commanders, and eight senior staff officers. It was seen as a scarcely veiled hint of a military coup should Khatami fail to act.

Khatami broke his silence the next day. "I am sure these people have evil aims," he said of the protest organizers. "They intend to foster violence in society, and we shall stand in their way." Defense Minister Ali Shamkhani chimed in later that day, warning protesters against violence: "We will enforce security at any price."

With Khatami firmly on board, the regime launched its counterattack. On July 14 it bussed tens of thousands of government employees to Tehran to stage a pro-regime rally. It was a massive show of force. Addressing the crowd, Hassan Rouhani, one of Khatami's vice presidents, promised to arrest pro-democracy protesters and execute them.

"Two nights ago we received decisive instructions to deal with these elements," he announced. "And at dusk yesterday we received a decisive revolutionary order to crush mercilessly and monumentally any move of these opportunist elements wherever it may occur. From today our people shall witness how our law-enforcement force and our heroic Bassij shall deal with these opportunists and riotous elements, if they simply dare to show their faces."

Khatami had shown his true colors. As one disillusioned student remarked to an AFP reporter, "Now we can see he's just a mullah like all the others."

ROOZBEH

Later that day, Roozbeh Farahanipour was at a safe house near the university organizing the next demonstration when armed militiamen shot out the windows and burst through the door. He was blindfolded and taken away along with eleven party activists to the infamous Towhid, where political prisoners were taken to be broken.

During his first interrogation, they asked him his name. When he answered normally, they said, "No, Farahanipour is dead. From now on, you are number 607." That was the number of his cell.

Because he was a writer, his jailers paid special attention to his hands, breaking his fingers repeatedly. At the time, no one even knew where the secret prison was located, or who was in charge.

The most brutal torture was the "chicken kabob." His jailers manacled his hands behind his back and shackled his feet, inserted a long metal bar like a skewer between them, and hoisted him onto a hook that was hanging from the ceiling, where they beat him with electric cable all over his body. As he was about to lose consciousness, one of them laughed. "Now we're going to barbecue you like chicken kabob."

A few days later he was taken to meet with a mullah who was sitting on a carpet, and managed to glimpse his face through the bottom of his blindfold. "So what's your involvement with these groups, young man?" the mullah asked. Farahanipour's interrogator told the cleric his name. "So this is the famous Farahanipour? Why can he still walk with his feet?"

Later, Farahanipour saw a picture of the mullah who was so eager to break his feet. It was Ali Yunesi, the "moderate" minister of intelligence, named by Khatami after the Forouhar murders.

KHOSROW SEIF

Khosrow Seif was arrested along with top IPP leaders Bahram Namizi and Farzin Mokbehr. Because of his age, they didn't physically torture him. Instead, they made him believe they had captured his son and were torturing him, by playing his screams in the cell block. Only later, did he find out it was faked.

They also played tapes with voices of friends, to make him think they were being tortured in front of his cell.

When he was first jailed, his interrogator was a picture of reasonableness. We have a problem, he admitted. But I believe there is a simple solution. We should execute you and three others, and it's all over.

After eight months, his jailers finally allowed him to make a single two-minute phone call to his family, who had feared he was dead. Seif believes he owes his eventual release to the intervention of the human rights groups in the West who constantly raised his case with the regime.

THE REGIME STRIKES BACK

With key leaders in jail, it was all over. The massive show of force by the regime on July 14 intimidated the students and they called it quits—at least for now. For the regime, the rest was just mopping up.

On July 17 and 18, plainclothes officers from the Intelligence Ministry, aided by armed Hezbollah's Helpers, set up roadblocks around Tehran and began methodically arresting students who had taken part in the protests.

On the eighteenth, MOIS announced it had arrested the head of the National Association of Iranian Students, Manuchehr Mohammadi, and his deputy, Gholamreza Mohajeri-Nejad. On the nineteenth and again on the twenty-sixth, state-run television broadcast heavily edited segments of Mohammadi's "confession." In the tape, he appeared swollen and drugged, and admitted that he had spent four months in Europe and America the previous year meeting with overseas Iranians, some of whom had contributed money to help him.

Mohajeri-Nejad spent the next thirty days in the Towhid. Just for fun, his jailers would bend one arm back behind his neck and the other one behind his back, twisting his body like a pretzel. Then they would wrap chains around his wrists and hoist him into the air, leaving him slowly twisting from a hook in the ceiling for hours. After six months in various jails, they released him. In 2001, at age thirty, he came to Los Angeles to join the exiles.

Farahanipour was also released on bail and managed to escape through Turkey to the United States, where he lives today.

Tabarzadi and Mohammadi are still in Iran and go in and out of Evin Prison, a very different place from the Towhid. The regime allowed Tabarzadi to set up two bank accounts with state-owned banks, so he could collect contributions from overseas. From time to time, while in Evin, he gave interviews to exile radio stations in Los Angeles.

Farahanipour smiled bitterly when he heard Tabarzadi denounce the regime during one of those interviews. "We call the place where he is staying 'Evin Hotel,' not Evin Prison," he said.

In the secretive world of Iran's clerical power brokers, nothing is as it seems. The army does not control Iran's military forces. The Law Enforcement Forces do not enforce the law. Iran's elected president does not control the government. Instead, decisions are made by small committees of clerics behind closed doors, then implemented through shadowy organizations.

The mullahs knew they were waging a twilight struggle. With 60 percent of the Iranian population born after the 1979 Revolution and yearning for freedom, it was only a matter of time before they faced serious challenges to their power.

The mullahs had won for now. But two clocks were ticking in a countdown to dramatic change.

First was the demographic bomb of Iran's pro-Western youth. Sooner or later they would break the yoke of fear and submission and stand by the thousands against the regime. Would the troops open fire? Would they murder their own children?

At then there was Iran's nuclear weapons program. If the clerics could get the bomb before the regime imploded, they figured no one would dare oppose them again.

CLINTON WASHES HIS HANDS

President Clinton ritually washed his hands of the students at a White House press conference on July 21, 1999.

"Frankly, I'm reluctant to say anything for fear that it will be used in a way that's not helpful to the forces of openness and reform," he began. He went out of his way to signal that the U.S. government had nothing to do with the demonstrations and was not supporting them in any way.

"I think that people everywhere, particularly younger people, hope that they will be able to pursue their religious convictions and their personal dreams in an atmosphere of greater freedom that still allows them to be deeply loyal to their nation," Clinton said. "I think the Iranian people obviously love their country and are proud of its history and have enormous potential. And I just hope they find a way to work through all this and I believe they will."

On July 27, 1999, the State Department formally lifted restrictions on the sale of food, medicine, and medical equipment to Iran, a loosening that prominent bazaaris close to Ayatollah Khamenei had been lobbying to achieve for several months.

It was just the beginning.

20

OCTOBER SURPRISE

If we abide by the Koran, we must mobilize to kill.

—Iranian president Mohammad Khatami
on state television, October 24, 2000

Bill Clinton wanted to leave a legacy behind him as a peacemaker. His last-minute attempt to force an agreement between Israeli prime minister Ehud Barak and Yasser Arafat at Camp David has been chronicled extensively. Virtually unknown to Americans, however, was an effort he undertook during his last eighteen months in office to craft a "grand bargain" with Iran's clerical rulers.

The "package deal" aimed to resolve twenty years of hostility between the United States and Iran. Clinton was hoping to renew diplomatic relations, restore commercial ties, and establish a new era of cooperation. He also figured the move would generate sizable donations to the Clinton Library in Little Rock from grateful corporations, which had been lobbying heavily to lift the Iran sanctions.

To the president's way of thinking, it was a win-win situation. Iran got investment, a new friend, perhaps even a protector. The United States lost a migraine headache. Gone from the mix was any attempt to pressure Iran to abandon its nuclear or missile programs.

Iran's pro-democracy students were not the only ones who would be on the receiving end of the new Clinton policy. So was Stephen Flatow, father of the twenty-year-old Brandeis University junior who was murdered on April 9, 1995, by an Iranian-backed bomber in Gaza.

Flatow's activism had prompted Democratic senator Frank Lautenberg and Republican congressman Jim Saxton to craft a provision in the 1996 Antiterrorism and Effective Death Penalty Act that allowed victims to sue foreign governments in U.S. courts. Three years later, Flatow received a default judgment from U.S. District Court in Washington, D.C., that ordered the Iranian government to pay $247.5 million in penalties and damages. He was flabbergasted. He had never expected the court case to go so far.

The problem was how to collect. Flatow and the families of other victims of terrorism wanted to seize Iranian government assets that had been frozen in the United States since the revolution. But the White House secretly maneuvered to prevent this from happening. The administration lied repeatedly to Congress and to the Flatow attorneys, claiming that no assets existed. It wanted to use the money as a negotiating chip with Tehran.*

"They had more Justice Department lawyers defending the government of Iran than they did working on the Microsoft antitrust suit," said Flatow family attorney Thomas Fortune Fay. "We thought they might avoid a question or two, but not that they would lie. We were naïve."

At one point, Deputy Secretary of the Treasury Stuart E. Eizenstat offered to set up a committee to study the question of Iran's assets. Flatow grunted when he heard that. Washington needs another committee like a moose needs a hat rack, he told me.

There was money, and lots of it. And the Iranians were determined to get it back. It was their greed that ultimately brought them to the negotiating table.

THE SPY CASE

On Passover Eve in the spring of 1999, twenty-three Jews were arrested during a police roundup in Iran's southern provincial capital, Shiraz. Among the victims were three rabbis, the keeper of a Jewish cemetery, a ritual butcher, and a sixteen-year-old student who was dragged out of his classroom by police. The regime was getting back into the hostage business.

Tehran Radio announced on June 7, 1999, that the authorities planned to try thirteen of the Shirazi Jews for spying on behalf of Israel. The prospective trial created a real problem for the Clinton administration, which had already made a series of "good faith" public gestures toward Iran.†

A few days after the arrests were made public, Ayatollah Ahmad Jan-

---

*In response to a query about the assets from Senator Frank Lautenberg, Assistant Secretary of State Barbara Larkin wrote falsely on June 10, 1998, "There are currently no Iranian assets held by or under the control of the United States Government which could be used to pay claims against Iran."

†On April 12, 1999, in remarks at the White House "Millennium dinner," the president recognized Iran's "historic grievances" against the United States, an admission that was received with derision and gloating in Tehran. A few days later the administration lifted a ban on the sale of food and medicines to Iran in an effort to quietly resume trade.

nati, the hard-line surrogate for Supreme Leader Ali Khamenei, said the regime would execute the thirteen Jews if they were found guilty. "Where on earth has a spy been allowed to go scot-free?" he asked during a Friday prayer sermon. "The United States itself has arrested spies, and the Americans have not shown any willingness to negotiate over their release. Neither will we." He then accused the United States of practicing a double standard because it continued to hold U.S. Navy analyst Jonathan Pollard, a spy for Israeli intelligence, despite Israeli efforts to win his release.

The mention of Pollard was no accident. Over the next year and a half Pollard's fate would become inextricably intertwined with the fate of the thirteen Iranian Jews and, more generally, with the course of U.S.-Iranian relations.

It started when Pollard heard about the arrest of the Shirazi Jews and decided to approach the Iranians directly with the idea of a three-way swap. It was a long shot. But, hey, when you're serving life without parole, no straw is too thin to grasp.

For Iran, there was the prospect of getting rid of the U.S. sanctions and renewing trade. For President Clinton, there was the public acclaim he would receive for having freed the Jews. For the Israelis, there was Pollard.

Unbeknownst to Pollard or to his wife, Esther, who kept trying to contact the Iranian mission to the United Nations in New York without success, they had stumbled into a minefield.

The real negotiations were under way.

THE GRAND BARGAIN

The Intermediary the Clinton White House had used on other occasions was pressed back into service to work the deal directly with the regime.

At the end of July 1999, the mood within President Khatami's office, the Nahad, was upbeat. Khatami's group had just cracked down on the students, beaten back the uprising, and solidified its relationship with the Supreme Leader. The Intermediary's main contact in the Nahad was an aide to Vice President Hassan Rouhani.

The Pollard gambit was intriguing, his contact said. Rouhani had brought it up during the previous Saturday's weekly NSC meeting, on July 24, when they were discussing how to resolve the situation of the Shirazi Jews.

So what's the package? How does it look? Rouhani's aide said they planned to have a full-blown session on the Shirazi Jews and the U.S. offers at next week's meeting, July 31.

In the meantime, National Security Adviser Sandy Berger dispatched his top Middle East hand, Bruce Reidel, to deliver a formal offer in Paris in late July. The CIA officer transmitted the carefully worded letter to Khatami to a diplomat from Oman, not to an Iranian government official. If word leaked out, the Iranians could then say they did not have direct talks with the Americans.

In the signed letter, Clinton outlined the "Grand Bargain" he believed could lead to renewed trade and diplomatic relations between the United States and Iran. It included the release of the Shirazi Jews, an end to the U.S. trade embargo, and a request for Iran's cooperation on the Dhahran investigation. The White House provided the names of the Saudi Hezbollah leaders it believed had carried out the attack, along with photographs of the Saudis taken by clandestine means while they sojourned in the Iranian cities of Qom, Mashad, Ahwaz, and Karaj.

It was a treasure trove of intelligence, on a par with the intelligence documents Clinton had authorized administration officials to release to the Russians and the Chinese to convince them of how much the United States knew about their involvement in Iran's nuclear missile programs. Jonathan Pollard had gone to jail for revealing classified documents to a U.S. ally. Clinton now authorized releasing such documents to avowed U.S. enemies.

In November, Deputy Secretary of State Strobe Talbott authorized the sale of upgrade kits for Iran's Boeing 747 cargo jets. This came despite concerns from the Pentagon that the deal would enhance Iran's military airlift capability.

Then, on March 17, 2000, Secretary of State Madeleine Albright tipped the administration's hand by announcing that the United States was seeking a "global settlement" with Iran. As an added sweetener, she made an unbidden apology for the U.S. role in the 1953 coup d'état that restored the shah after a power play by popular prime minister Mohammad Mossadeq.*

But still, the negotiations were going nowhere. The United States had offered all the carrots, and the mullahs in Tehran had eaten them all, without ever saying "thank you."

They needed more time.

*"The coup was clearly a setback for Iran's political development," Albright said. "And it is easy to see now why many Iranians continue to resent this intervention by America in their internal affairs."

"DON'T WORRY"

Gary Samore had an appointment at the Kremlin.

It's good to see you again, his Russian counterpart on the national security staff told him after guiding Samore through the labyrinthine corridors up to his threadbare office. Mr. Berger phoned ahead to my director. He said you had something very important to share with us.

I do indeed, Samore said. We're hoping to resolve this before the big bosses meet in New York for the Millenium summit.

Samore had been tracking Iran's nuclear program for well over a decade. The Iranians had been suspiciously low-key for the past two years. There was a lot of noise about their ongoing cooperation with Russia to complete the Busheir plant, but Samore believed that was a rat hole for the Iranian treasury more than a real proliferation concern. Through careful diplomacy, the United States had managed to shut down the worst of it. At least that's what he had thought until recently.

His doubts had begun when Khatami replaced the head of the Atomic Energy Organization of Iran with a real professional, former oil minister Gholamreza Aghazadeh. The old minister was known for his incompetence and corruption. Now maybe the organization was finally going to be run by a pro. That was definitely bad.

Then the Russians replaced Viktor Mikhailov as head of the atomic energy ministry with Yevgeny Admov, the former boss of NKIET, a top nuclear lab that, the Clinton administration had learned, planned to build a 40-megawatt graphite-moderated research reactor in Iran. No one who had looked at the technology had any doubt what the Iranians were after. The NKIET reactor was intended to produce large quantities of weapons-grade plutonium. It was a bomb plant, pure and simple, just like the one they had earlier tried to buy from the Chinese. During an earlier trip to the Kremlin, Samore had delivered the bad news that the Clinton administration was blacklisting NKIET. The Russian lab's main partner in the deal, the Mendeleyev Institute, was also blacklisted. It was planning to build a heavy water production plant in Iran.

Shortly after taking over at the Russian atomic energy ministry in late 1998, Adamov stunned U.S. negotiators Bob Gallucci and NSC envoy Jack Keraveli by admitting that Iran was developing nuclear weapons. But that was no reason for Russia to scale back nuclear cooperation, he added. He made a similar comment in public while still at NKIET. "I am sure that Iran is trying to create a nuclear arsenal," he told Reuters. "It would be foolish to suppose that they do not want to create one." The United States had sketchy reports that he was on the take from the Iranians as well.

As he sat in the Kremlin office, Samore got to the point. We've got some information we'd like you to look into about a laser enrichment deal, he told his Russian counterpart. He handed over a file on the D. V. Efremov Institute of St. Petersburg. They've signed a contract with Iran to build a small laser enrichment plant we believe is a demonstrator for a full-scale production plant for fissile material.*

The Russian didn't ask him where all the detail had come from, though he could guess. The Americans were notorious for intercepting faxes. The Russian services no longer had the money to sweep so broadly.

The summit is in September—that doesn't give us much time, Samore said.

Don't worry. I'll look into it, the Russian replied.

MONEY IN THE WATER

As Bill Clinton's second term drew to an end, the pace of the U.S.-Iran exchanges intensified, in hopes of crafting a last-minute deal before the 2000 presidential elections. The White House hoped it would be an "October surprise" of sorts.

The president gave his own wink and nod during the Millennium summit at the United Nations. Clinton opened the extravaganza on September 6, then pointedly took a seat in the hall to wait until Khatami took the podium, nearly an hour later, to address the delegates.

In Tehran, Clinton's behavior was given prominent play. The Islamic Republic News Agency noted that the American president "normally leaves the UN straight after his speech, but this time round, he waited for the speech by President Khatami and he listened attentively." Clinton "nodded his head several times, displaying his agreement with certain ideas of his Iranian counterpart." Among foreign correspondents, Clinton's attention to Khatami "was seen as a sign of his interest in renewing relations with the Islamic Republic of Iran," the Iranian state news agency reported.

Word of an impending deal with Iran quickly reached Washington, where lobbyists, lawyers, opportunists, and hangers-on could smell money.

*The technical term for the equipment Efremov was selling was Atomic Vapor Laser Isotope Separation, or AVLIS. Nuclear experts called the device "the Octopus," because it had so many tubes. Iraq had also worked on AVLIS enrichment during the 1990s.

Among them was a Bethesda, Maryland, fixer who claimed he could bring former top Clinton aide Lanny Davis to the table, along with other Clinton confidants and former administration officials.*

On September 14, 2000, Paul Geffert, who had done trade deals in Russia when business was dicey and who had a long-standing interest in Iran, faxed a letter to the Intermediary on stationery of his consulting company, Ventus, Inc., to be hand-carried to the authorities in Tehran.

"A concerted behind-the-scenes effort between now and President Clinton's departure from office can lead to the removal of U.S. trade sanctions with Iran," Geffert wrote. He had spoken with two top Washington law firms—Patton Boggs and Steptoe and Johnson—who could provide "experts with direct access to the President and his top appointees for international trade." Those experts, his letter went on, had "extensive experience with negotiating bilateral agreements."

Geffert suggested to the Iranians that their common goal should be "to remove barriers so citizens of Iran and America can find additional common ground through trade."

In addition to a commission on whatever business was generated, the Intermediary said he was told that grateful U.S. companies would be invited to make a contribution to the Clinton Library in Little Rock. To this day, a full contributor list to the $165 million library has never been disclosed, despite repeated Freedom of Information Act requests from media organizations.[1]

THE SPECIAL NEGOTIATOR

On September 19, 2000, President Clinton appointed former State Department legal adviser David R. Andrews as his "Special Negotiator for U.S./Iran Claims" and awarded him the "personal rank of ambassador" to enhance his status in dealing with the Iranian government.

It was the first time since the creation of the Iran-U.S. Claims Tribunal in 1981 that a U.S. president had made such an appointment. "The administration thought this job was important enough for it to have an important title," Andrews told me shortly after his appointment was announced.

His Iranian counterpart, Dr. Gudarz Eftekar-Jahromi, was also of high rank. Not only had he served successive Iranian presidents as legal adviser

---

*Davis had gone to work for gold-plated law firm Patton Boggs. His office denied he was involved in the effort to lift U.S. trade sanctions on Iran.

since 1982, but Eftekar-Jahromi was a former member of the Council of Guardians, the powerful body that oversees Iran's legislature and vets all candidates for office. He had Ayatollah Khamenei's ear, not just Khatami's.

Andrews met with Eftekar quietly before his appointment was announced. "The secretary wants this to get done as quickly as possible," he said. "If we can reach an agreement, our intent is to do it as quickly as possible." All the pieces seemed to be falling into place.

The first big sticking point was the money. At stake were billions of dollars in claims by U.S. citizens and companies who lost property during the revolution and counterclaims by the Islamic Republic.

Rafsanjani once asserted that the United States was holding $17 billion in frozen Iranian assets. U.S. officials dismissed that as "wildly exaggerated." It included, among other things, Iran's claim that the Americans were sheltering $10 billion stolen by the former shah and a demand that the United States pay damages incurred by Iran's state railways from Allied arms transports during World War II.

But the United States *was* still holding weapons and spare parts paid for by the shah's government, and a Foreign Military Sales (FMS) account frozen in 1979. The Islamic Republic filed twenty volumes of exhibits and affidavits in The Hague in 1996, claiming that with interest it was owed more than $1 billion from the FMS account, and another $2 billion for the military equipment.*

There were so many weapons and spare parts that the Pentagon had to build a huge secure warehouse outside of Dulles airport just to hold them. Inside the 160,000-square-foot, windowless facility, Iran's gear was stockpiled on pallets, carefully shrink-wrapped, reaching all the way up to the steel I-beams supporting the roof 30 feet above. See Appendix for exclusive photos.

Andrews didn't really care how much the twenty-five-year-old weapons and spare parts were actually worth. His marching orders were to reach a global settlement, then cut a check. Fast.

---

*Iran was demanding an additional $1 billion to compensate for U.S. military action against Iranian oil platforms in the Persian Gulf in 1987–88, in a separate case filed with the International Court of Justice. The United States rejected Iran's demands on the grounds that Iran was using the platforms to conduct acts of war against international shipping during the Iran-Iraq war.

KHARRAZI AT UCLA

Iran's clerics wanted to make sure that the settlement with the United States included formal U.S. acceptance of the regime's legitimate right to power, and an end to any support for the opposition. If Clinton would agree to that, they were home free.

In September 2000, just as the negotiations appeared to be nearing a conclusion, Ayatollah Khamenei dispatched Maurice Motamed, the only Jewish member of Iran's parliament, to carry a message to members of the American Jewish community. "Motamed told us that the decision to renew relations with the United States has been taken at the highest level in Iran," said Pooya Dayanim, whose Iranian Jewish Public Affairs Committee was leading the fight to win the freedom of the Shirazi Jews. "Motamed told us, 'This is not President Khatami's initiative: it has been decided by the Supreme Leader, Ayatollah Khamenei. Khamenei is willing to free the Shirzi Jewish hostages.' I found this game to be a very dangerous one."

Shortly after Motamed's arrival, Iranian foreign minister Kamal Kharrazi, a noted hard-liner, was granted a visa to visit California, where an estimated one million Iranian-Americans lived. It was the first time an Iranian government official had been allowed to travel outside of Washington, D.C., or New York since the 1979 revolution.

Kharrazi arrived just as ten of the Shirazi Jews were given stiff jail sentences on trumped-up charges of spying for Israel at the appellate level of Iran's judiciary. He was greeted by angry protesters at every stage of his four-day trip. Pressure from the protesters caused wealthy Iranian Jews operating under the banner of the Iranian American Jewish Federation, which had maintained communications with the Islamic Republic, to cancel a planned meeting with Kharrazi.

On September 21, Kharrazi planned to meet with a small crowd of carefully screened guests on the UCLA campus. The James West Alumni Center was ringed on four sides by barricades and police. Around two hundred protesters greeted Kharrazi with pictures of relatives who had been executed or jailed by the Iranian regime. "All I want to know is why they executed my husband twelve years ago," said one woman, tears streaming down her face.

Suzy Yashar was one of the protestors and remembers the day well. "We weren't allowed to go inside. I remember we had a fight with the pro-regime people [who had accompanied Kharrazi]. After the meeting, one woman came back from the covered parking lot and started swearing at us, calling us losers for opposing the regime."

The young woman with the foul tongue was named Susan Akbarpour. She was an Iranian journalist who had come to the United States just three years earlier and filed a request for political refugee status. She'd worked her way up in the community and was dating a prominent Silicon Valley high-tech entrepreneur. Now she was shouting out her support for Iran's clerical regime.

THE DEAL UNRAVELS

In the end, it was neither the weapons nor the shah's alleged assets that killed the deal. It was not even the harsh sentences meted out to the Shirazi Jews, which the administration saw as an Iranian negotiating tactic. It was the FMS account, and one very angry United States senator.

The FMS account was a revolving credit established in the 1960s to finance Iranian arms purchases. It was the mother lode of Iran's financial holdings in the United States. And Senator Frank Lautenberg wanted it.

Throughout the 1970s, the Iranian treasury regularly replenished the FMS account to cover arms deliveries as they occurred. The account was held in trust for the government of Iran by the Defense Security Assistance Agency (now known as the Defense Security and Cooperation Agency) with the United States Treasury.

Iran had a positive balance of $400 million in the FMS account when President Carter froze Iran's assets in November 1979. And then the Americans just forgot that it existed. At least that was what the State Department claimed when Senator Lautenberg asked repeatedly about Iran's frozen assets.

In testimony before a Senate Judiciary subcommittee in October 1999, Deputy Secretary of the Treasury Stuart E. Eizenstat claimed that after the resolution of the hostage crisis in 1981, "we transferred all of the assets basically to Iran and what is remaining is a relatively smaller amount in the Claims Tribunal."[2]

That was false. But it took yet more effort by Lautenberg and the Flatow attorneys to shake the truth out of the government. In a stunning letter to attorney Thomas Fortune Fay sent on June 23, 2000, the Justice Department revealed that Treasury had been caught destroying an estimated eight hundred to nine hundred files related to the case. The documents had been carefully protected for more than twenty years, the letter stated. They were destroyed only after they had been subpoenaed by Judge Royce Lamberth of the U.S. District Court in Washington, D.C.

Senator Lautenberg was fed up. Joining forces with Florida Republican Senator Connie Mack, he sponsored new legislation that would compel the Treasury Department to assist victims of terrorism in identifying and seizing the assets of foreign governments convicted of having murdered U.S. citizens. The Mack-Lautenberg bill, known as the Justice for Victims of Trafficking and Violence Protection Act, passed out of committee in July 2000 and lit a fire under the Iranians. They dispatched a senior government lawyer to Washington, who warned openly that the bill's passage would mean the collapse of the secret U.S.-Iranian talks.

The lawyer, Mohammad Hossein Zahedin Labbaf, was Iran's resident negotiator at the Iran-U.S. Claims Tribunal at The Hague. His July 24, 2000, presentation to Congress was sponsored by the American-Iranian Council, the same lobbying group that had been seeking for years to get U.S. trade sanctions lifted.

The bill passed the Senate unanimously on October 11, 2000, and was signed into law by President Clinton two weeks later. But in last-minute negotiations, the White House persuaded legislators to pay Flatow and other victims' families from the U.S. Treasury, leaving Iran's FMS account untouched.

Clinton still held out hope of a last-minute deal, perhaps even a historical trip to Iran. Better to let the taxpayers pay than compromise his legacy.

But Tehran's leaders had other plans.

THE WARNINGS

The training starts at the earliest age. For the past twenty years we have marched over the American flag. Every meeting starts by saying "Death to America" and "Death to Israel." It's not hidden. For twenty years this has been the policy of Iran.

—Former Iranian Revolutionary Guards colonel,
September 2004

The use of an atomic bomb against Israel would destroy Israel completely, while [the same] against the world of Islam only would cause damages. Such a scenario is not inconceivable.

—Ali Akbar Hashemi-Rafsanjani,
Jerusalem day sermon at Tehran University, December 14, 2001

Warnings of Iran's true intentions came hard and fast throughout 2000 and 2001. Indications that Iran had accelerated its nuclear weapons program were numerous, but instead of brandishing the stick, the U.S. unearthed more carrots to offer Tehran. Equally strong indicators of Iran's involvement with bin Laden's al-Qaeda organization appeared, but the White House sought instead to negotiate a global settlement with Tehran.

It was nonproliferation through bribery, counterterrorism through appeasement.

Clinton revealed his reasons for ignoring the regime's bad behavior in unusual remarks made at the World Economic Forum in Davos, Switzerland, on January 27, 2005.

Iran was the only country in the world, he argued, "including the United States, including Israel, including you name it, where the liberals, or the progressives, have won two-thirds to 70 percent of the vote in six elections: two for president; two for the parliament, the Majles; two for the mayoralities. In every single election, the guys I identify with got two-thirds to 70 percent of the vote. There is no other country in the world I can say that about, certainly not my own." It was all about politics, not U.S. national interest.

In January 2000, Khatami aide Hassan Rouhani, the increasingly powerful chairman of Iran's Supreme Security Council, met with Russian vice-premier Ilya Klebanov and said Iran wanted to expand nuclear cooperation with Russia. On the table was a heavy-water production plant, the laser enrichment plant, and more. Russia's commission on military industry, chaired by acting president Vladimir Putin, announced on January 14 that Russia would build two more power reactors at the Busheir site.

Just three days later the *New York Times* reported that the CIA had warned the White House that Iran was now able to produce nuclear weapons. This dramatic new assessment was based in part on NSA intercepts of an unnamed Iranian official, who boasted that Iran had "enough nuclear materials" to build a bomb.

In March the German federal intelligence service, BND, warned that Iran was "striving to control the nuclear fuel cycle, from uranium prospecting to reprocessing," and was gaining knowledge "that can be used to build nuclear weapons."

IAEA director general Mohammad El Baradei, the Egyptian lawyer who succeeded Hans Blix, ordered the agency's press secretary to sit on that one like a ton of bricks. At a news conference at IAEA headquarters in Vienna on March 23, 2000, David Kyd insisted that Iran was cooperating fully with the agency and had placed its nuclear facilities under IAEA safeguards. He added that the agency "has not received any intelligence" from the United States or other member states to indicate that Iran's nuclear program was anything but peaceful.

On April 2, an Iranian truck was stopped by Uzbekistan customs when special radiation detectors provided under a little-known U.S. aid program picked up emissions one hundred times the normal level. The truck was carrying ten containers of an unspecified (but highly radioactive) nuclear material. Initial reports from Moscow said the Iranian driver produced documents identifying a company in Quetta, Pakistan, as the ultimate owner of the goods. Quetta was an easy entry point to Iran favored by smugglers.

Baradei flew to Tehran in May 2000 to meet with President Khatami, Hassan Rouhani, and other officials. With great fanfare he announced that Iran's nuclear activities were entirely peaceful and compliant with Iran's obligations under the NPT. The Iranians asked the IAEA to help fund a new center for nuclear studies west of Tehran. Baradei agreed.

But Baradei was playing games. Iran had already broken ground on an industrial-scale uranium conversion facility in the rocky desert outside of Isfahan—the long-awaited "hex plant" that would allow Iran to transform large quantities of natural uranium into feedstock for its still-secret centrifuge enrichment facility.

U.S. intelligence assets had been tasked to hunt for a pilot plant, a smaller facility where the Iranians could test the concepts, experiment, prove the technologies. Instead the Iranians began to build a sprawling industrial complex that looked for all the world like just one more petrochemicals plant. They were using a complete set of blueprints purchased from the Chinese, which included equipment test reports and design information on each individual component of the gigantic chemical complex. Sure, it was complicated, but no more so than building a gigantic race car, complete with engine and hydraulics, out of LEGO blocks. The United States had underestimated them, again.

In Israel, General Amos Gilad, head of the military intelligence research division, could read the writing on the wall. He felt that the Iranians were finally pulling all the different threads together into a very dangerous shirt of many colors.

"I call this the year of decision because Iran is developing nuclear weaons," he declared in June. "Iran is trying to gather the resources to develop nuclear weapons. If they're not stopped now, in five or seven years, Iran will deploy nuclear weapons. In strategic terms, seven years is the blink of an eye."

Gilad had timed his statement to appear just as Clinton and Putin were meeting in Moscow. "Russia is opposed to the proliferation of weapons of mass destruction," said Leon Fuerth, national security adviser to Vice President Gore, who still chaired the U.S.-Russian committee that was supposed to shut down the Russian sales to Iran. "It is the execution that is the problem."

That was the understatement of the year.

The IAEA now says that Iran submitted "preliminary design information" for the hex plant on July 31, 2000, but there is no record that the agency communicated that information officially to the United States or to other member states.

The CIA eventually picked up Iran's efforts, because the building activity was clearly visible from U.S. satellites roaming overhead. The deputy director of the Agency's Nonproliferation Center, Norman Schindler, warned in a September 21 hearing before the Senate governmental affairs committee. "Iran is attempting to develop the capability to produce both plutonium and highly enriched uranium, and it is actively pursuing the acquisition of fissile material and the expertise and technology necessary to form the material into nuclear weapons."

The warning was vague enough that it went virtually ignored in the press. But it was a 100 percent accurate, concise summary of what the Iranians were doing.

Later, Aghazadeh admitted in an interview that when he gave the orders to his development teams to pursue a heavy-water production reactor for plutonium and uranium enrichment by centrifuge, he wasn't sure which one would work. He was pleasantly surprised when both teams reported success.

The Iranians had shifted into high gear. "By this point, they're really rolling," said nuclear analyst David Albright. "They raced to get the hex plant finished."

As Hamid Reza Zakeri told the CIA in July 2001, they had a deadline: 20 Shahrivar 1380. Or, as the CIA understood it, September 10, 2001.

THE KOSAR MISSILE

Steve B. was a missile analyst who worked for a Beltway consulting firm that did work for the U.S. intelligence community. His speciality was examining the wealth of technical data U.S. satellites acquired during foreign missile tests, and reaching judgments that ordinary mortals could comprehend.

One of the techniques the United States used to identify unidentified missiles was called "spectral analysis." It involved shooting a laser beam through the vapor trail generated by the rocket motor exhaust. Different missiles used different propellants, and propellants burned in unique ways. Each had a distinct spectral signature. By comparing the colors with known rocket motors, one could usually come up with a match.

After looking at more than a half-dozen Iranian rocket motor tests—in addition to the successful Shahab-3 launch in July 1998—Steve B. had come to a stunning conclusion: the Russians had not only provided sample RD-214 rocket motors from scrapped SS-4 missiles; they had also provided the more advanced RD-216, used in the longer-range SS-5. Both missiles had been banned under the 1987 INF treaty.

The SS-5 was first deployed in Cuba in 1962, and had an estimated range of approximately 2,640 miles. Its RD-216 motor used storable liquid nitric acid and hydrazine (UDMH). The new fuel gave the Iranians a precious advantage over the liquid oxygen used in the SS-4: stealth. They could fuel the new missiles well ahead of ever using them, whereas the liquid-oxygen boosters had to be fired immediately.

There could be no possible doubt: the Iranians had tested an RD-216 motor. The spectral signatures of the two motors were distinctly different.

The RD-216 was developed by Energomash, which had built most of Russia's liquid-fuel rocket engines over the past fifty years. Energomash was under the direct control of the Russian Space Agency (RSA), whose director general, Yuri Koptev, had been designated the "point man" for contacts with the United States over Russia's missile transfers to Iran.

Steve B. could hardly believe it. The United States was providing sensitive intelligence on Russian-Iranian missile transfers to the very man who was in charge of organizing the deals!

Other intelligence Steve B. had examined led him to the conclusion that Iran was making serious progress in developing a new multistage missile capable of hitting the United States with a nuclear warhead. The Iranians planned to cluster four RD-216 boosters together for the first stage, and use a Chinese-supplied solid-fuel rocket to deliver the payload into orbit. The only eventual sticking point would be Iranian pride: they insisted on developing their own engines based on the Russian, North Korean, and Chinese technology. That requirement was sure to slow down the program.

Israeli sources indicated that Iran had chosen a new name for the new missile, which earlier reports had referred to as Shahab-5 or Shahab-6. Now that it had left the drawing board, they called it "Kosar," a Koranic term that referred to the stream of eternal life in paradise.

The CIA's National Intelligence Officer for Strategic and Nuclear Programs delivered the bad news to a Senate governmental affairs subcommittee on September 21, 2000. Because of Iran and North Korea's recent progress, "the probability that a missile with a weapon of mass destruction would be used against U.S. forces or interests is higher today than during most of the Cold War, and will continue to grow," he said.

Over the next five years—that is, through 2005—Iran was "more likely to develop an intermediate-range ballistic missile (IRBM) based on Russian technology before developing an ICBM using that technology." Most intelligence community analysts believed Iran would also "develop and test" a three-stage ICBM by 2005 that "would be capable of delivering a nuclear weapon–sized payload to the United States," he added.

"The missiles need not be deployed in large numbers. They need not be highly accurate or reliable; their strategic value is derived from the threat of their use, not the near certain outcome of such use."

All the clerics had to do was buy a bit more time. The clock was ticking.

THE DEFECTORS

When Iranian intelligence operative Hamid Reza Zakeri walked into the U.S. embassy in Baku on July 26, 2001, he was sick and afraid.

After an initial meeting in the small private room off the reception area of the embassy, the CIA station chief told him to get some rest. "Joan" pointed out the window to a nearby street corner and said she'd pick him up later that afternoon. He should leave the embassy looking angry to allay suspicions, just in case he was under surveillance.

He went to a public bathhouse, washed, and took a nap. She picked him up at 5:00 p.m. in her Range Rover.

He was afraid because his boss, Mustafa Hadadian, had ordered him to go to Beirut. That's where they sent people who had become a liability. He thought they were getting ready to kill him and traveled instead to Baku, where he thought he would be safe.

Zakeri brought detailed information for the Americans on al-Qaeda's long-standing relationship with Iran. The Agency had inklings of that relationship, and when CIA "George" arrived to debrief him in Baku, he showed Zakeri photographs of a training camp in eastern Iran, some 20 kilometers before the Tayabad border crossing to Afghanistan.

That's an al-Qaeda camp, Zakeri said. There's another one outside of Kerman City they used to use ten years ago, until Rafsanjani made up with the Saudis and kicked them out.

Bin Laden's deputy, Ayman al-Zawahri, had been coming to Iran for more than a decade, he said. He had forged a close relationship with Revolutionary Guards brigadier general Mohammad Baqr Zolqadr in the Sudan in the early 1990s, when Zolqadr headed the Pasdaran training mission there. The grandson of slaves from Zanzibar, Zolqadr sympathized with the Egyptian doctor and asked if he couldn't help locate his relatives.

Recently, however, bin Laden's people had had a dispute with Iran over Northern Alliance leader Ahmad Shah Massoud, whom the Iranians were backing against the Taliban. When Zawahri came to Iran in early 2001, he said he wanted to bury the hatchet and go back to the more cooperative relationship they had enjoyed before. Their differences were insignificant when it came to working against their common enemy—the United States, Israel, and their lackeys.

The Agency had a problem with that. The Iranians were Shias, and bin Laden and his people were Sunnis—and not just any Sunnis, but radical Wahhabi extremists. Wahhabis ate Shias for breakfast. It was worse than Irish Catholics and Protestants, and another stroke against Zakeri's credibility.

Former CIA director Jim Woolsey gets apoplectic when asked why intelligence community analysts persisted in dividing the terror masters along sectarian lines.

"The convential wisdom is idiotic. I don't remember what so-called expert was saying that Shia Islamists will never cooperate with Sunni Islamists or with secular terrorists, but I've thought this line of reasoning on totalitarians was wrong since I was a sophomore in college," Woolsey said. It reminded him of the experts in the 1930s who said the Communists and the Fascists would never work together. "Then, whoops, here comes the Hitler-Stalin pact. Intellectuals get involved in policy analysis and they think the intellectual roots of a movement are more important than the fact that they are totalitarians. This is extremely dangerous. It's the same sort of nonsense as those who said that al-Qaeda would never have worked with the Baathists because they were secular. It's just stupid."

Colonel B, an Iranian defector I debriefed over a two-day period in September 2004 in a European capital, spent twenty years as a Pasdaran officer. From the very start, he told me, Ayatollah Khomeini had a plan to recruit Sunni terrorists in his war against the Great and Little Satans, the United States and Israel. He called it *Rahman-o Rahim*, taken from the Koranic injunction to prayer.

"The training starts at the earliest age. For the past twenty years, we have marched over the American flag. Every meeting starts by saying 'Death to America' and 'Death to Israel.' It's not hidden. For twenty years this has been the policy of Iran."

Under Khomeini's plan, still in force today, each government security organization set up a special department dedicated to helping foreign terrorist groups. Iran provided them with money, leadership, logistics, a command structure. He provided detailed information on al-Qaeda training camps in Iran, that operated all through the 1990s. "You combine all these things, and you have 9/11," he said.

Was Iran involved in 9/11? I asked.

"All I can say is, I don't see that al-Qaeda had this type of capability on its own," he laughed. "Iran tries to throw fire on Satan from afar, rather than light it directly under his feet. They prefer to act indirectly, through these other groups."

BIN LADEN'S BODYGUARD

The U.S. government had many indications that Iran was deeply involved with al-Qaeda in plotting terrorist strikes against America prior to 9/11. Some of that information came from al-Qaeda defectors working with U.S. prosecutors and the FBI but never reached intelligence analysts because of the famous "wall" dividing foreign intelligence gathering and analysis from the domestic crime-fighters, reinforced by Deputy Attorney Jamie Gorelick in 1995.

Ali Mohamed, bin Laden's personal bodyguard in the Sudan, provided extensive information on bin Laden's ties to Iran as part of a plea bargain he made with prosecutors in the Africa embassy bombing case.

The Egyptian-born Mohamed told the court he tried to penetrate U.S. intelligence agencies as a double agent for bin Laden in the early 1980s but was rejected by suspicious U.S. case officers. He immigrated to the United States, took U.S. citizenship, and joined an elite U.S. Army Special Forces unit as an instructor in Middle East politics at Fort Bragg, North Carolina.

In 1989 he traveled to Afghanistan, where he hooked up with Egyptian Islamic Jihad, part of bin Laden's broader al-Qaeda organization. By his own admission he trained al-Qaeda terrorists in "military and basic explosives" as well as intelligence-surveillance techniques for use in anti-American terrorist attacks.

Mohamed was called back to the United States as a material witness in the first World Trade Center bombing trial, but was then allowed to return overseas. Now he stood accused of having cased U.S. embassies in Kenya and Tanzania for the al-Qaeda strike teams, enabling their deadly attacks. The indictment charged him with two counts of conspiring to destroy U.S. property and three counts of conspiracy to murder, a capital offense. Ali Mohamed was no suicide bomber. He preferred life in jail to the threat of death by lethal injection.

In a brief appearance on October 20, 2000, before U.S. District Court judge Leonard B. Sand, just blocks away from the World Trade Center he described bin Laden's early ties to Iran in careful language.

"I was aware of certain contacts between al-Qaeda and al Jihad organization, on one side, and Iran and Hezbollah on the other side. I arranged security for a meeting in the Sudan between Mugniyeh, Hezbollah's chief, and bin Laden. Hezbollah provided explosives training for al-Qaeda and al Jihad. Iran supplied Egyptian Jihad with weapons.

"Iran also used Hezbollah to supply explosives that were disguised to look like rocks."[1]

By the time he met bin Laden in Khartoum, Mugniyeh had gone underground. According to Zakeri, who handled his personal potection during a pilgrimage to Mecca in May 1995 as part of an Iranian government delegation, he had surgically altered his appearance so that no one who knew him before would recognize him.

Before 9/11, Mugniyeh was the terrorist who had more American blood on his hands than any other. He was the regime's star planner, the man they parachuted into Argentina to organize the spectacular bombings against the Israeli embassy in 1992 and the Jewish community in 1994. He was the man who had trained Mikdad and other terrorists who infiltrated Israel to blow up airplanes in 1996.

Thanks to Ali Mohamed, the U.S. intelligence community knew without the slightest doubt or ambiguity that Mugniyeh was also the Iranian regime's dedicated liaison to Osama bin Laden.

And yet they chose to ignore it.

THE CONCEPT

The CIA's counterterrorism chief, Paul Pillar, established the new intelligence concept in a 1995 National Intelligence Estimate that abolished the notion of state-sponsored terrorism.

He called it "a new terrorist phenomenon." The old leviathans of the Cold War were gone, including the state sponsors of terror. Now the United States faced a jungle full of poisonous snakes, as CIA director Jim Woolsey liked to remind Congress.

But, unlike Woolsey, who counseled continued vigilance against America's enemies, Pillar suggested that terror had become a garden-variety nuisance. Without powerful states plotting attacks against the United States, all you had was a loose confederation of misfits and wackos. Johnny does bombs, Jimmy does hijackings, and Abu Mohammad in Fairfax can take video of a bridge. It was all who you knew, not structured organizations. They'd manage to kill people, but so would drunk drivers. Terrorism was the cost of doing business, he once famously told President Clinton.

When Pillar retired from the CIA, he expounded on his theory in a book called *Terrorism and U.S. Foreign Policy*, published by the liberal Brookings Institution just four months before the 9/11 attacks. It was welcomed by a coterie of former CIA officers who had reinvented themselves as media-savvy talking heads. What America really needed was better-trained law enforcement and more lawyers to indict the bad guys, they argued.

Until 1996, when pressure from the Saudis and the United States forced him to relocate to Afghanistan, Osama bin Laden depended on the direct support of the government of Sudan. Without its help, he would never have been able to establish training camps, gather his terrorists, train them, and arm them for murder. After 1996 the Taliban provided that same state support.

But neither Sudan nor Afghanistan used bin Laden as a tool of state policy. Iran did.

"ROSETTA STONE"

Jamal Ahmed al-Fadl was running scared when he walked into a U.S. embassy in Africa in the summer of 1996.

A Sudanese-born Arab, he was a top finance officer for bin Laden and a computer expert. According to the final report of the 9/11 Commission, bin Laden discovered that Fadl had skimmed $10,000 from one of his companies, and asked for restitution. "Fadl resented receiving a salary of only $500 a month while some of the Egyptians in al-Qaeda were given $1,200 a month. He defected and became a star informant for the United States," the report states on page 62.

Al-Fadl wanted protection from bin Laden's agents in Africa. And he was willing to give the United States information to buy that protection.

The original grand jury indictment against bin Laden, issued in June 1998, *before* the Africa embassy bombings, drew heavily on al-Fadl's information. It stated that al-Qaeda had "forged alliances with the National Islamic Front in the Sudan and with the government of Iran and its associated terrorist group Hezbollah for the purpose of working together against their perceived common enemies in the West, particularly the United States."[2]

Daniel Coleman, an FBI special agent who testified during the Africa embassy trial, called al-Fadl "the Rosetta Stone." Al-Fadl helped the FBI discover a safe house in Nairobi, which Coleman searched along with Kenyan police on August 21, 1997. The house belonged to Wadih El Hage and contained computer files of casing reports on the U.S. embassies in Nairobi and Dar es Salaam, which al-Qaeda destroyed the following year.

U.S. Attorney Pat Fitzgerald, the government's lead prosecutor in all the bin Laden cases, told 9/11 Commission investigators "the light went on" when he read al-Fadl's debriefings.

Al-Fadl knew all the secrets of bin Laden's organization. He knew about the *bayat*, the secret oath of loyalty to bin Laden that followers were made to pledge. He produced organization charts for the group's military committee, the finance committee, the intelligence structure. And he provided all of this to U.S. intelligence agencies in mid-1996.

Yet again, there was resistance. "We knew all six names on the finance committee because they'd been on the phone. They were out there. And all had been educated in the United States," a former U.S. intelligence analyst told me. "But the military committee were all unknown names. Some of the engineers and the bomb-makers had been educated in Baghdad."

Other bomb-makers were trained by Iranian Revolutionary Guards officers at Hezbollah camps in Lebanon, where they learned "how to explosives [*sic*] big buildings," al-Fadl told the court. Hezbollah's speciality, which they had learned from Imad Mugniyeh and his Iranian trainers, was simultaneous truck bombs—the same technique used to blow up the U.S. embassies in Africa in July 1998.

The Revolutionary Guards bomb-training began in 1993 after bin Laden and other top al-Qaeda leaders met with a senior Shiite cleric named Nomani at bin Laden's "Riyadh" guesthouse in Khartoum. Sheikh Nomani worked in an Iranian government office in Khartoum and had come to bury the hatchet with bin Laden, "because our enemy is one and because there is no reason to fight each other," al-Fadl said during his testimony.[3]

Bin Laden sent a dozen top operatives to Iran for training, including Abu Hajer al Iraqi (aka Mamdouh Mahmud Salim). Taken prisoner by Iran during the Iran-Iraq war, he was released in 1984 so he could join the Mujahedin to fight the Soviets in Afghanistan. The 9/11 Commission Report identified him as al-Qaeda's "chief weapons procurement officer" in the Sudan.

Wiretaps discovered by the commission showed that Salim had traveled to Manila at the same time that convicted Oklahoma City bomber Terry Nichols was reportedly there to learn how to make fertilizer bombs. "That's one hell of a coincidence, if that's all it was," a source who reviewed transcripts of the November 26–28, 1994, phone calls told me.*

Iran understood the advantage of having a Sunni Muslim group as an ally in their twilight struggle against America. They were fanatics, they had resources, and they were deniable.

But in the United States, no one got it.

---

* Salim was arrested in Germany on September 16, 1998, and extradicted to the United States, where he was convicted in the Africa embassy conspiracy.

THE ASSET

In April 2001 the warnings became more alarming. A longtime FBI informant known as "the Asset" told his controllers that al-Qaeda was training suicide pilots for devastating terror strikes in the United States and in Europe. He didn't know the specifics of the plot, but his source for the information was a former Iranian intelligence officer in Hamburg, Germany.

The Asset had been a top SAVAK officer in Afghanistan during the 1970s, who now lived in exile in the United States. FBI translator Behrouz Sarshar, also a SAVAK officer under the shah, had known him before the 1979 Revolution, and had maintained contact with him ever since. Normally the Asset brought information on Revolutionary Guards troop movements, personnel changes, and the like. Although this item was part of his normal "laundry list," it troubled him.

The FBI officer conducting the interview took note of the information, but expressed no surprise or particular interest, and asked no follow-up questions. He reported it to the Washington field office in his 302—the standard FBI witness report.

One month later the FBI sought to reinterview the Asset. He was part of a fraternity of former SAVAK officers and was considered to be a reliable source of information. He hesitated to bring up the report about pilot training again, because he wasn't entirely certain what it meant. He didn't believe al-Qaeda would be able to train pilots in Afghanistan. Neither did the FBI. They never asked him about his source in Hamburg.

Again they filed a 302, but it got lost as it moved up the food chain to FBI headquarters. The Asset's information was never seen by the intelligence officers who drafted the controversial August 6, 2001, presidential daily brief that reported "patterns of suspicious activity in this country consistent with preparations for hijackings or other types of attacks."

In hindsight, an unnamed FBI official told *Chicago Tribune* reporter John Crewdson, the Asset's reporting made it appear that "somebody in Iran had some knowledge of something" related to September 11.[4]

WITNESS C

Abdolghassem Mesbahi, a former Iranian intelligence officer who now lived in Hamburg, Germany, received a flash message ten days before the September 11 attacks from a close friend in Tehran who had ongoing access to intelligence plans. *Shaitan der artash*, the friend said. *Satan on fire.*

He knew exactly what the coded message meant. The plan Iran's leaders had been working on for over a decade had been activated. Iran was about to deliver a devastating blow to the United States through proxies, probably Arabs.

Mesbahi had direct knowledge of the plan from his many years as an MOIS operative with access to the top leaders of the regime. While in Switzerland in 1987, he played a peripheral role in the Iran-Contra negotiations with the United States. He fled Iran in 1996 when he learned of a plot to kill him. Former president Abolhassan Banisadr introduced him to a German court, where he provided damning testimony that led to the conviction of Iran's top leaders on terrorism charges in 1997. Throughout the Mykonos proceedings, the court referred to him as "Witness C."

Mesbahi's contact in Tehran phoned him again on September 4, 2001. *Shaitan der artash.* Satan on fire.

The calls made Mesbahi nervous. He had tried calling the legal attaché at the U.S. embassy in Berlin—the local FBI outpost—but had been unsuccessful despite several attempts. On September 10 he phoned his contact with the German police, and asked if he could reenter the witness protection program. He had important information he wanted to convey, but he was afraid and needed help.

Iranian-backed terrorists were planning to hijack commercial jets and crash them into major U.S. targets, including the Pentagon and the World Trade Center, he told his German police contact.

Iran's leaders initially developed the plan in retaliation for the downing of an Iranian Airbus by the USS *Vincennes* in 1988. (The United States has always insisted that the captain of the *Vincennes* acted appropriately, when radar identified the incoming aircraft as an Iranian F-14.) Since Khatami's election, the leadership had set up a shadow intelligence organization outside of MOIS to run foreign terrorist operations, he said. The man in charge was a cleric named Ibrahim Mir-Hejazi, a deputy in Khamenei's office. Mesbahi had worked with him for a year when he was at MOIS in 1985.

Eighteen months before 9/11, a private company connected to the Iranian government purchased a Boeing 757/767/777 simulator through the European Airbus consortium, Mesbahi said. The Iranian who purchased the simulator was in the United States on September 11.

Hours after the September 11 attacks, Mesbahi phoned Manoucher

Ganji in Dallas, who he believed maintained close contacts with U.S. intelligence agencies. Ganji phoned his local FBI contact, who spoke with Mesbahi repeatedly by phone. But when the FBI special agent tried to contact the CIA, they blew him off. Mesbahi was unreliable, a intelligence officer—just another messy human source, he was told.

Ganji then phoned a close friend who worked for Senator Joseph Lieberman. You've got to get the CIA to send somebody to see this guy in Germany, he said. This man has important information.

Senator Lieberman personally telephoned his former Senate colleague Dan Coats, who had just gone to Berlin as U.S. ambassador. He urged Coats to send someone to interview Mesbahi, but nothing ever came of his initiative.

By that point, the CIA had missed so many warnings they had no interest in helping to expose the truth of Iran's involvement in the 9/11 plot. And anyone who revealed that the emperor has no clothes, who broke the law of omerto and exposed their incompetencies and corporate sloth would be destroyed.

22

THE RAT LINE

It was nearly 9:00 a.m. when Ahmad Rezai rolled out of bed to pick up the phone that Tuesday morning in Los Angeles.

It was his father in Tehran. Are you watching television? he shouted.

No, why should I? Ahmad answered groggily. I was working late last night. I'm still in bed. He felt guilty that it was so late.

Turn on the TV, his father insisted. It doesn't matter. Any channel. Just turn it on.

It was nearly noon in New York, and both World Trade Center Towers had already come down. Ahmad couldn't believe it. He flipped the channel. It wasn't a trick. Every channel was playing the same horrific scene.

Are they showing the report about the Japanese Red Brigade? his father asked. In Iran, a television station had just reported that they had carried out the attacks in conjunction with bin Laden, he said.

Ahmad continued to channel-surf, but he saw nothing that resembled the report his father had described.

When I heard the story, I found it curious. The next day I asked a friend in Congress who monitored foreign media coverage of the attacks to look into it. What she found was even more intriguing. The only mention of a Japanese group claiming responsibility for the 9/11 attacks was aired on Al-Manar television in Lebanon at 0920 Pacific time, twenty minutes *after* Mohsen Rezai phoned his son.[1]

Al-Manar TV is owned and operated by Lebanon's Hezbollah and financed by Tehran.[2] Al-Manar was interviewing the editor of a Jordanian newspaper, who said he had received a call at his office from someone speaking in Arabic "with a foreign accent" claiming responsibility for the attacks in the name of the Japanese Red Army. The story was clearly a hoax.

Far more interesting was the fact that the former Revolutionary Guards commander, who now worked for Rafsanjani at the Expediency Council, had seen the report *before* it actually aired and that he provided a detail—the suspected tie between the Japanese group and bin Laden—that did not appear in the report as it was broadcast.*

Ahmad Rezai and his father were on speaking terms again. For two years after the younger Rezai's 1998 defection to the United States, his father had refused to talk to him. Once he paid an intermediary in Costa Rica to lure Ahmad outside of the United States and put him on a plane back to Tehran. To regime newspapers he claimed that Ahmad had been abducted by Zionist agents in Dubai, where he was undergoing treatment after a car accident. But the minute he realized Ahmad had fled Iran, he knew the truth. Like many of Iran's young people who had grown up in with the insanity of the Islamic regime, his twenty-one-year-old son was fed up and yearned for freedom, for normalcy.

Did you do this? Ahmad asked finally.

I doubt the United States will suspect us because they know we don't have the technology to coordinate such a complicated operation, he said. That was for the listeners. Then: Watch out for your own safety, Mohsen Rezai told his son.

He said he was ready to send his wife along with Ahmad's younger sister and brother to the United States so that the children could go to college. Ahmad had offered to help find a house for them months ago, but his father wouldn't consider it. Now he had changed his mind.

They shouldn't stay in Iran, said Mohsen Rezai. It could be dangerous.

Tehran's leaders feared a massive U.S. attack in reprisal for 9/11. They just assumed that with all of America's intelligence assets, the United States *knew* about their ties to bin Laden and would hold them accountable.

COLONEL B

On September 12, 2001, Revolutionary Guards commanders gathered in Tehran. General Mohammad Ahayi, a relative of Mohsen Rezai, gave a speech that started with a verse from the Koran:

"Whosoever battles with Allah, Allah will do battle with him."

General Ayahi then turned to his fellow commanders. Did you see how *we* (banging his fist into his chest) brought them down? How *we* brought America to its knees?

Colonel B, a Qods Ground Forces officer, was in the audience. Just the

---

*I first reported this phone call, and the al Manar allegation, in *Preachers of Hate: Islam and the War on America* (New York: Crown Forum, 2003).

year before, he had been assigned to a terrorist training camp northeast of Tehran, and had seen with his own eyes the Lebanese, Libyans, Azeris, Chechens, Iraqis, and others who had come to Iran to learn the disciplines of murder. He turned to the intelligence director of the Qods batallalion, a friend. Did we have anything to do with this event? he asked.

His friend smiled and admonished him with a shake of his finger. Don't dig into details. Leave it alone. You don't want to know more.

THE WOLFOWITZ BRIEFING

As the tall, dark-haired briefer from the Defense Intelligence Agency closed his red folder and prepared to leave, Deputy Defense Secretary Paul Wolfowitz just shook his head. How come I wasn't told about any of this before? he asked.

The date was October 26, 2001, and Wolfowitz had just learned about the al-Qaeda "rat line" that operated between Afghanistan and Europe, with the full knowledge and cooperation of the Iranian government.

Once they crossed the border into Iran, al-Qaeda operatives were welcomed at special camps outside the eastern Iranian city of Mashad, then given fresh travel documents so they could travel onward to Europe and America without arousing suspicion, the briefer said. The level of cooperation between Iran and al-Qaeda was stunning, and went against everything Wolfowitz thought he knew.

The briefer mumbled some excuse to Wolfowitz's question. But the real reason was almost as shocking as the information in the briefing itself: DIA higher-ups had forbidden the analysts from presenting the briefing to Wolfowitz earlier because it contradicted the Concept that Iran had no operational ties to al-Qaeda and had gotten out of the terror game with Khatami's election in 1997. It also violated the doctrine that had become a matter of faith among Middle East analysts and "experts" on Islam that there could be no cooperation between the Shia and Sunni fundamentalists.

Whenever intelligence personnel or journalists turned up evidence that al-Qaeda was working with Iran, those analysts made sure the reports were discredited. Bucking the conventional wisdom was an invitation to ridicule, as the briefer's colleagues at the DIA's tiny Iran unit at Bolling Air Force base knew well. The only way they had gotten approval to brief Wolfowitz was that he had explicitly tasked the DIA to examine the possibility of Iran/al-Qaeda ties—a possibility their political bosses at the DIA's Policy Support office in the Pentagon had discounted long ago.

Al-Qaeda had been working with Iran since at least 1992, when Revolutionary Guards general Mohammad Bagr Zolqadr was running a Revolutionary Guards training camp in the Sudan, the briefer said.

Zolqadr's ties to bin Laden had been brokered by Ayman al-Zawahri—the Egyptian terrorist known as "the Doctor"—who was wanted for his involvement in the 1981 assassination of Egyptian president Anwar Sadat.* Zawahri and his Egyptian Islamic Jihad group provided the muscle men for al-Qaeda, giving bin Laden access to a virtually unlimited pool of manpower. Zawahri was the man with the Iran contacts.

Throughout the 1990s, Zawahri traveled repeatedly to Iran as the guest of Minister of Intelligence and Security Ali Fallahian and the head of foreign terrorist operations, Ahmad Vahidi. Vahidi was the commander of the Qods Force and the man who supervised the Khobar Towers bombing in 1996.

It was not one trip or a chance encounter subject to interpretation. Zawahri and Vahidi were a couple. They had a steady date.

In the months before 9/11, Egyptian Islamic Jihad commanders transited in large numbers through the Iranian city of Mashad en route to Afghanistan to join bin Laden's ranks, the briefer said. They had solid reporting and hard evidence from human sources and from national technical means confirming the rat line.

Bin Laden preferred the Iranian route because he believed that U.S. intelligence officials were monitoring Pakistani airports and were responsible for the arrest of several of his top operatives during the last six years.†

Seven to ten days before the September 11 attacks, Iran suddenly closed the Mashad rat line to the Egyptian jihadis, the briefer said. Some sources believe it was because the Iranians knew a major terrorist attack was about to occur and didn't want to give the United States cause for military retaliation against Iran.

The latest piece of the puzzle was still being evaluated, he said. Just one week ago, the DIA had reports that Imad Mugniyeh had come to Mashad with Hossein Mosleh, Vahidi's deputy. According to one source, the two met with Iraqi intelligence chief Taher Jalil Haboosh.

---

*The regime named a Tehran street after Sadat's Islamic Jihad assassin, Khaled Islambouli, causing Egypt to rupture diplomatic ties with Iran. When Mubarak asked the Islamic republic to change the name in June 1999 as a prelude to a resumption of ties, Hezbollah's Helpers marched to the street and unveiled a gigantic four-story mural glorifying Sadat's assassin. His name is often transliterated as Eslambouli.

†Best known were Ramzi Yousef, the first World Trade Center bomber who was arrested in Pakistan in 1995, and Mir Aimal Kansi, who gunned down CIA employees as they turned off the highway to CIA headquarters. He was arrested in Pakistan in 1997.

NUKES "R" US

If we need nuclear plants, which we have already started, we need a complete fuel cycle.

—Iranian president Mohammad Khatami, February 9, 2003, on state television

They were waiting for President Khatami. At least that's what the Iranians said.

By the time IAEA director General Mohammad El Baradei finally traveled to Iran on February 21–22, 2003, they had been waiting for nearly six months. Skeptics in Washington said the IAEA had given the Iranians time to clean up.

Baradei hadn't come alone. The trip was sensitive, and he needed cover. So he brought with him his deputy director, the Belgian Pierre Goldschmidt; the head of Division B, the top-secret safeguards operations unit, Olli J. Heinonen; and a team of uranium enrichment experts.

Despite the pomp and the niceties with the Iranian president at the airport, none of them quite knew what to expect. When Iranian Atomic Energy chief Aghazadeh had agreed to allow them to visit Iran the previous September during an IAEA board meeting in Vienna, he'd made clear that the regime intended to set the record straight after the "lies" that had been told about Iran's clandestine uranium enrichment program by a violent opposition group, the MEK.

For several years, IAEA experts working for Heinonen at Division B had been viewing commercial satellite photographs of a site in the desert to the southeast of the central Iranian city of Kashan. The Iranians had excavated a huge area—some sources estimated it was over 25 acres—then buried it and surrounded the perimeter with barbed wire and an extensive air defense system.

Just 100 meters from the outer edge of the buried facility, the Iranians had erected five workshops above ground. No one knew whether the two facilities were connected or whether equipment brought into the aboveground workshops had been secretly installed in the buried plant. And no one knew for sure that either site was nuclear-related.

Aghazadeh took them down to Kashan by car—more than a four-hour drive from Tehran—and drove them back the same day. It was clear he had hoped to convince Baradei and his top aides that the site the experts had been watching was no cause for concern. It was just a project. It was still under construction. It was for the future.

When they arrived, they had tea with the project manager and his team. It was all very friendly, very civilized. The Iranian group were all wearing white lab coats. The older men had been trained in the United States, the younger ones in Iran. Goldschmidt, Heinonen, and their technical team were impressed by the breadth of their knowledge.

Iran's goal was to produce lightly enriched uranium to fuel the Busheir power plant, but they hadn't begun actual enrichment yet, the Iranian said. They were still at the pre-production phase. He had been instructed to share certain design information with the IAEA.

Baradei smiled and said that was why he had come. We are looking forward to touring the facilities.

The project manager was visibly nervous when Aghazadeh ordered him to open the heavy blast doors that led down the U-shaped tunnel to the cavernous underground halls. As they quickly scanned the vast space, Heinonen's enrichment experts were stunned by what they saw. They all had read the reports of Iran's clandestine procurement of centrifuge equipment. But none had expected to see a well-designed underground production plant, scaled to accommodate fifty thousand enrichment centrifuges and all the fittings: piping, chillers, power inverters—the works. It was not an industrial facility like any they had ever seen, but a hardened military plant, built to withstand a missile strike.

There were two square production halls, each roughly 320,000 square feet, the project manager said. It was big, impressive, and, until then, totally secret. The Iranians always had denied they had built an enrichment plant. Here was incontrovertible proof that they had been lying.

Heinonen's top expert did some quick math. Once all the centrifuges were installed, the facility reasonably would produce around 150,000 separative work units of low-enriched uranium (LEU) per year—barely enough to feed the mammoth Busheir plant, if that was indeed Iran's intention. But if they fed the LEU back into the cascade instead of extracting it for reactor fuel, they could produce roughly 500 kilograms per year of bomb-grade material—enough for twenty-five to thirty bombs, even with a lot of waste. The MEK referred to the site as Natanz, the name of a nearby town.

The project manager led them next door to the pilot plant, the five workshops built aboveground. It housed 164 centrifuges and it was clear they had already been spinning. He claimed they were conducting preproduction trials using an inert gas, not uranium. There were so many problems in getting the 6-foot-high metal cylinders to spin over one thousand times per second. The slightest imbalance caused the high-strength aluminum alloy to burst and threw the line into emergency shutdown. If they had pumped uranium hexafluoride gas into the works before it was fully tested, that type of accident would have generated a nuclear disaster of monumental proportions.

Aghazadeh explained that they had buried the production halls and fortified them to protect the site from air strikes. We saw what the Israelis did to Iraq, he said. He was referring to Israel's 1981 air strike that took out Saddam Hussein's French-built plutonium production plant. Don't forget, the manager said, we have lived through eight years of war.

When it was finished, the pilot plant would house a cascade of one thousand centrifuges, the Iranians said. They were adding more centrifuges every week, as soon as they had passed quality control. They planned to introduce UF6 feedstock into the pilot plant in June and begin full-scale production runs by 2005.

A member of Heinonen's centrifuge team had brought along one of B Division's black boxes, which he carried on a shoulder strap. You don't mind if we take a few samples, he asked.

The project manager blanched. Aghazadeh stepped in. This was not part of your initial request. If you wish, we can discuss this further back in Tehran. Baradei didn't insist.

The next day they toured the hex plant outside Isfahan. Although on the surface it ressembled a large petrochemical plant, it was surrounded by high security barriers and extensive air defenses.

This was the plant that Sandy Berger and his deputies claimed with pride that they had gotten the Chinese to cancel. And here it was. It was not a dream. It was not a project waiting to be completed. It was a fully functioning uranium conversion plant, built to the Chinese specifications. Another failure.

CLEANUP

Baradei returned to Vienna after the two-day tour, but left his deputies and the technical team behind for another week of discussions with Aghazadeh and his men. They had lots of questions, but it was clear the Iranians had reached the limit of what they were prepared to disclose.

Natanz was a pretty impressive achievement, one of Heinonen's centrifuge experts ventured. Only a handful of countries in the world had mastered industrial-scale uranium enrichment, and now Iran had become one of them. Where had Iran gotten the blueprints for the plant? Where did they get the power inverters? Who was welding the micro–ball bearings to the centrifuge endcaps?

Everything you have seen is Iranian, Aghazadeh said. The blueprints, the drawings, the overall plant layout, even the equipment. Everything we have done ourselves.

Heinonen's technical wizard believed *that* for about a nanosecond. Perhaps you could show us the production workshop, he asked.

I think you have seen enough for one visit, said Aghazadeh.

The Iranians had spent billions of dollars to get to this point. They had no intention of backing down now.

Besides, they needed time to clean up.

THE MEK REVELATIONS

The MEK revealed the existence of the secret uranium enrichment plant at Natanz and of a separate heavy-water production facility near Arak at a press conference in Washington on August 14, 2002.

They gave the precise location of the sprawling facility, 25 miles southeast of Kashan. They gave rough dimensions of the two production halls, and claimed they had been buried 25 feet below ground and covered with an 8-foot-thick slab of reinforced concrete. Excavation and construction had begun two years earlier by two Iranian companies, Jahad-e Towse'eh and Towse'eh-Sakhteman. They claimed the Supreme National Security Council had already spent $110 million on the project, outside of the regular state budget.

No one knew where the Mujahedin had gotten such detailed information. The group claimed they had informers inside Iran's nuclear establishment. And yet they made simple mistakes regarding the five buildings of the pilot plant that someone who had visited the buildings would not have made. Rival exile groups claimed the Israelis had leaked the information to the MEK, but provided no proof. Clearly someone had been feeding them.

At a follow-on press conference on February 20, 2003—just as Baradei was traveling to Iran—they claimed that the regime had begun removing machinery from the underground plant, following the initial leaks. They also revealed that Iran's Atomic Energy Organization had set up a front company in Tehran called Kala Electric that was procuring equipment for the facilities in India and China and was involved in overall project management. This was the production workshop Aghazadeh refused to let Heinonen's technical team visit. (The Iranians initially claimed it was a "watch factory.") The IAEA now refers to it as Kalaye Electric Company.

They also revealed that Mir Hossein Mousavi, an aide to the "moderate" president Mohammad Khatami, had gone to Natanz in early August 2002 on an inspection tour for the Supreme National Security Council.

As Khatami himself later made clear, the nuclear projects were embraced by all factions of the ruling clergy, hard-liners and "reformers" alike.

IAEA officials said that the agency had known about the sites revealed by the MEK for several years but had no authority to investigate without an outside catalyst.

"The MEK gave us an excuse, if you will," a senior official told me. "We had been following the construction of an underground site at Natanz using commercial satellite imagery for some years. But under the traditional safeguards arrangement we had with Iran, we had no good reason to ask them if we could go take a look at what they were doing. The MEK press conference gave us that excuse."

IAEA officials also claimed that no member government—including the United States—had ever given them information about Natanz or urged the agency to challenge the Iranians to open it to inspection.

U.S. officials I consulted said that was because no one—including the IAEA—had ever identified Natanz as a nuclear facility before the revelations by the MEK. All of them had been taken by surprise.

First to be shocked by the revelations at Natanz was U.S. Secretary of State Colin L. Powell. "Here we suddenly discover that Iran is much further along, with a far more robust nuclear weapons development program than anyone said it had," he told CNN's *Late Edition* on March 9, 2003. "It shows you how a determined nation that has the intent to develop a nuclear weapon can keep that development process secret from inspectors and outsiders, if they really are determined to do it."

Whatever information the intelligence community had about Natanz had not been kicked up to the policy makers. Another failure.

SLOW-ROLLER

Baradei was not in a hurry to force the issue. He presented a brief oral report to the IAEA board on his trip to Iran on March 17, 2003, just as U.S. troops were advancing on Baghdad. There were some safeguards issues with regard to Iran on which he would be reporting in more detail as the facts became clear, he said. It was not the lead item on the Board of Governors' agenda, and he offered no details of what he had actually seen. It was just one more bullet point of his activities over the previous quarter. The world had its sights turned elsewhere.

In the meantime, Division B sent several teams of specialists back to Iran, where they pressed Aghazadeh and his deputies for more information. They wanted to gain a better understanding of the history of the enrichment program. They wanted more information on centrifuge production. They wanted to visit the Kalaye Electric Company workshops in Tehran with the famous "black box" to take environmental samples. They wanted to return to Natanz and take samples there.

Kicking and screaming, the Iranians agreed to the IAEA requests one by one.

In May 2003, Aghazadeh came to Vienna and made a forceful presentation to the board of governors. From denial, Iran had decided to go on the offensive. Iran was fully within its rights as a signatory of the Nuclear Proliferation Treaty to enrich uranium, he said. And the nuclear powers were obligated under Article IV of the treaty to provide technical assistance to Iran, so long as its program was for peaceful purposes, which of course it was.

No one had discovered the slightest evidence to suggest that Iran was building a nuclear weapon, he insisted. Baradei was quick to agree.

In June the first results came back from the IAEA's state-of-the-art particles analysis lab at Seibersdorf, outside of Vienna. This was the same lab that had discovered North Korean cheating in 1994. Inside the agency, the environmental samples were known as "killers." The technique was simple but deadly.

Using ordinary cotton swabs, Division B inspectors collected samples from Natanz and Kalaye Electric. Back in Seibersdorf, the swipes were irradiated to determine which particles were of interest. Specialists then selected individual particles among millions under an electron microcrope, and sent them through a mass spectrometer to discover their secrets.

The Iranian samples came back full of enriched uranium. It was everywhere, even though the Iranians had spent months cleaning up.

Aghazadeh and his men had claimed Iran had never carried out enrichment experiments. The new data showed without any possible doubt that they had been lying.

That was when Baradei knew he had a problem.

EL BARADEI'S FIRST REPORT

On June 6, 2003, he made a more detailed presentation to the IAEA Board of Governors. His nine-page written report was couched in all the coded language of Vienna.

Secret workshops and materials stockpiles were called "Locations Outside of Facilities," or "LOFs," that had been declared to the IAEA. That was the ultimate no-no in Vienna-speak. It meant there was a strong suspicion that a country was trying to conceal weapons activities. Why else would they store or process nuclear materials at clandestine sites?

Not by accident, Baradei dropped that language in future reports. From then on, there were declared nuclear facilities, and "locations identified to date as relevant to the implementation of safeguards in Iran," or simply "other locations."[1]

The only thing the Iranians were lacking was time. The IAEA—and soon the European Union—helped buy them that time.

THE VERIFIER

Paula DeSutter was an old hand at decoding Vienna-speak. She'd been wrestling with the question of Iran's undeclared nuclear program for fifteen years.

During the Cold War, DeSutter worked at the Arms Control and Disarmament Agency (ACDA) and helped draft the State Department's annual noncompliance report. It examined arms control treaties and who was violating them. The arms controllers believed that treaties were the solution and made sure the U.S. adhered to them scrupulously. DeSutter and the verifiers argued that treaties were useless if the bad guys were allowed to violate them with impunity.

In her office suite on the sixth floor of the State Department she still keeps copies of the 1992 compliance report, delivered to Congress by President George H. W. Bush just days before he left office in January 1993. On page 17, it warned that "Iran has demonstrated a continuing interest in nuclear weapons and related technology that causes the U.S. to assess that Iran is in the early stages of developing a nuclear weapons program."[2]

"It's been over ten years that the United States has been saying that we think Iran has a nuclear weapons program," she told me. "It's time to recognize that Iran has violated its commitment to the Nonproliferation Treaty and refer them to the UN Security Council."

Feisty and uncompromising, DeSutter was put out to pasture during the Clinton years. She spent time at the National War College and at National Defense University Center for Counterproliferation Research, where, under the direction of Ambassador Robert Joseph, she analyzed Iranian WMD programs and how to deter Iranian use of WMD. By 1995 the pucker factor was high among her former colleagues at ACDA, and the language on Iran in the compliance reports was toned down. By 1998 the report dismissed Iran's nuclear effort as a "rudimentary program [that] has apparently met with limited success."

When President George W. Bush arrived in the White House, he brought Joseph to the NSC to head nonproliferation programs and appointed prominent conservative strategist John Bolton as undersecretary of state for arms control and international security. In 2002, Bolton recommended bringing DeSutter back and making her assistant secretary of state for verification and compliance. She was sworn in that August, thrilled to be back. They were going to kick butt.

The first problem the new team encountered was the entrenched bureaucracy at State. Bolton felt a bit like a field marshal without an army. Almost as soon as he took office he began tasking the Nonproliferation Bureau to examine the public record of Iran's nuclear program. "John Bolton put Iran on the front burner as of May 2001," DeSutter said. But the career officials and Clinton holdovers who ran the bureau that was in charge of the Iranian case refused to turn up the heat.

When Bolton saw how slowly the IAEA was moving on Iran, he asked DeSutter to send her principal deputy, Christopher Ford, to Vienna to light a fire under the U.S. delegation. A Yale-trained lawyer who had been general counsel to the Senate Intelligence Committee, Ford helped draft a Board of Governors resolution that was adopted on June 19, 2003, calling on Iran, as a "confidence-building measure," to drop its plans to introduce nuclear material into the pilot enrichment plant at Natanz. The Iranians scoffed and began enrichment trials just six days later.

The United States got the IAEA board to issue a second, more strongly worded resolution on September 12, calling on Iran to give agency inspectors full access and to provide a full accounting of its previously undeclared imports of nuclear materials and equipment.[3]

In October the Iranians delivered their report to Baradei, which he refused to share with the U.S. team in Vienna. The Iranians now admitted that they had been working on enriching uranium and extracting plutonium since 1981—over twenty-two years!—and had made the decision to build a centrifuge plant in 1985. Just two years later—precisely when Dr. Khan was making his first trips to Iran—they said they had acquired drawings of an early Urenco-model centrifuge "through an intermediary."

From 1985 through 1997, the Iranians said all work was done on the AEOI premises in Tehran and at Tehran University. Despite regular visits to these facilities during this period, agency inspectors never had a clue that Iran was cheating on them.

In 1997 the Iranians said they had moved centrifuge production and testing to Kalaye Electric in Tehran. But they never did any actual enrichment, they insisted.

If that's the case, former IAEA inspector David Albright told me, then Iran's program "is one of the slowest enrichment programs around." In a letter to the IAEA dated October 21, 2003, the Iranians admitted to having secretly imported massive quantities of uranium yellowcake over the past twenty years, starting with a 531-metric-ton shipment in 1982. (That shipment alone was more yellowcake than Brazil produces for its own nuclear fuel plants in an entire year.) They also admitted that they ran "bench scale experiments" to transform that yellowcake into uranium hexafluoride gas for enrichment. Iran received its first centrifuges in 1987 and another five hundred in 1995. They also purchased UF6 feedstock directly from China in 1991, which they never declared to the agency until late 2003. "And they are saying they never put it together to enrich uranium. It raises a question," Albright said.

The IAEA lab rats at Seibersdorf were now finding traces of highly enriched uranium in environmental samples taken at multiple sites. It suggested that the Iranians might have operated a clandestine enrichment cascade long enough to produce weapons-grade fuel. The Iranians claimed the contamination came from the country that had sold them the centrifuge components.

The sampling results forced Baradei to shift into full crisis mode. He sent another inspection team to Iran on October 13–22, 2003, and flew himself to Tehran on October 16 to meet with Hassan Rouhani, the Khatami deputy who also chaired the Supreme National Security Council.

Rouhani had been brought in to manage the cleanup operation. A tough negotiator who had no problem lying to Baradei's face and later admitting it, he was told to hold the line, buy more time. He again insisted that Iran was within its rights to enrich uranium. They had just made a few technical errors in not reporting all their activities at the appropriate time.

At the National Security Council, Ambassador Robert Joseph watched the crisis build, like a teapot slowly rising to a boil. Soon another pot began boiling as Libya's Colonel Qaddafi launched a secret overture to renew relations with the United States and Britain. Although the nonproliferation team didn't realize it at first, the Libyan adventure led straight back to Iran.

DR. KHAN'S BOMB DESIGN

On October 4, 2003, a U.S. warship, working in tandem with Italian customs, intercepted a German-registered vessel, the *BBC China*, as it was steaming out of the Suez Canal en route to Libya, and diverted it to Taranto, Italy. They were acting on highly sensitive intelligence obtained through NSA surveillance of Pakistani nuclear entrepeneur Dr. A. Q. Khan.

When they boarded the ship, they found five containers crammed full of centrifuge parts. U.S. officials later called the equipment "the guts" of Qaddafi's previously unknown uranium enrichment program. While Qaddafi had contacted U.S. and British officials that March in an effort to restore relations, it was seizure of the nuclear equipment on board the *BBC China* that convinced him the game was up. Without that equipment he would have to go back to square one.

From the NSA intercepts, first revealed by my colleague Bill Gertz of the *Washington Times*, the Americans knew that the centrifuge parts had been manufactured at Scomi Precision Engineering in Malaysia according to specifications provided by Dr. Khan. Shipped to Dubai, they were transferred onto the *BBC China* as "used machinery."

After the seizure, the Libyans began to come clean. Only then were U.S. and British intelligence teams allowed to visit previously closed nuclear sites, and to begin mapping out the true scope of the Libyan program.

Paula DeSutter was brought on board on December 20, 2003, the day after Qaddafi announced publicly that he was renouncing his previously secret nuclear weapons program. Over the Christmas holiday, she and her team of verifiers put together a conceptual plan of the sites, the people and the equipment they needed to see in Libya, in order to confirm that Qaddafi's stated intention of giving up his WMD programs was for real.

On New Year's Day she flew with Bolton to London to resolve outstanding issues with their British counterparts, before they met with the Libyans the following week. When all three parties had agreed on the approach, the action teams began rotating into Libya.

There were moments of comedy mixed with the drama. Because U.S. laws prohibited any economic exchanges with Libya—even by U.S. government officials—one of her lawyers had to "bust a piggybank" in London when they were scrambling to get Libyan visas and make travel arrangements. They needed a special license from the Treasury Department's Office of Foreign Assets Control to authorize them to spend money. Although they were going to Libya to dismantle Qaddafi's secret nuclear weapons program and to take possession of his missiles and chemical weapons, the team's airline reservations were kicked out by airline computers, so the tickets had to be handwritten.

Two weeks later, the first team had finished its work and was getting ready to board a chartered aircraft in Tripoli when a last-minute breakdown stranded them for several days. As they were waiting for the parts, the Libyans brought them an unexpected gift: an oversized briefcase that contained the top-secret nuclear bomb design Libya had purchased from the Khan network. Stunned, they communicated the news to Washington. One of the team members was handcuffed to the briefcase at all times as they waited for their plane to be repaired.

When they finally flew to Dulles Airport, they were expecting to discreetly leave the aircraft and deliver their precious cargo to DeSutter and her verifiers out in the parking lot. Instead, Energy Secretary Spencer Abraham sent plainclothes guards, wearing bomber jackets and packing heat, to greet them at the baggage carousel. It was definitely not discreet. The big black case was festooned with IAEA and Energy Department high-security seals. As the heavily armed men took control of the briefcase in front of the arriving passengers, they looked like a bunch of kooks out of *Dr. Strangelove*.

According to press reports, the sophisticated bomb designs were written in English and in Chinese. They were part of the nuclear bomb "package" the inimitable Dr. Khan had sold the Libyans. As the verifiers went over the files many weeks later, they realized that Dr. Khan had most likely sold the same package—if not better—to the Iranians as well. It was so obvious that they hadn't seen it until now.

Iran and Libya had been feeding from the same trough, one of

DeSutter's top aides said. The Iranians would be guilty of proliferation malpractice if they didn't get the bomb design, too.

"NO EVIDENCE"

Baradei issued his first full-scale report on Iran's previously clandestine enrichment programs on November 10, 2003. It ran thirty pages, single-spaced. Even couched in Vienna-speak, its findings were breathtaking.

The IAEA had now established that Iran had mastered the complete "front end" of the nuclear fuel cycle, "including uranium mining and milling, conversion, enrichment, fuel fabrication, heavy-water production, a light-water reactor, a heavy-water research reactor, and associated research and development facilities." And all of it, except for the light-water power plant at Busheir, had been kept secret.

Iran had "failed to report" large-scale imports of uranium metal, yellowcake, uranium hexafluoride, and depleted uranium and had "concealed many aspects of its nuclear activities, with resultant breaches" of its safeguards agreement.

And yet, Baradei concluded, "To date, there is no evidence that the previously undeclared nuclear material and activities referred to above were related to a nuclear weapons program."[4]

Thomas Cochran, a scientist with the Natural Resources Defense Council, told the *New York Times* that "it's dumbfounding that the IAEA, after saying that Iran for eighteen years had a secret effort to enrich uranium and separate plutonium, would turn around and say there was no evidence of a nuclear weapons program. If that's not evidence, I don't know what is."

Stephen G. Rademaker, assistant secretary of state for arms control, dismissed Baradei's conclusion as "simply impossible to believe." Addressing a forum hosted by the Lawrence Livermore National Laboratory in California on November 13, 2003, he said, "The United States believes that the massive and covert Iranian effort to acquire sensitive nuclear capabilities makes sense only as part of a nuclear weapons program."

It was time for the international community to step up to the plate and "declare Iran in noncompliance with its IAEA safeguards obligations," he added.

In Vienna-speak, that meant reporting Iran to the UN Security Council, which had the authority to mandate international sanctions to force Iran to comply, including military action.

THE MALAYSIAN POLICE REPORT

In Malaysia, Dr. Khan's business partner, B. S. A. Tahir, was singing to the police. He described a veritable Bombs "R" Us network of friends, cronies, and intermediaries around the world who were willing to work for the highest bidder. The Malaysian police released significant portions of his debriefings as well as documentary evidence in a sixteen-page report on February 20, 2004. "The Khan network may have changed the world in a big way," one of DeSutter's top aides told me.

Some of the names in the police report were familiar from the network of former Leybold employees and associates Dr. Khan had recruited in the 1980s to help Pakistan build its bomb. Dr. Khan simply had turned their talents to profit by selling the same technology to Libya, Iran, and North Korea.

In Switzerland, Dr. Khan had employed Friedrich Tinner, who helped purchase equipment for Pakistan through his Swiss company, CETEC. His son, Urs Friedrich Tinner, thirty-nine, became Tahir's partner. He brought the precision engineering expertise the network needed to build a centrifuge production plant in Malaysia. Urs Tinner was arrested in Germany on October 7, 2004.*

In Turkey, former Siemens employee Gunas Jireh had supplied dynamos and aluminum castings, while Selim Alguadis supplied electrical equipment, Tahir said.

In Germany, the late Heinz Mebus had been instrumental in selling Iran the centrifuge designs in the mid-1980s. Tahir also cited Gotthard Lerch, the former Leybold employee, whom the Germans had never succeeded in prosecuting. Lerch was eventually arrested in Switzerland in November 2004.

Lerch brought to the network his contacts with German engineer Gerhard Wisser, sixty-five, and sixty-six-year-old Swiss engineer Daniel Geiges. They had emigrated to South Africa years before and set up an engineering consultancy that helped design and build the vacuum-feed system to handle the flow of uranium hexafluoride for Libya's enrichment plant. They assembled and tested the equipment in a warehouse outside of

*On March 15, 2005, the criminal division of the Higher Regional Court in Cologne agreed to extradite Tinner to Switzerland, allegedly in accordance with a U.S. request. German press reports alleged that Tinner had become a U.S. informant who provided information leading to the seizure of the shipments to Libya.

Johannesburg over a three-year period, then dismantled it and packed it into eleven 40-foot shipping containers.

When police raided the Tradefin Engineering warehouse in September 2004, they claimed that the 200 tons of equipment were intended for a water purification plant. The pair were also accused of illegally purchasing and exporting to Libya a flow-forming lathe manufactured by a Spanish company that was intended to make centrifuge rotors in Libya.*

The United States had been watching Dr. Khan in the 1980s, but had lost interest in him for nearly eight years.

Former White House official Gary Samore told me that President Clinton delivered a "vague warning" about Dr. Khan to Pakistani prime minister Nawaz Sharif during a July 1999 meeting in the White House devoted mainly to the Kargill crisis in Kashmir. The United States had learned that Dr. Khan was attempting to make "freelance" sales of Pakistan's Ghauri missiles, a knock-off of the SCUD-Cs Pakistan had acquired from North Korea in the early 1990s, in exchange for centrifuge enrichment technology. A few months after the warning, Pakistani army chief of staff General Pervez Musharraf ousted Sharif in a bloodless coup.

But the United States intelligence community had completely missed Dr. Khan's nuclear network during the 1990s. It was yet another intelligence failure of monumental proportions that remains difficult to explain.[5]

Thanks to Tahir's cooperation, police in a half-dozen countries around the world began rolling up the network in 2004.

---

*Tradefin Engineering owner Johan A. M. Meyer, fifty-three, was arrested the day after the raid but cut a deal with prosecutors and turned state's evidence against his partners. Wisser and Geiges were later charged with trafficking in nuclear materials. Their consulting company—Krisch Engineering, based in Randberg, South Africa—was also raided by police.

24

THE EVIDENCE

One week before the 9/11 Commission was scheduled to send its final report to the printers in July 2004, Philip D. Zelikow, the Commission's staff director, gathered members together for an unusual briefing.

Commission staff members had discovered a document from a U.S. intelligence agency that described in detail Iran's ties to al-Qaeda, he said. It had been buried at the bottom of a huge stack of highly classified documents on other subjects that had been delivered to a special high-security reading room in an undisclosed location in Washington, D.C.

The document was a summary of raw intelligence reports gathered through intercepts and other means, and was uncovered when staff readers—on detail from different intelligence agencies—were turning over rocks before the report went to the printer, just to make sure no worm crawled out. When the chief analyst scanned through the references at the end, he whistled quietly. "There's trouble in River City," he recalls thinking. It footnoted seventy-five distinct source documents, labeled from Capital *A* to *sss*.

The commissioners realized that if their report was published and word of the missing documents leaked out later, it would discredit their entire investigation, so they ordered staff to make a last-minute panic run. Zelikow phoned the director of the intelligence agency that had prepared the summary and asked him to dig out all seventy-five source documents. He wanted to send his people over to read them in person the following morning at seven-thirty. He didn't care that it was Sunday. They had to see the documents immediately.

The team leader was a former CIA analyst who had spent decades reading highly classified SIGINT intercepts; he had been chosen for the commission staff because of his cosmic clearances and the breadth of his knowledge of how the vast U.S. intelligence community gathered, sifted, and analyzed raw data.

The problem was the Concept. Everything the CIA had been telling the commission up until that point was absolutely cut and dried: there was no connection between al-Qaeda and Iran. None, no way. Nada. "We found perplexing the settled CIA position as expressed by Paul Pillar in his book that there was no meaningful connection at all between al-Qaeda and Iran," one commissioner told me when I asked him about this incident.

The documents the team began reading that Sunday morning told a whole different story. After intense negotiations, commissioners agreed to a considerably scaled-back summary of what the staff had found, which appeared on pages 240–241 of the final report (and which is reproduced in this book's appendix).

But that brief summary gives no idea of the scope of the material the CIA had been sitting on, or the sheer number of intelligence reports. That story has never been told until now.

What the team leader found that Sunday morning was nothing less than a complete documented record of operational ties between Iran and al-Qaeda for the critical months just prior to September 11. "The documents showed Iran was facilitating the travel of al-Qaeda operatives, ordering Iranian border inspectors not to put telltale stamps on their passports, thus keeping their travel documents clean" the team leader told me. "The Iranians were fully aware that they were helping operatives who were part of an organization preparing attacks against the United States."

The U.S. intelligence community was also aware of the help Iran was providing bin Laden's men. But because the analysts were driven by the Concept, they consistently downplayed that relationship.

"Old School Ties" was the dismissive title of one post-9/11 analytical report issued by the CIA's CounterTerrorism Center that summarized the early days of bin Laden's cooperation with Iran. It included an account of his meetings in Sudan with Iranian officials in late 1991–1992, and the organizational meetings between bin Laden's Islamic Army Shura (Counsel) and the PLO, Hamas, and Hezbollah, meetings that were brokered by Sudan's Islamist leader Hassan Turabi. Other reports, from January 1997, detailed top bin Laden operatives' travels to Iran and to Hezbollah camps in Lebanon for terrorist training, where bin Laden tasked them to learn the secrets of Hezbollah's speciality: how to set off large, simultaneous truck bombs. (The Iranians obliged and provided that training, the CIA concluded.) "By late 1993, early 1994 there had been a handshake between bin Laden and Iran," the team leader said. A handshake and operational cooperation.

The commission also reviewed CIA documentation on al-Qaeda's connection to Vahidi, Sherafi, and Ahmed al-Mughassil in preparing the

Khobar Towers bombing. Apparently, the information was too sensitive to have been shared with FBI director Louis Freeh, who told reporters after testifying in U.S. District court on the case that al-Qaeda played no role in the attack.[1]

Most troubling among the seventy-five documents the team read that Sunday morning in July were masses of reports on Iranian intelligence operative Imad Mugniyeh, who is described in the 9/11 Commission Report as "a senior Hezbollah operative." The raw reporting showed that well before 9/11, the United States had hard intelligence that the Tehran regime had appointed Mugniyeh as the point man for operational contacts with bin Laden's men. That coincided with the information Zakeri brought to the CIA in Baku four months before the attack.

If anyone had been on the radar screen of U.S. intelligence collectors it was Imad Mugniyeh. Before 9/11, he had killed more Americans than any other terrorist. Putting Mugniyeh together with bin Laden was like throwing a match onto a pile of oil-soaked rags. And yet no alarm bells seemed to have gone off. Mugniyeh is not even named in the final commission report.

The source reports showed that Mugniyeh coordinated the travel of eight to ten of the "muscle hijackers" between Saudi Arabia, Beirut, and Iran in October and November 2000. They revealed that Mugniyeh personally traveled to Saudi Arabia that November and then accompanied muscle hijacker Ahmed al Ghamdi on the plane to Beirut for his trip on to Iran. After that successful dry run, three more muscle hijackers came to Beirut and then flew as a group to Iran, accompanied by one of Mugniyeh's men.

Frustrated by their late discovery of the documents, which prevented them from investigating further, the authors of the 9/11 Commission Report's chapter 7 resorted to irony. It was always possible that so much coordination was simply a "remarkable coincidence" and that "Hezbollah was actually focusing on some other group of individuals traveling from Saudi Arabia during this same time frame, rather than the future hijackers."

Even in its post-9/11 reporting, which Tenet tried unsuccessfully to prevent the commission from reviewing, the CIA simply assumed that the hijackers were traveling *through* Iran, not *to* Iran, my sources on the commission said. It was the Concept again.* The fact that Mugniyeh had become al-Qaeda's travel agent never hit home. "Every time they came up with a

---

*The CIA spin on those trips to Iran is evident in *9/11 and Terrorist Travel*, a staff monograph released by the commission at the same time as its main report. It speaks of "lax immigration and border security" in Iran and claims that al-Qaeda resorted to "human smugglers" to arrange travel to and from Afghanistan "through Iran." See *inter alia* "Exploring the Link between Human Smugglers and Terrorists," p. 61.

smoking gun, the analysts came back and said, yes, that's interesting, but it's not actionable," one commissioner told me. It was the supreme putdown.

Despite a personal pledge from CIA director George Tenet to provide every assistance and to scour every file, the Agency never briefed the commission on Zakeri's walk-in warning before 9/11. My sources believe Tenet simply didn't know—because no one had ever thought to brief him.

The FBI appears to have been less affected by the Concept, at least during their post-9/11 investigation. They sent teams of Special Agents to the Middle East and Europe and acquired the original passenger manifests that documented the hijackers' travels with Mugniyeh.

U.S. interrogators learned firsthand about Iran's help in facilitating travel of al-Qaeda operatives involved in the 9/11 plot from al-Qaeda planner Khaled Sheikh Mohammad, liaison officer Ramzi Binalshibh, and, more generally, from "Khallad" (Tawfiq Bin Attash). All three were captured by the U.S. after the September 11 attacks. Khallad initially tried to get a U.S. visa so he could take part in the "airplanes" plot but was rejected by U.S. immigration authorities. He helped bomb the USS *Cole* in Yemen in October 2000 instead.

"TOTAL COLLABORATION WITH THE IRANIANS"

Tarek Charaabi was worried when an al-Qaeda travel "facilitator" told him to use the rat line through Iran. "Isn't there a danger in Iran?" he asked. The facilitator reassured him that al-Qaeda had "total collaboration with the Iranians" and had its own organization in Iran "that takes care of helping the Mujahedin brothers cross the border." Their March 10, 2001, conversation was wire-tapped by Italian police and presented in a Milan court the following year. It helped convict Charaabi and three other Tunisians of having provided logistical support to al-Qaeda in Europe.

Al-Qaeda had switched from using Pakistan as a transit point, the facilitator said, because "in these past years there's too many secret services." Charaabi was instructed to go to the Iranian embassy in London to pick up a visa "because it's very smooth and then everything's well organized all the way to the training camps."[2]

In Hamburg, Germany, a Syrian Muslim brother named Mohammad Haydar Zammar boasted of having recruited 9/11 pilots Mohammad Atta and Ziad Jarrah and encouraging them to join bin Laden's jihad in Afghanistan. When the three-hundred-pound Zammar boasted, people around him took notice.

Zammar's frequent travels to Iran and his ties to the al-Qaeda cell in Hamburg were known to the CIA well before 9/11. In the late 1990s, a CIA operations officer named Tom V. was quietly asked by the German authorities to leave the country for having attempted to recruit Zammar and a colleague named Ma'moun Darkanzanli, who by then had acquired German citizenship.

Former Pentagon official Mike Maloof investigated Zammar and Darkanzanli and believes the CIA buried its reporting on the Iran–al-Qaeda ties in an effort to cover its tracks. "They had developed post–Cold War sources and didn't want to blow them," he said. In some cases the CIA, al-Qaeda, and Iran were all providing operational support to the same people and the same causes. "That's what happened in Bosnia and in Kosovo" with the Kosovo Liberation Army (KLA), he added.

Maloof stumbled upon the clandestine infiltration routes used by al-Qaeda into the Caucasus in 2000 while working on assignment with customs authorities in the former Soviet republic of Georgia. "I reported what I had learned back to the CIA, and they simply freaked out. It turned out they had the Muj [Mujahedin] from Afghanistan stage in Chechnya, then go to Bosnia and Macedonia." And the Iranians were in the game, handling the first leg of the rat line.

Zammar also recruited Ramzi Binalshibh, according to German intelligence reports provided to the 9/11 Commission. Identified by the commissioner as the "coordinator" of the 9/11 plot, Binalshibh met repeatedly with lead hijacker Mohammad Atta in various cities in Europe, then traveled to Afghanistan to convey operational details to bin Laden and his deputy, Ayman al-Zawahri. On his way, he always stopped in Iran, where Zawahri had set up an operation liaison team following his January 2001 meetings with top Iranian government officials.

For some reason the 9/11 Commission Report fails to mention Binalshibh's trips to Iran, although it references intelligence reports on Binalshibh's activities in Germany that the German federal criminal police, the BKA, made available.[3] One of those reports, which I reviewed in Germany, shows that Binalshibh traveled to Iran on his own passport after getting a visa from the Iranian embassy in Berlin.[4]

Roughly two weeks before Hamid Reza Zakeri walked into the U.S. embassy in Baku on July 26, 2001, Binalshibh traveled to Spain for his final face-to-face meeting with Mohammad Atta.

Atta initially had planned to carry out the attacks over the summer but had to push back the date because he didn't have enough pilots. It was during this meeting that Atta told Binalshibh the final date for the attack, investigators say. Binalshibh then traveled to Iran and eventually to Afghanistan. Zawahri traveled to Iran at the same time, according to Zakeri.

It is hard to believe that the presence in Iran of a top 9/11 planner and bin Laden's right-hand man just two months before the September 11 attacks was a coincidence.

20 SHAHRIVAR

The afternoon before the 9/11 attacks, Zakeri received an unsettling phone call in Baku. The caller spoke Persian with an American accent.

It's the tenth of September, he said. Now can you tell me what's going to happen?

Zakeri thought the caller was the Persian-speaking CIA officer who had dismissed his claims five weeks earlier. He was playing mind games. That's what they did in the intelligence business. They f—ed with your mind.

Zakeri had never checked a calendar himself to verify the date. To this day he believes his former boss in Iran had been off by one day.

In fact, it was CIA "George" who had made a mistake. The date Zakeri had given the CIA—20 Shahrivar—was September 11.

AL-QAEDA MOVES TO IRAN

Twenty days after the United States began bombing Afghanistan in October 2001, a convoy of late-model Toyota LandCruisers pulled up at the Dorgharoun border crossing into Iran. For years the customs outpost had been virtually closed. There wasn't even a village in the vicinity. But the border guards, under direct orders from the Revolutionary Guards intelligence chief, Morteza Rezai, were expecting visitors.

Although they were refugees of sorts, they weren't fleeing Afghanistan with mattresses and cheap cookstoves and bed linens strapped to the roofs. Their rugged four-wheel-drive vehicles had been carefully packed. The nineteen Arab men had brought a few suitcases, weapons, cash, uncut diamonds, and nine women and children.

Eleven of the men were high-ranking al-Qaeda members, including Saif al Adel, the Egyptian who was bin Laden's top military planner and a top computer specialist. Revolutionary Guards officers flew them to the "al-Madhi" housing complex in Lashkarak, northeast of Tehran. They were put up in family quarters in the Shahid Haj Hemmat bloc, which was reserved for Revolutionary Guards' guests. They stayed there until mid-February 2003, when word of their presence leaked out.

Saad bin Laden—the eldest son—was with them, as was one of his nephews. The Iranians referred to the Arabs as "Taliban" when talking among themselves.

Not long afterward, the al-Qaeda fighters started to stream across the border. According to my Iranian sources, nine hundred of them came with their families over the next few weeks. Many of them belonged to a group called Ansar al Islam, and went on to fight in Iraq against U.S. forces. Some of the fighters were taken to camps near Marivan in Iranian Kurdistan, but the Saudis stood out because they had long beards with no mustaches, and because the Afghan trousers they liked to wear were too short.

The United States also picked up al-Qaeda's move into Iran. "It wasn't just by road," one U.S. intelligence officer told me. "We saw helicopters and even fixed-wing aircraft being sent to Heart [Afghanistan] to evacuate al-Qaeda fighters and their families." This was the type of post-9/11 reporting that George Tenet specifically excluded from the documents turned over to the 9/11 Commission. It clearly demonstrated a deep, ongoing *operational* relationship between Iran and al-Qaeda. It was precisely the type of detail federal prosecutors used to build a case for conspiracy, since it helped to establish a pattern of behavior.

Two months after 9/11, the office of Supreme Leader Ali Khamenei sent a letter to a close associate of bin Laden deputy Ayman Zawahri, the man who "owned" al-Qaeda's Iran connection. "In continuation of our relations," it informed the recipient, Khamenei had just transferred 1 million Swiss francs into his Swiss bank account.

I was shown a copy of this letter from a source who had personal access to Khamenei's office. The recipient was a then relatively unknown Jordanian born to Palestinian parents, named Abu Musab Zarqawi. The Iranian regime continues to finance Zarqawi and his brutal band of murderers, whose signature act became the kidnapping and gruesome videotaped beheading of foreign truckdrivers and aid workers in Iraq. Whenever U.S. forces closed in on him in Iraq, he simply fled across the border into Iran, where Revolutionary Guards units continued to give him protection, money, and arms.

After denying for eighteen months that any al-Qaeda operatives were present in Iran, on February 21, 2003, Foreign Minister Kamal Kharrazi claimed that the authorities had arrested more than four hundred al-Qaeda members and were holding them in jail.

But Saif al-Adel, Saad bin Laden, and their families never saw the inside of an Iranian jail. Instead they were transferred to Boostaneh Bostan, a more secure guesthouse run by Revolutionary Guards intelligence, according to IRGC defector Colonel B. Known to U.S. intelligence analysts as the site of a former army depot, it was located just before the Cheetgar Park turnoff on the road to Karaj, about 10 kilometers north of Tehran. They continued al-Qaeda operations unhindered.

The United States reportedly intercepted communications from Saif al-Adel in Mashad to al-Qaeda hit teams in Saudi Arabia just before their May 12, 2003, assault on three housing compounds in Riyadh. More than ninety-two people died during the running gun battles, which shocked the Saudi royal family and prompted the first serious crackdown on al-Qaeda and its supporters in the kingdom.

THE POLYGRAPH

Shortly after the Riyadh attacks, seven American intelligence officers flew to The Hague. After all that had happened, they had decided to contact Hamid Reza Zakeri. This time they planned to do things the "right" way.

CIA "George" had come back. With him were several other officials, including "Peter," "Dr. Bill," and a senior FBI special agent. ("They like to call themselves 'Doctor,' " a former clandestine officer told me. "That gives them more gravitas.") They were going to polygraph Zakeri.

Dr. Bill attached the various sensors to Zakeri's body and, through a translator, started the routine. He began by asking him his name. "Zakeri," of course, was an alias; virtually everyone in the Iranian government used phony names, from government ministers down to lowly security officers. The needles on Dr. Bill's machine registered Zakeri's subterfuge, and his questioning became more aggressive.

Are you working for a foreign intelligence agency? Dr. Bill asked. Zakeri said no. Are you seeking to do harm to the United States? Again, Zakeri shook his head. At both answers, the needles practically jumped off the chart.

Finally they took the wires off, and the man from the FBI had an idea. Look, he said. Let's just agree that everything you've told us so far is a lie—all right, let's call it a creative exaggeration. From here on out, we're going to do things differently.

When I asked a former clandestine officer about the polygraph, he rolled his eyes. "I thought we had put this issue to bed years ago," he said. "Agents prove their bona fides through production, not by polygraph. No

Arab or Iranian has ever passed a polygraph. But why is it that every one of our Cuban agents but one always passed their polygraphs?" All those Cubans, he explained, had turned out to be double agents, trained by Castro's security force to use psychological methods to beat the machine. "They were trained to believe that their lies were patriotic—so they felt no guilt at lying." And it worked every time.

Zakeri was furious. He repeated the information he had given the CIA in Baku about learning of a massive attack involving aircraft planned for 20 Shahrivar. "This is not my story," he insisted. "This is the truth I'm telling."

It just wasn't what they wanted to hear.

ALI M.

Congressman Curt Weldon (R-Pa.) was a bulldog. When he got hold of something, he never let go. He believed Iranian government agents in the United States were planning a series of spectacular terrorist attacks that would make September 11 look like amateur hour. Among their targets was the Seabrook nuclear power plant in New Hampshire, just north of Boston. But neither CIA director George Tenet nor his chief of operations, Steve Kappas, would listen.

The problem was Weldon's source—or, rather, a key contact of his source, Kappas said.

Weldon made several trips to Paris starting in early 2003 to speak with a former Iranian government minister, Ali M., who claimed to have information about Iran that could be of use to the United States. During that first meeting, Ali told Weldon that Osama bin Laden was then in Iran for medical treatment. He was staying at a Revolutionary Guards safe house near the town of Ladiz, in Iranian Baluchistan, 80 kilometers southeast of Zahedan. It was a wild area, just on the Iranian side of the border triangle where Iran meets Pakistan and Afghanistan. Bin Laden was under the personal protection of Iranian leader Ayatollah Khamenei.

The powerful Republican legislator wasn't sure what to make of the information, but he determined to pass it on to CIA director George Tenet, whom he knew well. He gave Ali a private fax number. The Iranian agreed to send updated information as he received it.

Even before he returned to Washington, Ali's faxes started coming in. He wrote them all by hand, in large awkward script. Soon Weldon had a stack of them several inches high.

In April 2003, Ali warned that Iran was crashing on its nuclear weapons program and was sending technicians to North Korea to help construct a secret underground uranium-enrichment plant. On May 4, Ali predicted that the United States would raise its terror alert to Orange because of specific Iranian threats. Three weeks later, on May 20, the Department of Homeland Security raised the alert level to Orange but didn't mention Iran.

Then, on May 17, Ali warned that Iranian-backed terrorists were planning to hijack airliners in Canada and crash them into a U.S. nuclear reactor on the East Coast. Ali's sources referred to the reactor as "SEA." Weldon concluded they probably meant Seabrook.

Weldon met with Tenet personally and described Ali and his information. In several cases already, he said, Ali's predictions had come true. Tenet said the Agency would reach out to him, and assigned Kappas to work with him.

Months later, Weldon returned to Paris to see Ali and asked if anyone from the CIA had met with him. No, he replied nervously. But the French had sent someone from the Interior Ministry's counterespionage service, the DST. The French berated him for talking to a U.S. congressman.

Weldon blew up. Back in Washington, he phoned Tenet, who admitted that the Paris station chief had preferred to ask his French contacts to "vet" Ali. That was the protocol in friendly countries. We don't run operations without letting the host service know what we're doing, he said.

On August 22, 2003, the *Toronto Star* reported that Canadian authorities had just arrested nineteen suspected terrorists for immigration violations, including a man taking flight lessons who had flown solo over an Ontario nuclear power plant. Weldon saw the arrests as dire confirmation of Ali's warning about the plot to hit the Seabrook plant.

In November 2003, Weldon sent a memo to the chairman of the House Permanent Select Intelligence Committee, Florida Republican Porter Goss, and to his counterpart in the Senate, Kansas Republican Pat Roberts. "This letter is to warn you of an intelligence failure in the process of happening," Weldon wrote. He attached a stack of Ali's memos several inches thick, with a memo that summarized his predictions and matched them to events later confirmed in the press.

Again he met with Tenet and Kappas. "We need to get Ali some money," he said. "He's paying his informants. That's how it's done. You pay guys to spy on their country."

What's your man's relationship to Manucher Ghorbanifar? Kappas asked finally. That's when Weldon realized he had hit a brick wall.

Manucher Ghorbanifar was the Iranian arms dealer at the center of the Iran-Contra scandal. The Agency had put out a "burn notice" on him after he failed a polygraph. It was Ghorbanifar who had introduced Weldon to Ali M.

"I asked Ghorbanifar about the polygraph," Weldon told me. "I met with him for six hours. He said, yeah, he failed the CIA polygraph. You know why? Because the CIA kept asking him to give up the identities of his sources in Iran. He said he couldn't do that."

In early June 2004, Weldon received a fresh fax from Ali. The Supreme Leader's office had just given the green light for major terrorist actions against the United States, he said. They would be run by a special unit of the Revolutionary Guards that specialized in overseas operations. Ali provided the names of the eight people who took part in the meeting and a detailed account of what they said.

Weldon was so frustrated by Tenet's inaction that when Ali sent him fresh information on bin Laden's whereabouts in Iran, he contacted a bounty hunter in Wisconsin. The man was a former CIA contract employee and knew how to operate in hostile environments. They worked out a plan to get him into Iran so he could take bin Laden.

When Weldon told Tenet his plan, the CIA director nearly dropped out of his chair. Weldon was planning to go to Iran himself with the bounty hunter. Ali said his sources were telling him that President Khatami would love to see the end of bin Laden, to improve his own position against the regime hard-liners who were providing bin Laden safe haven, and could arrange to get the Revolutionary Guards protection detail called away. Tenet just shook his head. Congressman, you can't get involved in this kind of thing, he said.

Former CIA operations director Clair George was the man who had issued the original "burn" notice on Ghorbanifar, but he was stunned when he heard Weldon's story. "I think I'm still professional enough to say that if some guy strolls in and says, 'I can prove to you that bin Laden is in Iran,' I would look into it."

The problem was George Tenet, he believed. "Tenet was a very astute politician. He spent more time buttering up the president than presenting him with facts, and it eventually did him in."

THE JUDGE

French counterterrorism judge Jean-Louis Bruguière arguably knew more about al-Qaeda than any westerner alive. Already in March 1995, he had tasked French intelligence to investigate bin Laden safe houses in Peshawar, Pakistan, and his training camps in Afghanistan. He was also the man who first pieced together the legal case against Iran's clerical rulers for the murder of Iranian dissidents overseas. His watershed investigation of the 1991 assassination of former prime mininster Shahpour Bakhtiar revealed that the hit teams were acting on orders from the highest authorities in Tehran. He had no illusions about the regime's involvement in terror.[5]

He had reams of information on the travels of al-Qaeda operatives to and from Iran, especially after 9/11.

In his view, the Tehran regime was "trying to bargain its way in" to al-Qaeda operations. It was seeking to oversee, not manage, specific terror attacks. The mullahs "want to increase the threat to the United States and Israel," he told me. While he had no doubt that the Iranians played a supporting role in the 9/11 attacks, he had seen no evidence that they were a front-line player. "They are trying to take advantage of the situation," he said.

With Bakhtiar and other dissidents, the regime was willing to take risks. It considered the dissidents a domestic problem, not an international one. The mullahs figured it was their right to murder whoever they judged presented a risk to their grip on power. With al-Qaeda it was slightly more nuanced. They recognized the dangers of tickling the tiger and didn't want to get caught in the act. Because of this, in 2003 and 2004 they arrested some of the lower-level al-Qaeda members in Iran to give the impression that they were cracking down. But they never shut down al-Qaeda's Iran-based operations.

Bruguière was not beholden to the CIA's Concept. For the past fifteen years he had been struck repeatedly by the Iranians' willingness to use Sunni Muslim extremist groups, and vice versa. "Al-Qaeda is not a threat to Iran because the Iranians see no opposition between Sunnis and Shiites," he said.

In October 2004, Bruguière wrapped up his investigation into the al-Qaeda plot to bomb Strasbourg Cathedral over Christmas 2000. The alleged leader of the plot, a Moroccan named Mohammad Ben Zakhriah, aka Meliani, had trained in Afghanistan with top al-Qaeda operatives Abu Zubaida and Abu Jaafa. Buried in the 4-foot-high stack of documents Bruguière sent over to prosecutors were copies of his passport and his travel records.

Like so many other al-Qaeda operatives, Ben Zakhriah traveled back and forth to Europe through Iran. So did the Moroccan group that blew up the Madrid commuter trains in March 2004, in an effort to get Spanish troops out of Iraq.

As Bruguière saw it, the Iranians were placing their bets. Just like the warnings before TWA Flight 800, the intelligence on Iran's involvement in the 9/11 conspiracy was not actionable—then.

But it is now.

SHOWDOWN

We won't accept any new obligations. Iran has a high technical capability and has to be recognized by the international community as a member of the nuclear club. This is an irreversible path.

—Iranian foreign minister Kamal Kharrazi, June 12, 2004

For Constantine Menges, a former special presidential assistant for national security affairs under President Reagan, the showdown began on April 4, 2004. That was when an Iranian-backed cleric in Baghdad, Moqtada al-Sadr, called on his followers to launch an uprising against U.S. troops and their Iraqi allies.

Iran had been building its base inside Iraq for decades. Since the early 1980s it had welcomed anti-Saddam dissidents to Tehran and provided them with offices, broadcasting facilities, and safe haven.

But this was different. Menges believed Iran was spending huge sums on Moqtada al-Sadr and his grassroots movement as part of a concerted strategy to evict the United States from Iraq, prevent a democratic successor regime from taking root, and expand Iran's own claim as leader of the Muslim revolt against Western imperialism. Some sources said Iran was funneling the equivalent of $75 million per year to al-Sadr and his group. "They certainly are not lacking resources to pay their militiamen," one U.S. intelligence officer observed.

One day after al-Sadr called on his troops to revolt, the U.S. proconsul in Iraq, L. Paul Bremer, sought to arrest him for the murder of Ayatollah Abdul Majid al-Khoie, who had returned to Iraq from exile in London one year earlier. The United States had been counting on the moderate, pro-Western Khoie to mobilize Iraqi Shiites against any attempt by Iran to install an Islamic republic in Iraq. Khoie was assassinated by a knife-wielding mob in the holy city of Najaf just days after he returned. Bremer was convinced that Iran had ordered his murder and that al-Sadr was the instrument.

Shortly after Khoie's assassination, a pro-Iranian cleric in Kut took over the mosque in that city of 300,000, declared himself mayor, and began ruling with the help of three hundred armed Iranian guards, a force that swelled to over one thousand in just a few days. He also had buckets of cash. Iranian Revolutionary Guards units were provided arms, money, and logistical backup. Iranian intelligence was swarming all over Iraq. There was absolutely no doubt that Iran's goal was to ensure that the United States failed in Iraq. Menges tried to warn the Bush administration of these events.

A key shortcoming in U.S. strategy in Iraq was broadcasting, Menges said. The Iranians were spending millions of dollars to get their message into Iraq. A survey by Radio Free Europe/Radio Liberty found that Iran was financing forty-one of the sixty-three AM/FM/TV broadcasts heard in Arabic inside Iraq. The United States was supporting just one. Efforts by former Voice of America chief Robert Reilly to bolster U.S. broadcasting in Iraq were stymied by State Department appointees with Bremer's Coalition Provisional Authority.

The Iranians are real pros, Menges warned. They're thugs and they're killers. In Iraq, the stakes were high and they were playing for keeps. They won't hesitate to murder anyone who gets in their way. Compared with the Iranians, we're just babes in the woods, he sighed.[1]

FUELING INSURGENCY IN IRAQ

The Revolutionary Guards celebrated the remodeling of the former U.S. embassy in Tehran—which they still referred to as *laneh jasoosi*, the "den of spies"—by slaughtering a lamb. Since the mid-1980s, the Pasdaran had used the building as a training center, where they taught foreign terrorist recruits and members of the Qods Force the intricacies of codes, document forgery, and clandestine communications. Now they were preparing to train top Pasdaran operatives to infiltrate Iraq to fuel the anti-American "insurgency."

Fifty-two top Pasdaran officers, including many generals, attended the final debriefing. They were photographed at what appeared to be school desks, filling out forms, before being sent into Iraq to run deadly terrorist networks. Pictures from that session appeared in the Pasdaran internal bulletin, circulated to top regime leaders, and were kept on file with the Revolutionary Guards archives.

Hamid Reza Zakeri acquired these photographs from the archives and shared them with me. It was an extraordinary "deck of cards" U.S. military leaders would benefit from distributing to troops on the ground in Iraq. But, of course, the CIA had determined that Zakeri was a "serial fabricator" and had no interest in the photographic evidence he had acquired.

Among the top undercover officers now operating in Iraq was IRGC Brigadier General Salihani, a well-fed man with thinning light-brown hair. In archive photos Zakeri showed me, Salihani could be seen undergoing counterterror training, leaning out of a speeding red Mercedes as it careened through an obstacle course on two wheels, firing off blasts from a submachine gun and a pistol. After the "graduation" ceremony at the former U.S. embassy, Salihani showed up at an "aid" center in Iraq, distributing Korans, television sets, and other "humanitarian" goods. Along with other "graduates," he posed for a Revolutionary Guards photographer in front of the famous Shiite shrine in Karbala, Iraq.

The interim Iraqi government arrested a number of these Pasdaran officers in late 2004 but treated their presence among the insurgents as a coincidence, when in fact it was policy.

Iran's Revolutionary Guards have been fueling the anti-U.S. insurgency in Iraq from the start, yet another front in their twenty-five-year war on America.

TARGETING AMERICA

Dr. Hassan Abassi was the top theoretician for the Revolutionary Guards. In the early 1980s he formulated the doctrine of export of the revolution that led to the creation of Hezbollah in Lebanon. He'd been inspiring and indoctrinating young Iranians ever since.

Abassi believed the Islamic Republic of Iran had a mission to expand the Dar al Islam—the House of Islam—until Islam had conquered the world. It had been the Prophet's mission at the birth of Islam. Imam Khomeini had made it Iran's mission today.

In late May 2004, Abassi addressed new recruits at the Revolutionary Guards' Al-Hussein University in Tehran, to inspire them to adopt that mission as Hezbollah's Helpers. He spoke at length about Tehran's secret strategy for destroying "Anglo-Saxon civilization."

It was supposed to be a closed ceremony, commemorating Iran's victory in evicting Iraqi invaders from the city of Khoramshahr twenty-two years earlier. But a videotape of his speech reached Iranian exiles in the United States and Britain.

He began by relating the story of a Jewish woman who was mistakenly released by the Palestinian hijackers at Entebbe who didn't realize she was Jewish. What's the point of having Israel if Jews still can be taken hostage? she complained to waiting TV cameras.

I'm going to surprise you, Abassi told the young recruits. The Jewish lady was right. Look at Iraq, he said. What's the point of having an Islamic Republic if the Americans can come to Najaf and do what they want? The goal of Iran's Islamic Republic was not to defend Iran, he said. It was to defend Islam and to spread Islam throughout the world.

He went on to blast President Khatami, whom he accused of having abandoned the goals and ideology that made the Islamic Republic strong.

The West sees us as terrorists, he said. But our struggle against world arrogance gives us strength. If our young people adopted Khatami's way, we would abandon this struggle. "I take pride in my actions that cause anxiety and fear to the Americans," he said.

The regime had a new plan to recruit twenty thousand suicide bombers, he said. The Americans claim we are making nuclear weapons, but we don't need them! There are six thousand nuclear weapons in the United States in various places, and we know where they are! Our martyrs will bring America to its knees. One martyr for the cause of Islam is more powerful than a nuclear bomb.

The United States was the head of the snake, struggling against Allah and the Muslims, but Iran was planning devastating strikes against America. "There are twenty-nine sensitive sites in the U.S. and in the West," he said. "We have already spied on these sites and we know how we are going to attack them."

Iran had missiles fueled, armed, and ready to strike American targets. "[A]s soon as the instructions arrive from the Leader [Ayatollah Khamenei], we will launch our missiles at their cities and installations."

If Israel chose to attack Iran's nuclear plant at Busheir before the Islamic Republic went on the offensive, Abassi said Iran's losses would be "very low, because [only] one structure will be destroyed, while we have means of attacking Israel's nuclear facilities and arsenals such that no trace of Israel will remain."[2]

Just one month after this speech—described as "inflammatory but brilliant" by exiles who watched the tape in full—the United States quietly expelled two Iranian diplomats in New York who had been caught taking video footage of U.S. landmarks using cameras hidden beneath their coats. When investigators viewed their tapes, it was clear they were focusing on St. Patrick's Cathedral and Rockefeller Center—high-profile targets where thousands of Americans could be killed.

DENIAL, DECEPTION, AND DELAY

For more than a year the United States played the IAEA game, trying to persuade other members of the Board of Governors to refer Iran to the UN Security Council for having violated its safeguards obligations. It was called consensus building, and it wasn't working. The Europeans felt more threatened by the U.S. challenge to enforce the NPT than by a radical Islamic regime armed with nuclear weapons.

John Bolton, Ambassador Robert Joseph, and Paula DeSutter were increasingly concerned as IAEA inspectors kept finding new evidence of clandestine nuclear activities in Iran and the Board refused to act. "We came to Vienna in November [2003] and they said, 'Come back in January.' In January they said the time wasn't right, 'Come back in March.' In March, they said, 'Wait until June,' " DeSutter said. And on it went. Germany, France, and Britain claimed they were making progress in getting Iran to "suspend" uranium enrichment and stop manufacturing new centrifuges. Every time the Iranians turned around and broke their pledge, the Europeans tut-tutted and trotted back to Tehran to try again.

During the March 2004 Board of Governors meeting in Vienna, DeSutter's lawyer, Christopher Ford, pulled the evidence of Iran's safeguards violations into a public "indictment" and essentially ordered the U.S. permanent delegate to the IAEA, Kenneth Brill, to deliver it. (Brill was a career State Department official who delighted in Vienna-speak and had been reluctant to push the Board on Iran. He retired in August 2004.) Iran was practicing "a policy of denial, deception, and delay," the United States said. Iran kept on changing its story. It tried to hide work on a new-generation centrifuge known as the P-2. It was concealing production equipment in nondescript workshops with names like "Pars Trash" and "Farayand Technique." It got caught trying to produce polonium 210, an isotope that has virtually no civilian use but is ideal for triggering the massive chain reaction needed to set off a nuclear bomb. The Iranians claimed they had "suspended" the production of centrifuges, and yet agency inspectors kept counting new batches leaving the assembly lines. It was time for the Board to act.

By April 2004, Iran had produced 1,140 centrifuge rotors—enough, once assembled, to equip the entire pilot plant at Natanz and make enough fissile material in a year for several bombs. Despite the clear pattern of cheat-and-retreat, Baradei continued to state there was "no evidence" of nuclear weapons activity.

Then, in June, former IAEA inspector David Albright released satellite photographs that seemed to confirm everyone's worst fear. Iran had been operating a facility within the huge Defense Industries Organization munitions works at Lavizan-Shian in Tehran that bore the hallmarks of a secret centrifuge plant.

Photographs taken by DigitalGlobe's Quickbird commercial satellite in August 2003 showed large buildings surrounded by heavy security within the already secure DIO complex. Photographs of the same site taken in March 2004 showed—nothing. Shortly after the existence of the secret site was revealed by the MEK, the regime razed it to the ground. Not only had the buildings been taken down, but even the roads and sidewalks were gone and the rubble carted away. Clearly, Iran was trying to sanitize the site, to foil the agency's environmental sampling that was turning up traces of enriched uranium just about everywhere. Albright believes the Iranians might have succeeded. "There are real outstanding issues at Lavizan," he said.[3]

A former DIO employee who worked at the nearby TOW missile plant at Lavizan-Shian in the mid-1990s confirmed to me that the "physics center," as it was called, was strictly off limits to all but a handful of employees. Even plant managers with high-level security clearances were barred from entering by armed guards.*

Baradei and the European Union diplomats had been claiming they had everything under control. Iran's program was now visible, its contours known. All of a sudden, even the agency's own inspectors began to wonder whether Iran had been operating a clandestine enrichment facility at Lavizan-Shian—possibly for years.

If so, Iran could already have enough highly enriched uranium material for a small nuclear arsenal, and all the inspections and the noise in Vienna were just a shadow play to prepare the world for a nuclear-armed Iran.

THE BOLTON SPEECH

John Bolton had overall responsibility for arms control and international security at the State Department. The reporting from Paula DeSutter's

*Iran lately claimed that the site was used to study nuclear defense and preparedness but had "no nuclear material" despite the presence of whole-body counters, used to measure radioactivity.

verifiers, the IAEA, and the intelligence community went directly to him, Secretary Powell, and the president. He had long been warning about Iran's nuclear intentions and for years had been tracking masses of public and uncontradicted evidence that suggested Iran was secretly pursuing the bomb. By August 2004, as he surveyed Iran's latest record of cheat and retreat, he knew it was crunch time.

Iran was pursuing two separate paths to nuclear weapons, he told an audience at the Hudson Institute, one that would use highly enriched uranium and one that would use plutonium. Over many years, Iran had secretly built dozens of facilities dedicated to producing highly enriched uranium and plutonium for its bomb program. There was the hex plant in Isfahan, the secret centrifuge production workshops in Tehran, the buried centrifuge plant in Natanz, and a laser enrichment plant at Lashkar Abad. In Arak, they were building a heavy-water production plant and planned to begin construction of a plutonium production reactor in 2005 that would use the heavy water and natural uranium to produce plutonium.

"The costly infrastructure to perform all of these activities goes well beyond any conceivable peaceful nuclear program," he said. "No comparable oil-rich nation has ever engaged, or would be engaged, in this set of activities—or would pursue them for nearly two decades behind a continuing cloud of secrecy and lies to IAEA inspectors and the international community—unless it was dead set on building nuclear weapons."

Iran's cover stories were simply not credible. For instance, they were investing huge sums of money to mine, process, and enrich uranium, ostensibly because they could not purchase reactor fuel from foreign suppliers. But for at least the next decade, Iran would have at most a single nuclear power reactor, the one the Russians were building at Busheir. In addition, Iran's uranium reserves were limited; they didn't have enough uranium to fuel even one reactor over its lifetime. But they had quite enough to make a small arsenal of nuclear bombs. "We are being asked to believe that Iran is building uranium enrichment capacity to make fuel for reactors that do not exist from uranium Iran does not have," he said.

And Busheir itself was a problem. Although the reactor was under IAEA safeguards, and Russia had agreed to provide and reprocess the fuel, if Iran should withdraw from the NPT and renounce its agreement with Russia, "the Busheir reactor would produce enough plutonium each year for about thirty nuclear weapons," he said.

This was called the "breakout" strategy, and it was probably the biggest headache of all. Using the benefits that NPT membership afforded them, Iran could quite legally and openly acquire enough fissile material to make dozens of nuclear bombs. They could design the weapons and even build the bombs—without the fissile cores—without ever breaking the NPT. Once they were ready, they simply announced their intention to withdraw from the treaty and began assembling their weapons. In a matter of weeks, it was all over. Busheir was scheduled to be fueled sometime in 2005.

Iran was skillfully gaming the international system, Bolton believed. As the IAEA inspected, took samples, and asked for more information, Iran continued to lie, cheat, deny, and build. Inadvertently, perhaps, Baradei and the IAEA were buying more time for Iran to complete the facilities it needed to build the bomb. "If we permit Iran's deception to go on much longer, it will be too late. Iran will have nuclear weapons," he said.

Bolton laid his cards on the table. "Clearly, the time to report this issue to the Security Council is long overdue."

When he got back to his office, he told his staff to get ready for show time in Vienna.

VIENNA RULES

The chief German delegate, Friedrich Gröning, was outraged. As Germany's ambassador for Arms Control and Disarmament, he understood the international system. There were rules and procedures; and, most important of all, there was consensus. This was the Spirit of Vienna. These unknown Americans who had shown up for the September 2004 IAEA Board of Governors meeting were not playing by the rules. If they thought that he and his European colleagues were going to hand President Bush a diplomatic victory just two months before the U.S. elections, they had another thing coming.

For two days of a delicious Indian summer in Vienna, Gröning lectured the Americans on the Spirit of Vienna. The Iranians were complying, he said in private meetings away from the fourth-floor Council chamber. They were cooperating with the agency. All that remained were a few technical details to clear up about Iran's past activities. Hadn't the Americans read the director general's report?

Actually, we *have* read the latest DG report, said the new chief U.S. delegate, Jackie Wolcott Sanders. A tough, no-nonsense negotiator, Sanders was the U.S. ambassador to the Conference on Disarmament in Geneva and a special representative of the president for the nonproliferation of nuclear weapons. She was also a Bolton protégé.

What we find particularly disturbing in that report is to discover that the Iranians are preparing to process 37 tons of yellowcake at the Uranium Conversion Facility in Isfahan, she said. The Iranians are calling it a test, but we think that much uranium means a production run. Do you understand, Mr. Ambassador, how much highly enriched uranium the Iranians could make from that 37 tons of yellowcake?

Gröning didn't see the relevance of her question, so she spelled it out. Once processed and enriched, 37 tons of yellowcake could supply enough fissile material for up to five nuclear weapons, even by unclassified IAEA calculations.

By this point, the German was sputtering. We have no evidence that the Iranians are seeking to build weapons, he said. The DG has stated that repeatedly. We think your administration has got a political agenda, and we're not going to let you hijack this agency for such purposes.

It is not within the director general's mandate to determine whether Iran has a weapons program, Sanders noted. The DG's only job is to determine whether Iran has violated its safeguards commitments, and on this the evidence should be clear.

Like the other Europeans in the room, Gröning was convinced that George W. Bush was going to lose the November 2004 presidential elections, so he felt there was no reason to acquiesce to the U.S. request to take a tougher line on Iran. He told his Iranian friends as much when he met with them in the corridors. Married to an Iranian wife, Gröning prided himself on his ability to speak Farsi and made sure the Americans saw him conversing with the Iranian delegates and their official press. To his astonishment, however, Sanders and her delegation were holding firm. This was not the way the U.S. bureaucracy had usually acted. The Americans were fighting back, and not just in Vienna, but in Berlin, Brussels, and London as well. They had put on the diplomatic equivalent of a full-court press.

As the meetings got under way at IAEA headquarters on Monday, September 13, British foreign minister Jack Straw told EU foreign ministers in Brussels that Iran's behavior had become alarming. He reminded them that the EU had been standing up to the United States on Iran's behalf because the Iranians had pledged in June to stop building centrifuges and to suspend uranium enrichment.

"Since then they have said they are going to restart part of that process," Straw said. According to the IAEA, in fact, Iran had never completely stopped producing centrifuge components. In mid-July, Iran broke IAEA seals on centrifuge production equipment and began ramping up production of key components, and on July 28 the IAEA reported that Iran had resumed production of UF6. "That has undermined confidence in the international community in Iran's intention. What Iran has to understand is that it cannot turn the issue of confidence on and off like a tap."

When that wire report came into the U.S. delegation meeting room on the curving seventh-floor corridor overlooking the Danube, an aide to Sanders quickly photocopied it and went down three floors to hand it out to the press, who had pooled in front of the main council chamber, waiting for Baradei to emerge.

And then he began to spin. Straw's comments were evidence that the Europeans were "finally coming around" to the U.S. view of the gravity of the Iranian threat, he told reporters. "The Europeans now are calling for a permanent cessation of Iran's enrichment program, just as we are. So while there used to be a U.S. approach and a European approach, now they are virtually identical. We'd all like to see this program end."

For four days the Europeans resisted the U.S. efforts to put "backbone" into the joint resolution they planned to introduce to the Board of Governors. The United States wanted it to be crystal clear that the board would refer Iran to the UN Security Council if it resumed uranium enrichment or failed just once more to comply with IAEA demands. The Europeans were resisting, tooth and nail.

"Look, it's a bit like accusing someone of being a sex molester," an agency official explained. "Everyone knows there is a stigma to being found in violation of the NPT, and it puts everyone here in a quandary. Do you accept the DNA evidence, or do you believe the defendant's protests of innocence? Because once you accept the evidence, it marks them for life."

For the journalists waiting hours on end for delegates to emerge from the sealed council chambers, it was a bit like a papal council. "Any whiffs of white smoke?" one joked to the Sanders aide at the end of the second day. "Not even the beginning of a cloud," he replied. But he made a point of smiling. Meanwhile, delegates kept slipping out of the council chambers through a back door away from the news cameras, to continue negotiations in the private meeting rooms each delegation had been assigned.

Iran sent a deputy national security adviser, Hossein Mohammad Mousavian, who from the start staked out Iran's uncompromising refusal to abandon uranium enrichment. "Enrichment is the legitimate right of Iran as of any [NPT] member. We believe the suspension of enrichment cannot continue for a long time," he said. Iran's agreement to suspend enrichment temporarily had been a goodwill gesture toward the Europeans, but Iran was now insisting that it be allowed to go ahead. He confirmed plans to process 37 tons of uranium into enrichment feedstock. Regardless of what happened in Vienna, Iran was steaming ahead.

At one point, a member of the U.S. negotiating team left the door to the seventh-floor meeting room unlocked for a few moments and came back to find an Iranian delegate trying to hack into a computer. He claimed he was trying to check his Hotmail account.

Unabashed at getting caught, he sauntered back to the Iranian delegation room, three doors down the hall.

THE GERMANS BACK DOWN

Wednesday dawned to rain. With the bad weather, the mood among the Europeans sharpened and positions appeared to harden. The wire services began to report an unbridgeable "rift" between the Americans and the Europeans.

Reuters reporter Louis Charbonneau knew exactly who was to blame. "The people the Americans have sent this time are a bunch of freaks," he told an IAEA official I was meeting in the cafeteria for lunch. They had been selected by Bush administration "ideologue" John Bolton. "The Bush people don't have a clue about Iran," he added.

By late afternoon the agency announced the board would not meet on Thursday, so delegates could continue their negotiations. One reason for the delay, I learned, was a rift—not between the Americans and the Europeans, but among the Europeans themselves. "While the wire services were reporting that we were throwing chairs at each other in there, in fact it was the Germans who were arguing among themselves," one delegate said. "It was bizarre." Apparently, Gröning's pedantry finally had worn out the patience of his own colleagues.

On Thursday night, British foreign minister Jack Straw called his German counterpart, Jochka Fischer, to resolve the logjam.

Fischer was married to the daughter of a prominent Iranian dissident, and had a healthy suspicion of the mullahs in Tehran. On Friday, Gröning was instructed by Berlin to accept the American proposal, which now only obliquely threatened to refer Iran to the Security Council in the event of future violations. The resolution called for an immediate suspension of Iran's enrichment activities and demanded that Iran make a complete, detailed accounting of its entire nuclear program, including its black-market supply network, by the next Board of Governors meeting, November 25.

It took another day for Gröning to back down, but for Sanders and Bolton it was a big win. Despite the hedged language, they had finally gotten the IAEA to adopt a firm deadline for Iran to come clean on its clandestine nuclear program, not just another resolution "deploring" Iran's repeated failures to comply.

But it wasn't enough.

THE AYATOLLAH'S DEADLINE

The Iranians were in a hurry. The same day the diplomats issued their resolution in Vienna, the Revolutionary Guards missile force fired off another Shahab-3, which was declared operational on July 20, 2003, during an official ceremony with Supreme Leader Ayatollah Khamenei.

Several batteries of the missiles were now deployed in buried depots in Bakhtaran province along the Iraqi border and in Khouzestan in the southwest, facing Israel. The Israeli air force knew exactly where the missiles were located, and regularly practiced pinpoint bombing drills to take them out by collapsing the entrances to the buried sites.

It was not the first time an operational Shahab-3 had been tested, but it was the first time the Revolutionary Guards missile units had fired the new missile during large-scale military exercises, code-named Ashura-5. The September 18, 2004, launch gave the missile units critical experience in deploying, fueling, and launching a strategic missile. It also showed that Iran had a large enough stockpile of missiles to train actively with them.

As the Revolutionary Guards prepared the launch, Ayatollah Khamenei met with top advisers in Tehran and agreed to unblock funding to accelerate nuclear weapons development. Funds for weapons development were now authorized by the Leader's Office, which had established four "special organs" outside the Atomic Energy Organization of Iran to perform the weapons work.

Khamenei told the nuclear team to have the first bomb ready for launch by the start of the Persian new year, according to press accounts. The Iranian year began on March 21.

One of the special units was the Defense Ministry's Center for Readiness and New Defense Technology. They had operated and then razed the suspected enrichment plant at Lavizan-Shian to prevent an IAEA inspection. Even the normally cautious Baradei acknowledged that Iran's concealment efforts had been a success.*

Iran was not operating two separate nuclear programs that duplicated efforts. It had simply divided the work according to sensitivity. Iran was counting on the European Union and the Non-Aligned Movement to support its "right" under the Nonproliferation Treaty to enrich uranium, so long as the weapons work remained secret. For the strategy to work, they had to conceal the weapons until the last possible moment.

COLIN POWELL'S REVELATIONS

Secretary of State Colin Powell had been bitten on Iraq. Even though he had spent days at CIA headquarters going over the intelligence supporting every detail on Iraq's weapons of mass destruction, the CIA analysts had been wrong. Powell felt they had made him look like a fool. He wasn't about to repeat the experience with Iran.

Shortly after the U.S. presidential elections, however, a walk-in brought more than one thousand pages of documents on Iran's secret nuclear weapons program that changed Powell's mind. This was not hearsay or analysts reading tea leaves. It was the real thing. Among the technical documents were drawings of the warhead design Iran planned to use and production drawings detailing modifications that had to be made to the Shahab-3 missile to accommodate it.

Powell felt comfortable with the intelligence, which was briefed to him and other senior cabinet members in early November 2004, because it was tightly focused on the technical problems of mating the warhead to Iran's missiles. The walk-in didn't talk about other aspects of Iran's nuclear program, just the reentry vehicle.

The briefing was classified "No Forn"—meaning Powell and his cabinet colleagues were forbidden from disclosing it to foreign leaders. But President Bush considered it so important that he decided to share portions of it with British prime minister Tony Blair, a trusted friend and key U.S. ally.

Despite that move, the British government took the lead in negotiating a sweeping agreement with Iran, announced on November 14, which offered European technology and other assistance to Iran's nuclear programs, in exchange for a mere pledge that Iran would not pursue weapons.

---

*Soil samples taken eight months after the site was dismantled came up negative, but Baradei acknowledged that "detection of nuclear material in soil samples would be very difficult in light of the razing of the site." Director General's report to the IAEA Board of Governors, GOV/2004/83, November 15, 2004, p. 22.

The EU-Iran agreement committed the Europeans to opposing any U.S. effort at the IAEA to refer Iran to the UN Security Council. At Iran's insistence, the EU3 dropped a key demand from their working draft that Iran *indefinitely* suspend uranium enrichment "until we reach an acceptable long-term agreement." Instead, the agreement made clear that the suspension was only temporary, calling it "a voluntary confidence building measure" but not a legal obligation. Furthermore, Iran's commitment to suspend enrichment was made contingent upon an extensive package of technical, economic, and political support, aimed at thwarting U.S. efforts to roll back the nuclear program. "We stayed within our red lines, and this red line meant we could suspend enrichment but not stop it," foreign ministry spokesman Hamid Reza Asefi triumphantly told reporters in Tehran. "The talks [with Europe] will be for a short period of time . . . and in the agreement it has been emphasized that Iran has the right to develop peaceful nuclear technology," he added.

The Europeans announced the agreement with all the smug finality of Neville Chamberlain returning from Munich. The EU3, led by Britain, had delivered "peace in our time."

It was the British betrayal that convinced Powell he had to speak out. On November 17 he sprang the news on reporters traveling on his plane en route to an economic conference in Chile.

"I have seen some information that would suggest that [the Iranians] have been actively working on delivery systems. . . . You don't have a weapon until you put it in something that can deliver a weapon," he said. "I'm not talking about uranium or fissile material or the warhead; I'm talking about what one does with a warhead."

Asked for more details, he added that the new information "suggests that they were working hard as to how to put the two together. There is no doubt in my mind—and it's fairly straightforward from what we've been saying for years—that they have been interested in a nuclear weapon that has utility, meaning that it is something they would be able to deliver, not just something that sits there."

Powell's comments created a media and political frenzy. Congressman Gary Ackerman (D-N.Y.) took a swipe at the administration. "After crying wolf for so long about Iraq, how are we going to have any credibility on this?" he said. Others suggested that Powell had spoken out of school, but the White House put an end to that. Anonymous "intelligence souces" began briefing reporters on the walk-in and his information, trying to walk back the dramatic nature of Powell's revelations by saying they came from a "single source" that had not been verified.

Powell shot back from Santiago, Chile, in an interview with a local television network. He confirmed that the information showed that Iran was working on modifying its missiles to accommodate a nuclear warhead. "This shouldn't be brand-new news," he said. "This shouldn't surprise anybody. If they had been working on a nuclear weapon and designed a warhead, certainly they were also trying to figure out how they would deliver such a warhead."

The walk-in had just provided a key missing piece to the puzzle.

UNANSWERED QUESTION

Jackie Sanders was losing patience. It was Thanksgiving weekend and they were back in Vienna and they might as well never have left. The hard deadline they thought they had worked into the last IAEA Board resolution on Iran had fallen in the pan like a French soufflé.

Counselor? she said for the umpteenth time, turning to her colleague and compliance lawyer, Christopher Ford. How many times could you "note" Iran's bad behavior, its cheat-and-retreat with IAEA inspectors, and still fail to acknowledge that the Islamic Republic was in violation of the Nonproliferation Treaty?

Apparently, six times, he said. This would be the sixth resolution the IAEA Board of Governors had passed since Baradei began reporting on Iran's previously undisclosed uranium enrichment and plutonium programs in March 2003. And Iran continued to flaunt its commitment, including its pledge to the EU3 not to enrich uranium or produce UF6 feedstock. How about "note with concern"? he ventured.

Mr. Ford, British ambassador Peter Jenkins said testily, we've already been down that road and you know we are not going to play your games. We have reached an agreement with the Iranian government, and we intend to keep it. The Iranians are complying, and so shall we.

How do twenty sets of centrifuge components meet your standard of compliance? he replied.

Jenkins turned to Sanders huffily. I will not sit here and be cross-examined by some Harvard-trained lawyer, he said.

Ford chuckled to himself, but held his peace. John Bolton was a fellow Yale Law School graduate and would never send a Harvard man to do an honest day's work.

Baradei had stunned the Board—including the Europeans—when he announced in passing on opening day that the Iranians had just informed the agency that their agreement to "suspend" enrichment would not apply to a small cascade they wanted to operate for R&D purposes. Even the Europeans understood the significance of that exception. The Iranians reportedly believed the high-pitched whine from the permitted cascade would mask the noise from a clandestine enrichment cascade operating nearby.

Mr. Ford, you have to trust us, said Friedrich Gröning. You can't possibly know all that we discussed with the Iranians or the assurances they gave us, because you weren't there. We know what was said behind closed doors, and we are convinced the Iranians will uphold their side of the bargain. You can take my word on that.

Sanders sat without batting an eyelash as Herr Gröning lectured her legal adviser, but inwardly she was screaming. Take your word? You've got to be kidding! We're supposed to take assurances from a German diplomat whose country is Iran's number-one trading partner and just wants to make this whole thing go away?

The Americans were keeping lists of unanswered questions, and from time to time they handed them out to the press. The more they learned about the Iranian nuclear program, the longer grew the list of what they didn't know.

- Was Iran producing the more advanced P2 centrifuge? They acknowledged they had received a full set of production drawings in 1995 from Dr. Khan but swore up and down to Baradei that they never considered moving to the more reliable, easier-to-produce carbon composite centrifuge rotors, as Pakistan had done.
- What if Natanz was a ploy? What if Iran had separated out the really critical production equipment before the IAEA inspectors ever arrived, and was now using it in a clandestine enrichment facility at one of the many sites they refused to allow inspectors to visit?
- Why had Iran destroyed Lavizan-Shian? They had never provided a convincing reply or allowed inspectors to search a nearby facility identified as a possible enrichment site.
- Why was Iran still stonewalling the agency request to visit the Parchin munitions works, which had been identified as a possible site for centrifuge manufacture and possibly weaponization work?
- Why had Iran dismantled "temporary facilities" at the Gchine uranium mine near Bandar Abbas, after producing "several hundred kilograms" of yellowcake? Was the military in charge of the mine?
- Why had the Iranian government never pushed the Majles to ratify

the IAEA's enhanced safeguards agreement, known as the Additional Protocol? Baradei had touted Iran's agreement to apply the more rigorous inspection regime, but so far it was still an ad hoc arrangement, which the Iranians could renounce without cost at any time.

- Why was Iran refusing to suspend its uranium conversion work, even after the agreement with the EU? Why the urgency to those Iranian efforts?
- What did Iran intend to do with the UF6 it produced?
- Why did Iran produce polonium-210 and import large quantities of beryllium, which, combined with Po-210, forms a neutron initiator for the type of bomb design Iran was believed to have received from the Khan network?
- Had Iran carried out clandestine plutonium separation, as the IAEA suspected?
- What was the extent of military involvement in Iran's nuclear activities? Had military officials taken part in the thirteen meetings Iran acknowledged between 1994 and 1997 with Dr. Khan's procurement network?
- What other facilities, not yet revealed by Baradei to the Board, had the agency asked to visit and been refused access by the Iranians?
- Had the Khan network supplied highly enriched uranium or UF6 that Iran had not declared to the IAEA?

TUNNELS IN ISFAHAN

While they were meeting in Vienna, the German news magazine *Der Spiegel* issued a brief report based on information from an "unnamed intelligence agency" that Iran had dug a secret tunnel near the Isfahan hex plant to prepare raw uranium for enrichment, despite Iran's pledge to the Europeans to cease such activities.

Ayatollah Khamenei ordered the construction of the underground facility in October, *Der Spiegel* reported, and instructed the special military unit assigned to do the tunneling to take every precaution to avoid detection by spy satellites. Once the site was completed, the Iranians planned to make additional UF6 for a clandestine centrifuge enrichment cascade, the magazine asserted.[4]

Asked to comment on the *Der Spiegel* report, Iranian Foreign Ministry spokesman Hamid Reza Asefi said, "Lots of tunnels are being built across the country nowadays by the Ministry of Roads and Transportation." The idea that a tunnel of "such enormity" could be built without detection was absurd, he told the regime's news agency on November 28.

Just three days earlier, Iran's Mehr news agency quoted a provincial official who announced that Iran had established a factory near Qom to manufacture state-of-the-art tunnel-boring machines. The new machines would be capable of boring holes up to 4.5 meters in diameter. R&D on the machines was being done in Isfahan, he added.[5]

Burrowing underground was a pastime Iran shared with its longtime nuclear and missile partner, North Korea, which had buried hundreds of missile bases, production plants, and clandestine nuclear facilities.

In January 2005, Iranian officials admitted that they had built secret tunnels in Isfahan to protect UF6 production equipment from air attack. The machines they used for the task were not Iranian-made, however, but imported from Germany. And Isfahan was not the only secret underground facility they had made.

END OF THE ROAD IN VIENNA

As Jackie Sanders listened to IAEA director general Mohammad El Baradei present his case during the closing session of the Board of Governors meeting on November 29, 2004, it was clear the United States had reached the end of the road. The effort to take Iran to the Security Council would go nowhere, at least as long as this new agreement held.

For the past eighteen months the agency had worked together with the Iranians to bring their previously undeclared nuclear programs under IAEA control, Baradei said. There were a few minor outstanding issues, but Iran was committed to resolving them.

Baradei's message was clear: Iran had sinned. Iran had confessed. And now, Iran should be forgiven.

If that's the case, Sanders wondered out loud, what's the point of the NPT or the IAEA? Under Article 12C of the agency's charter, the Board was obligated to report an NPT member state that had violated its safeguards commitments to the United Nations Security Council for punitive action. And yet the Board had repeatedly deferred action.

The world might now conclude that proliferation was a "no lose" proposition. If no one catches you, you get the Bomb. And if you're caught, all you have to do is admit whatever has been discovered, and all will be forgiven—until the next time.

For an administration frequently criticized for "going it alone," the U.S. team had expended a tremendous effort to build consensus in Vienna. But the Europeans and the Chinese—who had just signed a massive $70 billion oil and gas agreement with Tehran and sent their foreign minister to Tehran in solidarity the day the Board of Governors meeting began—were intent on giving the Iranians more time. And time was the one thing the experts believed Iran still needed to complete work on its nuclear arsenal.

In light of the IAEA Board's "continuing inability to hold Iran accountable for its violations," the United States might be compelled to act unilaterally, "not just to freeze Iran's destabilizing enrichment-related work, but to end it," Sanders said. For example, the United States could accelerate the interception of equipment bound for Iran, as it had done with Libya. And in case the Board still refused to take action on Iran's safeguards violations, the United States was authorized under Article 35(1) of the Charter of the United Nations to bring Iran to the attention of the Security Council itself as a threat to international peace and security.

Heads turned when she said that; pencils scratched on paper. But the voting was over and the United States had lost.

The IAEA had rectified many of its earlier failings. It had become a first-rate inspection agency, not just a nuclear accountant. But it was still limited by what the consensus-driven Board would permit.

Diplomacy would continue, but not in Vienna.

THE WAY AHEAD

Definitely we can't stop our nuclear program and won't stop it. You can't take technology away from a country already possessing it.

—Hojjat-ol eslam Ali Akbar Hashemi-Rafsanjani, March 6, 2005

The students at Tehran University were chanting, jeering, clapping, and whistling, and President Mohammad Khatami couldn't stand it. "Shame on you! Shame on you!" they shouted. "Where are your promised freedoms?"

"Be human!" he shouted in heavily accented English, visibly taken aback. "If you are the representatives of the people, then I am the enemy of the people."

Former student leader Roozbeh Farahanipour thought Khatami's confrontation with the students on December 6, 2004, was so funny, he had recorded it on his Palm Pilot and played it to anyone who would listen. It revealed President Khatami for what he really was—a die-hard supporter of absolute clerical rule, and not the smiling "reformer" analysts in the West had tried to create.

"Don't be fooled by people who have run away from Iran," Khatami went on, his voice becoming hoarse as he tried to shout over the din from the chanting students. "Thank God my period as president is soon at an end. I don't owe anyone."

Two months later, in an extraordinarily candid speech carried live on Iranian TV, Khatami blasted opponents of the regime who were seeking to hold a referendum on whether Iran should continue as an Islamic Republic or adopt some form of secular government.

"It will be impossible to establish democracy here without the help of Islam," he said. "Not only is it impossible to establish a nonreligious democracy, but we don't want it."

Khatami had no intention of declaring war on a regime that he supported on principle. Besides, who would help this Western-style democracy that opponents of the regime were calling for? Were Iranians planning on asking the United States for help?

"I'm not claiming that the Islamic Republic is faultless," he said. "I'm not claiming that there are no human rights violations in some places. I'm not claiming that writers and journalists are always treated justly. I'm not claiming that our situation is ideal, from the Islamic point of view. But this I say, loud and clear: Even by current standards, we are better off than all our neighbors."

Among Pakistan, Afghanistan, and Iraq—where Iranian-sponsored and -funded terrorists were doing their best to wreck the first nationwide elections in two generations—the comparison fell flat. "If, indeed, the Islamic Republic is gone, democratic rule will not be established in this country," he said finally. If that happened, it would be America's fault.[1]

UNDETERRED

The Iranians violated their latest promise to the Europeans and the IAEA almost immediately, just as they had violated the earlier ones.

Just three weeks after the November Board of Governors meeting in Vienna, Tehran announced that it was continuing to process uranium for enrichment. "It is natural that the Islamic Republic continues all its nuclear activities," said Hossein Mousavian, the deputy National Security Council official who had been delegated to the IAEA. "Iran has only suspended the fuel cycle voluntarily, in the framework of its policy to build trust, without any legal obligations." The Europeans fretted that Iran might be violating "the spirit" of their agreement, while Iran fed all 37 tons of natural uranium into the process line.

Ayatollah Ahmad Jannati, a close ally of Supreme Leader Ayatollah Khamenei, told regime supporters during a televised Friday prayer sermon that Iran had no intention of upholding its side of the agreement with the EU. "Our hands are not tied," he said. "Our hands are free for the future. Make it clear that this agreement will be violated by both sides. . . . Our people, our senior officials, and our institutions, from our dear leader down, stand firm in their decision and determination to obtain nuclear technology." The nuclear issue, he added, is "where we draw the line."[2]

On February 2, 2005, Khamenei's representative to the Supreme National Security Council, Ali Larijani, derided the Europeans for thinking they could entice Iran into suspending uranium enrichment for five years.

"This is one of the jokes of our times," he told Iranian TV. "The success of the negotiations depends upon Iran's having a nuclear fuel cycle. Otherwise, there is no reason to continue in this path."[3] The hard-line Larijani was Khamenei's preferred candidate in the presidential election scheduled for June 2005.

A leading cleric of Iran's Hezbollah movement reassured supporters that they, not the government of President Khatami, owned Iran's nuclear weapons. "We have oil, gas, and all other natural resources and thus we don't need interaction with other countries," said Hojjat-ol Eslam Baqer Kharrazi. "We are able to produce atomic bombs and we will do that. We shouldn't be afraid of anyone. The U.S. is no more than a barking dog." Hezbollah's Helpers would take care of any government official who tried to compromise with the IAEA or the Europeans, he added. "And if necessary we will select our own president, ministers, and parliament members. For without the Hezbollah forces the Islamic Revolution will collapse from within."[4]

President Khatami was on the same page. "If we feel others are not meeting their promises, under no circumstances would we be committed to continue fulfilling ours," he said on February 9, 2005. "And we will adopt a new policy, the consequences of which are massive and would be the responsibility of those who broke their commitments."

With pomp and ceremony, the regime hosted a two-day nuclear technology conference in Tehran on March 5–6, 2005, inviting fifty foreign scientists and analysts, including former National Security Council official Gary Samore. Rafsanjani told them Iran would never agree to a permanent halt on enriching uranium. "Definitely we can't stop our nuclear program and won't stop it. You can't take technology away from a country already possessing it."

The mullahs were laughing all the way to Armageddon.

BREAKOUT

The IAEA now believes it has a comprehensive understanding of Iran's nuclear capabilities. These include previously secret uranium processing and enrichment facilities.

But the agency has been unable to determine whether Iran operated a smaller-scale enrichment plant during the 1990s. If so, using the equipment it is known to have imported, Iran could have as much as twenty-five bombs' worth of fissile material today. In addition to this, no Western intelligence agency has been able to put to rest persistent rumors that Iran acquired a small number of nuclear warheads in 1991–92 from black marketers in the former Soviet Union.*

Potentially even more dangerous is the massive Busheir nuclear power plant. A study released in September 2004 by the Nonproliferation Policy Education Center, run by former Pentagon official Henry Sokolski, concluded that "if Iran's overt program all stays on schedule, Tehran, in fact, could get a large arsenal of nuclear weapons—fifty to seventy-five bombs by 2006."

Iran's "breakout" scenario was not far-fetched or technically difficult, Sokolski concluded. It entailed operating the Russian-built power reactor at Busheir for twelve to fifteen months, then separating plutonium from the spent fuel and converting it into metal, a process that might take an additional twelve to sixteen weeks.

"Under the Nuclear Nonproliferation Treaty, all of this is legal. It is also legal under the NPT for Iran to make as many implosion devices (sans fissile cores) as one might want and have them ready to receive metal plutonium cores. At this point, sometime by or before 2006, Iran could break out of the NPT and have a large arsenal of weapons in a matter of weeks or days."[5]

Sokolski commissioned a panel of national authorities on nuclear chemistry, commercial nuclear power reactors, and nuclear weapons designs to examine the suitability of a light-water power reactor of the type Russia was completing at Busheir for a nuclear weapons program. The panel's conclusions were disturbing:

- The large amounts of plutonium Busheir would produce were "near weapons grade." Bombs built with this material "would not be significantly different from those based on weapons-grade plutonium."
- The design and technology for building a small plutonium reprocessing facility was affordable and readily available.
- Because of its small size (less than 65 square feet), such a reprocessing facility probably would not be detected by the IAEA or by spy satellites.
- Alternatively, if Iran chose to divert fuel obtained from Russia *before* it was introduced into the reactor, it could break the fuel pellets and

*These rumors resurfaced in 2002, when congressional aide and author Yossef Bodansky asserted that Iran succeeded in purchasing two 40-kiloton warheads for a SCUD-type missile, a gravity bomb, and one 152-mm nuclear artillery shell, all of which "reached initial operational status in late January 1992 and full operational status a few months later." Cf. Yossef Bodansky, *The High Cost of Peace: How Washington's Middle East Policy Left America Vulnerable to Terrorism* (Roseville, CA: Prima Publishing, 2002), 77.

convert them into enrichment feedstock. This would reduce the time needed to spin the uranium up to weapons grade "by a factor of five."

- Without real-time monitoring of its surveillance cameras, the IAEA would not detect the diversion of fuel from the Busheir plant for ninety days, by which time Iran would have produced a large arsenal of bombs.[6]

FACING A NUCLEAR IRAN

How will Iran's clerical rulers behave once they have a nuclear arsenal? Much as they have in the past, but on steroids.

The mullahs have long sought to drive U.S. forces out of the Persian Gulf. With the U.S. invasions of Afghanistan and Iraq, they now fear direct encirclement. A nuclear-ready Iran is likely to step up subversion in Iraq, where the bulk of U.S. forces in the region are deployed, and to launch increasingly bold terrorist strikes on U.S. bases in Afghanistan, Oman, Yemen, Bahrain, Qatar, and Kuwait, directly and through proxies.[7]

Former CIA director R. James Woolsey is of the view that aquiring a nuclear weapon would embolden Iran to become more aggressive in a number of ways against the Iraqi government. Some analysts believe Tehran may seek to provoke a war with a new, pro-American regime in Baghdad as a means of directly confronting U.S. troops and U.S. allies in the region who come to the aid of the Iraqi government.

Nuclear capability also will embolden the regime to stamp out domestic dissent ruthlessly, wherever it appears. At the same time, it will actively seek ways of lashing out at what it sees as the sources of that dissent: the United States and Israel. Regime leaders fear foreign support for the prodemocracy movement and are alarmed by the proliferation of satellite radio and television broadcasts beaming into Iran from abroad, however ineffective they may be. Massive protests inside Iran, whether fueled by outside forces or not, will be blamed on the United States and Israel.

Signs that the mullahs are seeking to step up military tensions throughout the region are already appearing. Following the January 2005 election of Mahmoud Abbas (Abu Mazen) as Yasser Arafat's replacement, Palestinian security forces reported a dramatic increase in Iran's efforts to undermine revived peace talks with Israel.

In carefully orchestrated leaks to the press, senior political and security officials in the Palestinian Authority complained that Hezbollah had been trying to recruit suicide bombers from among Fatah/Al-Aqsa Martyrs'

Brigades terrorists "to carry out attacks which would sabotage the truce." One official told Reuters on February 9, 2005, that intercepted e-mail communications and bank transactions suggested that Hezbollah had raised its cash payment to prospective suicide bombers, and was now "willing to pay $100,000 for a whole operation [suicide bombing] whereas in the past they paid $20,000." Clearly, Tehran was footing the bill.

U.S. and Israeli intelligence officials saw a similar increase in Iranian meddling in Lebanon, following the assassination of former prime minister Rafic Hariri on February 14, 2005. And Jordanian intelligence detected an Iranian effort to destabilize the pro-Western King Abdallah in a recent wave of deadly car bombings. "Whenever we see the king, he doesn't want to talk about Israel, or the Palestinians, or the U.S., in Iraq. It's Iran, Iran, Iran," a senior Middle Eastern official told me after a visit to Amman in the spring of 2005.

Former Iranian president Abolhassan Banisadr believes the regime is intent on provoking a region-wide conflagration. "They go from crisis to crisis," he said. "This is how they have governed from the beginning." Khomeini provoked the 1980–88 war with Saddam Hussein simply to stay in power. Today's clerics could provoke a new war for the same reason, Banisadr and other exiles believe.

Iran's clerical leaders speak with a kind of millennial exaltation when evoking a nuclear exchange with Israel. But how far will the mullahs go? And how long can Israel, which sees itself on the receiving end of an Islamic bomb, sit back and watch as Tehran prepares for war?

Israeli leaders have been warning that it won't be long. On January 24, 2005, Mossad director Meir Dagan told Israeli parliamentarians that "by the end of 2005 the Iranians will reach the point of no return from the technological perspective of creating a uranium-enrichment capability." Once you have that capability, he added, "you are home free."

Israeli defense minister Shaul Mofaz repeated that assessment during a trip to London three days later, and asked the Europeans to join the United States to "stop as soon as possible this military nuclear program in Iran."

On February 17, Foreign Minister Silvan Shalom, also in London, said Israel believed Iran would have finished all the tests and experiments needed to build a weapon "in six months from today." Reuters reported the same day that Israel planned to buy five hundred "bunker buster" bombs from the United States, which would enhance its capability to hit hardened underground targets.

Vice President Dick Cheney let the cat out of the bag in impromptu comments on the Don Imus radio show on January 20, just before the inauguration in Washington, D.C. Iran was "right at the top" of the administration's list of world trouble spots, he said. If nothing was done about Iran's nuclear weapons program, there was concern that Israel "might well decide to act first" to destroy Iranian nuclear and missile sites and let others "worry about cleaning up the diplomatic mess afterwards."

"One of the concerns that people have is that Israel might do it without being asked," Cheney said. "If in fact the Israelis became convinced the Iranians had significant nuclear capability—given the fact that Iran has a stated policy that their objective is the destruction of Israel—the Israelis might well decide to act first."

Tehran's ruling clerics have repeatedly threatened to retaliate for any Israeli strike by launching nuclear missiles against Israel. "We are not worried about Israel and its threats," Rafsanjani told Al Jazeera television. "If Israel committed such an error, we would give it a slap it would never forget—not only during several years but for all its history."[8]

The Revolutionary Guards showed off Shahab-3 missiles during the annual military parade in Tehran on September 22, 2004, festooned with banners that read, "Israel must be wiped off the map."

In case the message wasn't clear, Revolutionary Guards spokesman General Massoud Jazaeri explained, "If Israel makes the mistake of threatening and endangering our country's interests, our response will certainly be strong and crucial. I have used the same expressions and said that we would destroy Israel and erase it from existence. These were not empty words."[9]

Now it is anybody's guess who will strike first.

LAUNCH ON RUMOR

In January 2005, when news reports surfaced that the United States had been secretly flying intelligence-gathering drones over Iranian territory, the Iranian press vehemently denounced the maneuvers as the first steps of a U.S. attack.

In February, Iranian officials tried to spin the news, revealing that they had given orders to air defense commanders in January not to engage the drones, so as not to reveal critical intelligence information to the Americans on radar frequencies and time to engagement. "The United States must have forgotten that they trained half our guys," an unnamed Iranian official told the *Washington Post*.

Intelligence Minister Ali Yunesi weighed in after the initial story ran, saying that the Iranian air force had been ordered to shoot down any unknown airborne intruders. "If any of the bright objects come close, they will definitely meet our fire and will be shot down," he said.

With nuclear weapons in the hands of radical Islamic clerics prone to conspiracy thinking, the potential for miscalculation becomes enormous. The Cold War policy of "launch on warning" could easily become "launch on rumor" in Iran.

On February 16, 2005, Iran's state-run television interrupted all programs with an urgent bulletin: "We have just received this breaking news: a loud explosion was heard this morning in the outskirts of the city of Deilam in Bushehr District in southern Iran. Eyewitnesses said that the explosion was the result of a missile fired by an unidentified airplane towards an unpopulated area twenty kilometers from the city. Iranian officials have not yet commented officially about this incident."

The apparent missile strike—perhaps just the first launch of a salvo of attacks—had occurred in the immediate vicinity of the Busheir nuclear power plant. The independent news monitoring agency MEMRI found the news flash so remarkable that it immediately sent the bulletin out by e-mail to thousands of subscribers around the world.[10] Subsequent reports suggested that an unidentified aircraft had dropped its fuel tank.

Iranian defense minister Ali Shamkhani warned ominously on February 17 that "any attack, whatever it is, against any site, whether it be nuclear or not, would produce a very rapid response." Iranians would know that a nuclear or other facility had been attacked "when the Iranian nation sees our crushing response to the enemy," he said. Two days later, it turned out the noise had been caused by a construction crew blasting a new road.

The Iranians were getting jittery.

UNDERGROUND ARSENAL

In March 2005, I traveled with Hamid Reza Zakeri to a country in the Middle East to continue our meetings. This is when he told me about the Islamic Republic's ongoing support for the insurgency in Iraq and provided the pictures of Revolutionary Guards officers responsible for coordinating Iran's support for the insurgency that appear in the appendix.

As I was preparing to leave, I asked him in an almost offhand manner what he knew of recent nuclear developments in Iran. What he told me was so astonishing I could scarcely believe it; yet it was so detailed and so precise, it invited further investigation.

Iran had built a series of still-clandestine sites, not declared to the

IAEA, where it was actively enriching uranium, he said. He had information on five of those sites and described one of them in detail, near the town of Behbehan around 50 kilometers southwest of Natanz. (That description appears in the Prologue of this book.) He claimed that in addition to a small uranium-enrichment cascade the tunnels housed Shahab-3 missiles and fifteen nuclear warheads—not material for fifteen warheads, but actual warheads. The missiles were aimed at Israel.

I asked him how I could verify his information, which he said came from a source who had worked at the site in 2004. After a moment's thought, he suggested I look at satellite imagery taken before construction began in 2002 and compare it to pictures taken while the tunneling was taking place. Before the Revolutionary Guards took over the site, nothing was there, he said. The only thing visible was an unpaved road from the village of Behbehan that dead-ended in the mountains. Construction companies working for the Revolutionary Guards widened the road and began digging. "You should be able to see that," he suggested. On current pictures, all that remains visible besides the new road is a small housing development that climbs the slope overlooking the river across from the tunnel entrance. Fifty North Korean workers live there, he said.

In the underground centrifuge hall, the Revolutionary Guards constructed a deep swimming pool to house irradiated nuclear material, he added. Around two hundred Revolutionary Guards missile troops live full time inside the buried site, with their own kitchen and dormitory facilities. Food is brought regularly in nondescript vehicles from the surrounding villages, he said.

Zakeri's description of the geological features was so precise that when I looked at a map it almost leapt out at me. I ran his information by sources in several U.S. intelligence agencies, and one foreign intelligence agency, and they confirmed that satellite imagery of the site clearly documented the construction he had described.

One classified report, from February or March 2005, identified Behbehan as a "suspected SSM (surface-to-surface missile)" launch site.

For Zakeri, this information was just a toss-off. He had not mentioned it to me earlier because he had no firsthand knowledge of the site. He believed the information was true, but it was secondhand. Here was clear and convincing proof that the man the CIA had dismissed as a "fabricator of monumental proportions" was no liar.

If the second part of his information is also true, Iran already possesses a significant nuclear force and the missiles to deliver them.

But that's not all.

UKRAINIAN MISSILES

Colonel B, the former Revolutionary Guards officer I debriefed in a European capital for several days in September 2004 and again in May 2005, worked in 1999–2000 at the Khaibar missiles base in Karaj, where he received training on a new missile Iran had purchased from Ukraine. The training center was led by Sardar Sohani, a Revolutionary Guards brigadier general. He told Colonel B that once the Revolutionary Guards mastered these new weapons, they would be "invincible." By September 2005, Iran would start producing the missiles on its own.

"One of the people who took the training course with me asked Sohani if this was an atomic bomb. He said, I'm not going to tell you that. But in five years, you will see that we will become the biggest power in the Islamic world." The general's boast so struck Colonel B that he repeated it to me twice, word for word.

Colonel B provided line drawings of parts of the warhead and the fuse assembly, and made a rough sketch of the missile, with its lateral fins at the rear. All the documents used in the training course were in Russian, he added. The missile was designed to carry a 500-kilogram high-explosive warhead made of PETN, which explodes with a force equivalent to approximately 20,000 kilograms of TNT. In his drawing, the Colonel omitted two tell-tale details: the fold-out wings and the small rocket motor at the rear, leading me to believe that he was describing a large air-dropped bomb. In fact, Colonel B had been training on a version of the Soviet-era KH-55 "Granat" nuclear-capable cruise missile. Sardar Sohani told him Iran was producing the missiles at a factory purchased by Rafsanjani from Ukraine in the 1990s. A senior military official confirmed in late April 2005 that Iran had reverse-engineered the missiles and was now producing them by itself.

On January 28, 2005, Ukrainian parliamentarian Hryhoriy Omelchenko sent an open letter to President Viktor Yushchenko, alleging that Ukraine had illegally sold 12 of these missiles to Iran sometime between 1999 and 2001. He included the name of the front companies and the middlemen used for the sale, as well as banking details. The KH-55 was initially designed to carry a 200-kiloton nuclear warhead, but like U.S. cruise missiles, it had been reconfigured to carry a conventional warhead.

When the Ukrainian federal prosecutor's office opened an inquiry into the sale, lawyers for the company cited in Omelchenko's open letter confirmed that the missiles had been shipped to Iran but argued that they were "not weapons," because they were missing key parts.

One particularity of the KH-55 is that it can be launched from ships or land-based vehicles, as well as from aircraft. Colonel B mentioned that Iran intended to use the new strategic missile as a ground-to-ground vector.

With its range of 3,000 kilometers, these Ukrainian cruise missiles could reach Israel as well as NATO bases in Europe. By flying under the radar, the Iranians may believe that the KH-55 will allow them to defeat U.S. and Israeli defensive systems. If so, this missile—even more than the Shahab-3—could encourage Iran's ruling clerics into dangerous brinkmanship.

BIN LADEN IN IRAN

In late 2004, Ayman al-Zawahri met again with top regime leaders, this time in a guesthouse to the north of Tehran. According to sources with direct knowledge of these meetings, the Egyptian deputy to Osama bin Laden was dressed with the turban and robes of an Iranian cleric, not in Arab-style clothing. He was living in Iran by this point, and traveled frequently around the country, keeping tabs on al-Qaeda operatives who were moving among different safe houses across Iran.

Although they were drinking Orange Crush and other soft drinks, this was not a social meeting. They were plotting the next phases of al-Qaeda's war on America.

Meeting Zawahri were Revolutionary Guards generals Qolam Ali Rashid and Mohammad Baqr Zolqadr, his old friend from the Sudan. Representing the leadership was Ayatollah Jannati, a top aide to the Supreme Leader and a key hard-liner. Security officers swept the meeting area nine days ahead of time to prepare the site. Jannati was assisted by an interpreter, since his grasp of Arabic was limited to the classical expressions of the Koran, not the Egyptian dialect Zawahri spoke.

After the first day of meetings, bin Laden himself was brought to the safe house. Like Zawahri, he wore Iranian clerical robes, not traditional Arab dress. On a table in the meeting room were Iranian flags; on the wall were pictures of Ayatollah Khomeini and Khamenei. An intravenous tube was strapped to the back of bin Laden's hand. He looked frail and old. At one point, Jannati placed his late-model cell phone on an end table.

Jannati said the regime was worried that the United States would convince the Europeans and Russia to take Iran's nuclear case to the UN Security Council. If that were to occur, Iran planned to counterattack. Jannati spread out a map of the world, and they discussed different places where bin Laden felt his men could launch spectacular new attacks against the

United States and its key allies. They discussed specific sites in Britain—outside London—Holland, and of course, the United States.

According to these same sources, bin Laden was scheduled to hold a follow-on meeting with Rafsanjani later that spring to finalize these plans.

APPEASEMENT OR WAR?

So what can the United States do? There are two main options: capitulation or war.

The United States might encourage Iran to become a "responsible" member of the nuclear club by opening a "dialogue" with the regime. In exchange for Iran's agreement to abide by "rules" such as no nuclear first use and no proliferation to third parties, the United States might choose to offer incentives such as

- a resumption of normal trade and investment
- a resumption of diplomatic relations
- an end to stigmatizing the Islamic Republic as a member of the Axis of Evil
- an end to "the language of regime change"[11]

Appeasement has powerful supporters, including among the National Security Council staff. A think-tank analyst from the liberal Brookings Institution, hired to the NSC in 2004, successfully pushed a proposal that formed the backbone of Bush's proposal during his February 2005 European tour to offer Iran more "incentives" to change its behavior.

The Council on Foreign Relations argues that the underlying rationale for Iran's nuclear weapons programs is its fear of the United States. "Ultimately, only in the context of an overall rapprochement with Washington will there be any prospect of persuading Iran to make the strategic decision to relinquish its nuclear program," the report states.

Under the CFR proposal, "Iran would be asked to commit to permanently ceasing all its enrichment and reprocessing activities, subject to international verification. In return, the international community would guarantee access to adequate nuclear fuel supplies, with assurances that all spent fuel would be returned to the country of origin, and to advanced power generation technology (whose export to Iran is currently restricted)."[12]

But Tehran's leaders have already rejected this approach. Saying pretty-please won't help.

The regime's negotiating record with the IAEA and the EU3—Britain,

France, and Germany—shows that the only nuclear bargain it finds of interest is one that runs out the clock, playing on the delusions of the willfully naïve and the appeasers until Iran has enriched enough fissile material for a credible arsenal.

The other option for the United States is preemptive war. If so, it will be war in splendid isolation, and with active opposition from Europe, Russia, China, the Organization of the Islamic Conference, and just about every UN member state except, possibly, Israel.

But Iran's clerics are unlikely to wait to be attacked. Only one Iranian nuclear-tipped missile needs to penetrate Israel's Arrow antimissile defenses to devastate Israel's highly concentrated population, destroy its economy, and effectively smash the state. Israel is a "one-bomb" country and the Iranians know it.

Even if Iran chose to detonate a nuclear warhead in the upper atmosphere, the massive Electro-Magnetic Pulse (EMP) generated by the explosion would knock out virtually every electronic device in Israel, from computers to cellphones and power stations. The ensuing blackout wouldn't just paralyze the economy; it would cripple Israel's ability to mobilize and launch an effective counterstrike. Israel has never faced a threat of this magnitude before.

As the Europeans fiddle and Washington agonizes, it's anyone's bet who will be first to pull the nuclear trigger.

WHAT AMERICA CAN DO

As night fell in Tehran on September 11, 2001, thousands of Tehran residents poured into the streets and began walking toward the Swiss embassy, home to the U.S. Interests section. When they arrived before the embassy gates in Mohseni Square, they lit candles in solidarity with the victims of the attacks on America. Many of them maintained the vigil all through the night responding to an appeal from Persian-language NITV in Los Angeles, which reaches Iran by satellite. For once, Hezbollah's Helpers stayed at home.

The spontaneous outpouring of sympathy gives an inkling of the true feelings of the Iranian people toward America. It should also provide a signpost for how the United States should deal with the ruling clerics, when the time comes.

Thomas Jefferson famously asserted that economic sanctions were the only policy option between appeasement and war. When Israeli prime minister Ariel Sharon met with President Bush at his Texas ranch on April 11, 2005, he urged the president to take Iran to the UN Security Council to impose economic and political sanctions. Sharon and his military advisers saw this as the only possible way to avoid war.

In his second inaugural address, however, President George W. Bush hinted at a third way: "And to the Iranian people, I say tonight: As you stand for your own liberty, America stands with you."

It was only a brief passage, but Iranians heard it from Los Angeles to Tehran. So did legislators in Washington, who quickly introduced bills to provide funding for opposition broadcasting and other anti-regime activities.

Iran is not the problem, as the repeated pro-democracy demonstrations by Iranian students and the outpouring of pro-American sympathy on the night of September 11 have shown. The problem is a regime that believes it is invincible and will do anything to stay in power, even if it means plunging the world into a nuclear nightmare.

A full-scale U.S. military strike on Iran would be costly, ineffective, and counterproductive. We would probably fail to take out all of Iran's hidden nuclear assets. In addition, U.S. intelligence officials argue in private, we would give the regime a winning argument to mobilize those citizens who might otherwise support pro-democracy forces.

Instead, we should empower the pro-democracy forces to change the regime. We should do so openly, and as a government policy. But we should support nongovernmental organizations, primarily Iranian, to do the work.*

The most important thing the United States can do is to delegitimize the government in Tehran. Negotiating with Tehran would be a mistake. Seeking a "global settlement," even if it gave the appearance of disarming the regime of its nuclear capabilities, would only embolden the regime. If we continue to treat as legitimate a clerical clique who believe the United States and Israel are emanations of the Devil (the Great Satan and the Little Satan), we will have more terror, more hostage-takings, more blackmail.

---

*Some Iranian dissidents have urged the United States to launch a "decapitation strike" against the clerical leadership using pinpoint bombing, cruise missiles, or special forces teams. Opportunities for such a strike abound; and while the clerics have been careful to establish multiple centers of decision making and competing institutions, the number of top leaders controlling the security apparatus is relatively small. Iranian dissidents argue that while highly risky, such a strike (or strikes) would be far more effective than an all-out military assault and would provide a catalyst to regime opponents to launch a generalized uprising. The ultimate downside to this approach is that violent overthrow favors groups specialized in armed rebellion, such as the Marxist-Islamist Mujahedin-e Khalq.

It's not the behavior of the regime that poses a threat to world security; it's the very existence of this regime.

Iranians are desperately crying out for secular government, not a "reformed" Islamic state. We should heed their call and help them.

Former student leader Roozbeh Farahanipour, now in Los Angeles, says the pro-democracy forces inside Iran need three things: organization, organization, and organization. But they also need a strategy. Supporters of Reza Pahlavi have found a strategy that has won support from Congress and from prominent dissidents from the Islamic regime in Tehran. They are calling for an internationally supervised referendum on the future of the Islamic Republic.

One of the initial supporters of a referendum is Mohsen Sazegara, a founder of the Revolutionary Guards who went on to publish prominent reformist newspapers that the regime shut down. Sazegara came out in favor of the referendum in 2003 and was jailed twice for speaking out. The state department granted him a visa to work on a temporary fellowship with the Washington Institute for Near East Policy in March 2005. Because of his background, many Iranian dissidents continue to suspect his sincerity although he has paid a heavy price for his convictions.

Certainly, the ultimate weapon of nonviolent regime change is the referendum. Like the guillotine, it will administer the coup de grace to the *velayat-e faghih*, the doctrine of absolute clerical rule that is enshrined in the Constitution of the Islamic Republic.

But a referendum is not the first weapon. The Islamic Republic knows how to run Soviet-style elections, and unless the ground has been prepared for a free, full, and fair debate, the mullahs are guaranteed to win a crushing victory in such a contest. Sazegara sees the referendum movement as a catalyst for a nonviolent popular uprising that could force the clerics to abandon power well before a vote could be held. First and foremost, he says, the United States must refuse to recognize any government issued from elections under the current constitution.

The United States can and must help pro-democracy forces inside Iran to organize, organize, organize. We must put pressure on the regime for its human rights abuses. We must name the heroes and ostracize the torturers. We must challenge every newspaper closure, every jailing of every dissident. We must help Iranians to create the momentum for nonviolent regime change, before the ticking nuclear clock reaches midnight.

And it is almost there.

Epilogue

THE PRICE OF FAILURE

Just days before Christmas, as Congress was hurrying to wind up business so members could travel home to spend the holidays with their families, sailors on board a tramp steamer registered under a Liberian flag of convenience swung open the metal doors to the cargo hold and activated a winch.

They were just north of Baltimore—one of hundreds of ships plying the crowded maritime corridor off the East Coast of the United States. As their giant cargo rose up onto the deck, the sailors stripped away the tarpaulins, revealing a long, low-slung, eight-wheeled vehicle with a distinctive, bug-eyed cab.

Initially produced in the Soviet Union during the Cold War, the MAZ-543 tractor-erector-launcher (TEL) was exported widely around the world to launch the SCUD missiles so popular in places such as Iran, Iraq, Syria, and Libya.

The vehicle had no markings to indicate to what nation it belonged, and the crew, who were carrying passports issued by the Philippines, Malaysia, Yemen, Egypt, and Turkey, all spoke English. The SCUD missile lying flat on the TEL was fueled. Its warhead was primed for launch.

On orders from the commander, the MAZ operators plugged in coordinates from the ship's commercial GPS system, raised the launch rail, and fired. The blast from the SCUD's liquid-fueled engines scorched the specially treated underside of the cargo bay doors and made the sailors' faces sting, but otherwise did no damage.

Less than thirty seconds later, the MAZ commander retracted the launch rail and the sailors ran back toward the vehicle, throwing the weighted tarpaulins over the top and fastening them hastily to either side. Within two minutes of launch, the launch vehicle disappeared back into the cargo hold, the metal doors slammed shut, and the vessel continued its route toward Baltimore.

One minute later the warhead detonated in the air over the National Mall in Washington, D.C., just a few hundred yards west of the Capitol building, almost directly in front of FBI headquarters at Pennsylvania Avenue and 9th Street.

In less than one ten-thousandth of a second, heat from the 250-kiloton blast reached several million degrees Celsius, so intense that it melted concrete, stone, asphalt, and glass.

The FBI building itself was kicked apart like a pile of twigs. The shockwave radiated out in all directions just fractions of a second later, hitting buildings along Pennsylvania Avenue like a gigantic piston. An immense fireball raced across the Mall and through the city streets at supersonic speeds. Although the reinforced structures of both the White House and the Capitol survived the initial fireball, everyone who was not in the blast-proof shelters below ground was killed. The fireball shattered the Washington Monument like so many toy bricks.

Within less than five seconds, the fireball hit restaurants and movie theaters in the Cleveland Park district along Connecticut Avenue, some 3 miles north of ground zero, flattening every structure that had not been built to withstand massive earthquakes. In the other direction, to the south and east, the blast wave devastated the densely populated slums along the Anacostia River, transforming brick and clapboard row houses into confetti. Huge slabs of concrete and asphalt were torn from bridges and overpasses.

Farther downriver, at Bolling Air Force Base, nearly every window and wall in the White Hotel—home of the Defense Intelligence Agency—was blown out, exposing a ripped skeleton of steel.

There was no warning before the warhead detonated, although it was carried into U.S. airspace by a ballistic missile.

Whoever was behind the devastating nuclear attack—and surviving U.S. intelligence agencies would later discover a tantalizing trail of signals intelligence that led to a previously unknown branch of Osama bin Laden's al-Qaeda—had understood the strategic hole in America's ballistic missile defenses, recently deployed by President Bush. . . .

Experts refer to this type of terrorist strike as "SCUD in a bucket," and it is a scenario that has been war-gamed repeatedly. Although the capabilities involved are those of a state, intelligence analysts fear that Iran's clerical leaders will attempt to create a false trail leading to others.

The threat of a third-world nation like Iran acquiring the capability to launch such a strike against America was revealed after intense debate by the Commission to Assess the Ballistic Missile Threat to the United States—otherwise known as the Rumsfeld Commission—in the unclassified version of its landmark report. Some of the commissioners did not want to reveal America's dreadful vulnerability, especially since the tens of billions of dollars Congress wanted to spend on the National Ballistic Missile Defense System contained not one dollar to protect against such an attack.

"A ballistic missile or cruise missile launched from a cargo ship close to our shores would be able to fly in beneath our detection radars," ballistic missile analyst Scott McMahon told me when the Rumsfeld Commission Report first appeared. "If a rogue state such as Iran were to launch a missile off the East Coast of the United States, it could hit Washington, D.C., or New York before an interceptor missile could reach it."

In addition to raising the specter of sea-launched missiles, the Rumsfeld Commission warned that Iran could have nuclear warheads for such a missile before the United States could detect them. "Because of significant gaps in our knowledge, the U.S. is unlikely to know whether Iran possesses nuclear weapons until after the fact," the report stated.

That was in July 1998.

As Donald Rumsfeld and his fellow commissioners were completing their final draft, they were briefed on sensitive U.S. intelligence that Iran had just successfully tested a sea-launched missile from a barge in the Caspian Sea.

That classified U.S. intelligence report persuaded reluctant commissioners to sound the alarm. "We launched a Polaris missile off of a commercial ship back in 1962 and it works fine," said former undersecretary of state William Schneider, who served on the panel. "There is no reason to believe it is not being done by others."

Dr. J. David Martin, who was then the Ballistic Missile Defense Organization's deputy director for strategic relations, acknowledged that the United States was unable to counter this type of threat. "Sea-launch is a difficult problem," he said. "The NMD [National Missile Defense] is being developed against an ICBM-range missile launched from overseas."

That has been America's problem for generations. We are always fighting the previous war. It was precisely this type of failure that led to the 9/11 attacks and that tomorrow could leave America unprepared for an Iranian nuclear strike.

We have very little time to get it right.

The stakes are high, and the price of failure is enormous.

Appendix

THE EVIDENCE

In more than two decades of reporting on the Islamic Republic of Iran, I have discovered startling evidence of the clerical regime's deadly ambitions and capabilities—and of repeated U.S. failures to deal with the Iranian threat. The documents and photographs shown here—most of which have never been published, and some of which were previously classified—offer a glimpse into Iran's covert nuclear weapons program as well as its active involvement with al-Qaeda and in major terrorist operations against Americans. Of course, this appendix represents only a small sampling of the documented record against Iran. Readers interested in seeing even more of the evidence can visit www.kentimmerman.com or www.iran.org.

The smoking gun

This never-before-published memorandum, dated May 14, 2001, comes directly from the Supreme Leader's Intelligence Office and sets the guidelines for Iran's cooperation with al-Qaeda on the September 11 plot. The English translation is opposite.

بسمه تعالی

خیلی محرمانه

جمهوری اسلامی ایران

سازمان اطلاعات رهبری

شماره ۰۴-۳۳۵-۸۱۰/م/س

تاریخ ۱۳۸۰/۲/۲۴

پیوست ندارد

طبقه بندی خیلی محرمانه

از : ریاست سازمان اطلاعات رهبری

به : مدیر کل محترّم اداره‌عملیاتی ۴۳

موضوع : ابلاغ دستوردرخصوص تصمیمات مقام معظّم رهبری «دامت برکاته »

خدمت حجت الاسلام والمسلمین جناب آقای پورقناد «دامت توفیقاته »

بادعا وسلام

ضمن آرزوی موفقیت وبهروزی برای شماو کارمندان صدیق وشجاع آن اداره،نتایج گزارشات اخیرحضرتعالی درخصوص رفع ابهامات درجانبداری ازبرنامه های آتی القاعده ،نگرشهاودیدگاههای متفاوتی موردبررسی قرارگرفت والنهایه دررفع ابهامات موجودباتأکید مقام معظّم رهبری ،ایشان خاطرنشان فرمودند ،مبارزه بااستکبارجهانی ودرصدرآنان آمریکاواسرائیل ،جزء لاینفک ومقصداصلی نظام اسلامی می باشدومعیوب ساختن نظام اقتصادی وبی اعتبارساختن دیگرارکان این دودشمن متّحدنظام اسلامی درتسویه‌حسابهای سیاسی وبه خطرانداختن، اعتدال وامنیت آنهاواجب ولازم الاجرامی باشد،ایشان باتأکیدبرلزوم هوشیاری کامل درعرصه‌فعالیتهایتان خواستارتوجه بیشترگشتند،وهمچنین درتأکیدبه سنجش پیامدهای منفی وآتی درقبال این همکاری فرمودند،بااستادی کردن این مبارزه روندروبه رشدعرصه‌فعالیت دشمنان راهرچه بیشترباهمکاری نزدیکتربادیگرارکان اطلاعاتی وامنیتی داخلی وطرفداران خارجی تنگ نموده ،وسعی شوددربازتاب دستاوردهایتان کلیه‌امورزیرنظرمستقیم اداره‌حفاظت مرکزسازمان انجام گیرد.بالطبع تمیزوتشخیص آسیبهاجزء حیطه‌وظایف آن اداره‌زحمت کش وهوشیارمی باشد،همچنین مقرّرشدبرجلسات بعدی درارتباط بارفع موانع اصولی ومشکلات دستیابی به اهداف وتحقّق وپیشرفت اموردرخصوص توسعه‌همکاریهابامبارزین شبکه‌القاعده وحزب الله دررسیدن به یک هدف مشخص بحث وتبادل نظرگردد،درخاتمه ابراز رضایت مقام معظّم رهبری وحمایت کامل ایشان دراجرای برنامه های آتی آن اداره رااعلام وبادرک وظایف خطیرشما،ایشان تأکیدنمودند،کوچکترین ردّپایی درجانبداری ازالقاعده که مستوجب پیامدهای منفی وغیرقابل جبران گرددبرجای نماندوبه همان رابطه‌فعلی «عقنیه والزواهری» خلاصه گردد.ازخداوندمنّان تأییدات شمارامسئلت مینمایم.

… رحمت الله »

۲۰ صفر

علی اکبر ناطق نوری

رئیس سازمان اطلاعات رهبری

۱۳ جمهوری اسلامی ایران سازمان اطلاعات رهبری ۷۸

دبیرخانه اداره [illegible]

تاریخ ورود ۱۳۸۰/۲/۲۴

شماره ثبت [illegible]

مجتبی

خیلی محرمانه

برابر با اصل رونوشت به اداره حفاظت مرکز جهت اجرای فرامین ٪

Islamic Republic of Iran
Leader's Intelligence Organization

Date: 24 Ordibehesht 1380 (14 may 2001)

From: Director, Leader's Intelligence organization
[Hojjat-ol eslam Ali Akbar Nateq-Nouri]

To: Director, MOIS—Section 43 [Hojjat-ol eslam Mustafa Pourganad]

Subject: Tasking memo

We are very happy at the *Rahbar*'s [Supreme Leader's] office with all you have undertaken . . .

The Supreme Leader [Ayatollah Ali Khamenei] has seen your latest report regarding support and help for the future plan of al-Qaeda. Of course we are looking at different proposals for providing support, but all in all, after reviewing them, the Leader asked me to convey to you the following:

"Our emphasis should be the struggle with the Great Satan and Israel. This is our main agenda. It is not only important to us for tactical reasons, but for the greatness of Islam. Our main goal shall be to damage their economic structures and to damage their reputation and credibility. We shall concentrate on these two archenemies of the Islamic faith [the U.S. and Israel]. We must also strike at their internal peace and security. This is imperative. In this path, we should be very careful, and very clever, in order not to leave any evidence behind that can impact negatively on us in the future. Again I emphasize, we shall use our intelligence and internal security apparatus for this struggle and will coordinate with those foreign sources who share the same belief with us. These efforts should be centralized under the close supervision of our intelligence and security apparatus in order to be effective."

The Leader mentioned that at our next meeting we should analyze the ideological and logistical problems in reaching our goals and of improving our plans, especially in coordination with fighters of al-Qaeda and Hezbollah, to find one target [*haddaf*] that is beneficial to both sides. We need to set aside our ideological differences and analyze the problems that would hamper us from reaching our goal. In particular, we should examine the expansion and coordination with al-Qaeda (*Shabbakeh*) group and Hezbollah to reach our common objective.

The Leader has expressed his full support for the implementation of the future plans of your department [Section 43] and again emphasized that we should not leave any evidence of our support for al-Qaeda that could give us problems or prejudice our standing.

The Leader suggested that we limit our relations with al-Qaeda to only two people, as before (Imad Mugniyeh and Ayman Zawahri) and not go beyond them and deal only with them.

[Signature seal in green wax]
Ali Akbar Nateq-Nouri
Director, Leader's Intelligence Organization

[Rectangular stamp] Section 43—MOIS
Received by Mohebi
24 Ordibehesht 1380
Read: filed.

The defector

With Iranian defector Hamid Reza Zakeri set to appear as a German government witness in a 9/11-related trial, the BKA—the German equivalent of the FBI—presented a federal court in Hamburg with this report on the defector. The CIA has repeatedly tried to discredit Zakeri, but this report specifically affirms his employment at Department 12 of Iran's Ministry of Information and Security (MOIS).

Bundeskriminalamt
ST 24 – 014/04 (G)

Meckenheim, 21.01.2004

Eingang 30.1.04
8⁴⁰ Uhr

251 II
249 I (BND + 3AVerf)

VERMERK

Betreff
Ermittlungsverfahren gegen Said BAHAJI, Ramzi OMAR alias BINALSHIBH u. Zakariya ESSABAR wegen Verd. Der Mitgliedschaft in einer terroristischen Vereinigung i.T. mit Mord u. Angriffen auf den Luftverkehr
Az.: GBA 2 BJs 67/01-5
hier: Erkenntnisse zum iranischen Nachrichtendienst

Der im Rahmen des o.a. Ermittlungsverfahrens vernommene Zeuge hat u.a angegeben, er sei ab 1994 bis Herbst 1999 Büroleiter des Generaldirektors der Abteilung 12 (Abteilung für Sicherheit und Information) des iranischen Nachrichtendienstes MOIS gewesen.
Aus einem Organigramm dieses Dienstes, Stand 1999, geht hervor, daß es dort die Verwaltungen 11 – 18 gab. So war die Verwaltung 12 für den Schutz von Personen und Einrichtungen und die Verwaltung 15 für Auslandsaufklärung und Auswertung zuständig. Die Verwaltung 15 hatte 9 Abteilungen, u.a. auch eine Abteilung für Westeuropa und Nordamerika.
In diesem Zusammenhang wird auf die Aussage des Zeugen zu seinen Einsatz in Kanada (vor 1994) hingewiesen.

Zu einer angeblich nach 1999 neu gegründeten nachrichtendienstlichen Organisation (lt. Zeuge Nachrichtenorganisation des Führers) liegen hier keine Erkenntnisse vor.

Der vom Zeugen als Leiter einer Abteilung dieser Organisation und als erster VEVAK -Minister benannte REYSHEHRI ist hiesigen Unterlagen zufolge Mitbegründer des VEVAK gewesen. Die Schreibweise seines Namens lautet jedoch REYSHARI.

Zur Person des vom Zeugen darüber hinaus erwähnten Generaldirektors der Abteilung 12 und späteren Chefs der Abteilung 110, HADDADIAN sowie des Führers der Abteilung 43, Mostafa POURGHANNAD, liegen hier in nachrichtendienstlicher Hinsicht keine Erkenntnisse vor.

Walterschön, KHK

Confirmation

The German foreign intelligence service, the BND, filed an extensive report on Zakeri's bona fides to the Hamburg court hearing the 9/11 case.

VS - Nur für den Dienstgebrauch

2 Exemplare

2 Exemplar

ST 34 / Re

BND

BUNDESNACHRICHTENDIENST 82049 Pullach, 27 Januar 2004

47A - 43-21 - 47A-0028/04 VS-NfD

Kopie von ___ Ausf.

INFOTEC-Kontr. Nr. 047

Ausg. 27.01.04 Zeit: ...

E/ JAN 27 '04 000734

Bundeskriminalamt
ST34
53338 Meckenheim

über

Bundeskanzleramt
z.H. Herrn MinR Vorbeck
- o.V.i.A. -
10557 Berlin

Gesehen und weitergeleitet
BUNDESKANZLERAMT
Berlin, den 27. 01. 2004
Im Auftrag
Vorbeck

Betr.: Ermittlungsverfahren gegen Said Bahaji, Ramzi Omar alias Binalshibh und Zakariya Essabar wegen Verdachts der Mitgliedschaft in einer terroristischen Vereinigung u.a., Az GBA 2 BJs 67/01-5

hier: Zeuge Hamid Reza Zakeri

Bezug: BKA ST 34-067250/01 vom 23.01.2004

Zu Ihrem mit Bezug übersandten Fragenkatalog wird wie folgt gerichtsverwertbar Stellung genommen:

Seite 1 von 4

The e-mail

Zakeri showed the court this coded e-mail he received from a source in Iran. German prosecutors claimed the code revealed that the defendant, Abdelghani Mzoudi, was "involved in 9/11." Zakeri says the message was more vague—that his source had information on Mzoudi and his travels to Iran that he would transmit to Zakeri in person. But the German prosecutors never waited for Zakeri's source to provide that information. Just a few weeks after the Hamburg trial ended, the source did give a sworn deposition to a lawyer representing the German victims of 9/11.

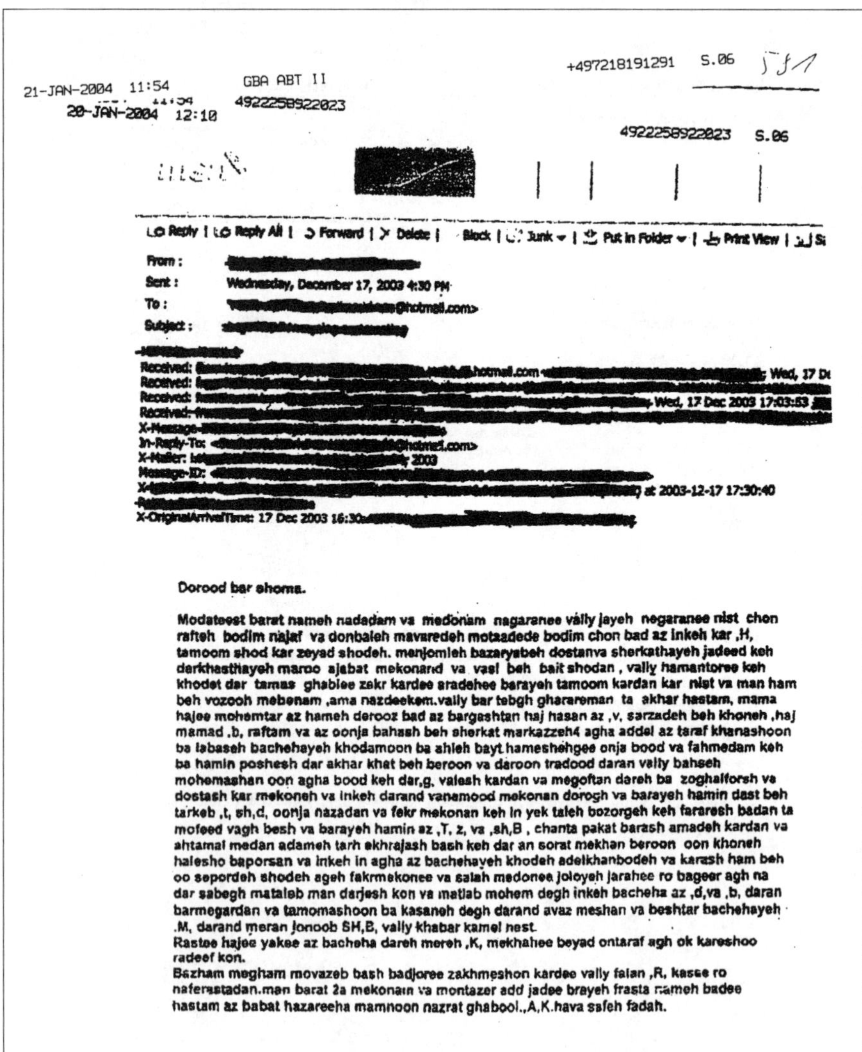

21-JAN-2004 11:54 GBA ABT II +497218191291 S.06

20-JAN-2004 12:10 4922258922023

4922258922023 S.06

Reply | Reply All | Forward | Delete | Block | Junk | Put in Folder | Print View |

From :

Sent : Wednesday, December 17, 2003 4:30 PM

To : @hotmail.com>

Subject :

Received: hotmail.com Wed, 17 De

Received:

Received: Wed, 17 Dec 2003 17:03:53

Received:

X-Message-

In-Reply-To: @hotmail.com>

X-Mailer: 2003

Message-ID:

X- at 2003-12-17 17:30:40

X-OriginalArrivalTime: 17 Dec 2003 16:30

Dorood bar shoma.

Modateest barat nameh nadadam va medonam nagaranee vally jayeh negaranee nist chon rafteh bodim najaf va donbaleh mavaredeh motaadede bodim chon bad az inkeh kar ,H, tamoom shod kar zeyad shodeh. menjomleh bazaryabeh dostanva sherkathayeh jadeed keh derkhasthayeh maroo ajabat mekonand va vasl beh bait shodan , vally hamantoree keh khodet dar tamas ghablee zekr kardee aradehee barayeh tamoom kardan kar nist va man ham beh vozooh mebenam ,ama nazdeekem.vally bar tebgh gharereman ta akhar hastam, mama hajee mohemtar az hameh derooz bad az bargashtan haj hasan az ,v, sarzadeh beh khoneh ,haj mamad ,b, raftam va az oonja bahash beh sherkat markazzeh4 agha addel az taraf khanashoon ba labaseh bachehayeh khodamoon ba ahleh bayt hameshehgee onja bood va fahmedam keh ba hamin poshesh dar akhar khat beh beroon va daroon tradood daran vally bahseh mohemashan oon agha bood keh dar,g, valesh kardan va megoftan dareh ba zoghalforsh va dostash kar mekoneh va inkeh darand vanemood mekonan dorogh va barayeh hamin dast beh tarkeb ,t, sh,d, oonja nazadan va fekr mekonan keh in yek taleh bozorgeh keh fararesh badan ta mofeed vagh besh va barayeh hamin az ,T, z, va ,sh,B , chanta pakat barash amadeh kardan va ahtamal medan adameh tarh ekhrajash bash keh dar an sorat mekhan beroon oon khoneh halesho baporsan va inkeh in agha az bachehayeh khodeh adelkhanbodeh va karash ham beh oo sepordeh shodeh ageh fakrmekonee va salah medonee joloyeh jarahee ro bageer agh na dar sabegh mataleb man darjesh kon va matlab mohem degh inkeh bacheha az ,d,va ,b, daran barmegardan va tamomashoon ba kasaneh degh darand avaz meshan va beshtar bachehayeh .M, darand meran jonoob SH,B, vally khabar kamel nest.

Rastee hajee yakee az bacheha dareh mereh ,K, mekhahee beyad ontaraf agh ok kareshoo radeef kon.

Bazham megham movazeb bash badjoree zakhmeshon kardee vally falan ,R, kasse ro naferastadan.man barat 2a mekonam va montazer add jadee brayeh frasta nameh badee hastam az babat hazareeha mamnoon nazrat ghabool.,A,K.hava safeh fadah.

Debriefing

One of my debriefings with Iranian defector Hamid Reza Zakeri in Paris, March 2005. *(Photograph by L. M.)* Zakeri provided me with a copy of his official identity card *(at bottom)*, which specifies that no one has the authority to arrest him for any reason.

جمهوری اسلامی ایران

(توجه)

۱- این کارت مخصوص کارمندان وزارت اطلاعات جمهوری اسلامی ایران می باشد

۲- دارنده این کارت بر طبق مصوبه شورای امنیت در هنگام هر گونه حادثه از بازداشت [illegible] مبراء می باشد .

۳- از کلیه نیروهای کشوری و لشکری تقاضای همکاری و مساعدت می گردد .

امضاء معاونت پرسنلی

امضاء معاونت حفاظت

Laughable accusation

The hard-line Tehran daily *Keyhan*, published by the Supreme Leader's office, has published numerous articles identifying me—incorrectly—as the head of the CIA's "human intelligence" effort to overthrow Iran's clerical regime. This front-page story, dated June 27, 2000 (column 1 above the fold), alleges that the calls for "democratic means of governing and renewal of the political structure of Iran are conspiracies planned by Kenneth Timmerman, the former CIA staffer in charge of Iran."
(Translation courtesy of Elham Yaghoubian)

سه شنبه ۷ تیر ۱۳۷۹ - ۲۴ ربیع الاول ۱۴۲۱ - ۲۷ ژوئن ۲۰۰۰
سال پنجاه ونهم - شماره ۱۶۸۳۳

در صفحات دیگر...

گفت و شنود | یادداشت روز | اخبار خارجی | مقالات | مقاله های بی متن | اخبار ورزشی | اخبار کشور
دور دنیا | اخبار ویژه | کیهان و خوانندگان | حوادث | پاورقی | بدون شرح

کیهان

نظرخواهی کیهان از مردم درباره تغییر ساعت کار بانکها

شورای امنیت خواستار قطع تجاوز اسرائیل به خاک لبنان شد

۱۶ صفحه

پاسخ رئیس قوه قضائیه به نامه نمایندگان
مجلس فرا جناحی عمل کند

خاتمی: تا خواسته‌های ملت ایران تأمین نشود
تحولی در رابطه با آمریکا صورت نخواهد گرفت

گزارش تحلیلی کیهان
از همسویی آمریکا و مدعیان اصلاح طلبی
در مورد قانون مطبوعات

عزت‌الله سحابی در ارتباط
با پرونده کنفرانس برلین
به زندان رفت

آغاز به کار دومین نمایشگاه
بین‌المللی خودرو در تهران

درخواست کمیته امداد از مجلس
برای کاهش بهای آب، برق و گاز
مصرفی خانواده‌های محروم

حوادث ایران و جهان

رباینده ۲۵ دختر بچه
در تهران به دار آویخته شد

هدف از حملات اخیر
به قوه قضائیه جلوگیری
از تعقیب جرائم کلان
اقتصادی است

کروبی: نگرانم که مجلس نتواند
نیازهای مردم را برآورده کند

گفتمان بی گفتمان: پاسخ را نخوانید!

Iran's terrorist master

These are the only known photographs of Iran's top terrorist, Imad Fayez Mugniyeh, one of the regime's key links to al-Qaeda. A French intelligence source gave me the photgraphs in 1988.

Photograph 1 is an early photo of Mugniyeh, probably as a teenager.

Photograph 2 was taken from Mugniyeh's passport in the early 1980s.

Photograph 3 was obtained from a French intelligence informer in Iran during one of Mugniyeh's many trips there in the early 1980s.

Photograph 4 is a suspect, believed to be Mugniyeh but never positively identified, photographed by French counterintelligence in Orly airport, Paris, circa 1986.

(All photographs copyright © 1988 by Kenneth R. Timmerman/MEDNEWS)

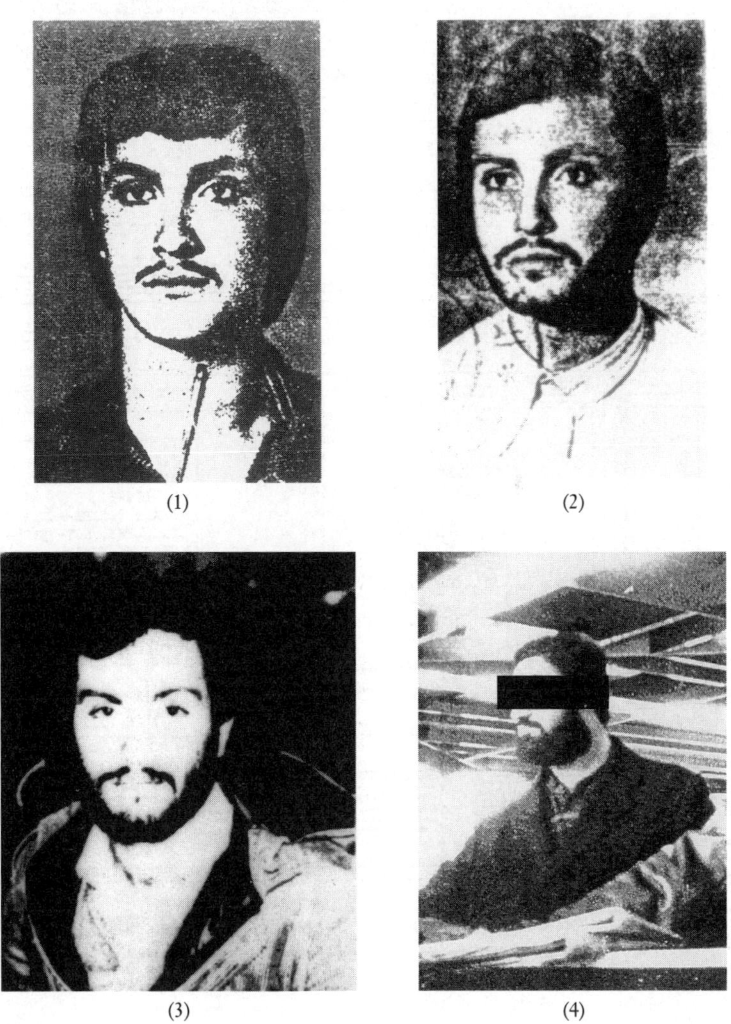

(1) (2)

(3) (4)

The nuclear Stop & Shop

This Air France bill of lading from 1985 is just a sample of the trove of documents seized by German and French customs officials investigating the nuclear supplier network of Pakistan's Dr. A. Q. Khan in the late 1980s. Despite detailed knowledge of Dr. Khan's nuclear black market, weak laws prevented prosecutors from shutting it down.

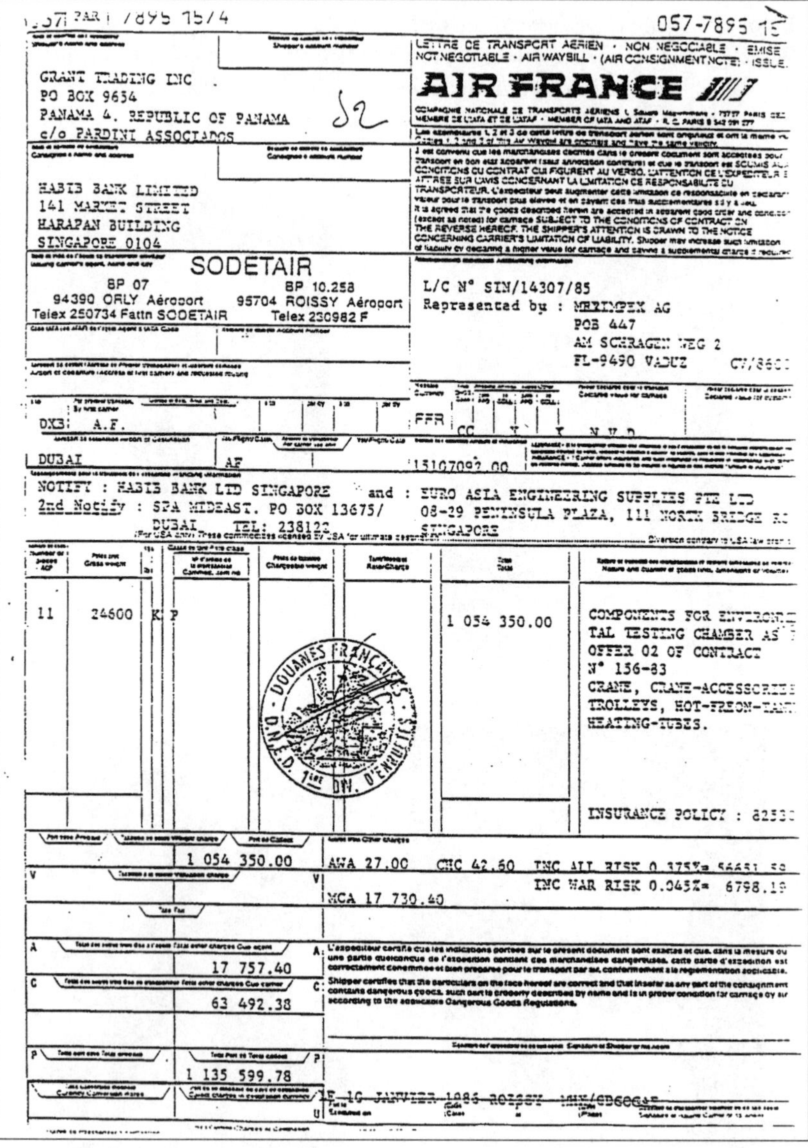

057 PAR 7895 1574

057-7895 15

LETTRE DE TRANSPORT AERIEN · NON NEGOCIABLE · EMISE
NOT NEGOTIABLE · AIR WAYBILL · (AIR CONSIGNMENT NOTE) · ISSUE.

AIR FRANCE

GRANT TRADING INC
PO BOX 9654
PANAMA 4. REPUBLIC OF PANAMA
c/o PARDINI ASSOCIADOS

HABIB BANK LIMITED
141 MARKET STREET
HARAPAN BUILDING
SINGAPORE 0104

SODETAIR
BP 07
94390 ORLY Aéroport
Telex 250734 Fattn SODETAIR
BP 10.258
95704 ROISSY Aéroport
Telex 230982 F

L/C N° SIN/14307/85
Represented by : MEKIMPEX AG
POB 447
AM SCHRAGEN WEG 2
FL-9490 VADUZ

DXB A.F.

FFR CC Y Y N V D

DUBAI AF 15107092.00

NOTIFY : HABIB BANK LTD SINGAPORE and : EURO ASIA ENGINEERING SUPPLIES PTE LTD
2nd Notify : SPA MIDEAST. PO BOX 13675/ 08-29 PENINSULA PLAZA, 111 NORTH BRIDGE RD
DUBAI TEL: 238122 SINGAPORE

11 24600 K P 1 054 350.00

COMPONENTS FOR ENVIRONMENTAL TESTING CHAMBER AS PER OFFER 02 OF CONTRACT N° 156-83
CRANE, CRANE-ACCESSORIES TROLLEYS, HOT-FREON-TANK HEATING-TUBES.

DOUANES FRANÇAISES D.N.E.D. 1ère DIV. D'ENQUÊTES

INSURANCE POLICY : 82533

1 054 350.00

AWA 27.00 CHC 42.60 INC ALL RISK 0.375%= 56451.58
INC WAR RISK 0.045%= 6798.19
MCA 17 730.40

17 757.40

63 492.38

1 135 599.78

L'expéditeur certifie que les indications portées sur le présent document sont exactes et que, dans la mesure où une partie quelconque de l'expédition contient des marchandises dangereuses, cette partie d'expédition est correctement dénommée et bien préparée pour le transport par air, conformément à la réglementation applicable.

Shipper certifies that the particulars on the face hereof are correct and that insofar as any part of the consignment contains dangerous goods, such part is properly described by name and is in proper condition for carriage by air according to the applicable Dangerous Goods Regulations.

LE 10 JANVIER 1986 ROISSY MHX/CD6064F

The Khan network's inner workings

French customs tracked shipments from Leybold subsidiaries in France to Merimpex in Vaduz, Liechtenstein, which they believed were ultimately destined for Dr. Khan's uranium enrichment plant in Pakistan.

.D. PARIS
Division

camion n°1 · camion n°2 · camion n°3 · camion n°4 · camion n°5 · camion n°6 · camion n°7 · camion n°8

OPERATION MERIMPEX AG. PO BOX 447 AM SCHRAGEN WEG 2 FL 9490 VADUZ.

N°, DATE, BUREAU	COLIS, CONTREMARQUE	POIDS KGS	TRANSPORTEUR	L.T.A.	DEST.	VOL / DATE
5, 27 DEC. 85, LA FERRIERE	[illegible] camion n°3	12.800	P/C SAIMA MILAN	78951563 78951574	KWI DXB	AF 1358/5.1. AF 3389/10.1
6, 27 DEC. 85, LA FERRIERE	2 : K1 et K2 1 : 135 B camion n°4	13.500	P/C SAIMA MILAN	78951563 78951574	KWI DXB	AF 1358/5.1. AF 3389/10.1
7, 27 DEC. 85, LA FERRIERE	[illegible] camion n°2	8.800	P/C SAIMA MILAN	78951563	KWI	AF 1358/5.1.
0, 19 DEC. 85, BUCHS	M22 : L1 et L2 camion n°1	9.000	SCHMID WETTINGEN (CH)	78951574	DXB	AF 3389/10.1
2, 07 JAN. 86, ANNECY	5 : [illegible] → n°8 → n°5	6.000	RAPID SAVOY SEYNOD (74600) P/C BONNIEUX ANNECY.	81960082	DHA	AF 1354/13.1
3, 07 JAN. 86, ANNECY	2 : H 2115 et 2121/3 → n°7 1 : 225808 → n°5	11.200	RAPID SAVOY SEYNOD (74600) P/C BONNIEUX ANNECY.	81960082 81960071	DHA DXB	AF 1354/13.1 AF 1356/14.1
1, 07 JAN. 86, ANNECY	2 : 25 B10 et [illegible]	6.600	CHAUDET ALFORVILLE (D4) P/C BONNIEUX ANNECY.	81960071	DXB	AF1356/14.1
1, 08 JAN. 86, ANNECY	7 : 1006BC11 et [illegible]	7.200	P/C BONNIEUX ANNECY	78951574	DXB	AF 3389/10.1
1, 27 JAN. 86, STUTTGART FEUERBACH	3 : E3/4 à E3/6	2.380	JS INTERNATIONAL AULNAY (93) P/C KUHNE ET NAGEL STUTTGART.	81969123	KWI	AF 1358/9.2.
1, 27 JAN. 86, STUTTGART FEUERBACH	3 : E3/1 à E3/3	6.900	FRITZ STUTTGART (RFA) P/C KUHNE ET NAGEL STUTTGART.	81969123	KWI	AF 1358/9.2.8
6, 30 JAN. 86, ROISSY.	16 : 1 à 16	9.000	DEBEAUX LIVRON (26) [illegible]	81991184	DHA	AF 1352/31.1.

Khan's middlemen

Among the intermediaries Dr. Khan used to sell nuclear technologies to Iran were B.S.A. Tahir *(above left)*, a Sri Lankan businessman who arranged the shipment of five hundred centrifuges in 1995, netting $3 million for Khan's network, and Tahir's partner in Germany, Urs Tinner (passport, *below left*; photo, *below right*). Tahir was arrested in Malaysia in November 2003, while Tinner was arrested in Germany in October 2004. Malaysian police seized the centrifuge rotor shown above right.

(Photographs from 2004 Malaysian police report)

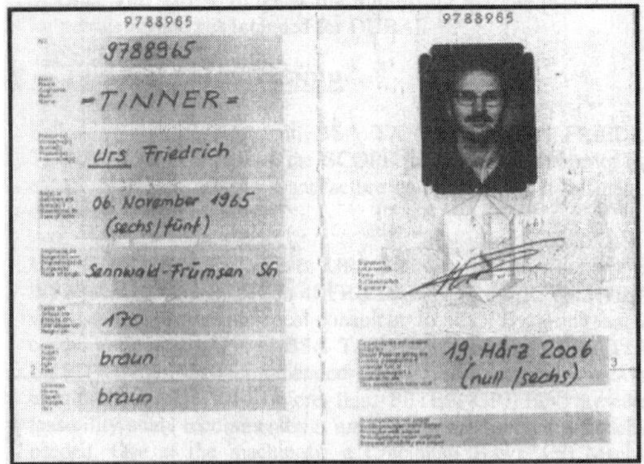

9788965

9788965

-TINNER-

Urs Friedrich

06. November 1965
(sechs/fünf)

Sennwald-Frümsen SG

170

braun

braun

9788965

19. März 2006
(null/sechs)

Missile sales

Iranian defense minister Ali Akbar Torkan *(at bottom, gesturing)*, a frequent visitor to North Korea along with Revolutionary Guards commander Mohsen Rezai, reviews models of Defense Industries Organization missiles offered for sale at the International Defense Equipment Exhibition in Abu Dhabi, 1993.

The hidden will

Shah Mohammed Reza Pahlavi was careful to hide tens of billions of dollars in special trust funds, managed by Swiss lawyer Jean Patry, as evidenced by this exchange from July 2, 1979. *(Source: Ahmad Ansari,* Me and Reza, *Tehran, 2000; unpublished English-language translation made available to author)*

Letter addressed to HIM Mohamed Reza Pahlavi on July 2nd, 1979 by Me Jean Patry

Free translation into English

Majesty,

According to your instructions given in Nassau on May 28, 1979, we executed the following :

1) We withdrew from the Union de Banques Suisses all the assets deposited under the name of the Foundation Lutecia and the Establishment Daletze, after having cashed the bonds which could be cashed.

2) We remitted to Me Jean-Pierre Cottier, attorney in Lausanne, a beige envelope, a brown packet and various documents containing 149 shares C. of the company limited by shares Bahia Las Rocas of Ptas 5.000.- each and 1.000 shares of the company limited by shares Marbe S.A. of Ptas 1000.- each, as well as documents concern the Establishment Daletze. You will find herewith photo-copy of receipts signed by ourselves in favour of the Union de Banques Suisses and by Me Jean-Pierre Cottier in our favour. We indicated to Me Cottier that you will give him instructions to realize at the best conditions the assets it represents.

3) We established in Liechtenstein the Foundations Niversa, Zarima and Rukam. These Foundations, for which we keep the respective files at your disposal, agreed with the Company Pallerga S.A., domiciled 15, boulevard des Philosophes, Geneva, to open each four accounts with respectively Unioñ de Banques Suisses, Geneva Branch, Crédit Suisse, Geneva Branch, Chase Manhattan Bank (Suisse) S.A. and Banque Gutzwiller Kurz Bungener S.A. The totality of the assets we withdrew from the Union de Banques Suisses, as mentioned hereabove, has been deposited on these accounts, with the exception of what we remitted to Me Jean-Pierre Cottier.

You will find herewith attached the composition as well as the distribution of these assets.

The files of the three Foundations mentioned contain a specimen of the fiduciary contracts signed with Pallerga S.A., which indicate to you the exact wording of the accounts open with the banking establishments.

4) We confirm to you irrevocably that all the assets withdrawn from the Union de Banques Suisses in Geneva (with the exception of what has been remitted to Me Cottier) have been remitted by yourself to the disposition of the Foundations Niversa, Rukam and Zarima. We also confirm that you are the sole person, with any proxy you could designate in writing to that effect, to be entitled to give instructions for the placement or in order to dispose of the assets held by these three Foundations. We irrevocably undertake to act only according to written instructions you could give us to that effect, either direcUy or to a proxy designated by yourselves in writing.

5) We thank you to confirm to us that in case you decease or in case you were unable to act for any reason whatsoever, we should act in order to have the assets of the three Foundations utilised as follows :

- 20 % to your wife
- 20 % to your elder son
- 15 % to your daughter Farahnaz
- 15 % to your daughter Leila
- 20 % to your younger son
- 8 % to your daughter Shanaz Djahanbani
- 2 % to your grand-daughter Mahnaz Zahedi.

If you agree with the foregoing, we ask you to return copy of that letter duly signed by yourself for approval.

Signed by Jean Patry

For approval :

signed by HIM Mohamed Reza Pahlavi

The corporate veil

The deposed shah's eldest son, Reza Pahlavi, drew these diagrams so he could better understand the complex financial structure set up to shield his assets from the Islamic Republic of Iran—and from U.S. taxes. *(Source: Reza Pahlavi;* Medina Development Company v. Ahmad Ali Masood Ansari, *United States District Court for the Eastern District of Virginia, 96-1519)*

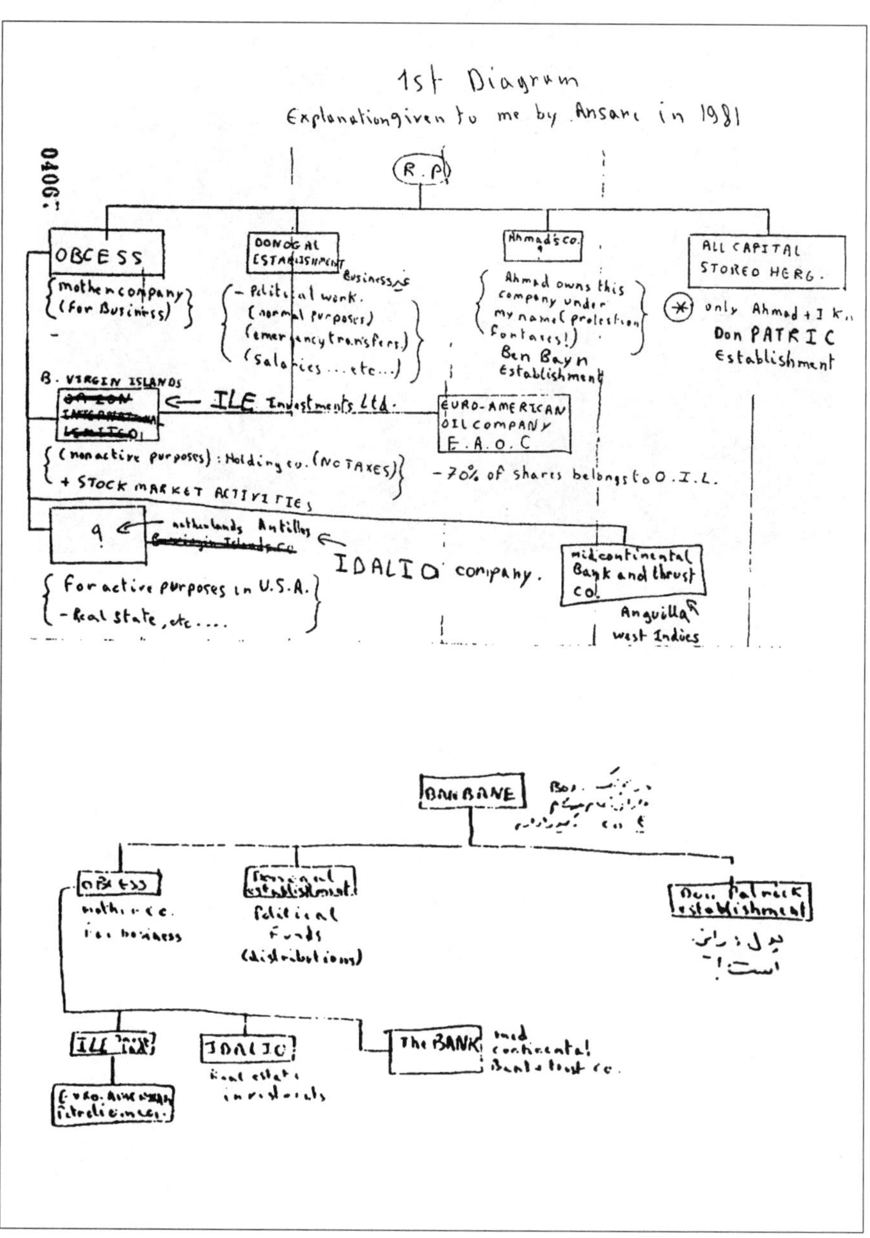

Face to face

The author meeting with Ahmad Ansari, March 2005.
(Photograph by Christina Timmerman)

The opposition

Dissident Ayatollah Mehdi Rouhani meeting with Iranian opposition leaders at my home outside Washington, D.C., 1997. From left to right: Sunni cleric Molavi Ali Akbar Mollahzadeh, Kurdish Democratic Party of Iran representative Awat Aliyar, Foundation for Democracy in Iran president Nader Afshar, former Iranian education minister Manoucher Ganji, me, Ayatollah Mehdi Rouhani, and Balouchi activists Dr. Hossein Bor and Prince Mohammad al Mohammad.

Masquerade

Bijan Sepasy, who continues to offer his services to groups opposing the Islamic Republic, was a registered lobbyist for the same regime he now says he opposes and set up a lobbying organization—the Forum on American-Iranian Relations—that took money from Tehran. These documents come from the Justice Department's Foreign Agent Registration database for the years 1991–1993. Sepasy claims he represented Tehran at the urging of U.S. government officials.

```
Bijan Adam Sepasy - Access U.S.A., Inc., #4560
     1850 K Street, N.W.
     Suite 200
     Washington, DC 20006

     Mission of Islamic Republic of Iran to the United Nations (t91)

     Registrant agreed to improve the image of the foreign principal
     through interactions with the media.  Registrant also agreed to
     monitor and report to the foreign principal on media coverage and
     developments in U.S. foreign policy.

     $15,000.00 received prior to registration on September 3, 1991.

     Political Propaganda:  None Reported
```

```
SXDSRU1A            REGISTRATION UNIT TRACKING SYSTEM                5/08/95
                          Record Update Search                      11:50:52
                                                        Filing    Term    Empl
Ln# Reg #  Typ Name                                 Sts  Date     Date    Code
*1  04560  PR Bijan Adam Sepasy - Access U.S.A., In  C  09/03/91 08/12/92 E018
*2  04702  PR Forum on American-Iranian Relations F  C  07/30/92 08/27/92 E021
*3  04703  PR Sepasy, Bijan Adam                     C  08/12/92 12/23/93 E021
                   ** End Of File **
```

Blacklist

In the early 1990s, the German government established a "blacklist" of end users in Iran that it suspected of involvement in WMD programs, and regularly warned exporters about them through this trade association.

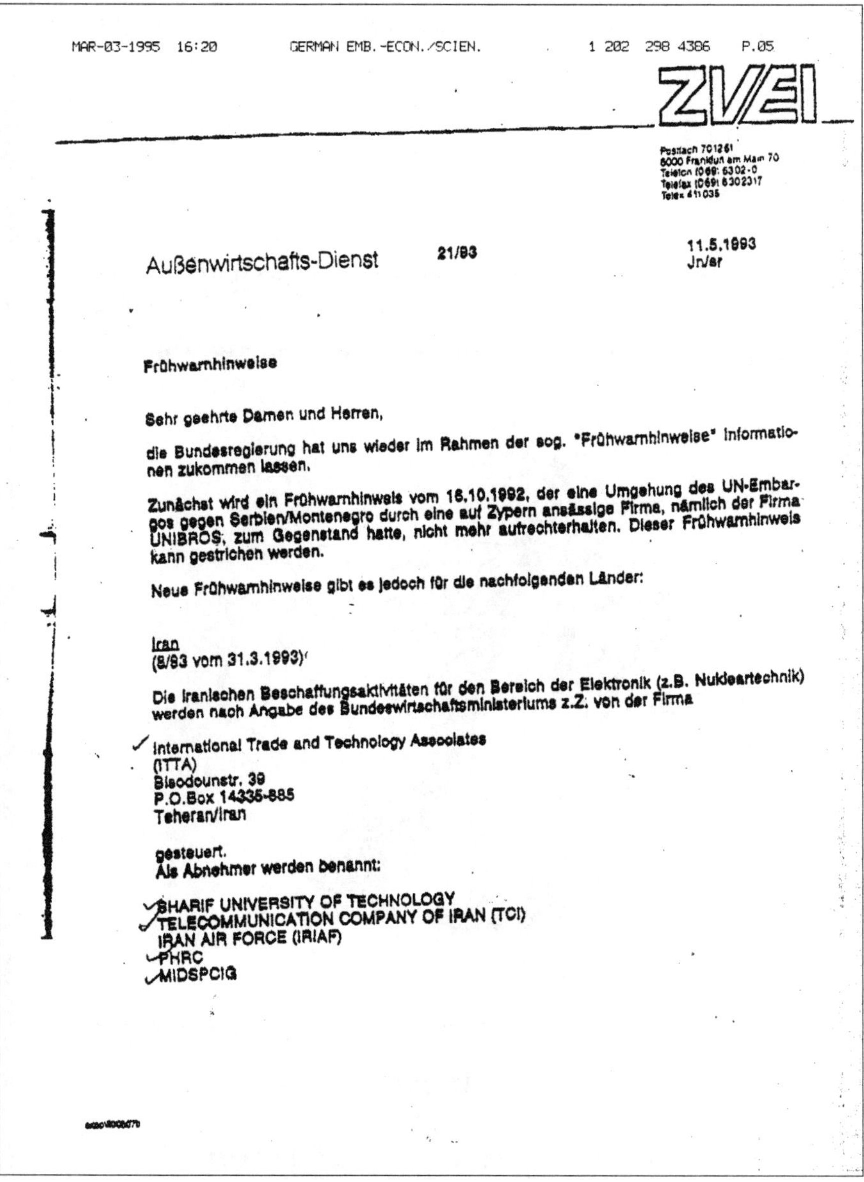

MAR-03-1995 16:20 GERMAN EMB.-ECON./SCIEN. 1 202 298 4386 P.05

ZVEI

Postfach 701261
6000 Frankfurt am Main 70
Telefon (069) 6302-0
Telefax (069) 6302317
Telex 411035

Außenwirtschafts-Dienst 21/93

11.5.1993
Jn/ar

Frühwarnhinweise

Sehr geehrte Damen und Herren,

die Bundesregierung hat uns wieder im Rahmen der sog. "Frühwarnhinweise" Informationen zukommen lassen.

Zunächst wird ein Frühwarnhinweis vom 16.10.1992, der eine Umgehung des UN-Embargos gegen Serbien/Montenegro durch eine auf Zypern ansässige Firma, nämlich der Firma UNIBROS, zum Gegenstand hatte, nicht mehr aufrechterhalten. Dieser Frühwarnhinweis kann gestrichen werden.

Neue Frühwarnhinweise gibt es jedoch für die nachfolgenden Länder:

Iran
(8/93 vom 31.3.1993)

Die iranischen Beschaffungsaktivitäten für den Bereich der Elektronik (z.B. Nukleartechnik) werden nach Angabe des Bundeswirtschaftsministeriums z.Z. von der Firma

International Trade and Technology Associates
(ITTA)
Bisodounstr. 39
P.O.Box 14335-885
Teheran/Iran

gesteuert.
Als Abnehmer werden benannt:

SHARIF UNIVERSITY OF TECHNOLOGY
TELECOMMUNICATION COMPANY OF IRAN (TCI)
IRAN AIR FORCE (IRIAF)
PHRC
MIDSPCIG

More warnings *(pages 338–339)*

The BND, Germany's foreign intelligence agency, issued this restricted-circulation report on Iran and other countries of proliferation concern in 1997. The report notes, "It is clear that Iran has been very aggressive in trying to obtain technologies related to uranium enrichment and nuclear weapons construction." In the section reproduced on the next page, the BND lists front companies used for overseas procurement, including the Dubai-based branch of the Mostazafan Foundation that I visited in 1995.

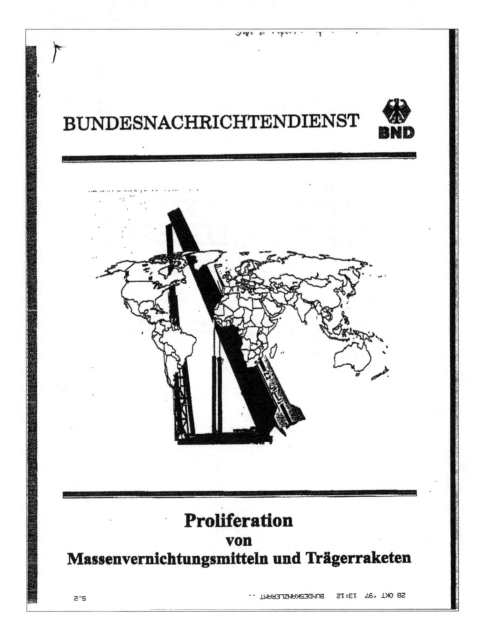

BUNDESNACHRICHTENDIENST

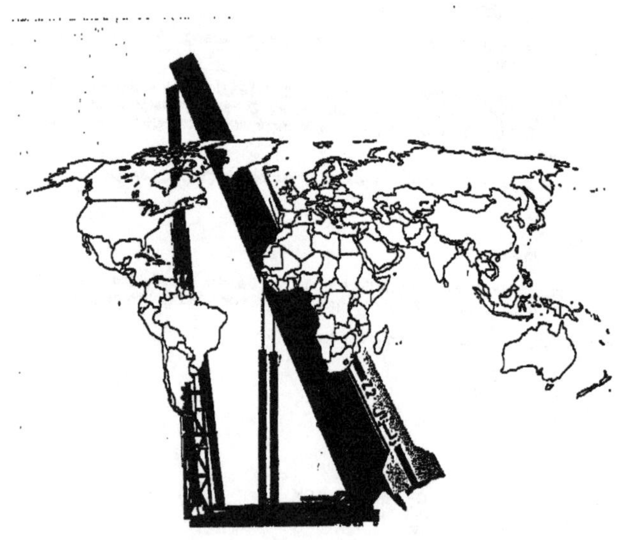

Proliferation
von
Massenvernichtungsmitteln und Trägerraketen

28 OKT '97 13:12 BUNDESKANZLERAMT .. S.2

Innerhalb der

DEFENCE INDUSTRIES ORGANIZATION (DIO)

ist die

MISSILE INDUSTRIES GROUP

zuständig für den Aufbau der Produktions- und Entwicklungsstätten. Ihr nachgeordnet sind für den Bereich der Festtreibstofftechnologie die

SHAHID BAGHERI INDUSTRIAL GROUP (SBIG)

und für die SCUD-Technologie die

SHAHID HEMAT INDUSTRIAL GROUP (SHIG).

Diese Organisationen treten auch nach außen als Einkäufer auf. Jedoch werden zunehmend unverdächtig klingende Adressen als Beschaffer verwendet, so daß ein rüstungsrelevanter Zusammenhang häufig nicht erkennbar ist.
Von besonderem Interesse für Iran sind in diesem Zusammenhang Werkzeugmaschinen, Luftfahrt-Werkstoffe, Treibstoffkomponenten, Ausrüstung zur Herstellung und Überprüfung von Navigationsgeräten (z. B. Kreisel) sowie luftatmende Kleintriebwerke.

Produktionsstätten des iranischen Raketenprogramms befinden sich in Parchin, Khorramabad, Esfahan, Mashhad, Semnan, Shiraz sowie im Großraum Teheran.

3.2.6 Die iranischen Beschaffungsorganisationen

An den iranischen Beschaffungen für Rüstungsgüter und Dual-use-Technologien und Waren sind, über die bereits erwähnten Institutionen hinaus, eine Vielzahl von Organisationen beteiligt.

Einkäufer für Konventionelle Rüstung/Ersatzteile für Rüstungsmaterial

Hier treten vor allem Firmen und Organisationen auf, die dem iranischen Verteidigungsministerium unterstehen bzw. eng mit diesem zusammenarbeiten und die primär als Beschaffer für militärische Zwecke auftreten wie z.B. das

MINISTRY OF DEFENCE AND ARMED FORCES LOGISTIC (MODAFL).

Wegen der Exportrestriktionen vieler ehemaliger Rüstungslieferanten des Iran nutzen die o.a. Organisationen auch Drittländer für ihre (Umweg-) Einkäufe.

Beschaffung von rüstungs- und proliferationsrelevanten Technologien

DEFENCE INDUSTRIES ORGANIZATION (DIO)

Für die Beschaffung proliferationsrelevanter Technologien sind Organisationen wie z. B. die DEFENCE INDUSTRIES ORGANIZATION (DIO), [auf FARSI: SAZEMANE SANAYE DEFA (SSD)] und/oder die BONAYD MOSTAZAFAN-STIFTUNG zuständig.
Unter der Leitung der DIO werden im Iran die Rüstungsbetriebe errichtet. Die DIO ist somit der Endnutzer für typische Dual-use-Technologien und -Waren.
Zur DIO gehören zahlreiche Industriebetriebe und Organisationen, deren Namen zumeist keine Zugehörigkeit zum Rüstungsbereich erkennen läßt.

BONAYD MOSTAZAFAN VE JANBAZAN STIFTUNG

Die BONAYD MOSTAZAFAN VE JANBAZAN STIFTUNG führt – neben „legalen" Einkäufen für ihre mehrere hundert Firmen im Iran – auch Beschaffungen für die ABC-Waffen und Raketenprogramme des Iran durch. Häufig werden hierfür Scheinfirmen im Iran und auch im Ausland zwischengeschaltet.

Umweglieferungen über Dubai / Vereinigte Arabische Emirate

Iran nutzt zu einem erheblichen Anteil Firmen in Dubai für die Beschaffung von Technologie. Die wichtigsten Beschaffungsfirmen in Dubai sind Tochter-unternehmen der BONAYD MOSTAZAFAN VE JANBAZAN STIFTUNG.

- 24 -

28 OKT '97 13:16 BUNDESKANZLERAMT .. S.7

Clinton ignores the warnings

Despite concern from U.S. allies and Congress, the Clinton administration actually relaxed export controls for Iran and allowed high-tech goods that previously had required a license to be shipped under G-DEST authority to be shipped license-free.

Page No. 1
09/02/93

1993 U.S. Total Exports of Selected Commodities to Iran

Code	Description	Quantity Unit	Value	Licence
** Month: January				
3002905050	TOXINS, CULTURES OF MICRO-ORGANISMS AND SIM PROD	0 X	11000	GDEST
8101930000	TUNGSTEN WIRE	13 KG	10125	GDEST
8411128000	TURBOJET TURBINES,EXC A/C, THRUST EXCEEDING 25 KN	1 NO	143428	GDEST
8414809000	AIR OR VACUUM PUMPS, NESOI	0 X	9172	GDEST2
8419600000	MACHINERY FOR LIQUEFYING AIR OR OTHER GASES	3 NO	23820	GDESTIN
8421190000	CENTRIFUGES, NESOI	2 NO	11260	GDEST
8421910000	PARTS OF CENTRIFUGES, INCLUDING CENTRIFUGAL DRYERS	0 X	5926	GDEST
8466100070	TOOL HOLDERS AND SELF-OPENING DIEHEADS, NESOI	0 X	2577	GDEST
8471200030	DIGITAL ADP MCH W CPU & INPUT/OUTPUT UNT,COLOR CRT	13 NO	47170	GDEST
8471200030	DIGITAL ADP MCH W CPU & INPUT/OUTPUT UNT,COLOR CRT	9 NO	32000	D161419
8471200030	DIGITAL ADP MCH W CPU & INPUT/OUTPUT UNT,COLOR CRT	5 NO	19195	D161419
8471200060	DIGITA[illegible] /OUTPUT,CRT EXC COLOR	[illegible]	[illegible]	[illegible]

Page No. 5
09/02/93

1993 U.S. Total Exports of Selected Commodities to Iran

Code	Description	Quantity Unit	Value	Licence
9027304080	ELEC SPECTROMETERS & SPECTROGRAPHS ETC., OPT RADTN	1 NO	3451	GDEST
9027304080	ELEC SPECTROMETERS & SPECTROGRAPHS ETC., OPT RADTN	1 NO	16258	GDEST
9027308080	SPECTROMETERS & SPECTROGRAPH,OPT RAD,NONELEC,NESOI	1 NO	8864	GDEST
9030100000	INST FOR MEASURING/DETECTING IONIZING RADIATIONS	1 NO	3170	GDEST
** Subtotal **				
		443	112978312	
** Month: June				
8414809000	AIR OR VACUUM PUMPS, NESOI	0 X	6755	GDEST
8421390040	GAS SEPARATION EQUIPMENT	3 NO	152000	
8466933000	PARTS OF METALWORKING MACH TOOLS FOR CUTTING GEARS	55 KG	6746	GDEST
8471200090	DIGITAL ADP MCH W CPU & INPUT/OUTPUT UNT, W/O CRT	14 NO	45400	GDEST
9027304040	SPECTROPHOTOMETERS USING OPTICAL RAD NONELECTRICAL	1 NO	3119	GDEST
9027304080	ELEC SPECTROMETERS & SPECTROGRAPHS ETC., OPT RADTN	2 NO	54510	GDEST
9027304080	ELEC SPECTROMETERS & SPECTROGRAPHS ETC., OPT RADTN	1 NO	35600	GDEST
9027304080	ELEC SPECTROMETERS & SPECTROGRAPHS ETC., OPT RADTN	18 NO	65330	GDEST
9027308020	SPECTROSCOPES USING OPTICAL RADIATIONS, NONELEC	1 NO	23833	GDEST
9030100000	INST FOR MEASURING/DETECTING IONIZING RADIATIONS	1 NO	173818	DGEST
9030200000	CATHODE-RAY OSCILLOSCOPES&CATHODE-RAY OSCILLOGRAPH	1 NO	8500	GDEST
** Subtotal **				
		97	575611	
*** Total ***				
			178668028	

Clinton's soft approach

This partially declassified State Department cable, dated April 15, 1994, shows how the Clinton administration unwisely allowed "dual-use" exports to Iran until congressional pressure forced the White House to impose a total trade embargo in May 1995. It was among scores of documents I obtained from the State Department in 2004 under a Freedom of Information Act request filed eight years earlier.

UNCLASSIFIED
RELEASED IN PART
B1, 1.4(D), 1.4(B)

Current Class: CONFIDENTIAL Page: 1
Current Handling: n/a
Document Number: 1994STATE099541 Channel: n/a

FR24

<<<>>>

PAGE 01 STATE 099541 150610Z
ORIGIN NEA-01

INFO LOG-00 AF 01 AMAD 01 ARA-01 CIAE-00 SMEC-00 COME-00
CEB-02 C-01 OASY-00 EAP-01 EB-01 EUR-01 EXIM-01
R-01 FRB-01 TEDE 00 INR 00 IO-16 ADS-00 MOFM-04
MOF-03 NSAE 00 OIG-04 P-01 SS-00 STR-01 TRSE-00
SA-01 /043R

DRAFTED BY: NEA/NGA:CPHENZEL:CPH
APPROVED BY: [redacted] B1
NEA:MRPARRIS NEA/NGA:DCLITT
[redacted] EB/IFD/OMA:EBENJAMINSON
E:BLOWRY P:RGRENIER
EUR/RPE:YWONG
------------------3C28DB 150611Z /38

P 150604Z APR 94
FM SECSTATE WASHDC
INFO IRAN COLLECTIVE PRIORITY
ALL EUROPEAN UNION POST COLLECTIVE

C O N F I D E N T I A L STATE 099541

E.O. 12356: DECL: OADR
TAGS: EFIN, IR, [redacted]
SUBJECT: OFFICIAL TRADE CREDITS TO IRAN

REF: [redacted]

CONFIDENTIAL

PAGE 02 STATE 099541 150610Z
1. CONFIDENTIAL - ENTIRE TEXT.

[redacted] B1

6. PLEASE MAKE THE FOLLOWING POINTS TO THE [redacted] AT AN APPROPRIATE LEVEL:

-- AS YOU MAY BE AWARE, THE UNITED STATES DOES NOT OPPOSE EXPORTS TO IRAN AS LONG AS THE PRODUCTS DO NOT HAVE POTENTIAL MILITARY OR DUAL USES. (U.S. EXPORTS TO IRAN IN 1993 WERE WORTH APPROXIMATELY USD 616 MILLION.)

The United States helps Iran

The Commerce Department allowed U.S. companies to ship spectrometers and other scientific instruments used in uranium enrichment to the Education Research Institute in Lavizan—a site the International Atomic Energy Agency (IAEA) now suspects housed a clandestine uranium enrichment plant during the 1990s.

U.S. DEPARTMENT OF COMMERCE — BUREAU OF THE CENSUS — INTERNATIONAL TRADE ADMINISTRATION

FORM 7525-V (1-1-88) **SHIPPER'S EXPORT DECLARATION** OMB No. 0607-0018

1a. EXPORTER (Name and address including ZIP code)
Thermo Jarrell Ash Corporation
8E Forge Parkway
Franklin, MA
ZIP CODE 02038

2/26/93

2. DATE OF EXPORTATION: 02 March 1993

3. BILL OF LADING/AIR WAYBILL NO.: 64063873/082-5727 3952

b. EXPORTER EIN (IRS) NO.: 04-2905275

c. PARTIES TO TRANSACTION: ☐ Related ☒ Non-related

4a. ULTIMATE CONSIGNEE
Education and Research Institute
Lavizan, Teharan, Iran

b. INTERMEDIATE CONSIGNEE
ATRANEF, BRUCARGO - BLDG. 739
B-1931 ZAVENTEN, BELGIUM

5. FORWARDING AGENT
FRITZ COMPANIES, INC.
440 Mc CLELLAN HIGHWAY
E. BOSTON, MA 02128

6. POINT (STATE) OF ORIGIN OR FTZ NO.: MA

7. COUNTRY OF ULTIMATE DESTINATION: IRAN

8. LOADING PIER (VESSEL ONLY): 04/17

9. MODE OF TRANSPORT (Specify): AIR

10. EXPORTING CARRIER: SN

11. PORT OF EXPORT: BOS

12. PORT OF UNLOADING (Vessel and air only): BRU

13. CONTAINERIZED (Vessel only): ☐ Yes ☐ No

14. SCHEDULE B DESCRIPTION OF COMMODITIES
15. MARKS, NOS., AND KINDS OF PACKAGES
(Use columns 17-19)

D/F (16)	SCHEDULE B NUMBER (17)	CHECK DIGIT	QUANTITY - SCHEDULE B UNIT(S) (18)	SHIPPING WEIGHT (Kilos) (19)	VALUE (U.S. dollars, omit cents) (Selling price or cost if not sold) (20)
	5 CARTONS				
	SPECTROMETER				
D	9027.30.4080	9	1 EA.	KGS. 1183.0	$170,000.

21. VALIDATED LICENSE NO./GENERAL LICENSE SYMBOL

22. ECCN (When required)

23. Duly authorized officer or employee — The exporter authorizes the forwarder named above to act as forwarding agent for export control and customs purposes.

24. I certify that all statements made and all information contained herein are true and correct and that I have read and understand the instructions for preparation of this document, set forth in the "Correct Way to Fill Out the Shipper's Export Declaration." I understand that civil and criminal penalties, including forfeiture and sale, may be imposed for making false or fraudulent statements herein, failing to provide the requested information or for violation of U.S. laws on exportation (13 U.S.C. Sec. 305; 22 U.S.C. Sec. 401; 18 U.S.C. Sec. 1001; 50 U.S.C. App. 2410).

Signature

Title: INTL. SALES ADMIN.

Date: 2/26/93

Confidential - For use solely for official purposes authorized by the Secretary of Commerce (13 U.S.C. 301 (g)).

Export shipments are subject to inspection by U.S. Customs Service and/or Office of Export Enforcement.

25. AUTHENTICATION (When required)

This form may be printed by private parties provided it conforms to the official form. For sale by Superintendent of Documents, Government Printing Office, Washington, D.C. 20402, and local Customs District Directors. The "Correct Way to Fill Out the Shipper's Export Declaration" is available from the Bureau of the Census, Washington, D.C. 20233.

The same old mistakes

The Commerce Department also turned a blind eye when a U.S. company declared that it was shipping radiation detection equipment to the Tehran office of a steel plant located hundreds of miles away, near Isfahan. Iran unilaterally destroyed similar equipment in Lavizan in 2004.

U.S. DEPARTMENT OF COMMERCE - BUREAU OF THE CENSUS - INTERNATIONAL TRADE ADMINISTRATION

FORM 7525-V (1-1-86)

SHIPPER'S EXPORT DECLARATION

1a. EXPORTER (Name and address including ZIP code)
DOSIMETER CORPORATION
11286 GROOMS ROAD
CINCINNATI, OHIO
ZIP CODE 45242

2. DATE OF EXPORTATION 1-18-93

3. BILL OF LADING/AIR WAYBILL NO. 32623916

b. EXPORTER'S EIN (IRS) NUMBER 31-0749263

c. PARTIES TO TRANSACTION ☐ Related ☒ Non-related

4a. ULTIMATE CONSIGNEE
MOBARAKEH STEEL COMPLEX, TEHRAN
~~XXXXXX~~ OFFICE, AVE. KHALED SLAMBOLY,
STREET 11, APT. 28, TEHRAN, IRAN

5. FORWARDING AGENT
BURLINGTON AIR EXPRESS INC.
3625 O'HARA ROAD
ERLANGER, KY 41018

6. POINT (STATE) OF ORIGIN OR FTZ NO. OHIO

7. COUNTRY OF ULTIMATE DESTINATION IRAN

9. MODE OF TRANSPORT (Specify) AIR

10. EXPORTING CARRIER BURLINGTON

14. SCHEDULE B DESCRIPTION OF COMMODITIES

15. MARKS, NOS., AND KINDS OF PACKAGES

SCHEDULE B NUMBER	QUANTITY	SHIPPING WEIGHT	VALUE (U.S. dollars)
9030.10.00003 RADIATION DETECTION EQUIPMENT	CARTON	25LBS	$7,990.00

21. VALIDATED LICENSE NO./GENERAL LICENSE SYMBOL G-DEST

22. ECCN (When required)

23. Duly authorized officer or employee — The exporter authorizes the forwarder named above to act as forwarding agent for export control and customs purposes.

24. I certify that all statements made and all information contained herein are true and correct and that I have read and understand the instructions for preparation of this document, set forth in the "Correct Way to Fill Out the Shipper's Export Declaration." I understand that civil and criminal penalties, including forfeiture and sale, may be imposed for making false or fraudulent statements herein, failing to provide the requested information or for violation of U.S. laws on exportation (13 U.S.C. Sec. 305; 22 U.S.C. Sec. 401; 18 U.S.C. Sec. 1001; 50 U.S.C. App. 2410)

Signature

Confidential - For use solely for official purposes authorized by the Secretary of Commerce (13 U.S.C. 301 (g)).

Title

Export shipments are subject to inspection by U.S. Customs Service and/or Office of Export Enforcement.

Date

25. AUTHENTICATION (When required)

The "Correct Way to Fill Out the Shipper's Export Declaration" is available from the Bureau of the Census, Washington, D.C. 20233.

The Iran lobby

The Clinton administration received support for its efforts to resume trade relations with Iran from major U.S. oil companies, which mounted a powerful lobbying campaign in favor of lifting U.S. sanctions. This ad appeared in the *Washington Times* on May 5, 1999.

Mixed signals. Mixed feelings.

April 28 was a give-and-take day for U.S. interests in a key part of the world—the Caspian.

It began with the Administration's announcement to lift the ban on the sale of food and medicine to Iran, Libya and Sudan. It was the right decision.

For one, the move sends a positive signal to Iran—a nation of strategic importance in the Middle East and Central Asia. It's an important first step toward rapprochement between our countries. Change is stirring in Iran. During the last two years, it has shown a new openness to the West and the forces of democracy. As we said several weeks ago, positive gestures from the U.S., like the sale of grain, are needed to demonstrate that our two nations can find common ground.

The decision also marks a shift in thinking on the use of U.S. unilateral sanctions. Both the Administration and Congress are rethinking sanctions and examining their effectiveness, with an eye to some reforms. We believe this is significant progress.

That April day also brought disappointment. The Administration denied Mobil's application for a license to swap a very limited amount of oil with Iran. We had submitted our application, as permitted by the president's Executive Order, so that we could move our crude oil out of the Caspian region, which lacks adequate pipelines, by swapping Turkmen oil for Iranian oil.

This route would have made our job of exporting cheaper and easier. And it would have brought meaningful advantage to our partner—the Turkmen government. But more importantly, we thought use of a southern export route supported the U.S. goal of strengthening the independence of the Caspian region by timely development of its oil resources. The denial of our request, we believe, sends a negative signal to those governments.

Two steps forward. One step back. At the end of the day, how did we feel? Pleased for the food that will be allowed to go where it's needed, but sad that the U.S. government missed the chance to help its Caspian friends.

Mobil The energy to make a difference.

The wall *(pages 345–346)*

This 1995 memorandum from Bill Clinton's deputy attorney general, Jamie S. Gorelick, created a "wall" between the FBI and the CIA that hampered their ability to share information on terrorism cases and arguably blinded both agencies to the growing threat from al-Qaeda before 9/11. Gorelick was a member of the 9/11 Commission when Attorney General John Ashcroft declassified and released the memo during sworn testimony.

~~SECRET~~

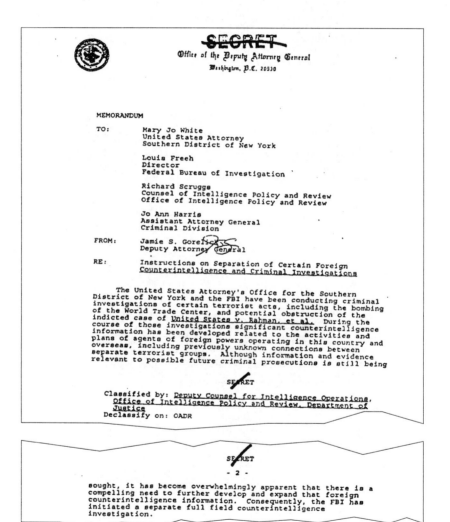

Office of the Deputy Attorney General
Washington, D.C. 20530

MEMORANDUM

TO: Mary Jo White
United States Attorney
Southern District of New York

Louis Freeh
Director
Federal Bureau of Investigation

Richard Scruggs
Counsel of Intelligence Policy and Review
Office of Intelligence Policy and Review

Jo Ann Harris
Assistant Attorney General
Criminal Division

FROM: Jamie S. Gorelick
Deputy Attorney General

RE: Instructions on Separation of Certain Foreign Counterintelligence and Criminal Investigations

The United States Attorney's Office for the Southern District of New York and the FBI have been conducting criminal investigations of certain terrorist acts, including the bombing of the World Trade Center, and potential obstruction of the indicted case of United States v. Rahman, et al. During the course of those investigations significant counterintelligence information has been developed related to the activities and plans of agents of foreign powers operating in this country and overseas, including previously unknown connections between separate terrorist groups. Although information and evidence relevant to possible future criminal prosecutions is still being

SECRET

Classified by: Deputy Counsel for Intelligence Operations, Office of Intelligence Policy and Review, Department of Justice
Declassify on: OADR

SECRET

- 2 -

sought, it has become overwhelmingly apparent that there is a compelling need to further develop and expand that foreign counterintelligence information. Consequently, the FBI has initiated a separate full field counterintelligence investigation.

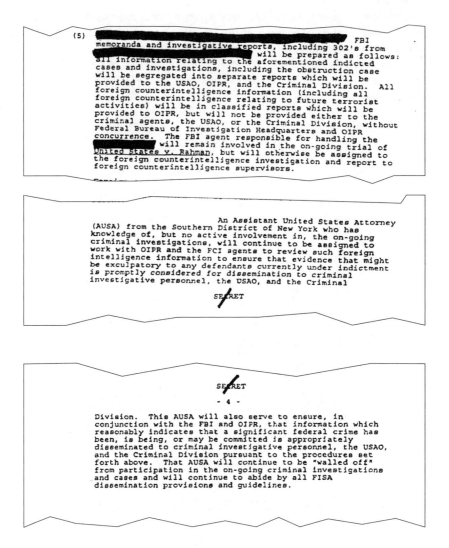

(5) [redacted] FBI memoranda and investigative reports, including 302's from [redacted] will be prepared as follows: all information relating to the aforementioned indicted cases and investigations, including the obstruction case will be segregated into separate reports which will be provided to the USAO, OIPR, and the Criminal Division. All foreign counterintelligence information (including all foreign counterintelligence relating to future terrorist activities) will be in classified reports which will be provided to OIPR, but will not be provided either to the criminal agents, the USAO, or the Criminal Division, without Federal Bureau of Investigation Headquarters and OIPR concurrence. The FBI agent responsible for handling the [redacted] will remain involved in the on-going trial of *United States v. Rahman*, but will otherwise be assigned to the foreign counterintelligence investigation and report to foreign counterintelligence supervisors.

An Assistant United States Attorney (AUSA) from the Southern District of New York who has knowledge of, but no active involvement in, the on-going criminal investigations, will continue to be assigned to work with OIPR and the FCI agents to review such foreign intelligence information to ensure that evidence that might be exculpatory to any defendants currently under indictment is promptly considered for dissemination to criminal investigative personnel, the USAO, and the Criminal

SECRET

SECRET

- 4 -

Division. This AUSA will also serve to ensure, in conjunction with the FBI and OIPR, that information which reasonably indicates that a significant federal crime has been, is being, or may be committed is appropriately disseminated to criminal investigative personnel, the USAO, and the Criminal Division pursuant to the procedures set forth above. That AUSA will continue to be "walled off" from participation in the on-going criminal investigations and cases and will continue to abide by all FISA dissemination provisions and guidelines.

The money trail

The Clinton administration repeatedly lied to Congress in asserting that the Iranian government had no significant assets in the United States. In fact, the Federal Reserve, the Treasury Department, and the IRS were regulating the activities of Iranian government banks and their subsidiaries. This listing shows the activity of Iranian government banks holding correspondent accounts in New York for the month of April 1995. In that month alone, three banks carried out 131 wire transfers for amounts in excess of $1 million. The month before, Bank Melli Iran reported doing *$382 million* of business with the Sanwa Bank California.

Iranian Accounts

Account Activity for Month of April, 1995

							Totals			Daily Averages		
Bank	Branch	Account No.	Total Wire Dr's	Avg. Daily Wire Dr's	Total Checks	Avg. Daily Checks	Wire Dr's 0-$10m*	Wire Dr's $10m-$1mm	Wire Dr's $1mm+ **	Wire Dr's 0-$10m	Wire Dr's $10m-$1m	Wire Dr's $1mm+
Saderat	New York	8033025905	691	35	138	7	276	371	44	14	2	1
	New York	8026114293	5	0	12	1	2	3	0	0	0	0
	Dubai	8900052856	683	34	0	0	557	125	1	28	0	1
Sepah	New York	8026115001	40	2	4	0	13	12	15	1	1	0
	Tehran	8033040939	24	1	0	0	21	2	1	1	0	0
Melli	New York	8033025854	145	7	329	16	87	7	51	4	3	0
	New York	8026019932	892	45	0	0	404	474	14	20	1	1
	Dubai	8033023627	16	1	10	1	4	7	5	0	0	0
	Tehran	8033041315	0	0	0	0	0	0	0	0	0	0
	Tehran	8900111161	13	1	0	0	12	1	0	1	0	0
		TOTALS:	2,509	125	493	25	1376	1002	131	69	7	3

Major assets

The Mostazafan Foundation, successor to the New York branch of the Pahlavi Foundation, owned substantial properties in the United States that victims of Iranian-government terrorist attacks have tried—unsuccessfully—to attach. This listing, prepared in 1995 by a U.S. government agency investigating Mostazafan, showed direct U.S. holdings valued at more than $124 million.

PROPERTY HELD DIRECTLY BY THE MOSTAZAFAN FOUNDATION

Address	Use	Total value
(a) 4836 Marconi Ave Carmichael, CA	School	$ 237,374
(b) 8100 Jeb Stuart Rd Montgomery Co, MD	Church with Resident	$ 321,570
(b) 8101 Jeb Stuart Rd Montgomery Co, MD	Residential	$ 4,214,230
(b) 12010 Seven Locks Rd Montgomery Co, MD	Residential Church	$ 210,500
(b) 7917 Montrose Rd Montgomery Co, MD	Residential Church	$ 143,740
(c) Mt. Airy Road Croton-On-Hudson, New York	Residential, Vacant Lot	$ 1,100*
(d) 11 Georgia Lane Croton-On-Hudson,New York	One-family Residence	$ 14,375*
(e) 839-57 3rd Ave NY, NY	Office Bldg	$ 48,300,800
(f) 231 Brooksite Dr Smithtown, New York	Residential Vacant Land	$ 800*
(g) 5511 Queens Blvd Queens, New York	Warehouse	$ 1,800,000
(h) 2313 S. Voss Harris Co., Texas	Office Bldg	$ 3,226,230
(i) 4300 Aldie Rd Prince William Co, VA	Vacant Land	$ 829,400
(i) 4204 Aldie Rd Prince William Co, VA	Vacant Land	$ 270,100
Total Value		**$ 59,570,219**

PROPERTY HELD BY 650 FIFTH AVENUE ASSOCIATES (CONTROLLED BY THE MOSTAZAFAN FOUNDATION

Address	Use	Total value
642-50 5th Ave, NY NY	Office Bldg	**$ 64,500,000**

Clinton's grand bargain

As part of his secret outreach to the mullahs in Tehran, President Clinton issued this Presidential Determination on October 21, 1998, blocking the efforts of U.S. victims of terrorism from collecting compensation or damages from Iranian government assets in the United States.

THE WHITE HOUSE
Office of the Press Secretary

For Immediate Release
October 21, 1998

October 21, 1998

Presidential Determination
No. 99-1

MEMORANDUM FOR THE SECRETARY OF STATE
THE SECRETARY OF THE TREASURY

SUBJECT: Determination to Waive Requirements Relating to Blocked Property of Terrorist-List States

By the authority vested in me as President by the Constitution and laws of the United States of America, including section 117 of the Treasury and General Government Appropriations Act, 1999, as contained in the Omnibus Consolidated and Emergency Supple-mental Appropriations Act, 1999 (approved October 21, 1998), I hereby determine that the requirements of section 117, including the requirement that any property with respect to which financial transactions are prohibited or regulated pursuant to section 5(b) of the Trading with the Enemy Act (50 U.S.C. App. 5(b)), section 620(a) of the Foreign Assistance Act of 1961 (22 U.S.C. 2370(a)), sections 202 and 203 of the International Emergency Economic Powers Act (50 U.S.C. 1701-1702), and proclamations, orders, regulations, and licenses issued pursuant thereto, be subject to execution or attachment in aid of execution of any judgment relating to a claim for which a foreign state claiming such property is not immune from the jurisdiction of courts of the United States or of the States under section 1605(a)(7) of title 28, United States Code, would impede the ability of the President to conduct foreign policy in the interest of national security and would, in particular, impede the effectiveness of such prohibitions and regulations upon financial transactions, and, therefore, pursuant to section 117(d), I hereby waive the requirements of section 117 in the interest of national security.

The Secretary of State is authorized and directed to publish this determination in the Federal Register.

WILLIAM J. CLINTON

Iran's deadly reach *(pages 350–351)*
The Khobar Towers indictment, unsealed by the Justice Department in June 2001, clearly implicates Iran's Revolutionary Guards and the MOIS in planning and funding the attack that killed nineteen U.S. servicemen in Dhahran, Saudi Arabia, in June 1996.

UNITED STATES DISTRICT COURT
EASTERN DISTRICT OF VIRGINIA
ALEXANDRIA DIVISION

	)	
	)	
UNITED STATES OF AMERICA	)	CRIMINAL NO: 01- ______ -A
	)	
	)	Conspiracy to Kill United States Nationals
-v-	)	(18 U.S.C. § 2332(b))
	)	(Count One)
	)	
AHMED AL-MUGHASSIL, aka "Abu Omran,"	)	Conspiracy to Murder United States Employees
	)	(18 U.S.C. §§ 1114, 1117)
(Counts 1-46)	)	(Count Two)
ALI AL-HOURI,	)	
(Counts 1-46)	)	Conspiracy to Use Weapons of Mass Destruction
HANI AL-SAYEGH,	)	Against United States Nationals
(Counts 1-46)	)	(18 U.S.C. §§ 2332a(a)(1), (a)(3))

INDICTMENT
June 2001 TERM – AT ALEXANDRIA

THE GRAND JURY CHARGES THAT:

COUNT ONE

Conspiracy to Kill United States Nationals

Introduction

Saudi Hizballah

1. From some time in the 1980s until the date of the filing of this Indictment, Hizballah, or "Party of God," was the name used by a number of related terrorist organizations operating in Saudi Arabia, Lebanon, Kuwait, and Bahrain, among other places. These Hizballah organizations were inspired, supported, and directed by elements of the Iranian government. Saudi Hizballah, also known as Hizballah Al-Hijaz, was a terrorist organization that operated primarily in the Kingdom of Saudi Arabia and that promoted, among other things, the use of violence against nationals and property of the United States located in Saudi Arabia. Because Saudi Hizballah was an outlaw organization in the Kingdom of Saudi Arabia, its members frequently met and trained in Lebanon, Syria, or Iran.

4. The "military wing" of Saudi Hizballah was headed at all relevant times by AHMED AL-MUGHASSIL, aka "Abu Omran," a native of Qatif, in the Eastern Province of Saudi Arabia. In his role as military commander, AL-MUGHASSIL was in charge of directing terrorist attacks against American interests in Saudi Arabia. AL-MUGHASSIL was actively involved in recruiting young Saudi Shi'ite men to join the ranks of Hizballah; arranging for those men to undergo military training at Hizballah camps in Lebanon and Iran; directing those men in surveillance of potential targets for attack by Hizballah; and planning and supervising terrorist attacks.

Hizballah Seeks a Target

16. In about 1993, AL-MUGHASSIL instructed AL-QASSAB, AL-YACOUB, and AL-HOURI to begin surveillance of Americans in Saudi Arabia. As a result, AL-QASSAB and AL-YACOUB spent three months in Riyadh conducting surveillance of American targets. AL-SAYEGH joined them during this operation. They produced reports, which were passed to AL-MUGHASSIL, then on to Saudi Hizballah chief AL-NASSER, and to officials in Iran. At the end of their mission, AL-MUGHASSIL came in person to meet with them and review their work.

18. In early 1994, AL-QASSAB began conducting surveillance, focusing on American and other foreign sites in the Eastern Province of Saudi Arabia, an area that includes Khobar. He prepared written reports, which were passed to AL-NASSER and Iranian officials.

19. In about Fall 1994, AL-MARHOUN, RAMADAN, and AL-MU'ALEM began watching American sites in Eastern Saudi Arabia at AL-MUGHASSIL's direction. They passed their reports to AL-MUGHASSIL, who was then spending most of his time in Beirut, Lebanon. At about the same time, AL-BAHAR began conducting surveillance in Saudi Arabia at the direction of an Iranian military officer.

Funding bin Laden

Iran also had business ties with Osama bin Laden going back to the early 1990s. This document, presented by the opposition Iranian People's Fedaii Guerrillas to the United Nations Security Council in 1996, details the purchase of Iraqi oil products smuggled through Iran by Iranian Revolutionary Guards in violation of UN sanctions. The ultimate purchaser was the Al Shamal Islamic Bank in Sudan, in which bin Laden had an ownership stake.

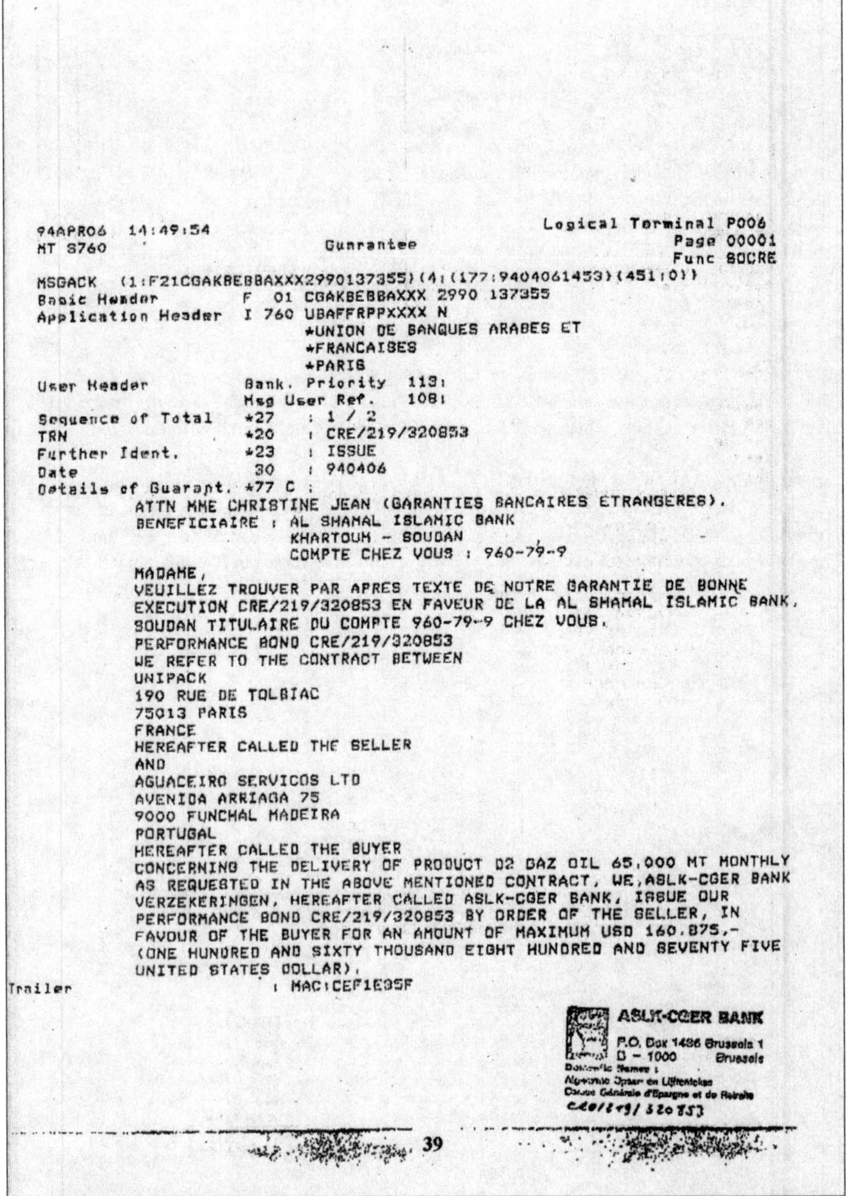

94APR06 14:49:54 Logical Terminal P006
MT S760 Guarantee Page 00001
Func SOCRE
MSGACK (1:F21CGAKBEBBAXXX2990137355)(4:(177:9404061453)(451:0))
Basic Header F 01 CGAKBEBBAXXX 2990 137355
Application Header I 760 UBAFFRPPXXXX N
*UNION DE BANQUES ARABES ET
*FRANCAISES
*PARIS
User Header Bank. Priority 113:
Msg User Ref. 108:
Sequence of Total *27 : 1 / 2
TRN *20 : CRE/219/320853
Further Ident. *23 : ISSUE
Date 30 : 940406
Details of Guarant. *77 C :
ATTN MME CHRISTINE JEAN (GARANTIES BANCAIRES ETRANGERES).
BENEFICIAIRE : AL SHAMAL ISLAMIC BANK
KHARTOUM - SOUDAN
COMPTE CHEZ VOUS : 960-79-9
MADAME,
VEUILLEZ TROUVER PAR APRES TEXTE DE NOTRE GARANTIE DE BONNE
EXECUTION CRE/219/320853 EN FAVEUR DE LA AL SHAMAL ISLAMIC BANK,
SOUDAN TITULAIRE DU COMPTE 960-79-9 CHEZ VOUS.
PERFORMANCE BOND CRE/219/320853
WE REFER TO THE CONTRACT BETWEEN
UNIPACK
190 RUE DE TOLBIAC
75013 PARIS
FRANCE
HEREAFTER CALLED THE SELLER
AND
AGUACEIRO SERVICOS LTD
AVENIDA ARRIAGA 75
9000 FUNCHAL MADEIRA
PORTUGAL
HEREAFTER CALLED THE BUYER
CONCERNING THE DELIVERY OF PRODUCT D2 GAZ OIL 65.000 MT MONTHLY
AS REQUESTED IN THE ABOVE MENTIONED CONTRACT, WE,ASLK-CGER BANK
VERZEKERINGEN, HEREAFTER CALLED ASLK-CGER BANK, ISSUE OUR
PERFORMANCE BOND CRE/219/320853 BY ORDER OF THE SELLER, IN
FAVOUR OF THE BUYER FOR AN AMOUNT OF MAXIMUM USD 160.875,-
(ONE HUNDRED AND SIXTY THOUSAND EIGHT HUNDRED AND SEVENTY FIVE
UNITED STATES DOLLAR).
Trailer : MAC:CEF1E35F

ASLK-CGER BANK
P.O. Box 1436 Brussels 1
B - 1000 Brussels
Caisse Générale d'Epargne et de Retraite
CRE/219/320853

39

The Moscow connection

This chilling 1995 study by the official think tank of the General Staff of the Russian Federation, obtained by Congressman Curt Weldon and translated at his request by the CIA, revealed that Russian strategists would readily arm Iran with long-range ballistic missiles and even nuclear weapons.

Institute of Defense Studies

INSTITUTE OF DEFENSE STUDIES

INOBIS

"APPROVED"

GENERAL DIRECTOR, INOBIS
DOCTOR OF TECHNICAL SCIENCES
PROFESSOR /s/ V. M. SURIKOV

CONCEPTUAL PROVISIONS OF A STRATEGY FOR COUNTERING THE MAIN EXTERNAL THREATS TO RUSSIAN FEDERATION NATIONAL SECURITY

MOSCOW **OCTOBER 1995**

An analysis shows that above all the United States is the main external force potentially capable of creating a threat to RF military security and to Russia's economic and political interests abroad and of exerting substantial influence on the economic and political situation within Russia and on Russia's mutual relations with former USSR republics. As a rule, the United States implements its policy in the Russian direction in coordination with other Western countries, Israel, and Japan. "Assistance to processes of democratization and of transition to a market economy with the help of the West and in

Finally, in case of a total break in relations with the United States, Russia has such convincing arguments for it as the nuclear-missile potential and the threat of proliferation of weapons of mass destruction around the world, which with skillful tactics can play the role of a kind of trading card. And in case Russia is persistently driven into a corner, then it will be possible to undertake to sell military nuclear and missile technologies to such countries as Iran and Iraq, and to Algeria after Islamic forces arrive in power there. Moreover, Russia's direct military alliance with some of the countries mentioned also should not be excluded, above all with Iran, within the framework of which a Russian troop contingent and tactical nuclear weapons could be stationed on the shores of the Persian Gulf and the Strait of Hormuz.

The Russian supply line

On July 13, 1999, I testified before the House Science Committee, presenting details on some twenty Russian companies that provided material assistance to Iran's long-range ballistic missile programs.

Russian Assistance to Iran's missile programs

Testimony by **Kenneth R. Timmerman**
before the Subcommittee on Space and Aeronautics of the
Committee on Science
U.S. House of Representatives
Washington, DC
July 13, 1999

Appendix 1: Russian suppliers of missile technology to Iran
(as compiled from public sources by the Middle East Data Project, Inc.

I. Entities providing design assistance and general purpose missile-related technologies.

1) Central Aerohydrodynamic Institute, a.k.a TsAGI.

TSAGI contracted in 1997 to build a wind tunnel in Iran, for use in aeronautical research projects. Their Iranian client was the Shahid Hemat Industrial Group, the Defense Industry Organization's liquid fuel missile development group. TSAGI also agreed to manufacture model missiles and to create missile design software for the Iranians.[1]

The State Department's International Science and Technology Center in Moscow was planning to fund a TsAGI project involving new aircraft design at the same time TsAGI engineers were traveling to Iran to work on Iranian missile projects. Funding was only withdrawn when TsAGI's Iran connection was leaked to the Washington Times.[2]

2) Bauman Technical University.

This is Moscow's leading aerospace research institute, something of the Russian equivalent of MIT. (It also happens to be the alma mater of Russia Space Agency boss Yuri Koptev). According to leaked U.S and Israeli intelligence reports, Bauman is helping the Iranians master production of the highly-corrosive liquid fuel—red fuming nitric acid—and the specialty steels needed to contain it.[3] U.S. missile experts say that without this steel, Iran will be unable to keep the missiles fueled and ready for more than a few hours at a time.[4] Bauman designers are also said to be helping Iran to adapt SS-4 technology to the North Korean Nodong missile which served as the basis for Iran's Shahab-3 missile.[5]

3) Baltic States Technological University.

The government of the Russian Federation has opened the doors to Iran of this formerly state-run institute in Saint Petersburg, which helped develop ICBM rocket motors during the Cold War. BSTU has contracted with the Shahid Bagheri facility in Tehran, and the DIO's Sanam College, to help Iran design long-range solid fuel rocket boosters. Both of these are attached to Department 140, the Missile Industries Group of DIO.[6] President Clinton imposed sanctions on BSTU by Executive Order on July 28, 1998.

4) Moscow Aviation Institute.

Iranian President Hashemi-Rafsanjani was the first to acknowledge the assistance from MAI in a little- noticed speech in February 1997, when he noted that MAI was providing aerospace instructors to Sheikh Bahaei University in Isfahan.[7] In November 1997, MAI was identified as being engaged in training Iranian "students" in aeronautics and ballistic design.[8] MAI had been receiving Nunn-Lugar funding for a project to develop high-tech plastic joints for the aerospace industry, but this was cut off in March 1998 because of MAI's Iran connections.[9]

The threat is real

Above: Iran's Shahab-3 missile being prepared for a test launch by a Revolutionary Guards missile unit. Note the Mercedes-Benz tractor for the missile launch vehicle. *(Photograph from the IRGC archives, provided to the author by Hamid Reza Zakeri). Below:* The area around Iran's nuclear research center in Isfahan, seen from the air in 1993. *(Photograph copyright © 2005 by Kenneth R. Timmerman)*

The warehouse

Iran claims the United States is holding $17 billion of its assets, including weapons and spare parts that fill a massive Victory Van warehouse near Washington's Dulles International Airport in Sterling, Virginia.

(Photograph copyright © 2000 by Kenneth R. Timmerman)

Shredding the evidence

In an astonishing admission to lawyers representing victims of Iranian government terrorism, the Treasury Department's Office of Foreign Assets Control reported in June 2000 that it had shredded hundreds of documents on Iran's assets in the United States. The shredding may have prevented the assets from being seized and handed over to the victims.

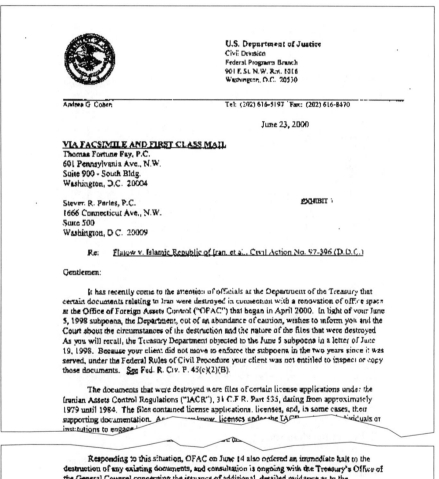

U.S. Department of Justice
Civil Division
Federal Programs Branch
901 E St. N.W. Rm. 1016
Washington, D.C. 20530

Andrea G. Cohen — Tel: (202) 616-5197 Fax: (202) 616-8470

June 23, 2000

<u>VIA FACSIMILE AND FIRST CLASS MAIL</u>
Thomas Fortune Fay, P.C.
601 Pennsylvania Ave., N.W.
Suite 900 - South Bldg.
Washington, D.C. 20004

Steven R. Perles, P.C.
1666 Connecticut Ave., N.W.
Suite 500
Washington, D.C. 20009

EXHIBIT

Re: <u>Flatow v. Islamic Republic of Iran, et al., Civil Action No. 97-396 (D.D.C.)</u>

Gentlemen:

It has recently come to the attention of officials at the Department of the Treasury that certain documents relating to Iran were destroyed in connection with a renovation of office space at the Office of Foreign Assets Control ("OFAC") that began in April 2000. In light of your June 5, 1998 subpoena, the Department, out of an abundance of caution, wishes to inform you and the Court about the circumstances of the destruction and the nature of the files that were destroyed. As you will recall, the Treasury Department objected to the June 5 subpoena in a letter of June 19, 1998. Because your client did not move to enforce the subpoena in the two years since it was served, under the Federal Rules of Civil Procedure your client was not entitled to inspect or copy those documents. <u>See</u> Fed. R. Civ. P. 45(c)(2)(B).

The documents that were destroyed were files of certain license applications under the Iranian Assets Control Regulations ("IACR"), 31 C.F.R. Part 535, dating from approximately 1979 until 1984. The files contained license applications, licenses, and, in some cases, their supporting documentation. A... know, licenses under the IAC... individuals or institutions to engage...

Responding to this situation, OFAC on June 14 also ordered an immediate halt to the destruction of any existing documents, and consultation is ongoing with the Treasury's Office of the General Counsel concerning the issuance of additional, detailed guidance as to the preservation of documents. I have been advised that only after such guidance has been issued will destruction of OFAC documents be resumed.

Sincerely yours,

Andrea G. Cohen
Trial Attorney

cc: The Honorable Royce C. Lamberth (w/ notice of filing)

The first report *(pages 358–360)*
In June 2003, IAEA director general Mohammad El Baradei made his first detailed report to the agency's Board of Governors in Vienna about Iran's previously clandestine nuclear research programs. The carefully couched language indicated that Baradei strongly suspected Iran was trying to conceal weapons activities. But the IAEA still did not move aggressively against Iran.

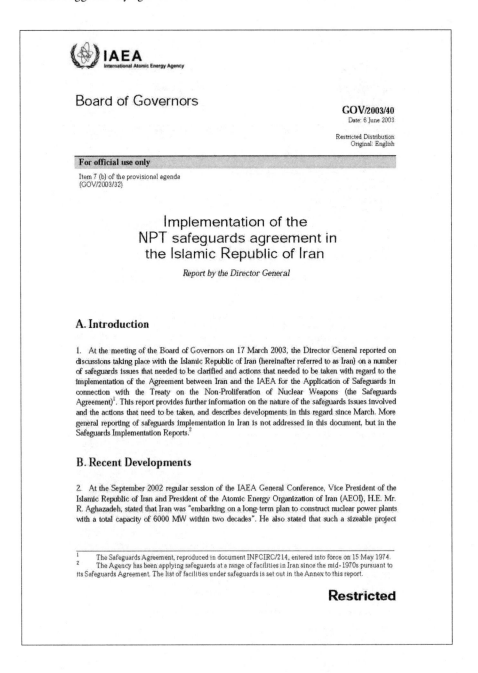

Board of Governors

GOV/2003/40
Date: 6 June 2003

Restricted Distribution
Original: English

For official use only

Item 7 (b) of the provisional agenda
(GOV/2003/32)

Implementation of the NPT safeguards agreement in the Islamic Republic of Iran

Report by the Director General

A. Introduction

1. At the meeting of the Board of Governors on 17 March 2003, the Director General reported on discussions taking place with the Islamic Republic of Iran (hereinafter referred to as Iran) on a number of safeguards issues that needed to be clarified and actions that needed to be taken with regard to the implementation of the Agreement between Iran and the IAEA for the Application of Safeguards in connection with the Treaty on the Non-Proliferation of Nuclear Weapons (the Safeguards Agreement)[1]. This report provides further information on the nature of the safeguards issues involved and the actions that need to be taken, and describes developments in this regard since March. More general reporting of safeguards implementation in Iran is not addressed in this document, but in the Safeguards Implementation Reports.[2]

B. Recent Developments

2. At the September 2002 regular session of the IAEA General Conference, Vice President of the Islamic Republic of Iran and President of the Atomic Energy Organization of Iran (AEOI), H.E. Mr. R. Aghazadeh, stated that Iran was "embarking on a long-term plan to construct nuclear power plants with a total capacity of 6000 MW within two decades". He also stated that such a sizeable project

[1] The Safeguards Agreement, reproduced in document INFCIRC/214, entered into force on 15 May 1974.
[2] The Agency has been applying safeguards at a range of facilities in Iran since the mid-1970s pursuant to its Safeguards Agreement. The list of facilities under safeguards is set out in the Annex to this report.

Restricted

GOV/2003/40
6 June 2003
Page 2

entailed "an all out planning, well in advance, in various field of nuclear technology such as fuel cycle, safety and waste management".

3. During the General Conference, the Director General met with the Vice President, and asked that Iran confirm whether it was building a large underground nuclear related facility at Natanz and a heavy water production plant at Arak, as reported in the media in August 2002. The Vice President provided some information on Iran's intentions to develop further its nuclear fuel cycle, and agreed on a visit to the two sites later in 2002 by the Director General, accompanied by safeguards experts, and to a discussion with Iranian authorities during that meeting on Iran's nuclear development plans.

4. The visit to Iran was originally scheduled for October 2002, but finally took place from 21 to 22 February 2003. The Director General was accompanied by the Deputy Director General for Safeguards (DDG-SG) and the Director of the Division of Safeguards Operations (B).

5. During his visit, the Director General was informed by Iran of its uranium enrichment programme, which was described as including two new facilities located at Natanz, namely a pilot fuel enrichment plant (PFEP) nearing completion of construction, and a large commercial-scale fuel enrichment plant (FEP) also under construction. These two facilities were declared to the Agency for the first time during that visit, at which time the Director General was able to visit both of them. Iran also confirmed that the heavy water production plant[3], referred to in paragraph 3 above, was under construction in Arak.

GOV/2003/40
6 June 2003
Page 6

C.2. Uranium Enrichment Programme

25. During the visit of the Director General in February 2003, the Vice President informed the Agency that over 100 of the approximately 1000 planned centrifuge casings had already been installed at the pilot plant and that the remaining centrifuges would be installed by the end of the year. In addition, he informed the Agency that the commercial scale enrichment facility, which is planned to contain over 50 000 centrifuges, was not scheduled to receive nuclear material in the near future.

26. The Agency has been informed that the pilot enrichment plant is scheduled to start operating in June 2003, initially with single machine tests, and later with increasing numbers of centrifuges. The Iranian authorities have also informed the Agency that the commercial enrichment plant is planned to start accepting centrifuges in early 2005, after the design is confirmed by the tests to be conducted in the pilot enrichment plant. Iran has also stated that the design and research and development work, which had been started about five years ago, were based on extensive modelling and simulation, including tests of centrifuge rotors both with and without inert gas, and that the tests of the rotors, carried out on the premises of the Amir Khabir University and the AEOI in Tehran, were conducted without nuclear material.

27. In May 2003, Iran provided preliminary design information on the enrichment facilities under construction in Natanz, which are being examined by the Agency. Since March 2003, Agency inspectors have visited facilities at Natanz three times to conduct design information verification and to take environmental samples at the pilot enrichment plant. A first series of environmental and destructive analysis samples has been taken at a number of locations. Additional samples are expected to be taken in the near future. Iran has co-operated with the Agency in this regard. The Agency has presented to the Iranian authorities a safeguards approach for the pilot enrichment plant.

GOV/2003/40
6 June 2003
Page 7

D. Findings and Initial Assessment

32. Iran has failed to meet its obligations under its Safeguards Agreement with respect to the reporting of nuclear material, the subsequent processing and use of that material and the declaration of facilities where the material was stored and processed. These failures, and the actions taken thus far to correct them, can be summarized as follows:

(a) Failure to declare the import of natural uranium in 1991, and its subsequent transfer for further processing.

On 15 April 2003, Iran submitted ICRs on the import of the UO_2, UF_4 and UF_6. Iran has still to submit ICRs on the transfer of the material for further processing and use.

(b) Failure to declare the activities involving the subsequent processing and use of the imported natural uranium, including the production and loss of nuclear material, where appropriate, and the production and transfer of waste resulting therefrom.

Iran has acknowledged the production of uranium metal, uranyl nitrate, ammonium uranyl carbonate, UO_2 pellets and uranium wastes. Iran must still submit ICRs on these inventory changes.

(c) Failure to declare the facilities where such material (including the waste) was received, stored and processed.

On 5 May 2003, Iran provided preliminary design information for the facility JHL. Iran has informed the Agency of the locations where the undeclared processing of the imported natural uranium was conducted (TRR and the Esfahan Nuclear Technology Centre), and provided access to those locations. It has provided the Agency access to the waste storage facility at Esfahan, and has indicated that access would be provided to Anarak, as well as the waste disposal site at Qom.

(d) Failure to provide in a timely manner updated design information for the MIX Facility and for TRR.

Iran has agreed to submit updated design information for the two facilities.

(e) Failure to provide in a timely manner information on the waste storage at Esfahan and at Anarak.

Iran has informed the Agency of the locations where the waste has been stored or discarded. It has provided the Agency access to the waste storage facility at Esfahan, and has indicated that access will be provided to Anarak.

33. Although the quantities of nuclear material involved have not been large[6], and the material would need further processing before being suitable for use as the fissile material component of a nuclear explosive device, the number of failures by Iran to report the material, facilities and activities in question in a timely manner as it is obliged to do pursuant to its Safeguards Agreement is a matter of concern. While these failures are in the process of being rectified by Iran, the process of verifying the correctness and completeness of the Iranian declarations is still ongoing.

[6] The total amount of material, approximately 1.8 tonnes, is 0.13 effective kilograms of uranium. This is, however, not insignificant in terms of a State's ability to conduct nuclear research and development activities.

Iran destroys the evidence

The Institute of Science and International Security (www.isis-online.org) has worked with DigitalGlobe to provide satellite imagery of many of Iran's once-secret nuclear sites. This series of three photos highlights the destruction of a suspected uranium enrichment site within the vast Revolutionary Guards military production facility at Lavizan-Shian in Tehran. *(Credit: DigitalGlobe/ISIS)*

Before -- August 11, 2003

After -- March 22, 2004

New -- May 10, 2004

"Bomb plant"

This February 27, 2005, satellite image of the Arak heavy water facility shows new construction of Iran's 40-megawatt research reactor, which U.S. analysts believe is a plutonium production "bomb plant." *(Credit: DigitalGlobe-ISIS)*

Covering their tracks

These satellite images from DigitalGlobe and GlobalSecurity.org show the underground production halls of the Natanz centrifuge enrichment facility just after they were covered over with dirt. *(Credit: DigitalGlobe/GlobalSecurity.org)*

Iran's 9/11 links

German intelligence determined that the coordinator of the 9/11 attacks, Ramzi Binalshibh, traveled to Iran en route to Afghanistan, where he carried information from lead hijacker Mohammad Atta to Osama bin Laden. On the trip described in this secret intelligence report, Binalshibh arrived in Iran in time to meet with bin Laden's top deputy, Ayman al-Zawahri.

000050

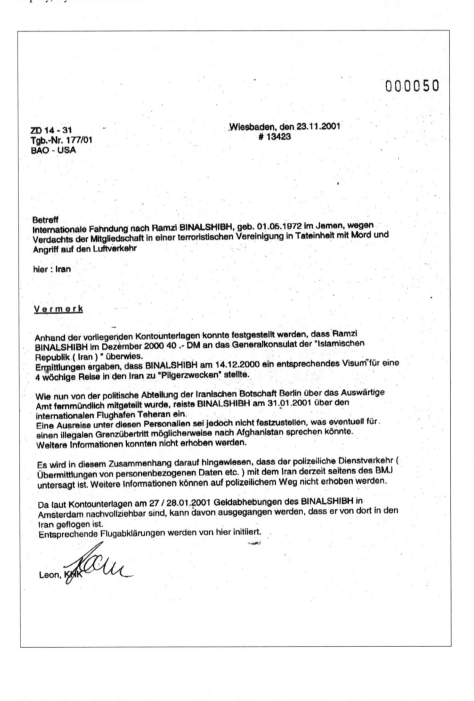

ZD 14 - 31
Tgb.-Nr. 177/01
BAO - USA

Wiesbaden, den 23.11.2001
13423

Betreff
Internationale Fahndung nach Ramzi BINALSHIBH, geb. 01.05.1972 im Jemen, wegen Verdachts der Mitgliedschaft in einer terroristischen Vereinigung in Tateinheit mit Mord und Angriff auf den Luftverkehr

hier : Iran

Vermerk

Anhand der vorliegenden Kontounterlagen konnte festgestellt werden, dass Ramzi BINALSHIBH im Dezember 2000 40 .- DM an das Generalkonsulat der "Islamischen Republik (Iran) " überwies.
Ermittlungen ergaben, dass BINALSHIBH am 14.12.2000 ein entsprechendes Visum für eine 4 wöchige Reise in den Iran zu "Pilgerzwecken" stellte.

Wie nun von der politische Abteilung der Iranischen Botschaft Berlin über das Auswärtige Amt fernmündlich mitgeteilt wurde, reiste BINALSHIBH am 31.01.2001 über den internationalen Flughafen Teheran ein.
Eine Ausreise unter diesen Personalien sei jedoch nicht festzustellen, was eventuell für einen illegalen Grenzübertritt möglicherweise nach Afghanistan sprechen könnte.
Weitere Informationen konnten nicht erhoben werden.

Es wird in diesem Zusammenhang darauf hingewiesen, dass der polizeiliche Dienstverkehr (Übermittlungen von personenbezogenen Daten etc.) mit dem Iran derzeit seitens des BMJ untersagt ist. Weitere Informationen können auf polizeilichem Weg nicht erhoben werden.

Da laut Kontounterlagen am 27 / 28.01.2001 Geldabhebungen des BINALSHIBH in Amsterdam nachvollziehbar sind, kann davon ausgegangen werden, dass er von dort in den Iran geflogen ist.
Entsprechende Flugabklärungen werden von hier initiiert.

Leon, KHK

Last-minute scramble *(pages 365–366)*

Just one week before their report was scheduled to be printed, staffers for the 9/11 Commission discovered an astonishing treasure trove of highly classified intelligence reports that documented Iran's assistance to al-Qaeda and to the terrorist attacks on America—documents that the CIA tried to keep from the commission. The staff scrambled to include this account of the Iran connection in the final report. A much more detailed account can be found in chapter 24 of this book.

240 THE 9/11 COMMISSION REPORT

his intended address as the Marriott Hotel, New York City, but instead spent one night at another New York hotel. He then joined the group of hijackers in Paterson, reuniting with Nawaf al Hazmi after more than a year. With two months remaining, all 19 hijackers were in the United States and ready to take the final steps toward carrying out the attacks.[119]

Assistance from Hezbollah and Iran to al Qaeda

As we mentioned in chapter 2, while in Sudan, senior managers in al Qaeda maintained contacts with Iran and the Iranian-supported worldwide terrorist organization Hezbollah, which is based mainly in southern Lebanon and Beirut. Al Qaeda members received advice and training from Hezbollah.

Intelligence indicates the persistence of contacts between Iranian security officials and senior al Qaeda figures after Bin Ladin's return to Afghanistan. Khallad has said that Iran made a concerted effort to strengthen relations with al Qaeda after the October 2000 attack on the USS *Cole*, but was rebuffed because Bin Ladin did not want to alienate his supporters in Saudi Arabia. Khallad and other detainees have described the willingness of Iranian officials to facilitate the travel of al Qaeda members through Iran, on their way to and from Afghanistan. For example, Iranian border inspectors would be told not to place telltale stamps in the passports of these travelers. Such arrangements were particularly beneficial to Saudi members of al Qaeda.[120]

Our knowledge of the international travels of the al Qaeda operatives selected for the 9/11 operation remains fragmentary. But we now have evidence suggesting that 8 to 10 of the 14 Saudi "muscle" operatives traveled into or out of Iran between October 2000 and February 2001.[121]

In October 2000, a senior operative of Hezbollah visited Saudi Arabia to coordinate activities there. He also planned to assist individuals in Saudi Arabia in traveling to Iran during November. A top Hezbollah commander and Saudi Hezbollah contacts were involved.[122]

Also in October 2000, two future muscle hijackers, Mohand al Shehri and Hamza al Ghamdi, flew from Iran to Kuwait. In November, Ahmed al Ghamdi apparently flew to Beirut, traveling—perhaps by coincidence—on the same flight as a senior Hezbollah operative. Also in November, Salem al Hazmi apparently flew from Saudi Arabia to Beirut.[123]

In mid-November, we believe, three of the future muscle hijackers, Wail al Shehri, Waleed al Shehri, and Ahmed al Nami, all of whom had obtained their U.S. visas in late October, traveled in a group from Saudi Arabia to Beirut and then onward to Iran. An associate of a senior Hezbollah operative was on the same flight that took the future hijackers to Iran. Hezbollah officials in Beirut and Iran were expecting the arrival of a group during the same time period. The travel of this group was important enough to merit the attention of senior figures in Hezbollah.[124]

Later in November, two future muscle hijackers, Satam al Suqami and Majed

Moqed, flew into Iran from Bahrain. In February 2001, Khalid al Mihdhar may have taken a flight from Syria to Iran, and then traveled further within Iran to a point near the Afghan border.[125]

KSM and Binalshibh have confirmed that several of the 9/11 hijackers (at least eight, according to Binalshibh) transited Iran on their way to or from Afghanistan, taking advantage of the Iranian practice of not stamping Saudi passports. They deny any other reason for the hijackers' travel to Iran. They also deny any relationship between the hijackers and Hezbollah.[126]

In sum, there is strong evidence that Iran facilitated the transit of al Qaeda members into and out of Afghanistan before 9/11, and that some of these were future 9/11 hijackers. There also is circumstantial evidence that senior Hezbollah operatives were closely tracking the travel of some of these future muscle hijackers into Iran in November 2000. However, we cannot rule out the possibility of a remarkable coincidence—that is, that Hezbollah was actually focusing on some other group of individuals traveling from Saudi Arabia during this same time frame, rather than the future hijackers.[127]

We have found no evidence that Iran or Hezbollah was aware of the planning for what later became the 9/11 attack. At the time of their travel through Iran, the al Qaeda operatives themselves were probably not aware of the specific details of their future operation.

After 9/11, Iran and Hezbollah wished to conceal any past evidence of cooperation with Sunni terrorists associated with al Qaeda. A senior Hezbollah official disclaimed any Hezbollah involvement in 9/11.[128]

We believe this topic requires further investigation by the U.S. government.

7.4 FINAL STRATEGIES AND TACTICS

Final Preparations in the United States

During the early summer of 2001, Atta, assisted by Shehhi, was busy coordinating the arrival of most of the muscle hijackers in southern Florida—picking them up at the airport, finding them places to stay, and helping them settle in the United States.[129]

The majority settled in Florida. Some opened bank accounts, acquired mailboxes, and rented cars. Several also joined local gyms, presumably to stay fit for the operation. Upon first arriving, most stayed in hotels and motels; but by mid-June, they settled in shared apartments relatively close to one another and Atta.[130] Though these muscle hijackers did not travel much after arriving in the United States, two of them, Waleed al Shehri and Satam al Suqami, took unusual trips.

On May 19, Shehri and Suqami flew from Fort Lauderdale to Freeport, the Bahamas, where they had reservations at the Bahamas Princess Resort. The two were turned away by Bahamian officials on arrival, however, because they

Attacking U.S. soldiers *(pages 367–368)*
Fifty-two top Revolutionary Guards officers attended a final debriefing before being sent into Iraq to fund, train, and arm the Iraqi "insurgency" after U.S. forces ousted Saddam Hussein. These exclusive photographs, obtained from Revolutionary Guards archives by Iranian defector Hamid Reza Zakeri, show the different faces of Revolutionary Guards Brigadier General Salihani.

Picture 1 shows him at the final debriefing in a specially constructed training center in the former U.S. Embassy in Tehran. Picture 2 shows Salihani *(right)* during counter-terrorism training. Picture 3 shows Salihani newly arrived in Iraq as a "humanitarian aid worker." Picture 4 shows him with other Iranian Revolutionary Guards officers inside the Imam Ali shrine in Kerbala, Iraq. *(Photographs courtesy of Hamid Reza Zakeri)*

(1)

(2)

(3)

(4)

Iran's advanced nuclear program *(pages 369–370)*
This table, which I assembled from IAEA reports, reveals Iran's key nuclear capabilities.

KEY IRANIAN NUCLEAR CAPABILITIES

Uranium Fuel Cycle—Recently declared facilities

TYPE	LOCATION	SAFEGUARDS STATUS
Uranium mine	**Saghand (Yazd)**	**Not under safeguards**

Work began in the early 1990s; Iran claims full production to begin in 2006, at 50 tons/year. Visited by IAEA inspectors in 2004.

Milling plant	**Ardakan (Yazd)**	**Not under safeguards**

Annual production of fifty tons of yellowcake from the nearby Saghand mine. Under construction in early 2005; production planned for 2006.

Uranium mine & mill	**Gchine (Bandar Abbas)**	**Not under safeguards**

Iran claimed this mine and milling plant produced only a "few hundred kilograms" of yellowcake. Dismantled before IAEA inspectors visited in 2004. Status of uranium unknown.

Centrifuge production	**Kala Electric Company (Tehran)**	**Additional protocol**

Manufacture of centrifuge components; centrifuge assembly and testing; pilot enrichment plant. Declared to the IAEA in 2003 after its existence was revealed by the MEK. Iran cleaned up the site in early 2003, while delaying IAEA visits. Equipment moved to Pars Trash (Tehran). Iran admitted centrifuge work began at this site in 1995; a subsequent declaration admitted work began in 1987. Two associated workshops—Farayand Technique and Pars Trash—also handled centrifuge manufacturing.

Uranium Conversion Facility (UCF)	**Isfahan**	**Additional protocol**

Production of uranium hexafluoride (UF6), uranium metal, and other compounds. Full-scale production set to begin in 2004; work temporarily suspended under 11/04 agreement with the EU. Hardened underground storage bunkers discovered in late 2004. Design capacity of 200 t/year of UF6 could produce fissile material for 20–30 bombs per year.

Enrichment plant	**Natanz**	**Additional protocol**

Pilot plant with 164 centrifuges was operational in 2003; the buried industrial-scale plant with 50,000 centrifuges is under construction; work temporarily suspended under 11/04 agreement with EU. Design capacity of 200,000 separative work units/year (roughly 500 kg of HEU) could produce fissile material for 20–30 bombs per year.

Uranium Fuel Cycle—Suspected Capabilities

TYPE	LOCATION	SAFEGUARDS STATUS
Uranium mines	**Various locations**	

In 1989, Iran announced it had discovered uranium reserves estimated at 3,500 tons at ten locations and intended to begin mining at all of them. Other sites, never visited by the IAEA but mentioned by the Iranians, include Khoshomi (possibly another name for Saghand), and unidentified locations in Azerbaijan and Sistan va-Baluchestan.

Pilot uranium conversion facility	**Unknown**	**N/A**

The IAEA continues to doubt Iran's claim that it built the industrial UCF in Isfahan without ever building a pilot plant to prove the processes and equipment.

(continued on next page)

KEY IRANIAN NUCLEAR CAPABILITIES

(continued)

Uranium Fuel Cycle—Suspected Capabilities (continued)

TYPE	LOCATION	SAFEGUARDS STATUS
Pilot enrichment plant	**Lavizan-Shian (Tehran)**	**N/A**

The IAEA is still investigating claims by the MEK that Iran operated a pilot enrichment plant within the giant Defense Industries Organization complex at Lavizan-Shian in Tehran, using centrifuges imported from the A. Q. Khan network. Iran razed the site to prevent environmental sampling, and moved production equipment to a nearby but still undisclosed site. If confirmed, by 2003 this plant could have produced enough fissile material for 20 to 25 bombs using UF6 imported through the A. Q. Khan network or produced at the suspected pilot UCF.

Plutonium Fuel Cycle

TYPE	LOCATION	SAFEGUARDS STATUS
Busheir Power Plant	**Busheir**	**Safeguards**

Construction complete in 2004; fuel loading planned for 2005; critical in 2006. Using Plutonium extracted from spent fuel, Iran could produce up to 70 bombs in less than two years.

Heavy water plant	**Arak**	**Not under safeguards**

Declared in 2003, after its existence was revealed by the MEK. Industrial-scale production of heavy water expected in late 2004; temporarily suspended under 11/04 agreement with EU.

40-MW research reactor	**Arak**	**In design phase**

Scheduled to be completed by 2014, this heavy water reactor will use natural uranium fuel and can produce enough weapons-grade Plutonium per year for several bombs. The MEK claimed in March 2005 that work on the reactor had been accelerated and that it would go critical by 2007.

Plutonium reprocessing	**Tehran**	**Violation**

Iran acknowledged in 2003 that it had carried out uranium reprocessing experiments at the Tehran Nuclear Research Center and elsewhere over an 18-year period, in violation of its existing safeguards agreement.

Notes

CHAPTER 1. THE DEFECTOR

1. Ayatollah Khomeini's designated successor, Ayatollah Ali Montazeri, was once presented to the press by then-exiled opponents of the shah as a living, breathing example of SAVAK brutality. To their great embarrassment, Montazeri told reporters, "I was not mistreated, besides the fact that I was imprisoned for no valid reason." In the end, his honesty got the better of him and he was stripped of his titles and placed under house arrest, only months before Khomeini's death in 1989. See Kenneth R. Timmerman, "Special Report: Iran's Leaders," *Middle East Defense News* (*MEDNEWS*) 2 (March 27, 1989): 12–13.
2. These five leaders were Ayatollah Khomeini, Majles speaker Hashemi-Rafsanjani, President Ali Khamenei, Mehdi Karrubi—then a lesser-known minor cleric, who was Rafsanjani's top aide for security matters—and Ayatollah Mohammed Reza Mahdavi-Kani, whom many in the CIA believed was a pro-Western "moderate" because of his longstanding contacts with British intelligence.
3. The German court acquitted Mzoudi in February 2004, after 9/11 planner Ramzi Binalshibh claimed that Mzoudi had no involvement in the plot.
4. Memorandum prepared for Minister R. Vorbeck, German Chancellor's Office, by the Bundesnachrichtendienst (BND)—the German equivalent of the CIA; three-page fax from the BundesamtfurVerfassungsschutz (BfV), Germany's counterintelligence organization, dated January 28, 2004 (Reference 4C2-183-S-450 039).
5. The other three members of the Leadership Council at that point were top clerics: Ayatollah Mohammad Yazdi, head of the Council of Guardians, which oversees Parliament; Ayatollah Mahmoud Hashemi Shahroudi, the Judiciary chief; and Ayatollah Ali Meshkini, the head of the Assembly of Experts, the group that picks the Supreme Leader.
6. Zakeri says that he stole the original document and gave it to the CIA. To test its authenticity, he says, the CIA analyzed the content of the paper, the watermark, even the green ink of Nateq-Nouri's seal. Zakeri claims the agency told him it thought the document was genuine. A half-dozen opposition sources to whom I showed the letter expressed doubts, although most believed that the contents were accurate.
7. After my initial article on Zakeri appeared in *Insight* magazine, *Chicago Tribune* reporter John Crewdson contacted me and asked how to reach Zakeri in Germany, where he was living in exile. Crewdson's excellent articles on Zakeri's testimony during the 9/11 trial of Mzoudi in Hamburg in January 2004 highlight the ambiguities of dealing with defectors from Iran, where lying, exaggeration, and self-aggrandizement often color hard intelligence.

CHAPTER 2. THE INTERCEPT

1. Timothy J. Geraghty interview, Dec. 12, 2003; testimony of Timothy J. Geraghty, March 17, 2003, in *D. Peterson et al. v. Islamic Republic of Iran*, U.S. District Court for the District of Columbia, Docket No. CA 01-2686; trial transcript pp. 24–25, 28, 41–43.
2. Testimony of Steve Edward Russell, March 17, 2003, in *D. Peterson, et al., v. Islamic Republic of Iran*, U.S. District Court for the District of Columbia, Docket No. CA 01-2686; trial transcript pp. 58–96.
3. *See* 9/11 Commission Report, p. 61.

4. Judge Royce C. Lamberth, Memorandum Opinion in *D. Peterson et al. v. Islamic Republic of Iran*, p. 12.
5. John Lehman interview, Dec. 16, 2003; Admiral James ("Ace") Lyons interview, Dec. 11, 2003; General John Vessey interview, Dec. 18, 2003. These were the first Tomahawks that had been retrofitted as conventional cruise missiles. The Tomahawk had been designed to deliver the W-80 thermonuclear warhead, which could be variably set to deliver a 5- to 160-kiloton yield.
6. Caspar Weinberger interview, Dec. 16, 2003.
7. Caspar Weinberger, *Fighting for Peace* (New York: Warner Books, 1990), pp. 161–62.
8. Bin Laden interview with ABC News reporter John Miller, May 28, 1998.
9. Department of State *Bulletin*, April 1984, pp. 29–30, cited by former Assistant Secretary of State John H. Kelly in Jeremy R. Azrael and Emil A. Payin, eds., *U.S. and Russian Policymaking with Respect to the Use of Force* (CF-129-CRES) (Santa Monica, CA: 1996), ch. 6.

CHAPTER 3. THE HIJACKER

1. *Richard L. Stethem et al. v. Islamic Republic of Iran*, U.S. District Court for the District of Columbia, C.A. No. 00-159, closing argument by Shale Stiller, Jan. 17, 2002, p. 11.
2. This description is taken from the decision and order by U.S. District Court Judge Thomas Penfield Jackson, dated April 19, 2002, in *Richard L. Stethem et al. v. Islamic Republic of Iran*, ibid, p. 6.
3. Robert Baer, *See No Evil: The True Story of a Ground Soldier in the CIA's War on Terrorism* (New York: Crown Forum, 2002), p. 99.
4. Kenneth R. Timmerman, "Imad Mugniyeh: The Real Story," *Middle East Defense News (MEDNEWS)*, 1, no. 15 (May 2, 1988).
5. Ibid.
6. Juan José Galeano interview, Oct. 21, 2001.

CHAPTER 4. ATOMIC AYATOLLAHS

1. Shyam Bhatia, *Nuclear Rivals in the Middle East* (London and New York: Routledge, 1988), 83, cited in Jack Boureston and Charles D. Ferguson, "Schooling Iran's Atom Squad," *Bulletin of the Atomic Scientists* 60, no. 3 (May 1, 2004): 31.
2. *Nuclear Engineering International* (Dec. 1984): 13.
3. Dr. A. Q. Khan, "Uranium Enrichment at Kahuta, a Decade of Pakistani Experience," *Dawn* (Karachi), Aug. 1, 1986. Reproduced in Zahid Malik, *Dr. A. Q. Khan and the Islamic Bomb* (Islamabad, Pakistan: Hurmat Publications, 1992), p. 96.
4. Ibid., 91.
5. Kenneth R. Timmerman, "Iran's Nuclear Program: Myth and Reality," Sept. 30, 1995, printed in *Fifty Years of Nuclear Weapons, Proceedings of the Sixth Castiglioincello Conference* (Milan, Italy: USPID, 1996).
6. Statement of deputy director general Pierre Goldschmidt to the IAEA Board of Governors, Vienna, March 1, 2005.
7. Leonard Spector, "Threats in the Middle East," *Orbis* (spring 1992), quoted by Henry Sokolski in "The Bomb in Iran's Future," *Middle East Quarterly* (June 1994).
8. Kenneth R. Timmerman, "Iran Trains Nuclear Engineers in Pakistan," *Middle East Defense News (MEDNEWS)* 2, no. 5 (Dec. 5, 1988).
9. Fereidoun Fesharaki, "Return to Iran: Impressions of an Ex-Official," *Newsday*, April 20, 1987, p. 56.
10. Eliyahu Ben Elissar, president of the Defense and Foreign Affairs Commission of the Israeli Knesset, interview, Jerusalem, May 16, 1992.
11. "Nuclear Nonproliferation: Major Weaknesses in Foreign Visitor Controls at Weapons Laboratories, Report to the Chairman, Committee on Governmental Affairs, U.S. Senate, General Accounting Office, Oct. 1988 (GAO/RCED-89-31), pp. 2–3. From

Jan. 1986 through Sept. 1987, eighteen Iranians visited Lawrence Livermore National Laboratory, five visited Los Alamos, and two visited Sandia.

12. "Nuclear Nonproliferation: Department of Energy Needs Tighter Control Over Reprocessing Information," report to the Honorable William Proxmire, U.S. Senate, General Accounting Office, Aug. 1987 (GAO/RCED-87-150), p. 20.
13. Under DoE procedures current in May 1988, the labs were required to release codes that were at least two years old, and were offering 870 of the 1,460 computer codes to "sensitive countries" including Iran and Pakistan. "Nuclear Nonproliferation: Better Controls Needed over Weapons-Related Information and Technology," report to the Chairman, Committee on Governmental Affairs, U.S. Senate, June 1989 (GAO/RCED-89-116), pp. 20–23.
14. David Kay, director of the Uranium Institute, interview, London, May 7, 1992.

CHAPTER 5. THE EXILES

1. Knaus has written an extraordinary account of this little-known chapter of the Cold War. See John Kenneth Knaus, *Orphans of the Cold War: America and the Tibetan Struggle for Survival* (New York: BBS Public Affairs Books, 1999), p. 146.

CHAPTER 7. THE BLIND SWEDE

1. Kenneth R. Timmerman, "New Nuclear Center Opens; More Planned," *The Iran Brief*, Serial 0118, Dec. 5, 1994.
2. "Amrollahi Says Uranium Being Mined in Yazd," *Resalaat*, Sept. 10, 1989, in *FBIS-NES*, Sept. 19, 1989.
3. "Uranium Bullion Plant to Be Set Up in Yazd," Tehran Domestic Service in Persian, Oct. 8, 1989, and "Survey of Uranium Samples Completed," Tehran Television Service in Persian, Oct. 10, 1989, both translated in *FBIS-NES*, Oct. 12, 1989.
4. Kenneth R. Timmerman, "Iran's Uranium Programs," *The Iran Brief*, Serial 0822, June 1, 1995.
5. Tehran radio announced the signing of the ten-year arms and technology agreement. See *FBIS-NES*, Jan. 21, 1990.

CHAPTER 8. THE GERMANY SYNDROME

1. Zahid Malik, *Dr. A. Q. Khan and the Islamic Bomb* (Islamabad, Pakistan: Hurmat Publications, 1992), p. 78.
2. Letter from French Customs, Investigation Directorate, Paris, dated July 6, 1988, included as Appendix 9 in the 1989 court case against Lerch and Heilingbrunner, 111Js 233–87.
3. Cited in Kenneth R. Timmerman, "Document: Cops & Robbers at Eschborn," *Middle East Defense News* (*MEDNEWS*) 4, nos. 12/13 (March 18, 1991): 6.
4. Interview with State Prosecutor Veilhaber, Sept. 30, 1992; see also Kenneth R. Timmerman, "The Case of the Missing Centrifuge Blueprints," *Middle East Defense News* (*MEDNEWS*), 6, nos. 1/2 (Oct. 12, 1992): 5.
5. Kenneth R. Timmerman, "The Leybold Law," *Middle East Defense News* (*MEDNEWS*) 5, no. 13 (March 30, 1992).
6. See Victor Gilinsky, Marvin Miller, and Harmon Hubbard, "A Fresh Examination of the Proliferation Dangers of Light Water Reactors" (Washington, DC: Nonproliferation Policy Education Center, October 22, 2004), p. 9. A detailed explanation and table of this calculation can be found on pp. 39–40. The full sixty-two-page report is available at www.npec-web.org.
7. Malik, *Dr. A. Q. Khan*, p. 105.
8. Kenneth R. Timmerman, "Customs Intercepts Iranian Rocket Pumps," *MEDNEWS* 4, no. 15 (April 29, 1991).

CHAPTER 10. LIFTING THE STONE

1. Shyam Bhatia and Daniel McGrory, *Brighter Than the Baghdad Sun* (Washington, DC: Regnery, 2000), p. 247. Other accounts of Kay's confrontation can be found in Alexander and Patrick Cockburn, *Out of the Ashes* (New York: HarperCollins, 1999), pp. 100–2, and Scott Ritter, *Endgame* (New York: Simon & Schuster, 1999), pp. 108–9.
2. Bhatia and McGrory, p. 249.
3. Bhatia and McGrory, p. 250. I heard the same anecdotes from inspectors who were present on the bus.
4. Blix complained to the director general of the institute, Pierre Goldschmidt, after Kay penned an article in the *Wall Street Journal* that called for transferring special inspection powers from the IAEA to the United Nations Security Council. Goldschmidt became deputy director general of the IAEA and head of the Department of Safeguards in May 1999.
5. The Habibi quote is from the *Tehran Times*, June 18, 1991. For more, see Kenneth R. Timmerman, "China-Iran Nuclear Cloud," *Middle East Defense News* (*MEDNEWS*) 4, no. 20 (July 22, 1991).

CHAPTER 11. THE VISITORS

1. Among the wares China was offering for sale were hot isostatic presses, used for shaping explosive lenses for nuclear warheads and manipulating nuclear material; high-speed streaking cameras, used in nuclear enrichment experiments; neutron generators, used in oil-well logging but also needed to trigger atomic explosions; missile accelerometers and gyros; high-vacuum valves and pumps, inverters, frequency converters, gas flowmeters, and cobalt ring magnets, all used in enrichment centrifuges; hot cells and remote manipulators to equip a research reactor facility for plutonium reprocessing. They also offered a variety of special materials with nuclear applications, including maraging steel, ion exchange resins, spherical aluminum powder, graphite, nickel powder, lithium, hafnium, and beryllium metal, heavy water, and uranium hexafluoride. U.S. Senate Committee on Governmental Affairs, *Proliferation Watch*.
2. Matt Kelley, "Pakistan Threatened to Give Iran Nukes," Associated Press, Feb. 27, 2004. Beg denied having ever made such a threat, but it was in line with Beg's very public posture on building an "Islamic bomb."
3. Kenneth R. Timmerman, "Mohsen Rezai to Pakistan," *Middle East Defense News* (*MEDNEWS*) 4, no. 21 (Aug. 5, 1991); Yosef Bodansky and Vaughn Forrest, House Republican Research Committee Task Force on Terrorism and Unconventional Warfare, "Iran's Nuclear Effort—Update," July 29, 1991.
4. "IAEA Visit to Iran," IAEA PR 92/11, Feb. 14, 1992.
5. Yossef Bodansky and Vaughn S. Forrest, "Addendum: The Ma'allem Kelayah Episode," House Republican Research Committee Task Force on Terrorism and Unconventional Warfare, Feb. 18, 1992. Although Bodansky's reports were widely circulated on Capitol Hill and to the U.S. media, they were frequently greeted with exasperation, since he refused to cite specific sources for his information.
6. Kenneth R. Timmerman, *Weapons of Mass Destruction: The Cases of Iran, Syria, and Libya* (Los Angeles: Simon Wiesenthal Center, 1992).

CHAPTER 12. LOOSE NUKES

1. "Iran Fires New Cruise Missile," Associated Press, Jan. 30, 1996.
2. According to the Al Watan al Arabi account of the nuclear buying teams, the "unprofessional" in charge of the project was Iranian vice president Atta'ollah Mohajerani, later a key "moderate" supporter of Rafsanjani's successor, Mohammad Khatami.
3. I tell the story of the China Plan in great detail in *Selling Out America: The American Spectator Investigations* (Philadelphia: Ex Libris, 2000), pp. 22–25.
4. Statement by Congressman Tom Lantos, Chairman, House Foreign Affairs Subcom-

mittee on International Security, International Organizations and Human Rights, "Rogue Regimes (Part II): Weapons Acquisition and Supplier Networks," Sept. 14, 1993.

5. William C. Potter, "The 'Sapphire' File: Lessons for International Nonprolifeartion cooperation, Transition, Nov. 17, 1995." For more on the Alfa class (Project 705) submarines, see http://spb.org.ru/bellona/ehome/russia/nfl/705.htm.

CHAPTER 13. RED LIGHT, GREEN LIGHT

1. Final Report of the Select Subcommittee to Investigate The U.S. Role in Iranian Arms Transfers to Croatia and Bosnia ("The Iranian Green Light Subcommittee"), House International Relations Committee, Oct. 10, 1996; 104th Congress, 2nd Session, pp. 2, 201.
2. Kenneth R. Timmerman, "The Islamic Bomb—Pakistani style," *Middle East Defense News* (*MEDNEWS*) 5, no. 4 (Nov. 25, 1991).
3. See Victor Gilinsky, Marvin Miller, and Harmon Hubbard, "A Fresh Examination of the Proliferation Dangers of Light Water Reactors" (Washington, DC: Nonproliferation Policy Education Center, 2004), p. 9. A detailed explanation and table of this calculation can be found on pp. 39–40. The full report is available at www.npec-web.org.

CHAPTER 14. THE PARTNERS

1. "Countering Propaganda about U.S.–Iran Trade," Feb. 10, 1995, 1995STATE-E034706, Confidential cable (declassified under FOIA); 5 pp.
2. Undersecretary of State Peter Tarnoff claimed during the March 16, 1995, Senate Banking Committee hearing that news of the Conoco deal with Iran came "out of the blue." But State Department records released shortly afterward showed that Tarnoff himself had been briefed on the negotiations during a swing through the Persian Gulf that began on Nov. 7, 1994. See "State Department Knew of Conoco deal," *The Iran Brief* 5 (April 3, 1995). My testimony at the hearing, "Conoco Deal Would Fuel Nuclear Weapons and Terrorism," is available at www.iran.org.

CHAPTER 15. THE PENETRATION

1. Knut Royce and Kevin McCoy, "Secretive Iranian Foundation Avoids Taxes," *Newsday*, May 26, 1995.
2. The paper I presented at the conference, "Iran's Nuclear Program: Myth and Reality," laid out a chronology of Iran's nuclear procurement and argued that it was using nuclear power as a "legend," or cover, for a covert nuclear weapons program. It is available online at www.iran.org. Hassan Mashadi's remarks were not transcribed.

CHAPTER 16. THUNDER

1. Details of the bombing were taken from *USA v. Ahmed al-Mughassil et al.*, Eastern District of Virginia, June 2001.
2. Author's notes of sworn testimony of Louis Freeh, Dec. 18, 2003, in a lawsuit against the Islamic Republic of Iran brought by the families of the nineteen Khobar Towers victims. U.S. Magistrate Judge Deborah A. Robinson, a Clinton appointee, tried to prevent Freeh and former FBI deputy director Dale Watson from providing evidence during the trial and sought unsuccessfully through direct questioning to disqualify their testimony relating to direct Iranian government responsibility for the Khobar Towers attack.

CHAPTER 17. THE COUNTDOWN BEGINS

1. See "Russia Steps Up Strategic Cooperation," *The Iran Brief*, Jan. 8, 1996.
2. Author's notes of Walpole's comments to a forum hosted by the Carnegie Endowment in Washington. See "Iran Building Missile Plants in Libya," *The Iran Brief*, Oct. 5, 1998.

CHAPTER 18. THE PRESIDENT, THE LEADER, AND THE MURDERERS

1. "Khatemi Tied to Mid-1980s Terror," *The Iran Brief*, Serial 3608, July 3, 1997.
2. For additional background, see "Ansar-e Hezbollah, Khamenei's Helpers," *The Iran Brief*, Serial 2307, June 3, 1996.

CHAPTER 20. OCTOBER SURPRISE

1. A congressional effort to require full disclosure of donors to presidential libraries, backed by the nonpartisan group Common Cause, stalled in 2001. *New York Sun* reporter Josh Gerstein traveled to Little Rock in November 2004 and consulted the single public computer terminal where limited donor information was available. His report, "Saudis, Arabs Funneled Millions to President Clinton's Library," appeared on November 22, 2004. See http://www.nysun.com/article/5137.
2. Eizenstat testified before the Senate Judiciary Subcommittee on Terrorism, Technology, and Government Information on Oct. 27, 1999.

CHAPTER 21. THE WARNINGS

1. In *USA v. Ali Mohamed*, U.S. District Court, Southern District of New York, S(7) 98 Cr. 1023 (LBS), Oct. 20, 2000. Portions filed under seal.
2. *United States v. Usama bin Laden*, 98-CR-539-ALL (S.D.N.Y.), p. 3. The indictment was unsealed in Nov. 1998, after the Africa embassy bombings, and substantially revised later on.
3. Trial testimony of Jamal Ahmed al-Fadl, *United States v. Usama bin Laden*, No S(7) 98 Cr. 1023 (S.D.N.Y), Feb. 6, 2001; transcript pp. 289–90.
4. John Crewdson, "As U.S. Steps Up Investigation, Iran Denies Assisting Al Qaeda," *Chicago Tribune*, July 21, 2004.

CHAPTER 22. THE RAT LINE

1. The time-stamped Al-Manar broadcast was translated by FBIS.
2. "Although al-Manar vociferously denies receiving any such funding, it is an open secret that Iran bankrolls the station. Al-Manar's budget currently stands at around $15 million—nearly half the size of Al-Jazeera's budget." Avi Jorisch, *Beacon of Hatred: Inside Hizballah's Al-Manar Television* (Washington, DC: Washington Institute for Near East Policy, 1994), p. xiii.

CHAPTER 23. NUKES "R" US

1. See, inter alia, "Implementation of the NPT Safeguards Agreement in the Islamic Republic of Iran," Report from the Director General, Nov. 10, 2003, GOV/2003/73, pp. 1–2. I have made this and other DG reports available at www.iran.org.
2. "Adherence to and Compliance with Arms Control Agreements and The President's Report to Congress on Soviet Noncompliance with Arms Control Agreements," ACDA, Jan. 14, 1993. Letter of transmittal to Congress signed by President George H. W. Bush on Jan. 19, 1993.
3. IAEA report, GOV/2003/69.
4. IAEA report, Nov. 10, 2003, GOV/2003/73, p. 10.
5. In his book *Treachery: How America's Friends and Foes Are Secretly Arming Our Enemies* (New York: Crown Forum, 2004), pp. 252–53, my colleague Bill Gertz describes a February 1998 NSA intercept that showed Dr. Khan was sending nuclear technicians from Pakistan to Russia for training. Gertz noted that this was "one of the first reports" to indicate the reach of the Khan network.

CHAPTER 24. THE EVIDENCE

1. Author's notes of Louis Freeh testimony and post-testimony comments, Dec. 18, 2003.

2. See Sebastian Rotella, "Terrorism Suspects Traced to Iran," *Los Angeles Times*, Aug. 1, 2004.
3. See, inter alia, chapter 5, nn. 80, 81, which cite BKA reports on Zammar, Binalshibh, and Jarrah (Commission Report, p. 495).
4. BKA cable number 13423, dated Nov. 23, 2001. Ref: N4 177/01. File 20.14-31.
5. I profiled Bruguière in the March 2002 issue of *Reader's Digest*, "Codes, Clues, and Confessions."

CHAPTER 25. SHOWDOWN

1. Conversations with the author. Menges made these arguments in private briefings to U.S. officials, in semi-official "Briefing Notes" issued by the Hudson Institute, where he worked as a senior fellow, and in op-eds published in the *Washington Times*. He tried to get the administration to become more active in countering Iranian "active measures" in Iraq and to support pro-democracy forces inside Iran right up until his death in July 2004.
2. Portions in quotes from *Al Sharq al Awsat*, London, May 28, 2004, as translated by the Middle East Media Research Institute (MEMRI), Special Dispatch 723, May 28, 2004 (available at www.memri.org). Other portions from author interviews with individuals who watched the original tape. Abassi's official title was director of the Revolutionary Guards Center for Doctrinaire Affairs of National Security Outside Iran.
3. The satellite photographs can be viewed at http://www.isis-online.org/publications/iran/lavizanshian.html.
4. "Nuclear Facility in Tunnel," *Der Spiegel*, 11/29/2004 (FBIS translated text). MEK foreign affairs spokesman Mohammad Mohaddessin told reporters in Paris on Oct. 26, 2004, that the regime was completing a major new site in Isfahan that would convert uranium yellowcake into UF6 for enrichment and that a test center with 120–180 centrifuges had been built nearby. Jennifer Joan Lee, "Group Discloses Secret Nuke Effort," *Washington Times*, Oct. 27, 2004.
5. "Official Says Iran to Establish Tunnel Boring Machines Production Plant in Qom," Tehran Mehr News Agency, 1210 GMT 25 Nov 04 (FBIS/World News Connection).

CHAPTER 26. THE WAY AHEAD

1. MEMRI TV Clip: "Iranian President Khatami Presents His Perception of Democracy," Iranian TV Channel 1, Feb. 13, 2005.
2. MEMRI TV Clip 384: "Tehran Friday Sermon by Ayatollah Ahmad Jannati: We Are Determined to Obtain Nuclear Technology," Nov. 30, 2004; http://www.memritv.org/search.asp?ACT=S9&P1=384.
3. MEMRI TV Clip 526: "Suspension of Uranium Enrichment Is Like Denying Iran Nuclear Technology," interview with Ali Larijani, Iranian TV, Channel 2, Feb. 3, 2005.
4. *Iran Emrooz* daily, Feb. 14, 2005, cited by IranMania.com.
5. "Iran: Breaking Out Without Quite Breaking the Rules," NPEC, October 2004; available at http://www.npec-web.org/projects/iranswu2.htm.
6. Victor Gilinsky, Marvin Miller, and Harmon Hubbard, "A Fresh Examination of the Proliferation Dangers of Light Water Reactors" (Washington, DC: Nonproliferation Policy Education Center 2004). The full sixty-two-page report is available at www.npec-web.org.
7. Iran's record of supporting so-called insurgents in Iraq is finally coming to light. See in particular Edward T. Pound, "The Iran Connection," *U.S. News & World Report*, Nov. 22, 2004. Pound writes that he was given access to "thousands of pages of intelligence reports . . . covering the period from July 2003 through early 2004" that were prepared by the CIA, the DIA, the Iraq Survey Group, the Coalition Provisional Authority, and various military commands and units in the field, including the V Corps and the Pentagon's Combined Joint Special Operations Task Force. The reports not only revealed

"the critical role Iran has played in aiding some elements of the anti-American insurgency after Baghdad fell," but raised "important questions about whether Iran will continue to try to destabilize Iraq after elections are held" in Jan. 2005.

8. "Iran's Rafsanjani warns Israel against attacking nuclear sites," AFP, Sept. 18, 2003. In his oft-cited Friday prayer sermon in Tehran on Dec. 14, 2001, Rafsanjani noted that an Iranian strike on Israel would cause Israel to be "removed from the region and the world of Islam as 'extraneous matter,'" and that "those who have gathered together in Israel will be dispersed again." See "Former Iranian President Rafsanjani on Using a Nuclear Bomb Against Israel," MEMRI Special Dispatch 325, Jan. 3, 2002.
9. MEMRI TV Clip 273, Sept. 22, 2004.
10. MEMRI TV Clip 555: "Iranian TV Reports a Missile Attack in Iran," Feb. 16, 2005.
11. Most of these proposals are drawn from the final report of a Council on Foreign Relations task force on Iran chaired by Robert Gates ("Iran: Time for a New Approach," CFR, July 2004).
12. Zbigniew Brzezinski, Robert Gates, et al., "Iran: Time for a New Approach," Council on Foreign Relations, July 2004, p. 39.

Acknowledgments

Many of the characters who appear in this book I have interviewed on multiple occasions over several years, some of them more than one hundred times.

In this regard, I want to thank Dr. Manoucher Ganji, Dr. Mehdi Rouhani, Shahriar Ahy, Ahmad Ansari, Reza Pahlavi, Ahmad Rezai, Roozbeh Farahanipour, Michael Maloof, James Swanson, Henry Sokolski, Gary Samore, Robert Einhorn, Dr. Stephen Bryen, David Kay, Daniel Poneman, John Lehman, Ed Ball, Abolhassan, Banisadr, Homayoun Moghadam, Constantine Menges, Hamid Reza Zakeri, Manoucher Moatamer, Thomas Fortune Fay, Steve Perlis, Congressman Curt Weldon, Assistant Secretary of State Paula DeSutter, Christopher Ford, Frederick Fleitz, and Jean-Louis Bruguière.

Many others have shared information and analysis, including Bill Royce, Nader Afshar, Patrick Clawson, Bob Baer, Pooya Dayanim, Fahriar Nikbakt, Asadollah Morovati, Manuchehr Bibyan, Zia Atabai, Sardar Haddad, Fuad Pashai, Mandana Zand-Karimi, Habib Momayez, Ahmad Oveissy, Bijan Kian, Mohammad Parvin, Gholamreza Mohajeri-Nejad, Bijan Kasraei, Khosrow Seif, Housang Ansary, Bahman Batmangelij, Bahman Maalizadeh, Behrouz Sarshar, Mohsen Sazegara, Michael Rubin, Pierre Villaros, Mark Gwozdecky, Randy Rydell, William Potter, Robert S. Norris, Gary Milhollin, "Bahram," Alireza Nourizadeh, George Cave, Marion Smoak, Clair George, John Kenneth Knaus, Vice Admiral (ret.) James "Ace" Lyons, Caspar Weinberger, Larry Wilkerson, Uri Lubrani, Reuven Ehrlich, Maj. Gen. Yaacov Amit-Dror, Shoshana Bryen, Frank Record, Gregg Rickman, Robert Armao, R. James Woolsey, Gordon Oehler, David Albright, and Corey Hinderstein.

Others I cannot name because of their ongoing work for U.S., European, and Middle Eastern government agencies. This includes sources inside Iran who have risked their lives to provide evidence of the regime's ongoing support for al-Qaeda and its secret nuclear weapons sites.

A special thanks to sometimes traveling companions Timothy Fleming, Rich Hailey, and J. D. Lee, who shared some of the adventure—and the uncertainty—of dealing with defectors from a hostile intelligence service.

I have been highly selective in writing this book. Readers seeking additional source documents and articles, as well as my congressional testimony on Iranian weapons programs, will find an extensive archive at www.kentimmerman.com and www.iran.org.

Finally, I would like to thank the IAEA for excellent cooperation throughout my research. I have tried to draw a clear distinction in this book between the agency's much-improved technical capabilities, which I believe have been instrumental in documenting Iran's violations of its safeguards commitments since February 2003, and the hopelessly inadequate political structure of the Board of Governors, which has consistently refused to step up to its responsibilities.

KENNETH R. TIMMERMAN
Washington, D.C./Athens/Paris/Ste. Maxime

Index